RESEARCH BIBLIOGRAPHIES IN AMERICAN LITERATURE
NUMBER 3
THEODORE DREISER

Other books in this series:

The Critical Reception of Robert Frost • Peter Van Egmond, No. 1

Edgar Allan Poe: An Annotated Bibliography of Books and Articles in English, 1827 - 1973 • Esther F. Hyneman, No. 2

A Bibliography of Writings By and About Harold Frederic • Thomas F. O'Donnell, Stanton Garner and Robert H. Woodward, No. 4

THEODORE DREISER:
A Primary and
Secondary Bibliography

Donald Pizer
Richard W. Dowell
Frederic E. Rusch

G. K. HALL & CO., 70 LINCOLN STREET, BOSTON, MASS.

Library of Congress Cataloging in Publication Data

Pizer, Donald.
    Theodore Dreiser.

    Bibliography: p.
    Includes index.
    1. Dreiser, Theodore, 1871-1945--Bibliography.
I. Dowell, Richard W., joint author. II. Rusch,
Frederic E., joint author. III. Title.
Z8241.7.P58 [PS3507.R55]   016.813'5'2   75-12891
ISBN 0-8161-1082-4

This publication is printed on permanent/durable acid-free paper.

MANUFACTURED IN THE UNITED STATES OF AMERICA

Preface

Bibliography is a cumulative scholarly activity. But since the degree of dependence on others and of incompleteness differs from instance to instance, it may be useful to outline briefly the history of Dreiser bibliography and to describe our own aims and limits.

Dreiser bibliography began in the late 1920s with the work of Edward D. McDonald and Vrest Orton. McDonald's bibliography, like so many of the time, was directed toward the interests of book collectors and therefore was particularly thin for Dreiser's periodical contributions and for writing about him. Orton's idiosyncratic Dreiserana corrected and supplemented McDonald but was still a limited endeavor. During the next four decades there was much useful work in special areas of Dreiser bibliography even though no full-scale bibliography appeared. John Huth and Walter Blackstock helped fill in our knowledge of Dreiser's periodical writing of the 1890s, and the major biographical and critical studies of Robert H. Elias, W. A. Swanberg, Ellen Moers, and Richard Lehan contributed, each in its own way, much important bibliographical information. For secondary bibliography, the situation was also that of gradual accretion of knowledge. Ralph N. Miller's mimeographed list of 1947 was long standard because there was no other separate compilation to rival it. Of the many secondary bibliographies appearing in books about Dreiser that in Kazin and Shapiro's The Stature of Theodore Dreiser (1955) was the most ambitious. Their list, however, was too inaccurate and undiscriminating to be more than a guide to future efforts. Two notable and more inclusive bibliographies appeared in 1971. Donald Pizer published in Proof the first attempt at a complete listing of Dreiser's published work since McDonald in 1928. And Hugh Atkinson made an effort--one marred by excessive selectivity and error--to compile a primary and secondary bibliography in the Kent State Serif series.

The present bibliography is thus the first which seeks to bring together in one book all that is known of primary and secondary materials concerning Dreiser. But once stated, this aim must be immediately qualified. First, we have not sought to describe the physical nature of Dreiser's books in a manner which conforms to the ideals of contemporary descriptive bibliography. The reader will not find in the descriptions of Dreiser's books which follow an exact reproduction of title-page typography or information on such matters as paper, gatherings, ornaments, and the like. These details are of importance primarily to textual editors who seek to establish a genealogy of textual variants by a genealogy of printing. And it is textual editors who no doubt can best prepare such a bibliography and profit from it, as appears to be the case in the numerous projects of the Center for Editions of American Authors now under way. Our aim has been to prepare a bibliography which will be of use primarily to scholars and critics of Dreiser whose interests are not professionally bibliographical, though it is hoped that those whose interests are principally bibliographical will also benefit from our work. In addition, we have lacked the personal and financial resources to make some portions of the bibliography as complete as we would have wished. Thus, for translations of Dreiser's works, we have limited ourselves to those physically present in the United States, and for publications about him, we have not sought to discover all articles in foreign journals. But in areas of greatest interest for the scholar and critic--Dreiser's books, contributions to books, periodical appearances, and significant writing about Dreiser in books, journals, and newspapers--we have sought completeness.

A further aim has been accuracy. With but a few exceptions which are noted in the text, we have seen every work cited either in its original form, in a clipping file or scrapbook in the Dreiser Collection at the University of Pennsylvania or the Theatre Collection of the New York Public Library, or in republished form. The Library of Congress symbols PU for the University of Pennsylvania and NN for the New York Public Library appear at the end of entries based on information found on clippings in files or scrapbooks in their collections.

With the exception of sections L, O and P, the first two digits in an entry number signify the year of publication. Other explanations of our methods and range can be found at the opening of the various sections of the bibliography. It only remains to note the division of labor in the project and to thank those who have aided us in our efforts.

Donald Pizer is responsible for sections A-E, G; Richard W. Dowell and Frederic E. Rusch for sections F, H-P.

Donald Pizer would like to thank the American Philosophical Society and the Tulane University Council on Research for grants in the summer of 1966 which permitted him to lay the foundation for his work in Dreiser bibliography; Neda Westlake, Curator of the Dreiser Collection of the University of Pennsylvania, whose unfailing knowledge and helpfulness in all matters Dreiserian have been invaluable;

PREFACE

Robert H. Elias for much bibliographical information over the years; Blair Bigelow for his aid in connection with Dreiser's newspaper writing between 1892 and 1895; Roberta Reeder for helping with East European title pages; Joseph Katz for supplying several rare issues of Ev'ry Month and also for permission to reuse material which originally appeared in Proof: The Yearbook of American Bibliographical and Textual Studies, 1 (1971), 247-92. Copyright © 1971 by Joseph Katz; and the many librarians who have answered letters or have guided him to the right places.

Richard W. Dowell and Frederic E. Rusch would like to thank the University Research Committee of Indiana State University for a grant that enabled them to visit libraries in Philadelphia, New York, Washington DC, and Chicago; Neda Westlake and her assistants for guiding them through the Dreiser Collection at the University of Pennsylvania; Karen Chittick for the many hours spent acquiring books, photocopied articles, and microfilms through interlibrary loan; Virginia Anderson, G. Ronald Dobler, Richard C. Frushell, Don Graham, and Louis Oldani for assistance in verifying items; Mary Jean DeMarr for helping with articles in Russian; and the librarians in charge of the newspaper collections at the Chicago Public Library, the Library of Congress, the New York Public Library, the New York State Library, the University of Chicago Library, and the University of Illinois Library for courteously meeting requests to see numerous issues of newspapers.

Contents

CONTENTS

A

BOOKS, PAMPHLETS, LEAFLETS, AND BROADSIDES

The description of the title page has been normalized as follows: differences in font are not noted; titles, subtitles, and proper names are regularized to initial capitalization for substantives; all other words on the title page are regularized to lower case only.

Only the earliest binding of the first impression is cited, and there has been no attempt to indicate the presence of decorative devices or illustrations on the covers.

Date of publication for copyrighted works is the date recorded by the Copyright Office of the Library of Congress. The publication date of material not deposited for copyright is determined by a source which is noted after the date or by information on the transcribed title page.

An asterisk after a new impression published in America indicates that the work is printed from the plates of the first American impression.

Only the first impression of a translation is cited. Later republication of the translation is omitted when the publisher, place, and translator are those of the first impression.

Translated works which appear in brackets are works which were published in a non-Latin alphabet. The information provided is transliterated from the original language.

WORKS BY - Books

A00-1   SISTER CARRIE

Sister Carrie / by / Theodore Dreiser / (publisher's device) / New York / Doubleday, Page & Co. / 1900

> 7 3/4 x 5 1/8, viii, 558 pp. (i-ii), half-title, verso blank; (iii-iv), title, verso copyright notice; (v-vi), dedication, verso blank; (vii-viii), fly-title, verso blank; (1)-557, text; (558-560), blank.

Red cloth, lettering on front and spine in black.

Published 8 November 1900.

Later Publication in English

1901--London: Heinemann (Dollar Library; abridged version).

1907--New York: Dodge (the 1900 plates except for lines 3-22, page 5; all later American impressions which use the 1900 plates incorporate this change).*

1907--New York: Grosset and Dunlap.*

1912--New York: Harper (includes a "Publisher's Note").*

1917--New York: Boni and Liveright.*

1927--London: Constable ("New Uniform Edition").

1929--New York: Liveright.*

1932--New York: Random House (Modern Library, with a "Publisher's Note" and Dreiser's "The Early Adventures of Sister Carrie," Colophon, Part 5, March, 1931).*

1935--London: Constable ("Popular Edition").

1939--New York: Limited Editions Club (illustrated by Reginald Marsh, with an introduction by Burton Rascoe; also published in a trade edition in 1939 by Heritage Press of New York).

1946--Cleveland: World.*

1949--New York: Pocket Books (abridged version, with an introduction by Maxwell Geismar).

SISTER CARRIE

1957--New York: Rinehart (Rinehart Edition, with an introduction by Kenneth S. Lynn).

1957--New York: Sagamore (American Century Series, with an
introduction by James T. Farrell).

1958--New York: Bantam (Bantam Classic).

1959--Boston: Houghton Mifflin (Riverside Edition, with an
introduction by Claude Simpson).

1960--New York: Dell (Laurel Dreiser, with a general introduction by Alfred Kazin).

1962--New York: New American Library (Signet Classic, with
an introduction by Willard Thorp).

1965--London: Oxford University Press (Classic American
Text, with an introduction by Michael Millgate).

1965--New York: Harper and Row (Perennial Classic, with an
introduction by Arthur Edelstein).

1967--New York: Airmont (Airmont Classic, with an introduction by Clarence A. Andrews).

1969--Cleveland: Charles E. Merrill (Merrill Standard
Edition, with an introduction by Louis Auchincloss; a
facsimile of the 1900 edition).

1969--New York: Johnson Reprint (with an introduction by
Jack Salzman; a facsimile of the 1901 Heinemann edition).

1970--New York: Norton (Norton Critical Edition, edited by
Donald Pizer).

1970--Indianapolis: Bobbs-Merrill (Library of Literature,
with an introduction by Jack Salzman).

1971--Cambridge, Mass.: Robert Bentley.

Translations

Czech

Sestra Carrie. Trans. unknown. Prague: Čin, 1931.

WORKS BY - Books

Danish

Søster Carrie. Trans. Tom Kristensen. Copenhagen:
Gyldendal, 1929.

Dutch

Carrie. Trans. Willy Cosari. 's-Gravenhage: H. P.
Leopold, 1931.

German

Schwester Carrie. Trans. Anna Nussbaum. Berlin: Paul
Zsolnay, 1929.

Schwester Carrie. Trans. Anna Nussbaum. Vienna: Paul
Zsolnay, 1949.

Schwester Carrie. Trans. Anna Nussbaum. Hamburg:
Rowohlt, 1953.

Schwester Carrie. Trans. Anna Nussbaum. Berlin: Aufbau,
1963.

Hungarian

Carrie Drágám. Trans. Pál Vámosi. Budapest: Európa
Könyvkiadó, 1967.

Italian

Il Cammino di una Donna. Trans. Mariquita Pizzotti.
Milan: N. Moneta [1946].

Nostra Sorella Carrie. Trans. Gabriele Baldini. Turin:
Einaudi [1951].

Gli Occhi Che Non Sorrisero. Trans. Agnese Silvestri
Giorgi. Milan: Baldini & Castoldi [1952].

Latvian

Māsa Kerrija. Trans. A. Mežsēts. Riga: Grāmatu Draugs
[1934].

SISTER CARRIE

Polish

    Siostra Carrie. Trans. Zofia Popławska. Warsaw:
      Ksiazka i Wiedza, 1949.

    Siostra Carrie. Trans. Zofia Popławska. Poznan:
      Wydawnictwo Poznańskie, 1959.

Portuguese

    Carolina. Trans. Moagir Augusto. Rio de Janiero:
      Edicão de Livraria do Globo, 1946.

Russian

    [Sestra Kerri. Trans. unknown. Riga: Academia, 1930].

    [Sestra Kerri. Trans. M. Volosov. Moscow: Checheno-
      Ingushkoe Knizhnoe Izdatel'stvo, 1958].

    [Sestra Kerri. Trans. M. Volosov. Moscow: Gosudarst-
      vennoe Izdatel'stvo Khuduzhestvennoi Literatury, 1960].

    [Sestra Kerri. Trans. Elenora Rzhevuts'ka. Kiev:
      Dnipro, 1971].

Serbo-Croatian

    Carrie. Trans. Vlatko Šarić. Zagreb: Zora, 1957.

Slovak

    Sestra Carrie. Trans. Ivan Krčméry, afterword Zora
      Studená. Bratislava: Slovenské Vydavetel'stvo
      Krásnej Literatury, 1965.

Slovenian

    Sestra Carrie. Trans. Mira Mihelič. Ljubljana:
      Slovenski Knjižni Zavod, 1955.

WORKS BY - Books

> Spanish
>
>> *Carolina*. Trans. Hector F. Miri. Buenos Aires:
>> Ediciones Mackern, 1941.
>
> Swedish
>
>> *Syster Carrie*. Trans. Teresia Eurén. Stockholm:
>> P. A. Norstedt, 1928.

A11-1   JENNIE GERHARDT

Jennie / Gerhardt / a Novel / by / Theodore Dreiser / author of /
"Sister Carrie" / (publisher's device) / Harper & Brothers Publishers / New York and London / M-C-M-X-I

> 7 3/8 x 4 7/8, viii, 434 pp. (i-ii), blank; (iii-iv), blank,
> verso frontispiece; (v-vi), title, verso copyright notice;
> (vii-viii), fly-title, verso blank; 1-(433), text; (434),
> blank.

> Mottled light blue cloth, lettering on front and spine in
> gold (uniform with Harper's *Sister Carrie* and *The Financier*
> and with John Lane's *The Titan*).

> .Published 19 October 1911.

Later Publication in English

> 1911--London: Harper.

> 1924--New York: Burt.* (Sometime between the first Harper
> impression and the A. L. Burt reprint of 1924, Dreiser
> cut the epilogue of *Jennie Gerhardt*, "In Passing,"
> pp. 432-33. Thus, some Harper impressions contain the
> epilogue and some do not, but all impressions and editions
> beginning with the Burt impression do not.)

> 1924--New York: Boni and Liveright.*

> 1928--London: Constable ("New Uniform Edition").

> 1932--New York: Liveright.*

> 1934--Garden City, N. Y.: Garden City.*

Theodore Dreiser: A Bibliography

1935--New York: Simon and Schuster.*

1935--London: Constable ("Popular Edition").

1946--Cleveland: World.*

1963--New York: Dell (Laurel Dreiser, with an introduction by Alfred Kazin).

1970--London: Panther (London Panther, with an introduction by T. G. Rosenthal).

Translations

Danish

> Jennie Gerhardt. Trans. Tom Kristensen. Copenhagen: Gyldendal, 1931.

Dutch

> Jennie Gerhardt. Trans. Van Jan Vogelaar. 's-Gravenhage: H. P. Leopold, 1929.

Finnish

> Jennie Gerhardt. Trans. Helvi Vasara. Helsinki: Kustannusosakeyhtiö Otava, 1939.

French

> Jenny Gerhardt. Trans. Marie Cresciani, intro. Jean de Fabrègues. Paris: Éditions du Siècle, 1933.

> Jenny Gerhardt. Trans. Marie Cresciani, intro. Jean de Fabrègues. Paris: Nouvelles Editions Latines, 1946.

German

> Jennie Gerhardt. Trans. Alfons Matthias Nuese. Berlin: Paul Zsolnay, 1928.

WORKS BY - Books

Italian

Jenny Gerhardt. Trans. Luigi x Taroni. Milan:
Edizioni Librarie Italiane, 1945.

Latvian

Dženija Gerhardt. Trans. A. Mežséts. Riga: Grámatu
Draugs, 1932.

Polish

Jennie Gerhardt. Trans. Jósefy Zydlerowej, intro.
Wiesław Furmanczyk. Warsaw: Czytelnik, 1956.

Portuguese

A Solteira (Jenny Gerhardt). Trans. Castelo de Morais.
Lisbon: Editorial-Século, 1934.

Russian

[Dzhenni Gergardt. Trans. Mark Volosov. Riga: Academia,
1929].

[Dzhenni Gerkhardt. Trans. unknown. Minsk: Akademiîa
Nauk BSSR, 1959].

Serbo-Croatian

Jennie Gerhardt. Trans. Mirko Jovič. Zagreb: Zora,
1961.

Sestra Carrie i Jennie Gerhardt. Trans. Vladislav Šarič.
Rijeka: Otokar Keršovani, 1963.

Slovak

Jennie Gerhardtová. Trans. Viera Szathmáry-Vlčkova.
Bratislava: Spoločnost Priatelov Krásnych Kníh, 1957.

Jennie Gerhardtová. Trans. Viera Szathmáry-Vlčkova.
Bratislava: Slovensky Spisovatel, 1966.

Slovenian

    <u>Jennie Gerhardtová</u>. Trans. Janko Moder. Ljubljana:
       Državna Založba Slovenije, 1964.

Spanish

    <u>Jenny Gerhardt</u>. Trans. Héctor Pedro Blomberg. Buenos
       Aires: Club del Libro A.L.A., 1941.

Swedish

    <u>Jennie Gerhardt</u>. Trans. Gerda Swedberg. Stockholm:
       P. A. Norstedt, 1930.

A12-1   THE FINANCIER

The / Financier / a Novel / by / Theodore Dreiser / author of /
"Jennie Gerhardt" "Sister Carrie" / (publisher's device) / Harper &
Brothers Publishers / New York and London / M-C-M-X-I-I

    7 5/16 x 4 7/8, viii, 780 pp. (i-iv), blank; (v-vi), title,
    verso copyright notice; (vii-viii), fly-title, verso blank;
    1-(780), text.

    Mottled light blue cloth, lettering on front and spine in
    gold (uniform with Harper's <u>Sister Carrie</u> and <u>Jennie Ger-
    hardt</u> and with John Lane's <u>The Titan</u>).

    Published 24 October 1912.

<u>Later Publication in English</u>

    1912--London: Harper.

    1915--New York: Burt.*

    1925--New York: Boni and Liveright.*

WORKS BY -- Books

A13-1   A TRAVELER AT FORTY

A Traveler / at Forty / by / Theodore Dreiser / author of   "Sister
Carrie," "Jennie Gerhardt," / "The Financier," etc., etc. / illus-
trated by / W. Glackens / (publisher's device) / New York / The
Century Co. / 1913

> 8 3/4 x 5 1/2, x, 526 pp. + a tipped-in, unpaginated frontis-
> piece and 15 additional tipped-in, unpaginated illustrations.
> (i-ii), half-title, verso blank; blank, verso frontispiece;
> (iii-iv), title, verso copyright notice; (v-vi), dedication,
> verso blank; (vii-viii), contents; (ix-x), list of illustra-
> tions, verso blank; (1-2), fly-title, verso blank; 3-526,
> text.

> Red cloth, lettering on front in blind within a gold box,
> lettering on spine in gold.

> Published 25 November 1913.

Previous Publication

Chapters I-III, V

> "The First Voyage Over," Century, 86 (Aug. 1913), 586-95.

Chapters VII-XI

> "An Uncommercial Traveler in London," Century, 86 (Sept.
> 1913), 736-49.

Chapter XIII

> "Lilly Edwards: An Episode," Smart Set, 40 (June 1913),
> 81-86.

Chapters XXI-XXIV

> "Paris," Century, 86 (Oct. 1913), 904-915.

Later Publication in English

1914--London: Grant Richards.

1930--New York: Liveright.*

A14-1   THE TITAN

The / Titan / by / Theodore Dreiser / author of / "The Financier,"
"Sister Carrie," / and "Jennie Gerhardt" / New York: John Lane
Company / London: John Lane, The Bodley Head / Toronto: Bell &
Cockburn MCMIV

> 7 1/4 x 4 7/8, viii, 552 pp. (i-ii), half-title, verso ad-
> vertisement; (iii-iv), title, verso copyright notice; (v-vi),
> contents; (vii-viii), fly-title, verso blank; 1-(552), text.
>
> Mottled light blue cloth, lettering on front and spine in
> gold (uniform with Harper's Sister Carrie, Jennie Gerhardt,
> and The Financier).
>
> Published 22 May 1914.
>
> > Note: The sheets for the first impression of
> > The Titan were prepared by Harper's. When
> > John Lane assumed publication of the novel,
> > these sheets were transferred to John Lane
> > and were used for the first John Lane im-
> > pression of The Titan.
>
> ### Later Publication in English

1915--London: John Lane.

1925--New York: Boni and Liveright.*

1928--London: Constable ("New Uniform Edition").

1935--Garden City, N. Y.: Garden City.*

1936--London: Constable ("Popular Edition").

1946--Cleveland: World.*

1959--New York: Dell (Laurel Dreiser, with a general introduction by Alfred Kazin).

1965--New York: New American Library (Signet Classic, with
an afterword by John Berryman).

1968--London: Panther (London Panther, with an introduction
by T. G. Rosenthal).

1972--Cleveland: World (included in A Trilogy of Desire,
with an introduction by Philip Gerber).*

WORKS BY - Books

Translations

Bulgarian

[Titan. Trans. Radka Krapcheve. Sofia: Dekembri, 1948].

Czech

Titán. Trans. Anna Novotná. Prague: Knihovna Klasiků,
1962.

German

Der Titan: Trilogie der Begierde. Zweite Roman: Der
Titan. Trans. Marianne Schön and Wilhelm Cremer.
Berlin: Paul Zsolnay, 1928.

Latvian

Titans. Trans. Anna Bauga. Riga: Latvijas Valsts
Izdevnieciba, 1951.

Norwegian

Titanen. Trans. Nils Lie. Oslo: Gyldendal, 1940.

Russian

[Titan. Trans. V. Kurell and T. Ozerskaîa. Kiev:
Derzhavne Vidavnitstvo Khudozhnoî Literatury, 1959].

Serbo-Croatian

[Titan. Trans. Olga Maryanovich. Belgrade: Prosveta,
1949].

Titan. Trans. Mira Kučić. Rijeka: Otokar Keršovani,
1956.

Financijer, Titan, Stoik (Trilogija). Trans. Vjekoslav
Susanić, Mira Kučić, and Franjo Bukovšek. Rijeka:
Otokar Kersovani, 1963.

Slovak

    Titan. Trans. Viera Szathmáry-Vlčkova, afterword Ján
      Boor. Bratislava, SPKK, 1966.

Slovenian

    Titan. Trans. Jože Stabej. Ljubljana: Državna Založba
      Slovenije, 1967.

Spanish

    El Titan. Trans. Jacobo Halperin. Buenos Aires:
      Editorial Futuro, 1945.

Swedish

    Titanen. Trans. Margaretha Odelberg, f. Frölich.
      Stockholm: P. A. Norstedt, 1930.

A15-1   THE "GENIUS"

The / "Genius" / by / Theodore Dreiser / New York: John Lane
Company / London: John Lane, The Bodley Head / Toronto: S. B.
Gundy MCMXV

    7 3/4 x 5 1/4, 736 pp. (1-2), half-title, verso advertisement;
    (3-4), title, verso copyright notice; (5-6), epigraph, verso
    blank; (7-8), divisional title, verso blank; 9-736, text.

    Red cloth, lettering in front in blind within a gold box,
    lettering on spine in gold.

    Published 1 October 1915.

Later Publication in English

    1915--London: John Lane.

    1923--Metropolitan Magazine, 56 (Feb.-Mar., 1923), 57 (Apr.-
      Sept., 1923), 58 (Oct.-Nov., 1923) (serialization of an
      abridged version).

    1923--New York: Boni and Liveright (with a foreword by
      Merton S. Yewdale).*

WORKS BY - Books

1928--London: Constable ("New Uniform Edition").

1931--New York: Liveright.*

1935--Garden City, N. Y.:   Garden City.*

1937--London: Constable ("Popular Edition").

1946--Cleveland: World.*

1967--New York: New American Library (Signet Classic, with
an afterword by Larzer Ziff).

Translations

German

> Das "Genie". Trans. Marianne Schön.   Berlin: Paul
> Zsolnay, 1929.

Hebrew

> [Ha Gaon.   Trans. A. Carmel.   Tel Aviv: A. Zalkovitz,
> n. d.].

Hungarian

> A Zseniális Ember.   Trans. Pál Tábori.   Budapest: Nova
> Irodalmi Intézet, 1937.

Serbo-Croatian

> Genije.   Trans. Berislav Lukić.   Rijeka: Otokar
> Keršovani, 1963.

Spanish

> El Genio.   Trans. Jacobo Halperin.   Buenos Aires:
> Editorial Futuro, 1944.

PLAYS OF THE NATURAL AND THE SUPERNATURAL

A16-1   PLAYS OF THE NATURAL AND THE SUPERNATURAL

Plays of the Natural / and the Supernatural / by / Theodore Dreiser / author of "The Titan," "The Genius," etc. / (publisher's device) / New York: John Lane Company / London: John Lane, The Bodley Head / MCMXVI

> 8 x 5 3/4, 228 pp. (1-2), half-title, verso advertisement; (3-4), title, verso copyright notice; (5-6), contents, verso blank; (7-8), divisional title, verso characters; 9-228, text.

> Light green boards, light brown linen spine; lettering on front in dark green, lettering on spine on a white paper label in green.

> Published 18 February 1916.

> > Note: The second issue of the first impression contains an added gathering at the close entitled "The Anaesthetic Revelation," paginated 1-4 and signed "The Author, New York, April, 1916." This gathering appears in this form in all later impressions and editions.

> > Contents and Previous Publications

> I.   The Girl in the Coffin

> > Smart Set, 41 (Oct. 1913), 127-40.

> II.   The Blue Sphere

> > Smart Set, 44 (Dec. 1914), 245-52.

> III.   Laughing Gas

> > Smart Set, 45 (Feb. 1915), 85-94.

> IV.   In the Dark

> > Smart Set, 45 (Jan. 1915), 419-25.

> V.   The Spring Recital

> > Little Review, 2 (Dec. 1915), 28-35.

THEODORE DREISER: A BIBLIOGRAPHY

WORKS BY - Books

VI. The Light in the Window

International, 10 (Jan. 1916), 6-8, 32.

VII. "Old Ragpicker"

Later Publication in English

1916--London: John Lane.

1922--New York: Dodd, Mead.*

1926--New York: Boni and Liveright.* (A second issue of this
    impression was created by the incorporation of a change
    on p. 53 in the last speech of "The Girl in the Coffin."
    In the 1916 impression, the speech reads: "She said I
    was to give you this. She said I was to say she died
    happy." In the 1926 impression, some copies contain this
    speech and some contain a revised version of it which
    reads: "She said I was to give you this. She said I
    was to say that she loved you and that it was all right."
    In addition, according to Vrest Orton, Dreiserana, 1929,
    p. 39, two special limited issues of the 1926 impression
    were prepared in late 1926. The first, of 12 copies,
    added Dreiser's plays "Phantasmagoria" and "The Court of
    Progress"; the second, of 10 copies, added these plays
    and Dreiser's "The Dream." These three added plays had
    previously been published in Hey Rub-a-Dub-Dub in 1920.
    Only the first of these two special issues has been
    examined; the two additional plays which it contains are
    printed from the plates of the 1920 Hey Rub-a-Dub-Dub.)

1969--New York: AMS (facsimile of the 1916 impression).

1970--St. Clair Shores, Mich.: Scholarly (facsimile of the
    1926 trade impression).

A16-2   A HOOSIER HOLIDAY

A Hoosier / Holiday / by / Theodore Dreiser / with illustrations /
by Franklin Booth / (ornament) / New York: John Lane Company /
London: John Lane / The Bodley Head / MCMXVI

9 3/8 x 6 1/8, 514 pp. + 31 tipped-in, unpaginated illustrations. (1-2), half-title, verso advertisement; (3-4), blank,
verso frontispiece; (5-6), title, verso copyright notice;
(7-8), dedication, verso blank; (9-10), contents; (11-12),
list of illustrations; 13-513, text; (514), blank.

Light green boards, olive green buckram spine; lettering on front in gold and red, lettering on spine in gold.

Published 17 November 1916.

> Note: Lines 29-34, page 173, of the first issue of the first impression read:
>
>> The war! The war! They were chasing German-American professors out of Canadian colleges, and making other demonstrations of hostility toward all others having pro-German leanings. I, with my German ancestry on one side and my German name and my German sympathies--what might they not have done to me!
>
> Shortly after publication, a new issue of this impression was created when a cancel for pages 173-74 was prepared and tipped in, with lines 29-34 of page 173 now reading:
>
>> Naturally there was much excitement, and on all sides were evidences of preparations being made to send armaments and men to the Mother Country. We had looked forward with the greatest pleasure to a trip to Canada, but the conditions were so unfavorable that we hesitated to chance it.

Later Publication in English

1925--New York: Boni and Liveright.*

1932--London: Constable.

A17-1 LIFE, ART AND AMERICA

The / Seven / Arts / Life, Art and America / by Theodore Dreiser / reprinted from the February, 1917, issue of / The Seven Arts

8 7/8 x 6, 28 pp. 1-27, text, (28), blank.

Wrappers.

Published Spring 1917.

Theodore Dreiser: A Bibliography

WORKS BY - Books

> Note: Pamphlet republication of Dreiser's
> article in the Seven Arts, 1 (Feb. 1917),
> 363-89; the essay was again republished in
> Hey Rub-a-Dub-Dub (1920).

A18-1   FREE AND OTHER STORIES

Free and Other / Stories / by Theodore Dreiser / author of "Sister
Carrie," "The Hand of the Potter," / "Jennie Gerhardt," etc. / (publisher's device) / Boni and Liveright / New York 1918

> 7 3/8 x 5, 370 pp. (1-2), free end paper, verso blank; (3-4),
> half-title, verso blank; (5-6), title, verso copyright no-
> tice; (7-8), contents, verso blank; 9-369, text; (370),
> blank.
>
> Blue cloth, lettering on front and spine in gold (uniform
> with Boni and Liveright's Twelve Men).
>
> Published 16 August 1918.

Contents and Previous Publication

Free

> Saturday Evening Post, 190 (16 Mar. 1918), 13-15, 81-89.

McEwen of the Shining Slave Makers

> Ainslee's, 7 (June 1901), 445-50 (as "The Shining Slave
>   Makers").

Nigger Jeff

> Ainslee's, 8 (Nov. 1901), 366-75.

The Lost Phoebe

> Century, 91 (Apr. 1916), 885-96.

The Second Choice

> Cosmopolitan, 64 (Feb. 1918), 53-58, 104, 106-107.

A Story of Stories

TWELVE MEN

Old Rogaum and His Theresa

Reedy's Mirror, 11 (12 Dec. 1901), 15-17 (as "Butcher
Rogaum's Door").

Will You Walk into My Parlor?

The Cruise of the "Idlewild"

Bohemian, 17 (Oct. 1909), 441-47.

Married

Cosmopolitan, 63 (Sept. 1917), 31-35, 112-15.

When the Old Century Was New

Pearson's, 11 (Jan. 1901), 131-40.

Later Publication in English

1918--New York: Boni and Liveright (Modern Library, with an
introduction by Sherwood Anderson).*

1971--St. Clair Shores, Mich.: Scholarly (facsimile of the
1918 Modern Library impression).

Translations

Hungarian

A Csapda. Trans. Borbála Farago. Budapest: Uj Magyar
Könyvkiadó, 1956 (selections).

Russian

[Neobyknovennaĩa Istoriĩa Drugie Rasskazy. Trans. T. and
V. Ravinskii. Leningrad: Mysl', 1930].

A19-1   TWELVE MEN

Twelve Men / by Theodore Dreiser / author of "Sister Carrie," "The
Hand of the Potter," / "Free and Other Stories," "Jennie / Gerhardt,"
etc. / (publisher's device) / Boni and Liveright / New York 1919

7 3/8 x 5, viii, 360 pp. (i-ii), half-title, verso advertisement; (iii-iv), title, verso copyright notice; (v-vi),

WORKS BY - Books

contents, verso blank; (vii-viii), fly-title, verso blank; 1-360, text.

Blue cloth, lettering on front and spine in gold (uniform with Boni and Liveright's Free).

Published 14 April 1919.

Contents and Previous Publication

I. Peter

II. A Doer of the Word

   Ainslee's, 9 (June 1902), 453-59.

III. My Brother Paul

IV. The Country Doctor

   Harper's Monthly, 13 (July 1918), 193-202.

V. Culhane, the Solid Man

   Based upon "Scared Back to Nature," Harper's Weekly, 47 (16 May 1903), 816.

VI. A True Patriarch

   McClure's, 18 (Dec. 1901), 136-44.

VII. De Maupassant, Jr.

VIII. The Village Feudists

IX. Vanity, Vanity

X. The Mighty Rourke

   McClure's, 37 (May 1911), 40-50 (as "The Mighty Burke").

XI. A Mayor and His People

   Era, 11 (June 1903), 578-84.

XII. W. L. S.

   Harper's Weekly, 45 (14 Dec. 1901), 1272-73 (as "The Color of To-Day").

THEODORE DREISER: A BIBLIOGRAPHY

THE HAND OF THE POTTER

Later Publication in English

1928--New York: Modern Library (with an introduction by Robert O. Ballou).*

1930--London: Constable.

1931--Leipsig: Tauchnitz (Collection of British and American Authors).

1937--London: Constable ("Popular Edition").

1962--Greenwich, Conn.: Fawcett (Premier Book, with an introduction by William C. Lengel).

1971--St. Clair Shores, Mich.: Scholarly (facsimile of the 1919 impression).

Translations

French

Douze Hommes. Trans. Fernande Hélie. Paris: F. Rieder, 1923.

A19-2   THE HAND OF THE POTTER

The Hand of the Potter / by / Theodore Dreiser / a Tragedy in Four Acts / (publisher's device) / Boni and Liveright / New York 1918

> 7 5/8 x 5, 210 pp. (1-2), free end paper, verso blank; (3-4), blank; (5-6), half-title, verso advertisement; (7-8), title, verso copyright notice; (9-10), epigraph, verso blank; (11-12), characters; (13-14), divisional title, verso blank; 15-209, text; (210), blank. Leaf (5-6) is a cancel in all copies examined.

> Light green boards, natural linen spine; lettering on front in dark green, lettering on spine on a white paper label in dark green.

> Published 20 September 1919.

>> Note: Although Boni and Liveright printed The Hand of the Potter in early 1918, the play was withheld from publication for over a year because it was being considered for production on the New York stage. A prepublication state of the play contains a variant text of pages 191-99.

21

WORKS BY - Books

A20-1 HEY RUB-A-DUB-DUB

Hey Rub-a-Dub-Dub / a Book of the Mystery and / Wonder and Terror / of Life / by Theodore Dreiser / author of "Sister Carrie," "The Hand of the Potter," / "Free and Other Stories," "Jennie / Gerhardt," etc. / (publisher's device) / Boni and Liveright / New York 1920

> 7 1/4 x 5, viii, 312 pp. (i-ii), half-title, verso advertisement; (iii-iv), title, verso copyright notice; (v-vi), contents, verso blank; (vii-viii), fly-title, verso blank; 1-312, text.

Dark blue cloth, lettering on front and spine in gold.

Published 15 January 1920.

Contents and Previous Publication

   I. Hey Rub-a-Dub-Dub

> Nation, 109 (30 Aug. 1919), 278-81.

  II. Change

> Pagan, 1 (Sept. 1916), 27-28 (two paragraphs only) and New York Call, 26 Jan. 1918, Call Magazine, p. 1.

  III. Some Aspects of Our National Character

  IV. The Dream

> Seven Arts, 2 (July 1917), 319-33.

  V. The American Financier

  VI. The Toil of the Laborer

> New York Call, 13 July 1913, p. 11.

  VII. Personality

  VIII. A Counsel to Perfection

  IX. Neurotic America and the Sex Impulse

  X. Secrecy--Its Value

  XI. Ideals, Morals, and the Daily Newspaper

XII.   Equation Inevitable

XIII. Phantasmagoria

XIV.   Ashtoreth

Reedy's Mirror, 28 (10 July 1919), 456-57.

XV.   The Reformer

XVI. Marriage and Divorce

XVII. More Democracy or Less? An Inquiry

Reconstruction, 1 (Dec. 1919), 338-42.

XVIII. The Essential Tragedy of Life

XIX. Life, Art and America

Seven Arts, 1 (Feb. 1917), 363-89.

XX.   The Court of Progress

Later Publication in English

1931--London: Constable.

A20-2   NOTICE

Broadside, 12 x 8 7/8.

Previous Publication

The Review, 2 (5 June 1920), 597 (as "Mr. Dreiser and the
Broadway Magazine").

Note: The broadside contains an undated letter
by Annie Nathan Meyer and Dreiser's rejoinder,
dated 16 May 1920, both of which had appeared
in The Review. The broadside was reproduced
in facsimile by Vrest Orton, Dreiserana (1929),
p. ii.

WORKS BY - Books

A22-1 A BOOK ABOUT MYSELF

A Book About / Myself / Theodore Dreiser / Boni and Liveright / Publishers New York

>8 1/2 x 5 5/8, viii, 504 pp. (i-ii), blank; (iii-iv), fly-title, verso advertisement; (v-vi), title, verso copyright notice; (vii-viii), fly-title, verso blank; 1-502, text; (503-504), blank.
>
>Red cloth, lettering on front in blind within a gold box, lettering on spine in gold.
>
>Published 15 December 1922.

Contents and Previous Publication

Chapters I, XIV

>"I. Chicago. Out of My Newspaper Days," Bookman, 54 (Nov. 1921), 208-17.

Chapters XX (in part), XXIV-XXV

>"II. St. Louis. Out of My Newspaper Days," Bookman, 54 (Jan. 1922), 427-33.

Chapters XLIV-XLV

>Free (1918) (as "A Story of Stories") and "III. 'Red' Galvin. Out of My Newspaper Days," Bookman, 54 (Feb. 1922), 542-50.

Chapter XLVI

>Free (1918) (as "A Story of Stories") and "IV. The Bandit. Out of My Newspaper Days," Bookman, 55 (Mar. 1922), 12-20.

Chapters LXXV-LXXVII

>"V. I Quit the Game. Out of My Newspaper Days," Bookman, 55 (Apr. 1922), 118-25.

Later Publication in English

1929--London: Constable.

THE COLOR OF A GREAT CITY

1931--New York: Liveright (published under the title <u>A His-</u>
<u>tory of Myself</u>: <u>Newspaper Days</u>, with an "Author's <u>Note"</u>).*

1937--London: Constable ("Popular Edition").

1962--Greenwich, Conn.: Fawcett (Premier Book).

1965--Greenwich, Conn.: Fawcett (Premier Book, published as
Volume II of <u>Theodore Dreiser: His Autobiography</u>).

<u>Translations</u>

German

<u>Das Buch über mich Selbst (Jahre des Kampfes)</u>. Trans.
Ernst Weiss. Berlin: Paul Zsolnay, 1932.

<u>Ein Buch über mich Selbst</u>. Trans. Edmund Th. Kauer.
Vienna: Paul Szolnay, 1950.

Russian

[<u>Reportazh pro Reportazh</u>. Trans. P. Slunimskĩa. Moscow:
Gosudartvennoe Izadtel'stvo Khudozestvennoi Literatury, 1955] (selections).

A23-1   THE COLOR OF A GREAT CITY

The Color of / a Great City / Theodore Dreiser / illustrations by /
C. B. Falls / (publisher's device) / Boni and Liveright / Publishers
New York

8 5/8 x 5 3/4, xvi, 288 pp. + a tipped-in, unpaginated
frontispiece and 30 tipped-in, unpaginated illustrations.
(i-ii), half-title, verso advertisement; blank, verso frontispiece; (iii-iv), title, verso copyright notice; v-x, foreword;
xi-xii, contents; xiii-xiv, list of illustrations; (xv-xvi),
fly-title, verso blank; 1-287, text; (288), blank.

Black cloth, lettering on front and spine in gold.

Published 6 December 1923.

<u>Contents and Previous Publication</u>

Foreword

The City of My Dreams

WORKS BY - Books

The City Awakes

The Waterfront

    Bohemian, 17 (Nov. 1909), 633-36.

The Log of a Harbor Pilot

    Ainslee's, 3 (July 1899), 683-92 (as "The Log of an Ocean
       Pilot").

Bums

The Michael J. Powers Association

The Fire

The Car Yard

The Flight of Pigeons

    Bohemian, 17 (Oct. 1909), 494-96.

On Being Poor

Six O'Clock

    1910, No. 4 (n.d.), unpaginated, 2 pp.

The Toilers of the Tenements

    Success, 5 (Apr. 1902), 213-14, 232 (as "The Tenement
       Toilers").
The End of a Vacation

The Track Walker

    New York *Daily News*, 3 Apr. 1904, Colored Section, p. 3
       (as "The Story of a Human Nine-Pin").

The Realization of an Ideal

The Pushcart Man

    New York *Call*, 30 Mar. 1919, Call Magazine, pp. 1, 7.

A Vanished Seaside Resort

THE COLOR OF A GREAT CITY

The Bread-Line

> Demorest's, 36 (Nov. 1899), 25-26 (as a portion of
> "Curious Shifts of the Poor") and Sister Carrie (1900)
> (Chapter XLVII).

Our Red Slayer

> Bohemian, 17 (Dec. 1909), 793-95.

When the Sails Are Furled

> Ainslee's, 2 (Jan. 1899), 593-601.

Characters

The Beauty of Life

A Wayplace of the Fallen

Hell's Kitchen

A Certain Oil Refinery

> New York Call, 16 Mar. 1919, Call Magazine, pp. 3, 5 (as
> "The Standard Oil Works at Bayonne").

The Bowery Mission

The Wonder of the Water

The Man on the Bench

> New York Call, 16 Nov. 1913, p. 9.

The Men in the Dark

> American Magazine, 73 (Feb. 1912), 465-68.

The Men in the Storm

> Demorest's, 36 (Nov. 1899), 24-25 (as a portion of "Curi-
> ous Shifts of the Poor") and Sister Carrie (1900)
> (Chapter XLVII).

The Men in the Snow

> New York Call, 23 Nov. 1913, p. 10 (as a portion of "Three
> Sketches of the Poor").

WORKS BY - Books

The Freshness of the Universe

The Cradle of Tears

New York Daily News, 27 Mar. 1904, Colored Section, p. 4.

Whence the Song

Harper's Weekly, 44 (8 Dec. 1900), 1165-66a.

The Sandwich Man

The Love Affairs of Little Italy

New York Daily News, 10 Apr. 1904, Colored Section, p. 3.

Christmas in the Tenements

Harper's Weekly, 46 (6 Dec. 1902), 52-53.

The Rivers of the Nameless Dead

Tom Watson's Magazine, 1 (Mar. 1905), 112-13.

Later Publication in English

1930--London: Constable.

Translations

French

La Couleur d'une Grande Cité. Trans. Mde. Pierre
Jeanneret. Paris: Librairie Stock, 1930.

Russian

[N'iu Iork. Trans. P. Okhrimenko. Moscow: Gosudarstvennoe Izdatel'stvo, 1927].

THEODORE DREISER: A BIBLIOGRAPHY

A25-1   AN AMERICAN TRAGEDY

An American / Tragedy / by / Theodore Dreiser / volume one / (publisher's device) / New York / Boni and Liveright / MCMXXV

> 7 3/8 x 5, viii, 432 pp. (i-ii), half-title, verso advertise-
> ment; (iii-iv), title, verso copyright notice; (v-vi), fly-
> title, verso blank; (vii-viii), contents, verso blank; (1-2),
> divisional title, verso blank; 3-431, text; (432), blank.

> Black cloth, lettering on spine in gold.

An American / Tragedy / by / Theodore Dreiser / volume two / (publisher's device) / New York / Boni and Liveright / MCMXXV

> 7 3/8 x 5, x, 410 pp. (i-ii), blank; (iii-iv), half-title,
> verso blank; (v-vi), title, verso copyright notice; (vii-
> viii), fly-title, verso blank; (ix-x), contents, verso blank;
> (1-2), divisional title, verso blank; 3-409, text; (410),
> blank.

> Black cloth, lettering on spine in gold.

> Published 17 December 1925.

Later Publication in English

1926--New York: Boni and Liveright (limited and signed
edition).*

1926--London: Constable.

1929--New York: Liveright (one volume edition).*

1934--Garden City, N. Y.:   Garden City.*

1935--London: Constable ("Popular Edition").

1937--New York: Sun Dial.*

1946--Cleveland: World (Memorial Edition, with an introduction by H. L. Mencken).*

1948--Cleveland: World (illustrated by Grant Reynard, with
an introduction by H. L. Mencken).

1949--Moscow: Foreign Languages Publishing House

THEODORE DREISER: A BIBLIOGRAPHY

WORKS BY - Books

1949--New York: New American Library (Signet Edition,
abridged and with an introduction by George Mayberry).

1954--New York: Limited Editions Club (illustrated by
Reginald Marsh, with an introduction by Harry Hansen;
also published in 1954 in a trade edition by Heritage
Press of New York).

1956--New York: Random House (Modern Library Giant).

1959--New York: Dell (Laurel Dreiser, with a general introduction by Alfred Kazin).

1962--Cleveland: World (Meridian Fiction, with an introduction by R. P. Warren).

1964--New York: New American Library (Signet Classic, with
an afterword by Irving Howe).

Translations

Czech

Americká Tragedie.   Trans. unknown.   Prague: Čin, 1930.

Americká Tragedie.   Trans. Karel Kraus.   Prague:
Nakladatelství, 1947.

Americká Tragedie.   Trans. Zdeněk Urbánek, intro. Zdeněk
Vancura.   Prague: Knihovna Klasiku, 1954.

Americká Tragedie.   Trans. Zdeněk Urbánek, intro. Zdeněk
Vančura.   Prague: Odeon, 1970.

Danish

En Amerikansk Tragedie.   Trans. Tom Kristensen.   Copenhagen: Gyldendal, 1928.

Dutch

Een Amerikaanse Tragedie.   Trans. J. W. F. Werumeus Buning.
Amsterdam: De Arbeiderspers, 1938.

Illusie Van Het Geluk (Een Amerikaanse Tragedie).   Trans.
J. W. F. Werumeus Buning.   Amsterdam: E. M. Querido,
1952.

AN AMERICAN TRAGEDY

Finnish

Amerikkalainen Murhenäytelmä. Trans. Lauri Miettinen.
Helsinki: Kustannusosakeyhtiö Tammi, 1947.

French

Une Tragédie Américaine. Trans. Victor Llona. Paris:
"Univers," A. Fayard et Cie, Éditeurs, 1932.

German

Eine Amerikanische Tragödie. Trans. Marianne Schön.
Berlin: Paul Zsolnay, 1927.

Eine Amerikanische Tragödie. Trans. Marianne Schön.
Vienna: Paul Zsolnay, 1951.

Eine Amerikanische Tragödie. Trans. Marianne Schön.
Hamburg: Rowohlt, 1951.

Eine Amerikanische Tragödie. Trans. Marianne Schön.
Berlin and Weimar: Aufbau, 1964.

Hungarian

Amerikai Tragédia. Trans. Soma Braun. Budapest:
Népszava-Könyvkereskedés Kiadása [1930].

Amerikai Tragédia. Trans. Andor Németh, postscript Imre
Szász. Budapest: Szépirodalmi Könyvkiadó, 1952.

Amerikai Tragédia. Trans. Andor Németh. Budapest:
Európa Könyvkiadó, 1961.

Amerikai Tragédia. Trans. Klára Szöllösy. Budapest:
Magyar Helikon, 1964.

Italian

Una Tragedia Americana. Trans. unknown. Milan: Casa
Editrice Nicola Moneta, 1930.

Una Tragedia Americana. Trans. Noemi Carelli. Milan:
Baldini & Castoldi [1951].

WORKS BY - Books

Japanese

An American Tragedy. Trans. unknown. Tokyo: Hayakawa
Shobo, 1950.

Norwegian

En Amerikansk Tragedie. Trans. Nils Lie. Oslo:
Gyldendal, 1938.

Polish

Tragedja Amerykánska. Trans. Jósefy Zydlerowej. Warsaw:
Bibljoteka Groszowa [1930].

Tragedia Amerykánska. Trans. Jósefy Zydlerowej. Warsaw:
Czytelnik, 1955.

Romanian

O Tragedie Americanā. Trans. unknown. Bucharest:
Editura de Stat Pentru Literaturā si Arta, 1954.

O Tragedie Americanā. Trans. Leon Levitchi and Pericle
Martinescu. Bucharest: Editura Pentru Literaturā
Universalā, 1961.

Russian

[Amerikanskaīa Tragediīa. Trans. Z. A. Vershininaīa,
foreword A. A. Elistratovaīa. Moscow: Gosudarstvennoe Izdatel'stvo Khudozhestvennoī Literatury, 1933].

[Zakon Likurga. Trans. N. Bazilevskiǐ. Moscow:
Vsekdram, 1934] (A Dramatic Version).

[Amerikanskaīa Tragediīa. Trans. Z. A. Vershininaīa,
intro. I. Anisimov. Moscow: Gosudarstvennoe Izdatel'stvo Khudozhestvennoi Literatury, 1959].

[Amerikanskaīa Tragediīa. Trans. unknown. Moscow:
Gosudarstvennoe Izdatel'stvo Khudozhestvennoi Literatury, 1969].

MOODS: CADENCED AND DECLAIMED

Serbo-Croatian

> Americka Tragedija.   Trans. Berislav Grgić.   Zagreb:
> Kultura, 1948.

> Americka Tragedija.   Trans. Berislav Grgić.   Rijeka:
> Otokar Kersovani, 1963.

> Americka Tragedija.   Trans. Berislav Grgić.   Zagreb:
> Naprijed, 1967.

Slovak

> Americká Tragédia.   Trans. Jozef Šimo.   Bratislava:
> Slovenské Vydavatel'stvo Krásnej Literatúry, 1963.

Spanish

> Una Tragedia Americana.   Trans. unknown.   Buenos Aires:
> Editorial Ayacucho [1945].

> Una Tragedia Americana.   Trans. Mariano Orta Manzano.
> Barcelona: Luis de Caralt, 1961.

Swedish

> En Amerikansk Tragedi.   Trans. Margaretha Odelberg, f.
> Frölich.   Stockholm: P. A. Norstedt, 1927.

Ukranian

> [Amerikans'ka Tragediîa.   Trans. I. Bushe, L. Smilîan'skii,
> and L. Iashchenko.   Kiev: Radîans'kii Pis'mennik,
> 1955].

A26-1⁻   MOODS: CADENCED AND DECLAIMED

Moods / Cadenced and Declaimed / by Theodore Dreiser / (publisher's
device) / 1926 / Boni and Liveright New York

> 8 7/8 x 5 3/4, xii, 328 pp. (i-ii), half-title, verso
> limited edition notice; (iii-iv), title, verso copyright
> notice; v-x, contents; (xi-xii), fly-title, verso blank;
> 1-328, text.

Marbled boards and black cloth spine, lettering on spine on
a green leather label in gold.

Published 1 July 1926.

> Note: The 1926 edition of Moods was a limited
> edition of 550 signed copies. Dreiser appar-
> ently felt that a limited edition did not con-
> stitute formal publication, for he published
> in Vanity Fair thirteen poems from the 1926
> edition after the appearance of this edition.
> The list which follows includes these periodi-
> cal appearances, which are also included in
> section C of the bibliography.

Contents and Previous Publication

The Poet

"Five Poems," New York Evening Post Literary Review, 20
Dec. 1924, p. 8.

The Visitor

Tall Towers

"Five Poems," New York Evening Post Literary Review, 20
Dec. 1924, p. 8, and My City (1929).

Proteus

"Four Poems," American Mercury, 1 (Jan. 1924), 8-10.

For I Have Made Me a Garden

Static

Song

The Sailor

Wood Note

"Four Poems," Smart Set, 49 (May 1916), 277-78.

The Guardian

Étude--Rain

Shadow

THEODORE DREISER: A BIBLIOGRAPHY

MOODS: CADENCED AND DECLAIMED

The Stream

   "Recent Poems of Life and Labour," Vanity Fair, 26 (Aug.
      1926), 61.

The Far Country

   "Recent Poems of Youth and Age," Vanity Fair, 27 (Oct.
      1926), 70.

The Riddle

Demons

For I Have Not Love

Formulae

Sky Imagery

Little Dreams, Little Wishes

The Hopeless Lover

The Gladiator

To a Wood Dove

Morituri Te Salutamus

Love Song [I]

The Cry

The Rival Gods

Diana

The Passing Freight

Geddo Street

   "Recent Poems of Life and Labour," Vanity Fair, 26 (Aug.
      1926), 61.

Ephemeron

Oh, You Who Find Beauty a Wanton

WORKS BY - Books

For A Moment the Wind Died

"Four Poems," Smart Set, 49 (May 1916), 277-78; "Four Poems," American Mercury, 1 (Jan. 1924), 8-10; and For A Moment the Wind Died: Song, Words by Theodore Dreiser, Music by Carl E. Gehring, London: Dolard, 1925.

Tethered

Him

The Perfect Room

The Beggar

Heyday

Related

April Weather

Amid the Ruins of My Dreams

Flaherty Junction

Oasis

Allegory

Life

Little Keys

Black Pools

The Young God

The Prisoner

All in All

The Dancer

The Victim Speaks

Vanity Fair, 27 (Feb. 1927), 40.

MOODS: CADENCED AND DECLAIMED

Oh, Little Flame

The Ensorcellor

The Greater Sea

Hosts and Guests

The Dreamer

Dirge--Winter

Zither--Spring

A Wine of Bitterness

Little Moonlight Things of Song

    "Recent Poems of Youth and Age," Vanity Fair, 27 (Oct. 1926), 70 (as "Little Moonlight Things").

The Victor

A Flower Speaks

The Toymaker

Differences

In A Country Graveyard

    "Five Poems," New York Evening Post Literary Review, 20 Dec. 1924, p. 8.

It

'Tis Thus You Torture Me

Acquaintances

Love Plaint

    "Recent Poems of Love and Sorrow," Vanity Fair, 27 (Sept. 1926), 54.

The Creator

So Weary I

WORKS BY - Books

Mirage

Love [I]

Rain

The Abyss

The Never Resting

The Beautiful

"Recent Poems of Love and Sorrow," Vanity Fair, 27 (Sept. 1926), 54.

Ego

Lament

The Wraith

The Furred and Feathery

To Loveliness

The Symbol

Exhortation

The Pilgrim

Nepenthe

The Sacrificed and Suffering

The Spell

The Great Blossom

Leonardo, Annual Magazine of the Leonardo da Vinci Art School, 1924/25 (1925), p. 54.

Phantasm [I]

The Voyage

The Galley Slave

MOODS: CADENCED AND DECLAIMED

Requiem

The Hidden God

   "Five Poems," New York Evening Post Literary Review, 20
      Dec. 1924, p. 8.

Moonlight--May

The Little Home

The Little Flowers of Love and Wonder

   "Four Poems," American Mercury, 1 (Jan. 1924), 8-10;
      Little Flowers of Love and Wonder: Song, Words by
      Theodore Dreiser, Music by Carl L. Gehring, London:
      Dolard, 1925; and "Recent Poems of Love and Sorrow,"
      Vanity Fair, 27 (Sept. 1926), 54 (as "Love and Wonder").

Night Voices

Take Hands

Egypt

The Weaver

Days

Suns and Flowers, and Rats, and Kings

The Time-Keeper

Youth

   "Recent Poems of Youth and Age," Vanity Fair, 27 (Oct.
      1926), 70.

The Beauty

Asia

Magic

Inquiry

I Lie Contending

WORKS BY - Books

Empty Rooms

The Wanderer

Shimtu

The "Bad" House

    "Recent Poems of Life and Labour," Vanity Fair, 26 (Aug. 1926), 61.

The Hell Pool

Heaven

Conquest

Cloudless Pleasure

Gold

Dakota Evening

The Master

The New Day

    "Five Poems," New York Evening Post Literary Review, 20 Dec. 1924, p. 8.

The Factory

    "Recent Poems of Life and Labour," Vanity Fair, 26 (Aug. 1926), 61.

Ye Ages, Ye Tribes

    "Four Poems," Smart Set, 49 (May 1916), 277-78.

Boom--Boom--Boom

The Rebel

Evensong

Protoplast

They Have Nourished as Abundant Rain

MOODS: CADENCED AND DECLAIMED

The Ancestor

October

To You

November

Where?

   "Recent Poems of Youth and Age," <u>Vanity Fair</u>, 27 (Oct.
     1926), 70.

The Haunted House

The Nestlings

The Humanist

Us

The Return

The Absolute

The Last Tryst

   "Recent Poems of Love and Sorrow," <u>Vanity Fair</u>, 27 (Sept.
     1926), 54.

For Answer

The Courting

The Artist

Storm

Prometheus

Fata Morgana

As It Is with the Living

The Guest

Proclamation

Theodore Dreiser: A Bibliography

WORKS BY - Books

The Runner

Sanctuary

The Little God

Intruders

Moon-Moth

Driven

The Ascent

Alembic

Enigma

They Have Conferred with Me in Solemn Counsel

This Living

The Husbandman

The Image of Our Dreams

Confession

The Greater Wisdom

Music

   Vanity Fair, 26 (June 1926), 68.

O Urgent, Seeking Soul!

Beyond the Tracks

The Face of the World

Defeat

They Shall Fall as Stripped Garments

   "Four Poems," Smart Set, 49 (May 1916), 277-78.

Seraphim

Avatar

Pastel

The Last Voice

As with a Finger in Water

A27-1   THE FINANCIER

The / Financier / a Novel / by / Theodore Dreiser / completely revised edition / (publisher's device) / New York / Boni & Liveright /
1927

> 7 3/8 x 5, vi, 506 pp. (i-ii), half-title, verso advertise-
> ment; (iii-iv), title, verso copyright notice; (v-vi), fly-
> title, verso blank; 1-503, text; (504-506), blank.

Blue cloth, lettering on front and spine in gold.

Published 16 April 1927.

Later Publication in English

1927--London: Constable ("New Uniform Edition").

1936--London: Constable ("Popular Edition").

1946--Cleveland: World.*

1961--New York: Dell (Laurel Dreiser, with a general introduction by Alfred Kazin).

1967--New York: New American Library (Signet Classic, with
an afterword by Larzer Ziff).

1968--London: Panther (London Panther, with an introduction
by T. G. Rosenthal).

1972--Cleveland: World (included in A Trilogy of Desire,
with an introduction by Philip Gerber).*

Translations

Czech

> Finančnik.   Trans. Emanuela and Emanuel Tilschovi.
> Prague: Knihovna Klasiku, 1961.

43

WORKS BY - Books

German

Der Titan: Trilogie der Begierder. Erster Roman: Der
Finanzier. Trans. Marianne Schön and Wilhelm Cremer.
Berlin: Paul Zsolnay, 1928.

Der Finanzier. Trans. Marianne Schön. Berlin and
Weimar: Aufbau, 1964.

Italian

Il Finanziere. Trans. Franca Violani Cancogni. Turin:
Einaudi, 1955.

Lithuanian

Finansininkas. Trans. K. Viaras-Račkauskas. Vilna:
Valstybinė Grožinės Literaturos Leidykla, 1958.

Russian

[Finansist. Trans. Mark Volosov. Moscow: Gosudarstvennoe Izdatel'stvo Khudozhestvennoĭ Literatury, 1944].

[Finansist. Trans. Mark Volosov. Kiev: Derzhavne
Vidavnit'stvo Khudozhnoĭ Literatury, 1959].

Serbo-Croatian

Financijer, Titan, Stoik (Trilogija). Trans. Vjekoslav
Susanić, Mira Kučić, and Franjo Bukovšek. Rijeka:
Otokar Keršovani, 1963.

Slovenian

Finančnik. Trans. Joze Stabej. Ljubljana: Državna
Založba Slovenije, 1966.

Spanish

El Financiero. Trans. Manuel Pumarega. Madrid:
Ediciones Hoy, 1930.

CHAINS

El Financiero. Trans. Manuel Pumarega. Buenos Aires:
Editorial Futuro, 1943.

Swedish

Finansmannen. Trans. Margaretha Odelberg, f. Frölich.
Stockholm: P. A. Norstedt, 1929.

A27-2   CHAINS

Chains / Lesser Novels and Stories by / Theodore Dreiser / (publisher's device) / New York / Boni & Liveright / 1927

7 1/2 x 5 1/8, iv, 428 pp. (i-ii), blank; (iii-iv), half-
title, verso blank; (1-2), title, verso copyright notice;
(3-4), foreword, verso blank; (5-6), contents, verso blank;
(7-8), fly-title, verso blank; 9-425, text; (426-428), blank.

Dark blue cloth, lettering on front and spine in gold.

Published 30 April 1927.

Contents and Previous Publication

Foreword

   I.   Sanctuary

      Smart Set, 60 (Oct. 1919), 35-52.

  II.   The Hand

      Munsey's, 66 (May 1919), 679-88.

 III.   Chains

      New York Tribune, 18 May 1919, Part 7, pp. 2-3
      (as "Love").

 IV.   St. Columba and the River

      Pictorial Review, 26 (Jan. 1925), 5-7, 51-52, 54,
      71 (as "Glory Be! McGlathery").

  V.   Convention

      American Mercury, 6 (Dec. 1925), 398-408.

WORKS BY - Books

 VI. Khat

 VII. Typhoon

   Hearst's International-Cosmopolitan, 81 (Oct. 1926), 42-45, 175-81 (as "The Wages of Sin").

 VIII. The Old Neighborhood

   Metropolitan, 49 (Dec. 1918), 27-30, 46, 48-50.

 IX. Phantom Gold

   Live Stories, 26 (Feb. 1921), 3-23.

 X. Marriage for One

   Marriage (1923).

 XI. Fulfilment

   Holland's Magazine, 43 (Feb. 1924), 7-9, 31.

 XII. Victory

   Jewish Daily Forward (New York), 24 Apr. 1927, English Section, pp. 12-13, 23.

 XIII. The Shadow

   Harper's Bazar, 59 (Aug. 1924), 84-85, 92, 94, 96 (as "Jealousy").

 XIV. The "Mercy" of God

   American Mercury, 2 (Aug. 1924), 457-64 (as "The Mercy of God").

 XV. The Prince Who Was a Thief

Later Publication in English

1927--New York: Boni and Liveright (limited and signed edition).*

1928--London: Constable ("New Uniform Edition").

1937--London: Constable ("Popular Edition").

A27-3   THE HAND OF THE POTTER

The Hand of the Potter / by / Theodore Dreiser / a Tragedy in Four
Acts / (publisher's device) / Boni and Liveright / Publishers New
York

> 7 1/2 x 5 1/8, 206 pp. (1-2), free end paper, verso blank;
> (3-4), blank; (5-6), half-title, verso advertisement; (7-8),
> title, verso copyright notice; (9-10), epigraph, verso blank;
> (11-12), characters; (13-14), divisional title, verso blank;
> 15-205, text; (206), blank.
>
> Red cloth, lettering on front in blind within a gold box,
> lettering on spine in gold.
>
> Published 17 November 1927 (Orton, Dreiserana, 1929, p. 55).
>
> > Note: Dreiser's revision of the 1919 edition
> > consists of the cutting of approximately four
> > pages from the last act of the play.

A28-1   MOODS: CADENCED AND DECLAIMED

Moods / Cadenced & / Declaimed / by / Theodore / Dreiser / with
fifteen symbols by / Hugh Gray Lieber / New York / Boni & Liveright /
1928

> 8 1/8 x 5 1/2, xiv, 386 pp. + a tipped-in, unpaginated
> frontispiece and 14 tipped-in, unpaginated illustrations.
> (i-ii), half-title, verso blank; blank, verso frontispiece;
> (iii-iv), title, verso copyright notice; v-xi, contents;
> (xii), blank; (xiii-xiv), list of illustrations, verso blank;
> 1-385, text; (386), blank.
>
> Light brown boards, blue cloth spine, lettering on front and
> on spine in gold.
>
> Published 30 July 1928.
>
> > Note: The 1928 edition of Moods contains all
> > the poems in the 1926 edition and 29 addi-
> > tional poems. The 1926 plates were used for
> > the initial 327 pages of the 1928 edition; the
> > new poems were then added to form pages 328-
> > 384; and the last poem of the 1926 edition,
> > "As with a Finger in Water" (p. 328), was
> > shifted to become the last poem in the 1928
> > edition (p. 385).

WORKS BY -- Books

Contents and Previous Publication

All the poems of the 1926 edition of Moods; see the note
    above and Moods (1926).

Eyes

Marriage

Pastel Twilight

Trees

Fugue

Decadence

The Great Voice

The Brook

The Fool

The March

Dreams

Fire of Hell

Lilies and Roses

By the Waterside

The Deathless Princess

You Are the Silence

Love Song [II]

Divine Fire

In the Park

Regret

To a Windflower

The One and Only

DREISER LOOKS AT RUSSIA

The Road I Came

The Evanescent Moment

Phantasm [II]

The House of Dreams

Pierrot

The Old South

Links

Later Publication in English

1929--London: Constable.

A28-2   DREISER LOOKS AT RUSSIA

Theodore Dreiser / Dreiser Looks / at Russia / (publisher's device) / New York / Horace Liveright 1928

> 8 1/8 x 5 3/8, 264 pp. (1-2), half-title, verso blank; (3-4), title, verso copyright notice; (5-6), contents, verso blank; (7-8), fly-title, verso blank; 9-264, text.

> Black cloth, lettering on front and spine in gold.

> Published 1 November 1928.

Previous Publication

Chapter I, pp. 9-15

> "Soviet Plan to Spread to U.S., Dreiser Thinks," New York World, 18 Mar. 1928, pp. 1, 8.

Chapter I, pp. 15-21

> "Dreiser Looks at Russia," New York World, 19 Mar. 1928, p. 13.

Chapter III

> "Russia: The Great Experiment," Vanity Fair, 30 (June 1928), 47-48, 102.

Theodore Dreiser: A Bibliography

WORKS BY - Books

Chapter VI, pp. 74-81

"Dreiser Looks at Russia," New York World, 20 Mar. 1928,
p. 15.

Chapter VI, pp. 81-88

"Dreiser Looks at Russia," New York World, 21 Mar. 1928,
p. 15.

Chapter VII, pp. 89-92

"Dreiser Looks at Russia," New York World, 23 Mar. 1928,
p. 15.

Chapter VII, pp. 97-99

"Dreiser Looks at Russia," New York World, 24 Mar. 1928,
p. 17.

Chapter VII, pp. 99-101

"Dreiser Looks at Russia," New York World, 26 Mar. 1928,
p. 15.

Chapter IX, pp. 120-21

"Dreiser Looks at Russia," New York World, 24 Mar. 1928,
p. 17.

Chapter IX, pp. 121-23

"Dreiser Looks at Russia," New York World, 25 Mar. 1928,
p. 6.

Chapter XVI

"Citizens of Moscow," Vanity Fair, 31 (Oct. 1928), 55-56,
102, 104.

Chapter XVII

"Russian Vignettes," Saturday Evening Post, 200 (28 Apr.
1928), 18-19, 80-82.

Chapter XVIII, pp. 245-54

"Dreiser Looks at Russia," New York World, 22 Mar. 1928,
p. 15.

THE CARNEGIE WORKS AT PITTSBURGH

Chapter XVIII, pp. 254-59

"Dreiser Looks at Russia," New York World, 28 Mar. 1928, p. 17.

Later Publication in English

1929--London: Constable.

Translations

German

Sowjet-Russland. Trans. Richard Hoffmann. Berlin: Paul Zsolnay, 1929.

A29-1 THE CARNEGIE WORKS AT PITTSBURGH

The / Carnegie Works / at Pittsburgh / Theodore Dreiser / decorations by Martha Colley / (illustration) / printed privately at Chelsea, New York

A limited edition of 177 copies in two states:

27 numbered copies: 9 1/2 x 6 1/4, 42 pp. (1-2), half-title, verso blank; (3-4), title, verso blank; (5-6), fly-title, verso blank; 7-38, text; (39-40), blank, verso limited edition notice; (41-42), blank, with edges folded to make a pocket in which is laid a leaf from the original holograph manuscript of Dreiser's article; red cloth, lettering on front in gold.

150 numbered copies: 9 x 6 1/4, iv, 44 pp. (i-iv), blank; (1-2), half-title, verso blank; (3-4), title, verso blank; (5-6), fly-title, verso blank; 7-38, text; (39-40), blank, limited edition notice; (41-44), blank; boards with a black and white design, light tan cloth spine; lettering on front on a white paper label in black.

> Note: The most problematical of Dreiser's separate publications. Both the physical state of the laid in manuscript and internal historical references date the composition of the essay as 1899, but it was apparently not published in article form at that time. (The essay is not to be confused with Dreiser's "A Monarch of Metal Workers," Success, 2 (3 June 1899), 453-54.) Moreover, Dreiser did not

WORKS BY - Books

> authorize the publication of the essay in its
> limited edition form. He wrote in a copy now
> in the Cornell University Library, "This is an
> unauthorized publication. Pirates seem to have
> been at work. Theodore Dreiser. Mt. Kisco,
> N. Y. May--1938." A probable explanation for
> the appearance of the book is that the manu-
> script was acquired by a New York collector or
> dealer--Chelsea is an area of Manhattan just
> north of Washington Square--who then had a
> limited edition prepared for his own amusement
> or profit. No printer or publisher is named and
> even the date of publication is uncertain. It
> is variously dated 1927 and 1929. Since McDonald
> does not mention it in his bibliography, which
> is complete to late 1927, and Orton does mention
> it in his 1929 Dreiserana, 1929 appears to be
> the more probable date.

A29-2   THE ASPIRANT

The Aspirant / by Theodore Dreiser / (publisher's device) / Random
House, New York / 1929

> 9 7/8 x 6 1/4, 8 pp. (1-2), blank; (3-4), title, verso blank;
> (5-6), text, verso limited edition and copyright notices;
> (7-8), blank.

> Light mauve wrappers.

> Published Spring 1929 (Random House records).

> > Note: Published in the Random House Poetry
> > Quarto series in an edition of 475 copies.

A29-3   A GALLERY OF WOMEN

A Gallery of / Women / Theodore / Dreiser / in two volumes / volume
I / (publisher's device) / New York / Horace Liveright / 1929

> 7 1/2 x 5 1/8, 428 pp. (1-2), half-title, verso blank; (3-4),
> title, verso copyright notice; (5-6), contents, verso blank;
> (7-8), fly-title, verso blank; (9-10), divisional title,
> verso blank; 11-428, text.

> Brown cloth, lettering on front and spine in gold.

A GALLERY OF WOMEN

Contents and Previous Publication

Reina

    Century, 106 (Sept. 1923), 695-716.

Olive Brand

    Hearst's International-Cosmopolitan, 84 (May 1928), 47-49, 130-34.

Ellen Adams Wrynn

Lucia

Giff

Ernita

Albertine

A Gallery of / Women / Theodore / Dreiser / in two volumes / volume II / (publisher's device) / New York / Horace Liveright / 1929

    7 1/2 x 5 1/8, vi, 398 pp. (i-ii), half-title, verso blank; (iii-iv), title, verso copyright notice; (v-vi), contents, verso blank; (429-30), divisional title, verso blank; 431-823, text; (824-826), blank.

Brown cloth, lettering on front and spine in gold.

Published 30 November 1929.

Contents and Previous Publication

Regina C--

    Hearst's International-Cosmopolitan, 84 (June 1928), 55-58, 144-49.

Rella

    Hearst's International-Cosmopolitan, 84 (Apr. 1928), 36-39, 199-204.

Ernestine

    Bookman, 66 (Sept. 1927), 2-14 (as "Portrait of a Woman").

WORKS BY - Books

Rona Murtha

Ida Hauchawout:

Century, 106 (July 1923), 335-48.

Emanuela

Esther Norn

Bridget Mullanphy

Later Publication in English

1929--New York: Liveright (limited edition).*

1930--London: Constable.

1930--Leipsig: Tauchnitz (Collection of British and American authors).

1962--Greenwich, Conn.: Fawcett (Premier Book, with an introduction by William C. Lengel).

Translations

German

Die Frau: Fünfzehn Lebensschicksale. Trans. Marianne
    Schön. Berlin: Paul Zsolnay, 1930.

Polish

Galerja Kobiet. Trans. Z. Popławskiej. Warsaw: Świat,
    [1933].

Russian

[Gallereĩa Zhenshchîn. Trans. V. Stanevich and V.
    Barbashovaĩā, intro. S. S. Dinamov. Moscow: Gosudarst-
    vennoe Izdatel'stvo Khudozhestvennoi Literatury, 1933].

Serbo-Croatian

Galerija Žena. Trans. Vjekoslav Susanič. Rijeka: Otokar
    Keršovani, 1963.

54

PLAYS, NATURAL AND SUPERNATURAL

A29-4   MY CITY

My City / by Theodore Dreiser / illustrated / with eight etchings /
in color by / Max Pollak / published / in New York by Horace
Liveright

> 14 7/8 x 11, 20 pp. (1-2), half-title, verso copyright no-
> tice; (3-4), limited edition notice, verso blank; (5-6),
> title, verso illustration; (7-8), illustration; (9-17), text
> and illustrations; (18), colophon; (19-20), blank.

> Boards with wood-grain design, lettering on front in black.

> Published 16 December 1929.

>> Note: Published in a limited edition of 275
>> signed copies.

Previous Publication

> The entire work (poetry and prose) appeared in the
> New York Herald-Tribune, 23 Dec. 1928, Section 3, p. 1;
> the poetry portion appeared as "Tall Towers" in "Five
> Poems," New York Evening Post Literary Review, 20 Dec.
> 1924, p. 8, and in the 1926 and 1928 editions of Moods.

A30-1   PLAYS, NATURAL AND SUPERNATURAL

Plays / Natural and Supernatural / by / Theodore Dreiser / London /
Constable & Co Ltd / 1930

> 7 7/8 x 5, viii, 392 pp. (unpaginated leaf), blank; (i-ii),
> half-title, verso advertisement; (iii-iv), title, verso copy-
> right notice; v-vi, contents, verso blank; (1-2), divisional
> title, verso characters; 3-389, text; (390-92), blank.

> Marbled boards, light mauve cloth spine, lettering on spine
> in gold.

> Published February 1930 (Whitaker's).

Contents and Previous Publication

> I. The Girl in the Coffin

>> Plays of the Natural and the Supernatural (1916).

WORKS BY - Books

II.   The Blue Sphere

    <u>Plays</u>

III.   Laughing Gas

    <u>Plays</u>

IV.   In the Dark

    <u>Plays</u>

V.   The Spring Recital

    <u>Plays</u>

VI.   The Light in the Window

    <u>Plays</u>

VII.   "Old Ragpicker"

    <u>Plays</u>

VIII.   Phantasmagoria

    <u>Hey Rub-a-Dub-Dub</u> (1920)

IX.   The Court of Progress

    <u>Hey</u>

X.   The Dream

    <u>Hey</u>

XI.   The Anaesthetic Revelation

    <u>Plays</u>

XII.   The Hand of the Potter

    <u>The Hand of the Potter</u> (1919)

A30-2   EPITAPH

Epitaph / a Poem / by Theodore Dreiser / decorations by / Robert
Fawcett / Heron Press Incorporated New York

A limited edition of 1200 copies in three states:

Numbers 1-200:   11 1/2 x 8 5/8, 64 pp. (1-2), half-title,
verso limited edition notice; (3-4), ornament, verso illustration; (5-6), title, verso copyright notice; (7-8), fly-
title, verso ornament; (9-58), text and ornaments; (59-60),
ornament, verso blank; (61-64), blank; black leather,
lettering on front and spine in gold.

Numbers 201-400:   11 3/4 x 8 7/8, 64 pp. (1-2), half-title,
verso limited edition notice; (3-4), ornament, verso illustration; (5-6), title, verso copyright notice; (7-8), fly-
title, verso ornament; (9-58), text and ornaments; (59-60),
ornament, verso blank; (61-64), blank; black silk, lettering
on front and spine in silver.

Numbers 401-1200:   11 3/4 x 8 7/8, 64 pp. (1-2), half-title,
verso limited edition notice; (3-4), ornament, verso illustration; (5-6), title, verso copyright notice; (7-8), fly-
title, verso ornament; (9-58), text and ornaments; (59-60),
ornament, verso blank; (61-64), blank; black cloth, lettering
on front and spine in gold.

Published 24 May 1930.

Note: The poem also appears in the 1935
edition of Moods.

A30-3   JOHN REED CLUB ANSWER

Broadside, 12 15/16 x 8 7/16.

Note: A reply, dated "Portland, Oregon, June
10, 1930," to a request by the John Reed Club
of New York to comment on political persecution
in America.

A30-4   FINE FURNITURE

Fine / Furniture / by / Theodore / Dreiser / (publisher's device) /
Random House   New York / 1930

WORKS BY - Books

8 1/4 x 5 1/4, iv, 40 pp. (i-ii), blank; (iii-iv), half-title,
verso blank; (1-2), title, verso limited edition and copyright notices; 3-35, text; (36-40), blank.

Light blue wrappers, lettering on spine on a white label in
black.

Published 27 December 1930.

> Note: Published in the Random House Prose
> Quarto series in a limited edition of 875
> copies. Dreiser's contribution was Number 6
> in the series.

Previous Publication

Household Magazine, 29 (Nov. 1929), 5-7; 29 (Dec. 1929),
4-5, 29-32.

A31-1   DAWN

A History of Myself / Dawn / Theodore / Dreiser / Horace Liveright,
Inc. / New York

9 3/8 x 6 1/4, vi, 590 pp. (i-ii), blank; (iii-iv), half-
title, verso advertisement; (v-vi), title, verso copyright
notice; (1-2), fly-title, verso blank; 3-589, text; (590),
blank.

Red cloth, black cloth spine, lettering on front and spine
in gold (uniform with Liveright's A History of Myself: Newspaper Days, the 1931 impression of A Book About Myself).

Published 8 May 1931.

Later Publication in English

1931--New York: Liveright (limited and signed edition).*

1931--London: Constable.

1937--London: Constable ("Popular Edition").

1958--Greenwich, Conn.: Fawcett (Premier Book).

1965--Greenwich, Conn.: Fawcett (Premier Book, published as
Volume I of Theodore Dreiser: His Autobiography).

TRAGIC AMERICA

Translations

German

> Das Buch über mich Selbst (Jugend). Trans. Marianne
> Schön. Berlin: Paul Zsolnay, 1932.

A31-2   TRAGIC AMERICA

Tragic / America / by / Theodore Dreiser / (publisher's device) /
Horace Liveright, Inc. / New York

> 8 1/16 x 5 1/2, x, 438 pp. (i-ii), blank; (iii-iv), half-
> title, verso advertisement; (v-vi), title, verso copyright
> page; (vii-viii), contents; (ix-x), fly-title, verso blank;
> 1-426, text; 427-435, index; (436-438), blank.

Mottled grey cloth, lettering on front and spine in gold.

Published 30 December 1931.

> Note: A prepublication state exists which con-
> tains a number of verbal variants from the pub-
> lished volume. Those variants initially noted
> by Merle Johnson and confirmed by me are:

	Prepublication	Published
p. 49, 1. 14	filched	pocketed
p. 100, 1. 13	fraudulent	excessive
p. 130, 1. 4	corruption	subservience
p. 380, 1.4 up	pirates	figures

Later Publication in English

1932--London: Constable.

Translations

French

> L'Amérique Tragique. Trans. Paul Nizan.   Paris: Les
> Éditions Rieder, 1933.

German

> Die Tragik Amerikas. Trans. Marianne Schön.   Berlin:
> Paul Zsolnay, 1932.

WORKS BY - Books

Hungarian

A Dollár Uralma Alatt. Trans. Iván Boldizsár. Budapest:
Szépirodalmi Könyvkiadó, 1951.

Russian

[Tragicheskaia Amerika. Trans. E. Kalashnikovaia and O.
Kholmskaia, intro. I. Anisimov. Moscow: Gosudarstvennoe Izdatel'stvo Khudozhestvennoi Literatury, 1952].

A33-1 TOM MOONEY

Tom Mooney / by Theodore Dreiser / 10¢

9 x 6, 8 pp. (1-8), text.

Wrappers.

Published April 1933 (advertisement for the Free Tom Mooney
Cabaret Ball on verso of front wrapper).

A35-1 MOODS: PHILOSOPHIC AND EMOTIONAL (CADENCED AND DECLAIMED)

Moods / Philosophic and Emotional / Cadenced and Declaimed / Theodore
Dreiser / (publisher's device) / Simon and Schuster / New York / 1935

7 7/8 x 5 1/2, xviii, 426 pp. (i-ii), publisher's device,
verso blank; (iii-iv), title, verso copyright notice; v-viii,
introduction by Sulamith Ish-Kishor; ix-xvii, contents;
xviii, blank; (1-2), fly-title, verso blank; 3-423, text;
424, "About the Author"; (425-426), blank.

Aquamarine cloth, lettering on front and spine in gold.

Published 10 June 1935.

Note: For the 1935 edition of Moods, Dreiser
revised the 1928 edition by omitting 37 poems,
carrying over 173 poems, and adding 77 poems.
In noting previous publication below, I abbre-
viate the 1926 edition as M (26) and the 1928
edition as M (28).

MOODS: PHILOSOPHIC AND EMOTIONAL (CADENCED AND DECLAIMED)

Contents and Previous Publication

Introduction

1. The Poet

    M̲ (26, 28).

2. Individuality

3. The Sailor

    M̲ (26, 28).

4. Decadence

    M̲ (28).

5. The Broken Ship

6. Arizona

7. The Toymaker

    M̲ (26, 28).

8. Tall Towers

    M̲ (26, 28), "My City," New York Herald-Tribune, 23
    Dec. 1928, Section 3, p. 1, and My City (1929).

9. Proteus

    M̲ (26, 28).

10. For I Have Made Me a Garden

    M̲ (26, 28).

11. Karma

12. Zither--Spring

    M̲ (26, 28).

13. Brahma

14. Song

   M (26, 28).

15. Etude--Rain

   M (26, 28).

16. The Little Flowers of Love and Wonder

   M (26, 28).

17. The Muffled Oar

   Nation, 128 (27 Feb. 1929), 258.

18. Suns and Flowers, and Rats, and Kings

   M (26, 28).

19. Moonlight--May

   M (26, 28).

20. Marriage

   M (28).

21. The Ensorcellor

   M (26, 28).

22. River Dirge

23. Desire--Ecstasy

24. Intruders

   M (26, 28).

25. Evening--Mountains

   "Three Poems," American Spectator, 2 (Feb. 1934), 4.

26. The Great Blossom

   M (26, 28).

MOODS: PHILOSOPHIC AND EMOTIONAL (CADENCED AND DECLAIMED)

27. Chief Strong Bow Speaks

"Three Poems," <u>American Spectator</u>, 2 (Feb. 1934), 4.

28. Wood Note

<u>M</u> (26, 28).

29. The Weaver

<u>M</u> (26, 28).

30. The New Day

<u>M</u> (26, 28).

31. Epitaph

<u>Epitaph: A Poem</u> (1930).

32. Night Voices

<u>M</u> (26, 28).

33. A Wine of Bitterness

<u>M</u> (26, 28).

34. Trees

<u>M</u> (28).

35. Geddo Street

<u>M</u> (26, 28).

36. The Myth of Possessions

37. The Great Face

38. But I Have Not Love

<u>M</u> (26, 28).

39. Formula

<u>M</u> (26, 28) (as "Formulae").

WORKS BY - Books

40. The Evil Treasure

41. Conclusion

42. Two by Two

43. "Material" Possessions

44. The Passing Freight

M (26, 28).

45. The Rival Gods

M (26, 28).

46. Links

M (28).

47. Fire of Hell

M (28).

48. Love Song [II]

M (28).

49. Him

M (26, 28).

50. Pastel

M (26, 28).

51. Machine

"Five Moods in Minor Key," Esquire, 2 (Mar. 1935), 25.

52. The Savage

53. Flower and Rain

54. The Ultimate Necessity

55. Static

M (26, 28).

MOODS: PHILOSOPHIC AND EMOTIONAL (CADENCED AND DECLAIMED)

56. The Guardian

M (26, 28).

57. The Fool

M (28).

58. The Beauty

M (26, 28).

59. Pierrot

M (28).

60. The Never Resting

M (26, 28).

61. The Factory

M (26, 28).

62. Marsh Bubbles

63. For Answer

M (26, 28).

64. The "Bad" House

M (26, 28).

65. The Little Home

M (26, 28).

66. The Martyr

American Spectator, 1 (July 1933), 4.

67. The Watch

68. The Little God

M (26, 28).

69. April Weather

   M̲ (26, 28).

70. The Thinker

71. The Brook

   M̲ (28).

72. The Granted Dream

73. The Galley Slave

   M̲ (26, 28).

74. The Psychic Wound

75. Fugue

   M̲ (26, 28).

76. Eunuch

77. Equation

78. The Riddle

   M̲ (26, 28).

79. St. Francis to His God

80. The Light House

   M̲ (26, 28) (as "The Cry").

81. Tigress and Zebra

82. By the Waterside

   M̲ (26, 28).

83. Sky Imagery

   M̲ (26, 28).

84. Protoplast

   M̲ (26, 28).

MOODS: PHILOSOPHIC AND EMOTIONAL (CADENCED AND DECLAIMED)

85. For a Moment the Wind Died

    M (26, 28).

86. Shadow

    M (26, 28).

87. All Thought--All Sorrow

88. Machines

89. Flaherty Junction

    M (26, 28).

90. The Perfect Room

    M (26, 28).

91. The Beggar

    M (26, 28).

92. The Reformer Speaks

93. The Hopeless Lover

    M (26, 28).

94. Related

    M (26, 28).

95. Oasis

    M (26, 28).

96. The Victim Speaks

    M (26, 28).

97. Lydian Measure

    M (26, 28) (as "Love Song [I]").

98. The Furred and the Feathery

    M (26, 28).

99. All in All

   M (26, 28).

100. The Master

   M (26, 28).

101. The Traveler

102. Lust

   M (26, 28) (as "The Victor").

103. Sidereal

104. Improvisation

   "Five Moods in Minor Key," Esquire, 2 (Mar. 1935), 25.

105. Egypt

   M (26, 28).

106. The Prisoner

   M (26, 28).

107. In a Country Graveyard

   M (26, 28).

108. The Greater Sea

   M (26, 28).

109. Tethered

   M (26, 28).

110. Little Dreams, Little Wishes

   M (26, 28).

111. Before the Accusing Faces of Billions

112. The Last Tryst

   M (26, 28).

MOODS: PHILOSOPHIC AND EMOTIONAL (CADENCED AND DECLAIMED)

113. I Lie Contending

M̲ (26, 28).

114. Heaven

M̲ (26, 28).

115. Diana

M̲ (26, 28).

116. The Young God

M̲ (26, 28).

117. The Dreamer

M̲ (26, 28).

118. Revolt

119. The Dancer

M̲ (26, 28).

120. The Stream

M̲ (26, 28).

121. To a Wood Dove

M̲ (26, 28).

122. Lilies and Roses

M̲ (28).

123. The Hidden God

M̲ (26, 28).

124. Gold

M̲ (26, 28).

125. Cloudless Pleasure

M̲ (26, 28).

WORKS BY - Books

126. They Have Conferred with Me in Solemn Counsel

M (26, 28).

127. Beyond the Tracks

M (26, 28).

128. The Sower

M (26, 28) (as "The Husbandman").

129. The Old South

M (28).

130. Thought

131. The Nestlings

M (26, 28).

132. The Greater Wisdom

M (26, 28).

133. The Humanist

M (26, 28).

134. The Visitor

M (26, 28).

135. The Road I Came

M (28).

136. Sunset and Dawn

137. Wood Tryst

138. Cat Tails--November

American Spectator, 1 (Jan. 1933), 3.

139. This Living

M (26, 28).

MOODS: PHILOSOPHIC AND EMOTIONAL (CADENCED AND DECLAIMED)

140. Differences

M (26, 28).

141. Oh, You Who Find Beauty a Wanton

M (26, 28).

142. The Balance

143. The Love Death

144. The Beautiful

M (26, 28).

145. The Gladiator

M (26, 28).

146. Oh, Little Flame

M (26, 28).

147. 'Tis Thus You Torture Me

M (26, 28).

148. The Symbol

M (26, 28).

149. Asia

M (26, 28).

150. Messenger

151. Rain

M (26, 28).

152. Ye Ages, Ye Tribes

M (26, 28).

153. The Rebel

M (26, 28).

WORKS BY - Books

154. The Courting

   M (26, 28).

155. The Guest

   M (26, 28).

156. Alembic

   M (26, 28).

157. Little Keys

   M (26, 28).

158. Storm

   M (26, 28).

159. Moon Moth

   M (26, 28).

160. The Abyss

   M (26, 28).

161. The Miracle

162. The Deathless Princess

   M (28).

163. They Shall Fall as Stripped Garments

   M (26, 28).

164. If Beauty Would But Dwell with Me

165. The Creator

   M (26, 28).

166. Home

167. The Spell

   M (26, 28).

MOODS: PHILOSOPHIC AND EMOTIONAL (CADENCED AND DECLAIMED)

168. In the Park

  $\underline{M}$ (28).

169. November

  $\underline{M}$ (26, 28).

170. Dirge--Winter

  $\underline{M}$ (26, 28).

171. The Plaintiff

  $\underline{M}$ (26, 28) (as "So Weary I").

172. Morituri Te Salutamus

  $\underline{M}$ (26, 28).

173. The Process

  "Appearance and Reality," American Spectator, 1
  (Feb. 1933), 4.

174. Tribute

  "Five Moods in Minor Key," Esquire, 2 (Mar. 1935), 25.

175. Factory Walls

176. Something Is Thinking

177. To a Windflower

  $\underline{M}$ (28).

178. Tenantless

179. Ambition

180. Allegory

  $\underline{M}$ (26, 28).

181. The Hidden Poet

182. Sutra

WORKS BY - Books

183. Music

    M (26, 28).

184. The Ascent

    M (26, 28).

185. To You Who Lurk in the Shadow

186. Query

187. The Runner

    M (26, 28).

188. Evensong

    M (26, 28).

189. Love [II]

190. Nature

    M (26, 28) (as "The Artist").

191. Dakota Evening

    M (26, 28).

192. They Have Nourished as Abundant Rain

    M (26, 28).

193. Boom--Boom--Boom

    M (26, 28).

194. Empty Rooms

    M (26, 28).

195. Avatar

    M (26, 28).

196. The Time-Keeper

    M (26, 28).

MOODS: PHILOSOPHIC AND EMOTIONAL (CADENCED AND DECLAIMED)

197. The Pilgrim

    M̲ (26, 28).

198. Take Hands

    M̲ (26, 28).

199. Interrogation

    M̲ (26, 28) (as "Inquiry").

200. Ephemeron

    M̲ (26, 28).

201. The Face of the World

    M̲ (26, 28).

202. Shimtu

    M̲ (26, 28).

203. The Dole

    M̲ (26, 28) (as "Nepenthe").

204. Requiem

    M̲ (26, 28).

205. Night Song

    M̲ (26, 28) (as "Lament").

206. The New World

207. The Wraith

    M̲ (26, 28).

208. Confession

    M̲ (26, 28).

209. "Reality"

WORKS BY - Books

210. Love [I]

    M (26, 28).

211. The Ancestor

    M (26, 28).

212. Search Song

213. Wounded by Beauty

214. Demons

    M (26, 28).

215. Phantasm [I]

    M (26, 28).

216. Pastel Twilight

    M (28).

217. The Wanderer

    M (26, 28).

218. Seraphim

    M (26, 28).

219. The Voyage

    M (26, 28).

220. The Return

    M (26, 28).

221. Regret

    M (28).

222. Contest

223. Fata Morgana

    M (26, 28).

MOODS: PHILOSOPHIC AND EMOTIONAL (CADENCED AND DECLAIMED)

224. The Loafer

"Five Moods in Minor Key," Esquire, 2 (Mar. 1935), 25.

225. A Flower Speaks

M (26, 28).

226. Little Moonlight Things of Song

M (26, 28).

227. Borealis

228. Amid the Ruins of My Dreams

M (26, 28).

229. Etching

230. The Multitude

231. The Far Country

M (26, 28).

232. The Unterrified

"Three Poems," American Spectator, 2 (Feb. 1934), 4 (as "Love").

233. The Sacrificed and Suffering

M (26, 28).

234. The Kiln

235. The Possible

236. Mirage

M (26, 28).

237. Black Pools

M (26, 28).

238. Acquaintances

    M (26, 28).

239. Light and Shadow

240. All

241. Us

    M (26, 28).

242. Escape

    "Five Moods in Minor Key," Esquire, 2 (Mar. 1935), 25.

243. Defeat

    M (26, 28).

244. Phantasmagoria

245. Love Plaint

    M (26, 28).

246. Proclamation

    M (26, 28).

247. Life

    M (26, 28).

248. Selah

249. The Last Voice

    M (26, 28).

250. As with a Finger in Water

    M (26, 28).

A REQUEST AND AN ANSWER

A39-1   THE DAWN IS IN THE EAST

Broadside, 12 3/8 x 8 7/16.

Publication Elsewhere

International Literature, no. 11 (Nov. 1939), pp. 109-111 and
  Common Sense, 8 (Dec. 1939), 6-7.

> Note: Written in response to a request from the
> editors of Common Sense for an opinion about the
> war in Europe. The request is printed in the
> broadside.

A40-1   CONCERNING DIVES AND LAZARUS

Broadside, 16 1/2 x 6 1/8.

Publication Elsewhere

Soviet Russia Today, 8 (Apr. 1940), 8-9 (as "The Soviet-
  Finnish Treaty and World Peace").

> Note: Written in response to a request from
> Jessica Smith, editor of Soviet Russia Today,
> dated 15 March 1940, for a comment on the end
> of the Russian-Finnish War. Miss Smith's tele-
> gram is printed in the broadside.

A40-2   WAR

Broadside, 11 15/16 x 5 5/16.

Publication Elsewhere

People's World, 6 Apr. 1940, p. 7 (as "Theodore Dreiser
  Condemns War").

A40-3   A REQUEST AND AN ANSWER

Broadside, 14 1/2 x 6.

> Note: Dated 16 July 1940. Written in response
> to a request from S. Bayard Colgate, dated 10
> July 1940, for a contribution to the Boys
> Brotherhood Republic. Colgate's letter is
> printed in the broadside.

WORKS BY - Books

A40-4   EDITOR & PUBLISHER

Broadside, 15 3/8 x 6 3/16.

Publication Elsewhere

People's World, 2 Oct. 1940, p. 5 (as "Theodore Dreiser and
the Free Press").

> Note: Dated 18 September 1940. Written in
> response to a request by Walter E. Schneider,
> editor of Editor & Publisher, dated 9 September
> 1940, for a comment on a free press in America.
> Schneider's letter is printed in the broadside.

A40-5   U.S. MUST NOT BE BLED FOR IMPERIAL BRITAIN

Four page leaflet, 7 15/16 x 5 3/16.

Publication Elsewhere

People's World, 12 Nov. 1940, p. 6.

> Note: A headnote on page 1 explains that the
> contents of the leaflet were given as an ad-
> dress by Dreiser on 9 November 1940 over the
> Columbia Broadcasting System on behalf of the
> American Peace Mobilization.

A41-1   AMERICA IS WORTH SAVING

Theodore / Dreiser / America / Is Worth / Saving / Modern Age Books /
New York

> 8 3/8 x 5 5/8, 294 pp. (1-2), half-title, verso advertisement;
> (3-4), title, verso copyright notice; (5-6), contents; (7-8),
> fly-title, verso blank; 9-292, text; (293-296), blank.

> Blue cloth, lettering on front and spine in gold.

Published 20 January 1941.

Previous Publication

Chapter 11

"What Is Democracy?", Clipper, 1 (Dec. 1940), 3-7.

Chapter 16

"Our Democracy: Will It Endure?", New Masses, 38 (21 Jan. 1941), 8-9.

Translations

Spanish

América Debe Ser Salvada. Trans. unknown. Buenos Aires: La Cruz del Sur, 1941.

A41-2 CONCERNING OUR HELPING ENGLAND AGAIN

Four page leaflet, 8 x 5 1/2.

Publication Elsewhere

New Masses, 38 (18 Feb. 1941), 35-36 (as "This Is Churchill's 'Democracy'").

A41-3 MRS. FRANKLIN DELANO ROOSEVELT

Broadside, 11 15/16 x 8 1/2.

> Note: A letter by Dreiser to Mrs. Roosevelt, dated 25 April 1941.

A41-4 TO THE WRITERS' LEAGUE OF AMERICA

Four page leaflet, 7 3/16 x 4 1/2.

> Note: Dated 13 May 1941. A headnote explains that Dreiser is writing in response to a request for an opinion about the political activities of the League of American Writers.

A42-1 EDITORS

Four page leaflet, 9 3/8 x 5 3/4.

> Note: Consists of Dreiser's letter to "Editors," dated 6 October 1942, followed by his undated letter to the Writers War Board explaining his remarks in Toronto.

THEODORE DREISER: A BIBLIOGRAPHY

WORKS BY - Books

A46-1   THE BULWARK

Theodore Dreiser / The / Bulwark / a Novel / (ornament) /
Doubleday & Company Inc. / Garden City 1946 New York

    8 3/8 x 5 5/8, x, 342 pp. (unpaginated), blank; (i-ii), half-
title, verso advertisement; (iii-iv), title, verso copyright
notice; v-viii, introduction; 1-337, text; (338-342), blank.

    Light blue cloth, lettering on front and spine in gold.

    Published 21 March 1946.

Later Publication in English

1946--New York: Book Find Club.*

1947--London: Constable.

1960--New York: Popular Library.

Translations

Danish

    Bolvaerket. Trans. Tom Kristensen. Copenhagen:
      Gyldendal, 1948.

Dutch

    Het Bolwerk. Trans. F. W. B. Engler. Amsterdam: Allert
      de Lange, 1947.

German

    Solon der Quäker. Trans. Carl Bach. Zurich: Humanitas,
      1948.

Hungarian

    Omló Bástya. Trans. Tivadar Szinnai. Budapest: Dante
      Könyvkiadó, 1947.

THE STOIC

Norwegian

Jeg Og Mitt Hus. Trans. A. W. Gammelgaard. Oslo:
Nasjonalforlaget, 1951.

Polish

Szaniec. Trans. Tadeusz Jakubowicz. Warsaw: Ksiazka i
Wiedza, 1950.

Spanish

El Baluarte. Trans. Horacio Laurora. Buenos Aires:
Editorial Guillermo Kraft [1947].

Swedish

Bål Verket. Trans. Aida Törnell. Stockholm: Albatross/
Norstedts, 1947.

A47-1   THE STOIC

The Stoic / Theodore Dreiser / Garden City, New York / Doubleday &
Company, Inc. / 1947

8 3/8 x 5 5/8, viii, 312 pp. (i-ii), blank; (iii-iv), half-
title, verso advertisement; (v-vi), title, verso copyright
notice; (vii-viii), fly-title, verso blank; 1-310, text;
(311-312), blank.

Grey-blue cloth, lettering on spine in gold.

Published 6 November 1947.

Later Publications in English

1952--Cleveland: World.*

1972--Cleveland: World (included in A Trilogy of Desire,
with an introduction by Philip Gerber).*

WORKS BY - Books

Translations

Czech

Stoik. Trans. Anna Novotná. Prague: Knihovna Klasiků, 1964.

Italian

Lo Stoico. Trans. Romano Giachetti. Rome: Editori Riuniti, 1963.

Romanian

Stoicul. Trans. Nic Popescu. Bucharest: Editura Univers, 1971.

Russian

[Stoik. Trans. M. Bogoslovskaia and T. Kuriavtsevaia, Tallin, Estonia: Estonskoe Gosudarstvennoe Izdatel'stvo, 1957].

[Stoik. Trans. M. Bogoslovskaia and T. Kuriavtsevaia. Kiev: Derzhavne Vidavnitstvo Khudozhoi Literatury, 1959].

Serbo-Croatian

Financijer, Titan, Stoik (Trilogija). Trans. Vjekoslav Susanić, Mira Kučić, and Franjo Bukovšek. Rijeka: Otokar Keršovani, 1963.

Slovenian

Stoik. Trans. Jože Stabej. Llubljana: Državna Založba Slovenije, 1968.

A74-1   NOTES ON LIFE

Notes on Life / by / Theodore Dreiser / edited by / Marguerite
Tjader / and / John J. McAleer / The University of Alabama Press /
University, Alabama

> 9 1/4 x 6, xiv, 346 pp. (i-ii), half-title, verso blank;
> (iii-iv), title, verso copyright notice; v-ix, foreword by
> Marguerite Tjader; x-xiv, introduction by John Cowper Powys;
> (1-2), contents, verso blank; 3-333, text; 334-346, notes by
> John J. McAleer.

Mottled black cloth, lettering on spine in gold.

Published May 1974.

> Note: An edition of Dreiser's previously un-
> published philosophical essays and notes.

B

CONTRIBUTIONS TO BOOKS AND PAMPHLETS

Included in this section are Dreiser's contributions to books and pamphlets when these contributions constitute initial publication.

Only the first impression of each title is cited unless a later impression or edition contains a significant variation affecting Dreiser's contribution.

B97-1   Respectfully Inscribed to Miss Mary E. South, Terre Haute, Ind. / On the Banks / of the Wabash, / Far Away. / Song & a Chorus / by / Paul Dresser... / Published by / Howley, Haviland & Co., / 4 East 20th Street, New York. / London, Chas. Sheard & Co.

Published July 1897.

> Note: Dreiser often claimed that he wrote the first verse and the chorus of this famous song. See particularly his "My Brother Paul" in Twelve Men (1919) and his introduction to The Songs of Paul Dresser (1927). This claim has recently been disputed by Richard W. Dowell in "'On the Banks of the Wabash': A Musical Whodunit," Indiana Magazine of History, 66 (June 1970), 95-109.

B98-1   Spanish-American War Songs / a Complete Collection of News-paper Verse dur- / ing the Recent War with Spain / com-piled and edited / by Sidney A. Witherbee / Sidney A. Witherbee, Publisher, / Detroit, Mich. / 1898

Published late December 1898 (Publisher's Weekly).

"Exordium," pp. 276-77.

Theodore Dreiser: A Bibliography

B00-1   A Princess of / Arcady / by / Arthur Henry / New York / Doubleday, Page & Co. / 1900

Published 3 October 1900.

Chapter XIII, pp. 299-307.

> Note: For Dreiser's claim that he wrote the final chapter of Henry's novel, see his letter to H. L. Mencken, 13 May 1916; Letters of Theodore Dreiser (1959), I, 214.

B01-1   The Success / Library / Dr. Orison Swett Marden / editor-in-chief / George Raymond De Vitt, M.A. / managing editor / ten volumes / volume nine--parts XXV, XXVI, XXVII... / New York / The Success Company / Publishers

Published 13 December 1901.

"How an Agricultural Society Markets Fruits and Vegetables," pp. 5215-17; republished in Orison Swett Marden, Choosing a Career, Indianapolis: Bobbs-Merrill, 1905, pp. 233-40 (as "The Career of a Farmer: Cooperation in Marketing Fruit").

B14-1   Life in a / Garrison Town / the Military Novel / Suppressed by the / German Government / by Lieutenant Bilse / ...with a foreword by Theodore / Dreiser... / New York: John Lane Company / London: John Lane, The Bodley Head / MCMIV

Published 12 December 1914.

Foreword, pp. v-xiii.

B20-1   Caius Gracchus / a Tragedy / by / Odin Gregory / with / an introduction / by / Theodore Dreiser... / Boni and Liveright / Publishers New York

Published 10 August 1920.

Introduction, pp. 3-9.

> Note: Odin Gregory was the pseudonym of J. G. Robin.

WORKS BY

B20-2   Jurgen / and the Censor / Report of the Emergency Committee /
         Organized to Protest Against the / Suppression of James
         Branch Cabell's / Jurgen / privately printed for the
         emergency committee / Edward Hale Bierstadt Barrett H.
         Clark Sidney Howard / one thousand nine hundred and
         twenty / New York

         Published September 1920 (reviews).

         Letter, dated 23 February 1920, p. 47.

B23-1   Ebony and Ivory / by / Llewelyn Powys / with a preface by /
         Theodore Dreiser / 1923 / American Library Service /
         New York

         Published 5 January 1923.

         Preface, pp. vii-ix.

              Note: The English edition of Ebony and Ivory,
              published by Grant Richards in 1923, does not
              contain Dreiser's preface.

B23-2   Marriage / Short Stories of Married Life by American Writers /
         Tarkington Delano Hopper Dreiser... / Garden City New
         York / Doubleday, Page & Company / 1923

         Published 30 April 1923.

         "Marriage--For One," pp. 238-58; republished in Chains
         (1927).

              Note: The English edition of Marriage, pub-
              lished by Holder and Stoughton in 1923, also
              contains Dreiser's story.

B25-1   Thomas Hardy / Notes on His Life / and Work / Publishers /
         Harper & Brothers / New York and London

              Published 1925 (Helmut Gerber and W. Eugene Davis, Thomas
              Hardy: An Annotated Bibliography..., De Kalb, Ill.:
              Northern Illinois University Press, 1973).

              Contribution to "Tributes from American and English
              Writers," p. 15.

Contributions to Books

Note: A 32 page advertising brochure issued by Harper's.

B25-2 The / Man Mencken / a Biographical and Critical Study / by Isaac Goldberg... / Simon and Schuster / New York 1925

Published 16 November 1925.

"Henry L. Mencken and Myself," dated 24 August 1925, pp. 378-81.

B26-1 Lilith / a Dramatic Poem / by / George Sterling / New York / The Macmillan Company / 1926 / all rights reserved

Published 27 April 1926.

Introduction, pp. vii-xii.

B27-1 Poorhouse / Sweeney / Life in a County Poorhouse / by Ed Sweeney / with a foreword by / Theodore Dreiser / illustrated by the author... / New York / Boni & Liveright / 1927

Published 25 March 1927.

Foreword, pp. v-xi.

B27-2 The Sandgate Edition / Tono-Bungay / by / H. G. Wells / with an introduction to the edition by / Theodore Dreiser / New York / Duffield and Company / 1927

Published 30 June 1927.

"Introduction to the Sandgate Edition of H. G. Wells," pp. v-xi.

Note: Dreiser's introduction appears only in Tono-Bungay.

B27-3 The Songs of / Paul Dresser / with an introduction by / his brother / Theodore Dreiser / published by / Boni & Liveright New York / 1927

Published Fall or Winter, 1927 (trade announcements).

"Concerning the Author of These Songs," pp. v-x.

B28-1   A Bibliography / of the Writings of / Theodore Dreiser / by /
        Edward D. McDonald / with a foreword by Theodore
        Dreiser... / Philadelphia / The Centaur Book Shop / 1928

        Published 24 January 1928.

        Foreword, dated 26 February 1927, pp. 11-12.

            Note: Republished in facsimile in 1968 by Burt
            Franklin of New York.

B28-2   The Road / to Buenos Ayres / by Albert Londres / with an
        introduction by / Theodore Dreiser / the translation is
        by / Eric Sutton / London / Constable & Co. Ltd. / 1928

        Published March 1928 (Whitaker's).

        Introduction, pp. v-xviii.

            Note: The American edition, published by Boni
            and Liveright in 1928, does not contain
            Dreiser's introduction.

B28-3   The Crime of Dr. Garine / by / Boris Sokoloff / with an in-
        troduction by / Theodore Dreiser / woodcuts by Roger
        VanGindertail / New York / Covici Friede Publishers /
        1928.

        Published 23 November 1928.

        Introduction, pp. vii-xii.

B28-4   McTeague / a Story of San Francisco / by / Frank Norris /
        with an introduction by / Theodore Dreiser / volume
        VIII... / 1928 / Doubleday, Doran & Company, Inc. /
        Garden City, New York

        Published 28 November 1928.

        Introduction, pp. vii-xi.

THEODORE DREISER: A BIBLIOGRAPHY

Note: The Argonaut Manuscript Limited Edition
of Frank Norris' Works. A trade edition was published early in 1929.

B29-1 Catalogue of an Exhibition / of / Paintings / by Jerome Blum /
with a foreword by / Theodore Dreiser / January 28th-
February 9th / the Anderson Galleries... / New York /
1929

Published January 1929.

"Jerome Blum," pp. 2-3.

Note: A four page exhibition catalog.

B30-1 The Symbolic Drawings / of Hubert Davis for / An American
Tragedy / by Theodore Dreiser / Horace Liveright Publisher

Published 10 November 1930.

Foreword, pp. vii-x.

Note: Published in a limited edition of 525
copies.

B31-1 Little Blue Book No. 1590 / edited by E. Haldeman-Julius /
How the Great Corporations Rule the United States /
Theodore Dreiser / Haldeman-Julius Publications / Girard,
Kansas

Published 24 February 1931.

"How the Great Corporations Rule the United States" appears on pp. 5-12 of this 62 page pamphlet; the pamphlet
also contains variously titled articles by seven other
writers.

B32-1 Harlan Miners Speak / Report on / Terrorism in the Kentucky
Coal Fields / prepared by / members of the National Com-
mittee / for the Defense of Political Prisoners /
Theodore Dreiser / Lester Cohen... / Harcourt, Brace and
Company / New York

Published 31 March 1932.

Introduction, dated 23 December 1931, pp. 3-16; portions of this introduction appeared in the New Masses, 7 (Jan. 1932), 1-2 (as "Individualism and the Jungle") and Crawford's Weekly, 2 Jan. 1932, p. 6 (as "Individualism and the Jungle").

> Note: Dreiser also appears as an interrogator in much of the testimony published in Harlan Miners Speak. The book was republished in facsimile by Da Capo Press of New York in 1970.

B33-1   Forced Labor / in the / United States / by / Walter Wilson / with an introduction by / Theodore Dreiser / International Publishers / New York

Published 21 March 1933.

Introduction, pp. 7-8.

> Note: The London edition of Forced Labor in the United States, published by Martin Lawrence in 1933, also contains Dreiser's introduction.

B33-2   Tom / Mooney / introduction by / Theodore Dreiser / Story in Pictures / by Anton Refregier / 5¢ published by / International Labor Defense

Published 1933 (trade announcements).

Introduction, p. 2.

> Note: A 32 page pamphlet.

B34-1   Mr. President: / Free the Scottsboro Boys!

Published 1934 (copyright page notice).

"Mr. President: Free the Scottsboro Boys!" pp. 3-4.

> Note: A 30 page pamphlet published by the International Labor Defense. Dreiser's contribution is the introduction to the entire pamphlet.

B35-1   Magnificent / Hadrian / a Biography of Hadrian / Emperor of
        Rome by / Sulamith Ish-Kishor / introduction by Theodore
        Dreiser... / New York / Minton, Balch & Company

        Published 21 March 1935.

        Introduction, dated 18 February 1935, pp. 1-5.

            Note: The London edition of Magnificent Hadrian,
            published by Gollancz in 1935, does not contain
            Dreiser's introduction.

B35-2   Waiting for Nothing / by / Tom Kromer / with an introduction /
        by / Theodore Dreiser / and a portrait / Constable & Co
        Ltd / London / 1935

        Published July 1935 (Whitaker's).

        Introduction, pp. xi-xix.

            Note: The American edition of Waiting for
            Nothing, published by Knopf in 1935, does not
            contain Dreiser's introduction.

B35-3   So Red the Nose / or / Breath / in the Afternoon / edited by
        Sterling North / and Carl Kroch / illustrated by Roy C.
        Nelson / Farrar & Rinehart / Incorporated / on Murray
        Hill New York

        Published 29 November 1935.

        "Theodore Dreiser's American Tragedy Cocktail," p. 30.

B36-1   Samuel Butler / The Way of / All Flesh / pictures by Robert
        Ward Johnson / introduction by Theodore Dreiser / New York
        1936 / The Limited Editions Club

        Published 21 January 1936.

        Introduction, Volume One, pp. v-xxx.

            Note: Dreiser's introduction also appears in
            the trade edition published by Heritage Press
            of New York in 1936.

THEODORE DREISER: A BIBLIOGRAPHY

WORKS BY

B37-1   Paintings / and / Drawings / by / Biala... / February 23-
         March 13 / Gallery of / Georgette Passedoit...

         Published February 1937.

         "Biala," p. 2.

             Note: A four page exhibition catalog.

B37-2   Hubert Davis / Lithographs / Saturday, March 13 / to
         Saturday, March 27th / Art Service Company / Studio,
         405 Carnegie Hall

         Published March 1937.

         "Theodore Dreiser Writes," dated February 1937, pp. 2-3.

             Note: A four page exhibition catalog.

B38-1   Of / Human Bondage / by W. Somerset Maugham. With an
         intro- / duction by Theodore Dreiser & sixteen / etchings
         by John Sloan. In two volumes / volume one / printed for
         the members of the Limited / Editions Club at the printing-
         office of / the Yale University Press New Haven / 1938

         Published 21 January 1938.

         Introduction, pp. iii-xiv.

B38-2   Writers Take Sides / Letters about the War in Spain / from
         418 American Authors / published by / the League of
         American Writers / 381 Fourth Avenue, New York City

         Published May 1938 (copyright page notice).

         "Theodore Dreiser," pp. 20-21.

B38-3   Hubert Davis / Lithographs Drawings / May 16, through June 4,
         1938 / Cooperative Gallery / ...Newark, N. J.

         Published May 1938.

         "Foreword," p. 2.

             Note: A four page exhibition catalog.

Contributions to Books

B39-1   "We Hold These / Truths..." / Statements on Anti-Semitism /
        by 54 Leading American / Writers, Statesmen, Educators, /
        Clergymen and Trade-Unionists. / Published by / the
        League of American Writers / 381 Fourth Avenue, New York,
        N. Y.

        Published March 1939 (copyright page notice).

        "Theodore Dreiser," pp. 45-47.

B39-2   The Living Thoughts of / Thoreau / presented by / Theodore
        Dreiser / the Living Thoughts Library / edited by Alfred
        O. Mendel / Longmans, Green and Co. / New York   Toronto

        Published 21 March 1939.

        "Presenting Thoreau," pp. 1-32.

                         Translations

        Portuguese

            O Pensamento Vivo de Thoreau.   Trans. Lauro Escorel.
            São Paulo: Livraria Martins Editoria, 1939.

        Spanish

            El Pensamiento Vivo de Thoreau.   Trans. Luis Echávarri.
            Buenos Aires: Editorial Losada, 1940.

B39-3   I Believe / the Personal Philosophies / of Certain Eminent /
        Men and Women / of Our Time / edited, with an introduc-
        tion / and biographical notes, by / Clifton Fadiman /
        1939 / Simon and Schuster   New York

        Published 15 August 1939.

        "Theodore Dreiser," pp. 355-62.

            Note: The English edition of I Believe,
            published by Allen & Unwin in 1940, does not
            contain Dreiser's essay.

WORKS BY

B40-1   Shall It Be War for America? / Theodore Dreiser Introduces
         Browder to Radio Audience...

         Published October or November 1940.

         Introduction, pp. 1-2.

              Note: A four page pamphlet containing Dreiser's
              introduction and Earl Browder's speech. Both
              were delivered on 29 October 1940 over the Mutual
              Broadcasting System in support of Browder's can-
              didacy for President.

B41-1   More / Dangerous / Thoughts / by Mike Quin / introduction
         by / Theodore Dreiser / illustrated by / Rosalie Todd
         and / Chuck / published by / the People's World / San
         Francisco

         Published 1941 (copyright page notice).

         Introduction, pp. 7-8.

              Note: Mike Quin was the pseudonym of Paul
              William Ryan.

B41-2   U.S.S.R. Society for Cultural Relations with / Foreign
         Countries (Voks) / In Defense of Civilization Against
         Fascist Barbarism / Statements, Letters and Telegrams
         from / Prominent People / Moscow 1941

         Published 1941.

         "Russia's Cause Is True Democracy's Cause," p. 89.

B43-1   The Truth about / Reader's Digest / by Sender Garlin / illus-
         trations by William Gropper / published by / Forum Pub-
         lishers / P. O. Box 228, Station D / New York, N. Y.

         Published May 1943.

         Uses as a preface Dreiser's letter to Garlin, dated 28
         April 1943, p. 2.

              Note: Only the fourth printing of Garlin's pam-
              phlet contains Dreiser's letter; the first three
              printings, published earlier in 1943, do not.

C

CONTRIBUTIONS TO PERIODICALS (NEWSPAPERS AND JOURNALS)

An asterisk after an entry indicates that the item was published anonymously or pseudonymously; a note on attribution immediately follows all items so designated.

When the nature of an item is not apparent from its title or from its republication, a brief description--poem, story, sketch--is supplied. In particular, the subject of biographical sketches and of book and drama reviews is provided when this information is not available in the title.

Only the first periodical republication and the first book republication of an item are presented except in instances when the omission of a second periodical or book republication would cause confusion. For syndicated articles, only one syndicated appearance is noted. When a title changes significantly in republication, the altered title is supplied. No attempt has been made to indicate textual changes in connection with republication.

It may be helpful to briefly note some of the more significant areas for which Dreiser or his biographers cite periodical publication but for which no publication is cited in this bibliography. A good many newspaper articles which Dreiser attributed to himself in his autobiography have not been located by several researchers. These include a number of his contributions to the St. Louis Globe-Democrat and St. Louis Republic between November 1892 and February 1894, and all his reporting for the Cleveland Leader in April 1894 and for the New York World during the winter of 1894-95. In addition, Dreiser's claim that he was the theatre critic of the Globe-Democrat and that he also wrote many of the "Heard in the Corridors" paragraphs for that newspaper has not led to the attribution of this material to Dreiser. Both of these responsibilities were evidently shared by several reporters and it is impossible to distinguish more than a few specific items as undoubtedly by Dreiser. Finally, Dreiser's columns in the Pittsburg Dispatch during 1894 involve a number of problems in attribution. These problems are discussed in the headnote accompanying the appendix to section C.

WORKS BY

Dreiser's tenure as editor and principal contributor to Ev'ry
Month during 1895-97 also presents several difficulties in location
and attribution. The first two issues of the journal--October and
November 1895--have never come to light and thus Dreiser's contributions to them cannot be determined. Also, though a number of pseudonyms used by Dreiser in Ev'ry Month have been conclusively identi-
fied, it is impossible to determine the extent of his responsibility
for some of the anonymous features which appeared regularly in the
magazine, such as the decorative notes column. No Ev'ry Month item
not undoubtedly by Dreiser has been included, but this practice
should not be equated with a belief that Ev'ry Month does not contain other material written by Dreiser.

Other matters involving attribution are discussed when they arise
in the list which follows.

In citing the republication of Dreiser's Success articles, three
short titles are used:

How They Succeeded (1901)--How They Succeeded: Life Stories
of Successful Men Told by Themselves, by Orison Swett
Marden, Boston: Lathrop, Lee, and Shephard, 1901.

Little Visits with Great Americans (1905)--Little Visits
with Great Americans, ed. Orison Swett Marden, 2 vols.,
New York: Success Co., 1905.

Talks with Great Workers (1901)--Talks with Great Workers,
ed. Orison Swett Marden, New York: Crowell, 1901.

References to the Dreiser Collection in the Attribution commentary of section C are to the Theodore Dreiser Collection of the University of Pennsylvania Library. See G-11.

1892

C92-1 "Cleveland and Gray the Ticket," Chicago Daily Globe, 21
June, p. 1.*
Attribution: A Book About Myself (1922), pp. 56-58.

C92-2 "Cheyenne, Haunt of Misery and Crime," Chicago Sunday Globe,
24 July, p. 3.*
Attribution: A Book About Myself (1922), pp. 65-67.

C92-3 "The Copper Grinned," Chicago Daily Globe, 15 Sept., p. 2.*
Attribution: A Book About Myself (1922), pp. 76-81.

The first in a series of articles about fake auction
houses.

C92-4   "Swindlers," Chicago <u>Daily Globe</u>, 6 Oct., p. 1.*
        Attribution: <u>See</u> C92-3.

C92-5   "At Last," Chicago <u>Daily Globe</u>, 7 Oct., p. 1.*
        Attribution: <u>See</u> C92-3.

C92-6   "Robbers," Chicago <u>Daily Globe</u>, 8 Oct., p. 1.*
        Attribution: <u>See</u> C92-3.

C92-7   "On the Run," Chicago <u>Sunday Globe</u>, 9 Oct., p. 2.*
        Attribution: <u>See</u> C92-3.

C92-8   "Fakes," Chicago <u>Daily Globe</u>, 10 Oct., p. 1.*
        Attribution: <u>See</u> C92-3.

C92-9   "Waiting," Chicago <u>Daily Globe</u>, 11 Oct., p. 2.*
        Attribution: <u>See</u> C92-3.

C92-10 "Fakes," Chicago <u>Sunday Globe</u>, 16 Oct., p. 1.*
        Attribution: <u>See</u> C92-3.

C92-11 "Fakes," Chicago <u>Daily Globe</u>, 18 Oct., p. 1.*
        Attribution: <u>See</u> C92-3.

C92-12 "Arrested," Chicago <u>Daily Globe</u>, 19 Oct., p. 1.*
        Attribution: <u>See</u> C92-3.

C92-13 "Zuckerman," Chicago <u>Daily Globe</u>, 20 Oct., p. 5.*
        Attribution: <u>See</u> C92-3.

C92-14 "Reap a Harvest," Chicago <u>Daily Globe</u>, 21 Oct., p. 2.*
        Attribution: <u>See</u> C92-3.

C92-15 "Plenty of Suckers," Chicago <u>Daily Globe</u>, 22 Oct., p. 3.*
        Attribution: <u>See</u> C92-3.

C92-16 "Still at Work," Chicago <u>Sunday Globe</u>, 23 Oct., p. 3.*
        Attribution: <u>See</u> C92-3.

C92-17 "The Return of Genius," Chicago <u>Sunday Globe</u>, 23 Oct., p. 4.*
        Attribution: Signed "Carl Dreiser".

C92-18 "Great Profit," Chicago <u>Daily Globe</u>, 24 Oct., p. 1.*
        Attribution: <u>See</u> C92-3.

WORKS BY

C92-19 "Fakes," Chicago Daily Globe, 25 Oct., p. 1.*
         Attribution: See C92-3.

C92-20 "Reports and Recommendations," Saint Louis Globe-Democrat,
         17 Nov., p. 9.*
         Attribution: A Book About Myself (1922), pp. 110-111.

         Terence Powderly's speech.

C92-21 "Greatest in the World. Inception and Progress of the St.
         Louis Union Depot Scheme," Saint Louis Globe-Democrat,
         11 Dec., p. 28.*
         Attribution: A Book About Myself (1922), p. 121.

                              1893

C93-1   "Mr. Watterson on Politics," St. Louis Globe-Democrat, 6 Jan.,
         p. 4.*
         Attribution: A Book About Myself (1922), p. 150.

         Henry Watterson.

C93-2   "Water Works Extension," St. Louis Globe-Democrat, 15 Jan.,
         p. 31.*

         Attribution: A Number of newspaper articles of 1893-94
         were attributed to Dreiser by Robert H. Elias on the basis
         of clippings which were at one time in the Dreiser Collec-
         tion but which now appear to have been misplaced. Here
         and elsewhere in instances of this kind, I cite Elias for
         attribution of Dreiser's authorship; Elias, Theodore
         Dreiser (1949), p. 313, n. 8.

C93-3   "Theosophy and Spiritualism," St. Louis Globe-Democrat,
         20 Jan., p. 12.*
         Attribution: A Book About Myself (1922), p. 150.

         Annie Besant.

C93-4   "Burned to Death," St. Louis Globe-Democrat, 22 Jan.,
         pp. 1-2.*
         Attribution: A Book About Myself (1922), pp. 156ff.

C93-5   "Sixteen Dead," St. Louis Globe-Democrat, 23 Jan., p. 10.*
         Attribution: A Book About Myself (1922), pp. 156ff.

                               100

C93-6   "The Black Diva's Concert," St. Louis Globe-Democrat, 1 Apr.,
        p. 8.*
            Attribution: A Book About Myself (1922), p. 184.

C93-7   "The Theatres," St. Louis Globe-Democrat, 1 May, p. 10.*
            Attribution: A Book About Myself (1922), pp. 200-203.
        Dreiser's reviews of performances which did not occur;
        for a report of the railroad washouts which prevented the
        arrival of the theatre companies, see the St. Louis Re-
        public, 1 May 1893, p. 3.

C93-8   "His Own Story. Train Robber Wilson Relates His Experience,"
        St. Louis Republic, 4 June, pp. 1-2.*
            Attribution: A Book About Myself (1922), pp. 286ff.

C93-9   "Fast Mail Train," St. Louis Republic, 19 June, pp. 1, 3.*
            Attribution: A Book About Myself (1922), p. 268.

C93-10 "The Trouble Still On," St. Louis Republic, 20 June, p. 4.*
            Attribution: A Book About Myself (1922), pp. 229-31.
        The first in a series of tongue-in-cheek reports of a
        forthcoming baseball game between the Owls and Elks.

C93-11 "The War Fever Spreads," St. Louis Republic, 21 June, p. 12.*
            Attribution: See C92-10.

C93-12 "With Wrinkled Fronts," St. Louis Republic, 22 June, p. 12.*
            Attribution: See C92-10.

C93-13 "Jawing and Jabbering," St. Louis Republic, 23 June, p. 7.*
            Attribution: See C92-10.

C93-14 "Sphere Twirling Art," St. Louis Republic, 24 June, p. 8.*
            Attribution: See C93-10.

C93-15 "Let the Owl Screech," St. Louis Republic, 25 June, p. 4.*
            Attribution: See C93-10.

C93-16 "Got It in for the Owls," St. Louis Republic, 28 June, p. 12.*
            Attribution: See C93-10.

C93-17 "Demands Fair Play," St. Louis Republic, 29 June, p. 12.*
            Attribution: See C93-10.

C93-18 "The O. and E. Ball Game," St. Louis Republic, 30 June,
        p. 12.*
            Attribution: See C93-10.

WORKS BY

C93-19 "No More Monkeying," St. Louis Republic, 1 July, p. 11.*
            Attribution: See C93-10.

C93-20 "Article 4 Hundred 47," St. Louis Republic, 2 July, p. 2.*
            Attribution: See C93-10.

C93-21 "All Torn Up the Back," St. Louis Republic, 4 July, p. 12.*
            Attribution: See C93-10.

C93-22 "Practiced at the Park," St. Louis Republic, 6 July, p. 7.*
            Attribution: See C93-10.

C93-23 "The Elks and the Owls," St. Louis Republic, 7 July, p. 12.*
            Attribution: See C93-10.

C93-24 "In Grim, Dead Earnest," St. Louis Republic, 8 July, p. 8.*
            Attribution: See C93-10.

C93-25 "Ready for the Fray," St. Louis Republic, 9 July, p. 9.*
            Attribution: See C93-10.

C93-26 "Professional Playing," St. Louis Republic, 11 July, p. 4.*
            Attribution: See C93-10.

C93-27 "Oraculous Opinion," St. Louis Republic, 12 July, p. 12.*
            Attribution: See C93-10.

C93-28 "Here Are the Facts," St. Louis Republic, 13 July, p. 7.*
            Attribution: See C93-10.

C93-29 "Portentous Pointers," St. Louis Republic, 14 July, p. 7.*
            Attribution: See C93-10.

C93-30 "A Presage of Disaster," St. Louis Republic, 15 July, p. 11.*
            Attribution: See C93-10.

C93-31 "Monday the Day," St. Louis Republic, 16 July, p. 2.*
            Attribution: See C93-10.

C93-32 "To Leave To-Day," St. Louis Republic, 16 July, p. 11.*
            Attribution: A Book About Myself (1922), pp. 223ff.
            The first in a series of articles about the excursion
        of a group of teachers to the Chicago World's Fair.

C93-33 "Pictures from Real Life," St. Louis Republic, 16 July,
            p. 24.*
            Attribution: Dreiser Collection clipping.

C93-34 "The Great Game To-Day," St. Louis Republic, 17 July, p. 2.*
Attribution: See C93-10.

C93-35 "Teachers at the Fair," St. Louis Republic, 18 July, p. 7.*
Attribution: See C93-32.

C93-36 "The Republic Teachers," St. Louis Republic, 19 July, p. 6.*
Attribution: See C93-32.

C93-37 "Third Day at the Fair," St. Louis Republic, 20 July, p. 4.*
Attribution: See C93-32.

C93-38 "Will See Everything," St. Louis Republic, 21 July, p. 2.*
Attribution: See C93-32.

C93-39 "Fifth Day at the Fair," St. Louis Republic, 22 July, p. 2.*
Attribution: See C93-32.

C93-40 "Gallagher," St. Louis Republic, 6 Aug., p. 9.*
Attribution: Elias, Theodore Dreiser (1949), p. 314,
n.27; See C93-2.

C93-41 "Fever's Frenzy. John Finn Tries to Kill His Four Children,"
St. Louis Republic, 9 Aug., pp. 1-2.*
Attribution: A Book About Myself (1922), p. 144
(falsely associated by Dreiser with the period during
which he worked on the St. Louis Globe-Democrat).

C93-42 "Almost a Riot," St. Louis Republic, 11 Aug., pp. 1-2.*
Attribution: A Book About Myself (1922), pp. 268ff.
The first in a series of articles about the spiritual-
ist Jules Wallace and the mind-reader Alexander Tyndall.

C93-43 "They Met and--Lunched," St. Louis Republic, 12 Aug., p. 5.*
Attribution: See C93-42.

C93-44 "Blindfolded He Drove," St. Louis Republic, 18 Aug., p. 1.*
Attribution: See C93-42.

C93-45 "Election of Officers. The World's Sunday School Convention
in Session," St. Louis Republic, 5 Sept., p. 3.*
Attribution: Elias, Theodore Dreiser (1949), p. 314,
n.22; See C93-2.

C93-46 "Jules Wallace, Faker, Fraud, Medium, Healer!", St. Louis
Republic, 9 Sept., pp. 1-2.*
Attribution: See C93-42.

WORKS BY

C93-47 "Wallace on Wallace," St. Louis Republic, 10 Sept., p. 6.*
        Attribution: See C93-42.

C93-48 "A Spiritualist Fraud," St. Louis Republic, 11 Sept., p. 3.*
        Attribution: See C93-42.

C93-49 "A Negro Lynched. Taken from Jail at Rich Hill, Mo., and
        Hanged--His Crime the Usual One," St. Louis Republic,
        17 Sept., p. 2.*
        Attribution: A Book About Myself (1922), p. 325, and
        "Nigger Jeff," Free (1918).

C93-50 "Unprovoked Murder," St. Louis Republic, 24 Sept., p. 2.*
        Attribution: A Book About Myself (1922), pp. 331ff.

C93-51 "A Deep Mystery," St. Louis Republic, 25 Sept., p. 1.*
        Attribution: See C93-50.

C93-52 "Will Wear the Medal," St. Louis Republic, 1 Oct., p. 29.*
        Attribution: See C93-50.

C93-53 "The Glittering Ballroom" and "The Ball at Midnight," in
        "Brilliant Beyond Compare. Annual Ball of the Veiled
        Prophets," St. Louis Republic, 4 Oct., pp. 1-2.*
        Attribution: A Book About Myself (1922), pp. 142-43
        and (for the two specific sections of the article)
        Dreiser Collection clippings.

C93-54 "Mystery of a Murder," St. Louis Republic, 19 Nov., pp. 9-10.*
        Attribution: A Book About Myself (1922), p. 268.

C93-55 "A Cosmopolitan Camp," St. Louis Republic, 17 Dec., pp. 30-
        31.*
        Attribution: Elias, Theodore Dreiser (1949), p. 314,
        n.25; See C93-2.

C93-56 "Bloodshed May Result," St. Louis Republic, 30 Dec., p. 5.*
        Attribution: The first in a series of humorous
        articles about a football game between the Builders'
        Exchange and the Merchants' Exchange; attributed to
        Dreiser on the basis of the close similarity of the series
        to his earlier series on the Owls and Elks baseball game.
        See also, Elias, Theodore Dreiser (1949), p. 214, n.24.

C93-57 "Miltenberger's Scheme," St. Louis Republic, 31 Dec., p. 28.*
        Attribution: See C93-56.

Theodore Dreiser: A Bibliography

1894

C94-1   "That Football Fracas," St. Louis <u>Republic</u>, 2 Jan., p. 8.*
Attribution: <u>See</u> C93-56.

C94-2   "Charity Teams Chosen," St. Louis <u>Republic</u>, 4 Jan., p. 5.*
Attribution: <u>See</u> C93-56.

C94-3   "Armed for the Battle," St. Louis <u>Republic</u>, 5 Jan., p. 2.*
Attribution: <u>See</u> C93-56.

C94-4   "This Is the Great Day," St. Louis <u>Republic</u>, 6 Jan., p. 3.*
Attribution: <u>See</u> C93-56.

C94-5   "The Merchants Win," St. Louis <u>Republic</u>, 7 Jan., p. 10.*
Attribution: <u>See</u> C93-56.

C94-6   "Fighting Now the Fad," St. Louis <u>Republic</u>, 22 Jan., p. 3.*
Attribution: Elias, <u>Theodore Dreiser</u> (1949), p. 314,
n. 23; <u>See</u> C93-2.

C94-7   "The Strike To-Day," Toledo <u>Blade</u>, 24 Mar., pp. 1, 6.*
Attribution: <u>A Book About Myself</u> (1922), pp. 272-73.

C94-8   "No Union Men," Toledo <u>Blade</u>, 24 Mar., p. 6.*
Attribution: Internal reference to Dreiser.

C94-9   "As If in Old Toledo," Toledo <u>Blade</u>, 28 Mar., p. 7.*
Attribution: <u>A Book About Myself</u> (1922), p. 373.

C94-10   "Hospital Violet Day," Pittsburg <u>Dispatch</u>, 12 May, p. 2.*
Attribution: Dreiser Collection clipping.

C94-11   "And It Was Mighty Blue," Pittsburg <u>Dispatch</u>, 15 May, p. 2.*
Attribution: Dreiser Collection clipping.

C94-12   "After the Rain Storm," Pittsburg <u>Dispatch</u>, 19 May, p. 2.*
Attribution: Dreiser Collection clipping.

C94-13   "Soldiers of Morganza," Pittsburg <u>Dispatch</u>, 5 July, p. 3.*
Attribution: Dreiser Collection clipping.

C94-14   "Reapers in the Fields," Pittsburg <u>Dispatch</u>, 6 July, p. 2.*
Attribution: Elias, <u>Theodore Dreiser</u> (1949), p. 316,
n. 13; <u>See</u> C93-2.

C94-15   "Odd Scraps of Melody," Pittsburg <u>Dispatch</u>, 7 July, p. 3.*
Attribution: Dreiser Collection clipping.

WORKS BY

C94-16 "Fenced Off the Earth," Pittsburg Dispatch, 19 July, p. 3.*
        Attribution: A Book About Myself (1922), p. 459.

C94-17 "With the Nameless Dead," Pittsburg Dispatch, 23 July, p. 3.*
        Attribution: Material reused by Dreiser; See Donald
        Pizer, "Dreiser's 'Nigger Jeff'...," American Literature,
        41 (Nov. 1969), 331-42.

C94-18 "Some Dabbling in Books," Pittsburg Dispatch, 14 Aug., p. 3.*
        Attribution: Dreiser Collection clipping.

C94-19 "Snap Shots at Pleasure," Pittsburg Dispatch, 18 Aug., p. 3.*
        Attribution: Dreiser Collection clipping.

C94-20 "Now the Pill Doctrine!" Pittsburg Dispatch, 20 Aug., p. 3.*
        Attribution: Material reused by Dreiser in "The Gloom
        Chasers," Ev'ry Month, 1 (Dec. 1895), 16-17.

C94-21 "Where Sympathy Failed," Pittsburg Dispatch, 25 Aug., p. 3.*
        Attribution: Dreiser Collection clipping and material
        reused by Dreiser in "Forgotten," Ev'ry Month, 2 (Aug.
        1896), 16-17.

C94-22 "Our Fleeting Shekels," Pittsburg Dispatch, 26 Aug., p. 2.*
        Attribution: Dreiser Collection clipping.

C94-23 "General Booth Says Farewell," Pittsburgh Dispatch, 12 Nov.,
        pp. 1-2.*
        Attribution: Dreiser Collection clipping.

                              1895

C95-1   "Review of the Month," Ev'ry Month, 1 (Dec.), 2-9.*
        Attribution: One of Dreiser's tasks as editor and
        principal contributor to Ev'ry Month was to write an in-
        troductory column of miscellaneous topical and philo-
        sophical commentary. Initially entitled "Review of the
        Month" and signed "The Prophet," the column was called
        "Reflections" with the issue of January, 1896, though it
        continued to be signed "The Prophet."
        The horse show, international marriages, New York ar-
        chitecture, sweatshop investigations, Emperor William II,
        the Atlanta Exposition, Eugene Field, Rockefeller's
        philantrophies, Bill Nye, canal trolleys, widespread
        praise of Ev'ry Month.

Contributions to Periodicals

C95-2   "We Others," Ev'ry Month, 1 (Dec.), 15-16.*
         Attribution: Signed "S. J. White." Dreiser used "S.
         J. White" as a pseudonym during his editorship of Ev'ry
         Month and "Sallie Joy White" for some of his Success
         articles of 1898-99; the name derives from that of his
         fiancee, Sallie White.
         Sketch.

C95-3   "The Gloom Chasers," Ev'ry Month, 1 (Dec.), 16-17.*
         Attribution: Signed "The Cynic"; material reused by
         Dreiser from "Now the Pill Doctrine!" Pittsburg Dispatch,
         20 Aug. 1894, p. 3.
         Sketch.

C95-4   "The Literary Shower: 'Out of India'," Ev'ry Month, 1 (Dec.),
         18.*
         Attribution: Signed "Edward Al." "Edward Al" was
         Dreiser's most commonly used pseudonym; the name derives
         from the first names of two of his brothers.
         Review of Out of India by Rudyard Kipling.

C95-5   "The Drama," Ev'ry Month, 1 (Dec.), 22-23.
         Review of Wizard of the Nile, a comic opera by H. B.
         Smith.

1896

C96-1   "Reflections," Ev'ry Month, 1 (Jan.), 2-11.*
         Attribution: Signed "The Prophet"; See C95-1.
         Intent of the "Reflections" column, the year's woes,
         dangers of anonymous journalism, political corruption,
         window displays on Broadway, Alexander Dumas, fils, cler-
         gymen in literature, a letter from James McCord, the new
         year.

C96-2   "Dramatic," Ev'ry Month, 1 (Jan.), 16-17.
         Review of The Heart of Maryland by David Belasco.

C96-3   "The Literary Shower," Ev'ry Month, 1 (Jan.), 21-22.*
         Attribution: Signed "Edward Al" on the cover of this
         issue; See C95-4.
         Reviews of Constantinople by Edwin A. Grosvenor, Under
         the Red Flag by Edward King, The Child's Garden of Song
         by William L. Tomlins, and Casa Braccio by F. Marion
         Crawford.

WORKS BY

C96-4   "Reflections," Ev'ry Month, 1 (Feb.), 2-6.*
             Attribution: Signed "The Prophet"; See C95-1.
             Current war scares, King Otto of Bavaria, art in
         photography, Alfred Austin, Spain, historical novels, the
         dismissal of Professor Bemis, New York society, the po-
         litical power of financiers.

C96-5   "The Literary Shower: A Daughter of the Tenements," Ev'ry
         Month, 1 (Feb.), 10-11.*
             Attribution: Signed "Edward Al"; See C95-4.
             Reviews of A Daughter of the Tenements by Edward L.
         Townsend, Rose of Dutcher's Coolly by Hamlin Garland, and
         brief comments on Paul Verlaine, Rudyard Kipling's Tommy
         Atkins of the Ramchunders, William Winter's Brown Heath
         and Blue Bells, and Quida's The Nurnberg Stove.

C96-6   "Wintry Landscapes," Ev'ry Month, 1 (Feb.), 18.*
             Attribution: Signed "S. J. White"; See C95-2.
             Sketch.

C96-7   "Reflections," Ev'ry Month, 1 (Mar.), 2-6.*
             Attribution: Signed "The Prophet"; See C95-1.
             The bond crisis, Paul Verlaine, hypnotism, scientific
         advances, March, the Turks, public corruption, the
         Venezuela dispute.

C96-8   "Literary Notes: As to the Jucklins," Ev'ry Month, 1 (Mar.),
         10-11.*
             Attribution: Signed "Edward Al"; See C95-4.
             Review of As to the Jucklins by Opie Read and brief
         comments on Hamlin Garland, Thomas Hardy, and Eugene Field.

C96-9   "Cometh in as a Lion," Ev'ry Month, 1 (Mar.), 16.*
             Attribution: Signed "S. J. White"; See C95-2.
             Sketch.

C96-10   "Dramatic," Ev'ry Month, 1 (Mar.), 22.
             Reviews of Izeyl by Armand Sylvestre and Eugene Morand,
         A Woman's Reason by Charles Brookfield and F. C. Philips,
         and brief comment on Richard Mansfield.

C96-11   "Reflections," Ev'ry Month, 2 (Apr.), 2-7.*
             Attribution: Signed "The Prophet"; See C95-1.
             Spring, the Cuban revolt, political corruption, nepo-
         tism in the Salvation Army, New York society, the success
         of Ev'ry Month, Bohemianism, life as a struggle.

Contributions to Periodicals

C96-12 "Literary Notes: The Day of Their Wedding," Ev'ry Month, 2
        (Apr.), 11.*
        Attribution: Signed "Edward Al"; See C95-4.
        Review of The Day of Their Wedding by William Dean
        Howells.

C96-13 "Dramatic," Ev'ry Month, 2 (Apr.), 22.
        Reviews of A Black Sheep by C. H. Hoyt, Marriage by
        Brandon Thomas and Henry Keeling, and brief comment on
        Mme. Duse.

C96-14 "Reflections," Ev'ry Month, 2 (May), 2-6.*
        Attribution: Signed "The Prophet"; See C95-1.
        The presidential campaign, sensational journalism, the
        popularity of musicians, the harm of tipping, women's
        duty, New York in spring.

C96-15 "Literary Notes: A Singular Life," Ev'ry Month, 2 (May),
        11-12.*
        Attribution: Signed "Edward Al"; See C95-4.
        Reviews of A Singular Life by Elizabeth Stuart Phelps,
        The Red Badge of Courage by Stephen Crane, and brief com-
        ments on Ernest McGaffey and Balzac.

C96-16 "I Shall Pass Through This World But Once," Ev'ry Month, 2
        (May), 17.*
        Attribution: Signed "S. J. White"; See C95-2.
        Poem.

C96-17 "Conditioned Ones," Ev'ry Month, 2 (May), 18.
        Poem.

C96-18 "The Drama," Ev'ry Month, 2 (May), 22.
        Reviews of Bohemia by Clyde Fitch and Madame by Charles
        Coghlan.

C96-19 "Reflections," Ev'ry Month, 2 (June), 2-6.*
        Attribution: Signed "The Prophet"; See C95-1.
        Baron Hirsch's philanthrophies, physical and mental
        strength, the sensitivity of plants, self-preservation and
        the Golden Rule, the Decadent school of art, suicide.

C96-20 "The Madding Crowd," Ev'ry Month, 2 (June), 17.
        Poem.

C96-21 "The Literary Shower," Ev'ry Month, 2 (June), 21-22.*
        Attribution: Signed "Edward Al"; See C95-4.
        Reviews of Tom Grogan by F. Hopkinson Smith, Personal

WORKS BY

> Recollections of Joan of Arc by Mark Twain, and comments
> on Richard Harding Davis, Paul Bourget, Rev. John Watson,
> and the relationship between journalism and literature.

C96-22 "Dramatic," Ev'ry Month, 2 (June), 26.*
Attribution: Signed "S. J. White"; See C95-2.
Reviews of His Absent Boy by Yarne and Fisher, Thor-
oughbred by Ralph Lumley, and comment on the season of
1895-96.

C96-23 "Reflections," Ev'ry Month, 2 (July), 2-6.*
Attribution: Signed "The Prophet"; See C95-1.
Political reform, the jury system, Sunday observance,
Sunday newspapers.

C96-24 "Some Notable Women in New York Society," Ev'ry Month, 2
(July), 10-11.*
Attribution: Signed "V. D. Hyde." "V. D. Hyde" is
the most problematical of Dreiser's pseudonyms in Ev'ry
Month. Unlike "Edward Al" and "S. J. White," he never
used it elsewhere, and the name itself has no immediate
association with Dreiser's background. Moreover, the
story "The Bayly to Paquita," Ev'ry Month, 2 (July 1896),
16-17, which is signed "V. D. Hyde," is almost certainly
not by Dreiser. Nevertheless, it is almost equally certain that he did use the name in Ev'ry Month for a series
of articles on notable women and for one article on
Grant's Tomb. The name does not appear in any other
journal of the period, and Dreiser later reused some of
the Ev'ry Month material signed "V. D. Hyde" in articles
which he published during 1898-1901. For example, compare
"Portia Come Again," Ev'ry Month, 4 (May 1897), 8, which
is signed "V. D. Hyde," and Dreiser's "The Career of a
Modern Portia," Success, 2 (18 Feb. 1899), 205-206.

C96-25 "Chevalier," Ev'ry Month, 2 (July), 18.*
Attribution: Signed "S. J. White"; See C95-2.
Albert Chevalier.

C96-26 "The Literary Shower," Ev'ry Month, 2 (July), 24-25.*
Attribution: Signed "Edward Al"; See C95-4.
Reviews of The XIth Commandment by Halliwell Sutcliff
and Underwoods by Robert Louis Stevenson.

C96-27 "Reflections," Ev'ry Month, 2 (Aug.), 2-7.*
Attribution: Signed "The Prophet"; See C95-1.
The work of Harriet Beecher Stowe, woman suffrage, in-
ternational marriages, American ambition, the poor in
America, strength, weakness, and pain in life.

C96-28 "Woes of Cats," Ev'ry Month, 2 (Aug.), 10-11.*
      Attribution: Signed "S. J. White"; See C95-2.
      Sketch.

C96-29 "Forgotten," Ev'ry Month, 2 (Aug.), 16-17.
      Story.

C96-30 "The Literary Shower," Ev'ry Month, 2 (Aug.), 21-22.*
      Attribution: Signed "Edward Al"; See C95-4.
      Reviews of Adam Johnstone's Son by F. Marion Crawford,
      The Folly of Eustace by Robert Hichens, and An Ambitious
      Man by Ella Wheeler Wilcox.

C96-31 "Reflections," Ev'ry Month, 2 (Sept.), 2-7.*
      Attribution: Signed "The Prophet"; See C95-1.
      The presidential election, the role of art, self-
      education, change in nature and in society.

C96-32 "A Royal Abdication," Ev'ry Month, 2 (Sept.), 16-17.*
      Attribution: Signed "S. J. White"; See C95-2.
      Queen Victoria.

C96-33 "The Literary Shower," Ev'ry Month, 2 (Sept.), 22-23.*
      Attribution: Signed "Edward Al"; See C95-4.
      Reviews of Yekl by Abraham Cahan, The Time Machine by
      H. G. Wells, and Lancashire Idylls by Marshall Mather.

C96-34 "Reflections," Ev'ry Month, 3 (Oct.), 2-7.*
      Attribution: Signed "The Prophet"; See C95-1.
      Patriotism, the liquor question, the orator, New York
      strikes.

C96-35 "Reflections," Ev'ry Month, 3 (Nov.), 2-7.*
      Attribution: Signed "The Prophet"; See C95-1.
      Political and judicial corruption, public education,
      social progress, charity, happiness and faith.

C96-36 "A Metropolitan Favorite," Ev'ry Month, 3 (Nov.), 22.
      R. F. Outcault.

C96-37 "Reflections," Ev'ry Month, 3 (Dec.), 2-7.*
      Attribution: Signed "The Prophet"; See C95-1.
      Christmas, the fall of a businessman, the Turks, abuses
      in the courts.

C96-38 "Caricatures and a Caricaturist," Ev'ry Month, 3 (Dec.), 10.*
      Attribution: Signed "S. J. White"; See C95-2.
      Homer Davenport.

WORKS BY

1897

C97-1   "Reflections," Ev'ry Month, 3 (Jan.), 2-7.*
        Attribution: Signed "The Prophet"; See C95-1.
        Hopes for the New Year, Cuba, weakness of the drama,
        American grand opera, a defense of the "Reflections"
        column.

C97-2   "William Gillette," Ev'ry Month, 3 (Jan.), 17.*
        Attribution: Signed "S. J. White"; See C95-2.

C97-3   "The Woman Journalist," Ev'ry Month, 3 (Jan.), 24-25.*
        Attribution: Signed "V. D. Hyde"; See C96-24.

C97-4   "Reflections," Ev'ry Month, 3 (Feb.), 2-7.*
        Attribution: Signed "The Prophet"; See C95-1.
        Financial speculators, Herbert Spencer, winter suffer-
        ing, Mars, charity, luxury.

C97-5   "Reflections," Ev'ry Month, 3 (Mar.), 2-6.*
        Attribution: Signed "The Prophet"; See C95-1.
        The Bradley-Martin Ball, the trust, journalism, Spring,
        the poor, telepathy.

C97-6   "Where Grant Is to Rest," Ev'ry Month, 3 (Mar.), 18-19.*
        Attribution: Signed "V. D. Hyde"; See C96-24.

C97-7   "Mary E. Tillinghast: Stained Glass Artist," Ev'ry Month, 3
        (Mar.), 20-21.*
        Attribution: Signed "V. D. Hyde"; See C96-24.

C97-8   "A Social Samaritan: Rose Hawthorne Lathrop's Mission to
        the Afflicted," Ev'ry Month, 3 (Mar.), 25.*
        Attribution: Signed "S. J. White"; See C95-2.

C97-9   Ev'ry Month, 4 (Apr.), 20-21.*
        Attribution: From April through September, 1897, the
        "Reflections" column was transferred to the rear of Ev'ry
        Month and appeared untitled and unsigned. The column is
        nevertheless still clearly the work of Dreiser.
        Women criminals, European political affairs, world-
        weariness, immigration, the seeking of notoriety.

C97-10 Ev'ry Month, 4 (May), 20-21.*
        Attribution: See C97-9.
        American worship of things European, public architec-
        ture, ideals of children, struggle in life.

Contributions to Periodicals

C97-11　"Portia Come Again," Ev'ry Month, 4 (May), 8.*
　　　　Attribution:　Signed "V. D. Hyde"; See C96-24.
　　　　Mrs. Clara Foltz.

C97-12　Ev'ry Month, 4 (June), 20-21.*
　　　　Attribution:　See C97-9.
　　　　Queen Victoria, American statesmen, aestheticism,
　　　　American schools, feminism, success.

C97-13　Ev'ry Month, 4 (July), 20.*
　　　　Attribution:　See C97-9.
　　　　Cities in the summer, schools, the Scotch, Independence
　　　　Day, poverty and hardship in America.

C97-14　Ev'ry Month, 4 (Aug.), 18.*
　　　　Attribution:　See C97-9.
　　　　Cheap books, an Indian famine, noise in the New York
　　　　streets, children and pets in New York, the United States
　　　　Senate.

C97-15　"A Finished Farce-Comedian," Ev'ry Month, 4 (Aug.), 27.*
　　　　Attribution:　Signed "S. J. W."; See C95-2.
　　　　James T. Powers.

C97-16　Ev'ry Month, 4 (Sept.), 14.*
　　　　Attribution:　See C97-9.
　　　　Perniciousness of banquets, patriotism, the collecting
　　　　fad, death.

C97-17　"New York's Art Colony.　The Literary and Art Retreat at
　　　　Bronxville," Metropolitan, 6 (Nov.), 321-26.*
　　　　Attribution:　Signed "Theodore Dresser".

C97-18　"Our Women Violinists," Puritan, 2 (Nov.), 34-35.

C97-19　"On the Field of Brandywine," Truth, 16 (6 Nov.), 7-10.

1898

C98-1　"The Haunts of Bayard Taylor," Munsey's, 18 (Jan.), 594-601.

C98-2　"A Talk with America's Leading Lawyer," Success, 1 (Jan.),
　　　　40-41.
　　　　Joseph Choate.
　　　　Repub:　Little Visits with Great Americans (1905).

WORKS BY

C98-3   "A High Priestess of Art," <u>Success</u>, 1 (Jan.), 55.*
         Attribution: Signed "Edward Al"; <u>See</u> C95-4.
         Alice B. Stephens.
         Repub: <u>Little Visits with Great Americans</u> (1905).

C98-4   "Henry Mosler, A Painter for the People," <u>Demorest's</u>, 34
         (Feb.), 67-69.

C98-5   "The Art of MacMonnies and Morgan," <u>Metropolitan</u>, 7 (Feb.),
         143-51.
         Frederick MacMonnies and E. Percy Morgan.

C98-6   "A Photographic Talk with Edison," <u>Success</u>, 1 (Feb.), 8-9.
         Repub: <u>How They Succeeded</u> (1901).

C98-7   "Historic Tarrytown," <u>Ainslee's</u>, 1 (Mar.), 25-31.

C98-8   "Work of Mrs. Kenyon Cox," <u>Cosmopolitan</u>, 24 (Mar.), 477-80.

C98-9   "Virtue," <u>Demorest's</u>, 34 (Mar.), 100.
         Poem.

C98-10 "A Club-Woman on Women's Clubs," <u>Success</u>, 1 (Mar.), 8-9.*
         Attribution: Signed "Sallie Joy White"; <u>See</u> C95-2.
         Mrs. Ellen M. Henrotin.

C98-11 "Anthony Hope Tells a Secret," <u>Success</u>, 1 (Mar.), 12-13.
         Repub: <u>Talks with Great Workers</u> (1901).

C98-12 "A Vision of Fairy Lamps," <u>Success</u>, 1 (Mar.), 23.*
         Attribution: Signed "Edward Al"; <u>See</u> C95-4.
         H. Barrington Cox.

C98-13 "Benjamin Eggleston, Painter," <u>Ainslee's</u>, 1 (Apr.), 41-47.

C98-14 "A Prophet, But Not Without Honor," <u>Ainslee's</u>, 1 (Apr.),
         73-79.*
         Attribution: Signed "Edward Al"; <u>See</u> C95-4.

C98-15 "The Harp," <u>Cosmopolitan</u>, 24 (Apr.), 637-44.

C98-16 "Resignation," <u>Demorest's</u>, 34 (Apr.), 137.
         Poem.

C98-17 "Art Work of Irving R. Wiles," <u>Metropolitan</u>, 7 (Apr.), 357-61.

C98-18 "How He Climbed Fame's Ladder," <u>Success</u>, 1 (Apr.), 5-6.
         William Dean Howells.
         Repub: <u>How They Succeeded</u> (1901).

TheodoreDreiser:ABibliography

THEODORE DREISER: A BIBLIOGRAPHY

Contributions to Periodicals

C98-19 "A Great American Caricaturist," Ainslee's, 1 (May), 336-41.
Homer Davenport.

C98-20 "The American Water-Color Society," Metropolitan, 7 (May),
489-93.

C98-21 "Of One Who Dreamed: W. Louis Sonntag, Jr., Obiit, May 11,
1898," Collier's, 21 (28 May), 2.
Poem.

C98-22 "A Painter of Travel," Ainslee's, 1 (June), 391-98.
Gilbert Gaul.

C98-23 "Where Battleships Are Built," Ainslee's, 1 (June), 433-39.*
Attribution: Signed "Edward Al"; See C95-4.

C98-24 "With Whom Is Shadow of Turning," Demorest's, 34 (June), 189.
Poem.

C98-25 "Artists' Studios," Demorest's, 34 (June), 196-98.

C98-26 "The Making of Small Arms," Ainslee's, 1 (July), 540-49.

C98-27 "Scenes in a Cartridge Factory," Cosmopolitan, 25 (July),
321-24.

C98-28 "Carrier Pigeons in War Time," Demorest's, 34 (July), 222-23.

C98-29 "Influences of College Life," Success, 1 (July), 8.*
Attribution: Signed "Sallie Joy White"; See C95-2.
Alice Freeman Palmer.

C98-30 "The Harlem River Speedway," Ainslee's, 2 (Aug.), 49-56.

C98-31 "Night Song," Ainslee's, 2 (Aug.), 73.
Poem.

C98-32 "The Sculpture of Fernando Miranda," Ainslee's, 2 (Sept.),
113-18.

C98-33 "Brandywine, the Picturesque, After One Hundred and Twenty
Years," Demorest's, 34 (Sept.), 274-75.

C98-34 "Mortuarium," Demorest's, 34 (Sept.), 279.
Poem.

C98-35 "Fame Found in Quiet Nooks," Success, 1 (Sept.), 5-6.
John Burroughs.
Repub: How They Succeeded (1901).

C98-36 "Thou Giant," Success, 1 (Sept.), 16.
        Poem.

C98-37 "Haunts of Nathaniel Hawthorne," Truth, 17 (21 Sept.), 7-9.

C98-38 "America's Sculptors," New York Times, 25 Sept., Illustrated
        Magazine Supplement, pp. 6-7.

C98-39 "Haunts of Nathaniel Hawthorne," Truth, 17 (28 Sept.), 11-13.

C98-40 "The Return," Ainslee's, 2 (Oct.), 280.
        Poem.

C98-41 "Great Problems of Organization. III. The Chicago Packing
        Industry," Cosmopolitan, 25 (Oct.), 615-26.

C98-42 "Supplication," Demorest's, 34 (Oct.), 302.
        Poem.

C98-43 "The Smallest and Busiest River in the World," Metropolitan,
        8 (Oct.), 355-63.

C98-44 "Life Stories of Successful Men--No. 10, Philip D. Armour,"
        Success, 1 (Oct.), 3-4.
        Repub: How They Succeeded (1901).

C98-45 "The Real Zangwill," Ainslee's, 2 (Nov.), 351-57.

C98-46 "Through All Adversity," Demorest's, 34 (Nov.), 334.
        Poem.

C98-47 "Birth and Growth of a Popular Song," Metropolitan, 8 (Nov.),
        497-502.

C98-48 "Life Stories of Successful Men--No. 11, Chauncey Mitchell
        Depew," Success, 1 (Nov.), 3-4.
        Repub: Talks with Great Workers (1901).

C98-49 "And Continueth Not," Ainslee's, 2 (Dec.), 477.
        Poem.

C98-50 "The Treasure House of Natural History," Metropolitan, 8
        (Dec.), 595-601.

C98-51 "Life Stories of Successful Men--No. 12, Marshall Field,"
        Success, 2 (8 Dec.), 7-8.
        Repub: How They Succeeded (1901).

Contributions to Periodicals

C98-52 "More Cargoes," Saturday Evening Post, 171 (10 Dec.), 384.*
        Attribution: Dreiser Collection correspondence.
        Review of More Cargoes by W. W. Jacobs.

C98-53 "A Leader of Young Mankind, Frank W. Gunsaulus," Success, 2
        (15 Dec.), 23-24.
        Repub: Talks with Great Workers (1901).

1899

C99-1 "When the Sails Are Furled: Sailor's Snug Harbor," Ainslee's,
        2 (Jan.), 593-601.
        Repub: New York Tribune, 22 May 1904, Sunday Magazine,
        pp. 3-5, 19.
        The Color of a Great City (1923).

C99-2 "Who Wills to Do Good," Ainslee's, 2 (Jan.), 667.
        Poem.

C99-3 "The Making of Stained-Glass Windows," Cosmopolitan, 26
        (Jan.), 243-52.

C99-4 "In Keeping," Demorest's, 35 (Jan.), 37.
        Poem.

C99-5 "Electricity in the Household," Demorest's, 35 (Jan.), 38-39.

C99-6 "A Golden Sorrow," Saturday Evening Post, 171 (28 Jan.), 496.*
        Attribution: Dreiser Collection correspondence.
        Review of A Golden Sorrow by Maria Louise Pool.

C99-7 "He Became Famous in a Day," Success, 2 (28 Jan.), 143-44.
        Paul W. Bartlett.
        Repub: Talks with Great Workers (1901).

C99-8 "The Chicago Drainage Canal," Ainslee's, 3 (Feb.), 53-61.

C99-9 "A Painter of Cats and Dogs," Demorest's, 35 (Feb.), 68-69.
        J. H. Dolph.

C99-10 "Karl Bitter, Sculptor," Metropolitan, 9 (Feb.), 147-52.

C99-11 "E. Percy Morgan and His Work," Truth, 18 (Feb.), 31-35.

C99-12 "His Life Given Over to Music," Success, 2 (4 Feb.), 167-68.
        Theodore Thomas.
        Repub: How They Succeeded (1901).

WORKS BY

C99-13 "America's Greatest Portrait Painters," <u>Success</u>, 2 (11 Feb.),
        183-84.

C99-14 "The Career of a Modern Portia," <u>Success</u>, 2 (18 Feb.), 205-
        206.
        Mrs. Clara Foltz.

C99-15 "Literary Lions I Have Met," <u>Success</u>, 2 (25 Feb.), 223-24.
        James B. Pond.

C99-16 "The Town of Pullman," <u>Ainslee's</u>, 3 (Mar.), 189-200.

C99-17 "Amelia E. Barr and Her Home Life," <u>Demorest's</u>, 35 (Mar.),
        103-104.

C99-18 "Edmund Clarence Stedman at Home," <u>Munsey's</u>, 20 (Mar.),
        931-38.

C99-19 "Bondage," <u>Ainslee's</u>, 3 (Apr.), 293.
        Poem.

C99-20 "The Real Choate," <u>Ainslee's</u>, 3 (Apr.), 324-33.

C99-21 "Japanese Home Life," <u>Demorest's</u>, 35 (Apr.), 123-25.

C99-22 "Women Who Have Won Distinction in Music," <u>Success</u>, 2
        (8 Apr.), 325-26.

C99-23 "A 'New Woman' from the Orient," <u>Success</u>, 2 (29 Apr.), 373.*
        Attribution: Signed "Sallie Joy White"; <u>See</u> C95-2.
        Madame Wu.

C99-24 "The Horseless Age," <u>Demorest's</u>, 35 (May), 153-55.

C99-25 "Woodmen," <u>Demorest's</u>, 35 (May), 159.
        Poem.

C99-26 "The Home of William Cullen Bryant," <u>Munsey's</u>, 26 (May),
        240-46.

C99-27 "Human Documents from Old Rome," <u>Ainslee's</u>, 3 (June), 586-96.

C99-28 "Concerning Bruce Crane," <u>Truth</u>, 18 (June), 143-47.

C99-29 "A Monarch of Metal Workers," <u>Success</u>, 2 (3 June), 453-54.
        Andrew Carnegie.
        Repub: <u>How They Succeeded</u> (1901).

Contributions to Periodicals

C99-30 "A Master of Photography," Success, 2 (10 June), 471.
        Alfred Stieglitz.
        Repub: Talks with Great Workers (1901).

C99-31 "The Foremost of American Sculptors," New Voice, 16 (17 June),
        4-5, 13.
        J. Q. A. Ward.

C99-32 "American Women as Successful Playwrights," Success, 2
        (17 June), 485-86.

C99-33 "American Women Who Play the Harp," Success, 2 (24 June),
        501-502.

C99-34 "The Log of an Ocean Pilot," Ainslee's, 3 (July), 683-92.
        Repub: The Color of a Great City (1923) (as "The Log
        of a Harbor Pilot").

C99-35 "An Important Philanthropy," Demorest's, 35 (July), 215-17.

C99-36 "From New York to Boston by Trolley," Ainslee's, 4 (Aug.),
        74-84.*
        Attribution: Signed "Herman D. White"; Dreiser
        Collection correspondence.
        Repub: American Review of Reviews, 20 (Aug. 1899),
        201 (excerpted).

C99-37 "A Notable Colony: Artistic and Literary People in the
        Picturesque Bronx," Demorest's, 35 (Aug.), 240-41.

C99-38 "If Force Transmutes," Demorest's, 35 (Aug.), 243.
        Poem.

C99-39 "John Burroughs in His Mountain Hut," New Voice, 16 (19
        Aug.), 7, 13.

C99-40 "Christ Church, Shrewsbury," New York Times, 27 Aug.,
        Illustrated Magazine Supplement, pp. 12-13.

C99-41 "C. C. Curran," Truth, 18 (Sept.), 227-31.

C99-42 "It Pays to Treat Workers Generously," Success, 2 (16 Sept.),
        691-92.
        John H. Patterson.
        Repub: Talks with Great Workers (1901).

C99-43 "American Women Violinists," Success, 2 (30 Sept.), 731-32.

119

WORKS BY

C99-44 "The Camera Club of New York," Ainslee's, 4 (Oct.), 324-35.

C99-45 "The Unrewarded," Demorest's, 36 (Nov.), 5.
        Poem.

C99-46 "Curious Shifts of the Poor," Demorest's, 36 (Nov.), 22-26.
        Repub: Sister Carrie (1900) (Chapters XLV-XLVII).
        The Color of a Great City (1923) (as "The Bread Line"
        and "The Men in the Storm").

C99-47 "American Women Who Are Winning Fame as Pianists," Success,
        2 (4 Nov.), 815.

C99-48 "Our Government and Our Food," Demorest's, 36 (Dec.), 68-70.

                        1900

C00-1 "The Trade of the Mississippi," Ainslee's, 4 (Jan.), 735-43.

C00-2 "Atkinson on National Food Reform," Success, 3 (Jan.), 4.*
        Attribution: Signed "Edward Al"; See C95-4.

C00-3 "The Story of a Song-Queen's Triumph," Success, 3 (Jan.),
        6-8.
        Lillian Nordica.
        Repub: How They Succeeded (1901).

C00-4 "The Railroad and the People," Harper's Monthly, 100 (Feb.),
        479-84.

C00-5 "Little Clubmen of the Tenements," Puritan, 7 (Feb.), 665-72.

C00-6 "The Real Howells," Ainslee's, 5 (Mar.), 137-42.
        Repub: Americana, 37 (Apr. 1943), 275-82 (as "Five
        Interviews with William Dean Howells").

C00-7 "New York's Underground Railroad," Pearson's, 9 (Apr.),
        375-84.

C00-8 "Good Roads for Bad," Pearson's, 9 (May), 387-95.

C00-9 "Champ Clark, the Man and His District," Ainslee's, 5
        (June), 425-34.

C00-10 "The Descent of the Horse," Everybody's, 2 (June), 543-47.

Theodore Dreiser: A Bibliography

C00-11　"Thomas Brackett Reed:　The Story of a Great Career,"
　　　　　Success, 3 (June), 215-16.

C00-12　"The Transmigration of the Sweat Shop," Puritan, 8 (July),
　　　　　498-502.

C00-13　"Apples:　An Account of the Apple Industry in America,"
　　　　　Pearson's, 10 (Oct.), 336-40.

C00-14　"Fruit Growing in America," Harper's Monthly, 101 (Nov.),
　　　　　859-68.

C00-15　"Whence the Song," Harper's Weekly, 44 (8 Dec.), 1165-66a.
　　　　　Repub:　The Color of a Great City (1923).

1901

C01-1　"Why the Indian Paints His Face," Pearson's, 11 (Jan.), 19-23.

C01-2　"When the Old Century Was New," Pearson's, 11 (Jan.), 131-40.
　　　　Repub:　Free (1918).

C01-3　"Delaware's Blue Laws," Ainslee's, 7 (Feb.), 53-57.

C01-4　"Rural Free Mail Delivery," Pearson's, 11 (Feb.), 233-40.

C01-5　"Lawrence E. Earle," Truth, 20 (Feb.), 27-30.

C01-6　"The Story of the States:　No. III--Illinois," Pearson's, 11
　　　　(Apr.), 513-44.

C01-7　"The Shining Slave Makers," Ainslee's, 7 (June), 445-50.
　　　　　Repub:　Free (1918) (as "McEwen of the Shining Slave
　　　　Makers").

C01-8　"Plant Life Underground," Pearson's, 11 (June), 860-64.

C01-9　"Nigger Jeff," Ainslee's, 8 (Nov.), 366-75.
　　　　　Repub:　Free (1918).

C01-10　"A True Patriarch," McClure's, 18 (Dec.), 136-44.
　　　　　Repub:　Twelve Men (1919).

C01-11　"Butcher Rogaum's Door," Reedy's Mirror, 11 (12 Dec.), 15-17.
　　　　　Repub:　Free (1918) (as "Old Rogaum and His Theresa").

WORKS BY

C01-12 "The Color of To-Day," Harper's Weekly, 45 (14 Dec.), 1272-73.
Repub: Twelve Men (1919) (as "W. L. S.").

1902

C02-1 "The New Knowledge of Weeds," Ainslee's, 8 (Jan.), 533-38.

C02-2 "A Cripple Whose Energy Gives Inspiration," Success, 5 (Feb.),
72-73.

C02-3 "A Touch of Human Brotherhood," Success, 5 (Mar.), 140-41,
176.

C02-4 "The Tenement Toilers," Success, 5 (Apr.), 213-14, 232.
Repub: New York Call, 24 Aug. 1919, Call Magazine,
pp. 6-7 (as "The Toilers of the Tenements).
The Color of a Great City (1923) (as "The Toilers of
the Tenements").

C02-5 "A Remarkable Art," Great Round World, 19 (3 May), 430-34.*
Attribution: Material reworked from Dreiser's "A
Master of Photography," Success, 2 (10 June 1899), 471.
Alfred Stieglitz.

C02-6 "A Doer of the Word," Ainslee's, 9 (June), 453-59.
Repub: Twelve Men (1919).

C02-7 "Christmas in the Tenements," Harper's Weekly, 46 (6 Dec.),
52-53.
Repub: The Color of a Great City (1923).

1903

C03-1 "True Art Speaks Plainly," Booklovers Magazine, 1 (Feb.),
129.
Repub: Modernist, 1 (Nov. 1919), 21.

C03-2 "Scared Back to Nature," Harper's Weekly, 47 (16 May), 816.*
Attribution: Material reused by Dreiser in his sketch
"Culhane, the Solid Man" in Twelve Men (1919).

C03-3 "A Mayor and His People," Era, 11 (June), 578-84.
Repub: Twelve Men (1919).

C03-4 "The Problem of the Soil," Era, 12 (Sept.), 239-49.

THEODORE DREISER: A BIBLIOGRAPHY

1904

C04-1   "Just What Happened When the Waters of the Hudson Broke into the North River Tunnel," New York Daily News, 23 Jan., Magazine Section, pp. 6-7.*
    Attribution: Material reused by Dreiser in his story "St. Columba and the River" in Chains (1927).

C04-2   "The Cradle of Tears," New York Daily News, 27 Mar., Colored Section, p. 4.*
    Attribution: Republished by Dreiser.
    Repub: Tom Watson's Magazine, 1 (May 1905), 349-50.
    The Color of a Great City (1923).

C04-3   "The Sowing," Ainslee's, 13 (Apr.), 135.
    Poem.

C04-4   "The Story of a Human Nine-Pin," New York Daily News, 3 Apr., Colored Section, p. 3.*
    Attribution: Republished by Dreiser.
    Repub: Tom Watson's Magazine, 1 (June 1905), 502-503 (as "The Track Walker").
    The Color of a Great City (1923) (as "The Track Walker").

C04-5   "The Love Affairs of Little Italy," New York Daily News, 10 Apr., Colored Section, p. 3.*
    Attribution: Republished by Dreiser.
    Repub: The Color of a Great City (1923).

C04-6   "Hunting for Swordfish," New York Tribune, 24 July, Sunday Magazine, pp. 11-12.

C04-7   "The Voyage," Ainslee's, 14 (Oct.), 136.
    Poem.

1905

C05-1   "The Old 10:30 Train," Tom Watson's Magazine, 1 (Mar.), 96.*
    Attribution: Signed "Marion Drace"; the Dreiser Collection contains an unidentified clipping of this poem (apparently a later printing) signed "Theodore Dreiser."

C05-2   "The Rivers of the Nameless Dead," Tom Watson's Magazine, 1 (Mar.), 112-13.
    Repub: The Color of a Great City (1923).

WORKS BY

C05-3   "A Word to the Public," <u>Smith's</u>, 1 (June), unpaginated advertising section, 3 pp.*
      Attribution: <u>Smith's Magazine</u> published its first number in April 1905, the month in which Dreiser became editor of the journal. The first two issues (April and May) contained a section of editorial commentary on the contents of the magazine called "The Publisher's Word." I am assuming that Dreiser changed the title of the column to "A Word to the Public" when he took over responsibility for this column in the June number, a responsibility which he made explicit in the August number when he began to call the column "What the Editor Has to Say." Although Dreiser resigned the editorship of <u>Smith's</u> in April 1906, he was responsible for the magazine's contents (and therefore presumably its editorial column) through the June 1906 number.

C05-4   "A Word to the Public," <u>Smith's</u>, 1 (July), unpaginated advertising section, 4 pp.*
      Attribution: <u>See</u> C05-3.

C05-5   "What the Editor Has to Say," <u>Smith's</u>, 1 (Aug.), unpaginated advertising section, 2 pp.*
      Attribution: <u>See</u> C05-3.

C05-6   "What the Editor Has to Say," <u>Smith's</u>, 1 (Sept.), unpaginated advertising section, 2 pp.*
      Attribution: <u>See</u> C05-3.

C05-7   "The Silent Worker," <u>Tom Watson's Magazine</u>, 2 (Sept.), 364.
      Repub: "Three Sketches of the Poor," New York <u>Call</u>, 23 Nov. 1913, p. 10.

C05-8   "What the Editor Has to Say," <u>Smith's</u>, 2 (Oct.), unpaginated advertising section, 2 pp.*
      Attribution: <u>See</u> C05-3.

C05-9   "The City of Crowds," <u>Smith's</u>, 2 (Oct.), 97-107.

C05-10   "The Loneliness of the City," <u>Tom Watson's Magazine</u>, 2 (Oct.), 474-75.

C05-11   "What the Editor Has to Say," <u>Smith's</u>, 2 (Nov.), unpaginated advertising section, 3 pp.*
      Attribution: <u>See</u> C05-3.

C05-12   "What the Editor Has to Say," <u>Smith's</u>, 2 (Dec.), unpaginated advertising section, 2 pp.*
      Attribution: <u>See</u> C05-3.

Contributions to Periodicals

1906

C06-1   "Smith's: The Magazine of Ten Million. What It Will Do
        During the Coming Year," Smith's, 2 (Jan.), unpaginated
        advertising section, 8 pp.*
        Attribution: See C05-3.

C06-2   "A Lesson from the Aquarium," Tom Watson's Magazine, 3 (Jan.),
        306-308.

C06-3   "What the Editor Has to Say," Smith's, 2 (Feb.), unpaginated
        advertising section, 3 pp.*
        Attribution: See C05-3.

C06-4   "What the Editor Has to Say," Smith's, 2 (Mar.), unpaginated
        advertising section, 2 pp.*
        Attribution: See C05-3.

C06-5   "What the Editor Has to Say," Smith's, 3 (Apr.), unpaginated
        advertising section, 3 pp.*
        Attribution: See C05-3.

C06-6   "What the Editor Has to Say," Smith's, 3 (May), unpaginated
        advertising section, 2 pp.*
        Attribution: See C05-3.

C06-7   "What the Editor Has to Say," Smith's, 3 (June), unpaginated
        advertising section, 2 pp.*
        Attribution: See C05-3.

C06-8   "New York and 'The New Broadway'," Broadway, 16 (June), vii-
        ix.*
        Attribution: Dreiser was editor of the Broadway
        Magazine from April 1906 to June 1907. I have attributed
        to Dreiser the unsigned editorial columns in the Broadway
        between June 1906, when the magazine announced a new
        editorial policy, and July 1907.

C06-9   "The Beauty of the Tree," Broadway, 16 (June), 130.
        Sketch.

C06-10 "$5,000 for Short Stories!", Broadway, 16 (July), iv.*
        Attribution: See C06-8.
        This editorial announcement was reprinted in the August
        and September numbers.

C06-11 "The Problem of Magazine Building," Broadway, 16 (July),
        v-vi.*
        Attribution: See C06-8.

WORKS BY

C06-12 "We Are Building This Magazine Along New Lines," <u>Broadway</u>,
     16 (Aug.), v-vi.*
       Attribution: <u>See</u> C06-8.

C06-13 "The Poet's Creed," <u>Broadway</u>, 16 (Aug.), 353.
       Poem.

C06-14 "The Peace of the Thousand Isles," <u>Smith's</u>, 3 (Aug.), 769-84.

C06-15 "As New as New York Itself," <u>Broadway</u>, 16 (Sept.), vii-viii.*
       Attribution: <u>See</u> C06-8.

C06-16 "Broadway Magazine for 1907," <u>Broadway</u>, 17 (Dec.), unpaginated
     front matter, 4 pp.*
       Attribution: <u>See</u> C06-8.

1907

C07-1 "Fruitage," <u>Broadway</u>, 17 (Feb.), 566.
       Poem.

C07-2 "Broadway for the American Home," <u>Broadway</u>, 18 (Apr.), un-
     paginated front matter, 4 pp.*
       Attribution: <u>See</u> C06-8.

C07-3 "What Broadway Means to America," <u>Broadway</u>, 18 (May), un-
     paginated front matter, 4 pp.*
       Attribution: <u>See</u> C06-8.

C07-4 "Broadway Is One Year Old This Number," <u>Broadway</u>, 18 (June),
     unpaginated front matter, 4 pp.*
       Attribution: <u>See</u> C06-8.

C07-5 "Broadway's Brilliant Mid-Summer Fiction," <u>Broadway</u>, 18
     (July), unpaginated front matter, 4 pp.*
       Attribution: <u>See</u> C06-8.

C07-6 "Concerning Us All," <u>Delineator</u>, 70 (Oct.), 491-92.*
       Attribution: Dreiser was editor of the <u>Delineator</u>
     from June 1907 to October 1910, though he did not become
     fully responsible for the magazine until the October 1907
     number. All <u>Delineator</u> items which I attribute to
     Dreiser were designated in the magazine as by the editor.
     These columns came to an end with the December 1909 number.

C07-7 "Interviews with the Editor," <u>Delineator</u>, 70 (Nov.), 649-50.*
       Attribution: <u>See</u> C07-6.

C07-8 "Concerning Us All," Delineator, 70 (Nov.), 732-33.*
   Attribution: See C07-6.

C07-9 "Your Magazine in 1908," Delineator, 70 (Dec.), 864-65.*
   Attribution: See C07-6.

C07-10 "Concerning Us All," Delineator, 70 (Dec.), 927-28.*
   Attribution: See C07-6.

1908

C08-1 "Just You and the Editor," Delineator, 71 (Jan.), 5-7.*
   Attribution: See C07-6.

C08-2 "Concerning Us All," Delineator, 71 (Jan.), 67-68.*
   Attribution: See C07-6.

C08-3 "Just You and the Editor," Delineator, 71 (Feb.), 161-63.*
   Attribution: See C07-6.

C08-4 "Concerning Us All," Delineator, 71 (Feb.), 221-22.*
   Attribution: See C07-6.

C08-5 "Just You and the Editor," Delineator, 71 (Mar.), 335-37.*
   Attribution: See C07-6.

C08-6 "Concerning Us All," Delineator, 71 (Mar.), 397-98.
   Attribution: See C07-6.

C08-7 "Summer-Time: A Conference," Delineator, 71 (Apr.), 508-509.*
   Attribution: The Delineator's "Just You and the
   Column"; See C07-6.

C08-8 "Concerning Us All," Delineator, 71 (Apr.), 575-76.*
   Attribution: See C07-6.

C08-9 "Just You and the Editor," Delineator, 71 (May), 710-11.*
   Attribution: See C07-6.

C08-10 "Concerning Us All," Delineator, 71 (May), 775-76.*
   Attribution: See C07-6.

C08-11 "Concerning Us All," Delineator, 71 (June), 971-72.*
   Attribution: See C07-6.

C08-12 "Concerning Us All," Delineator, 72 (July), 77-78.*
   Attribution: See C07-6.

WORKS BY

C08-13 "Just You and the Editor," Delineator, 72 (Aug.), 162-63.*
        Attribution: See C07-6.

C08-14 "Concerning Us All," Delineator, 72 (Aug.), 223-24.*
        Attribution: See C07-6.

C08-15 "Concerning Us All," Delineator, 72 (Sept.), 369-70.*
        Attribution: See C07-6.

C08-16 "Just You and the Editor," Delineator, 72 (Oct.), 468-69.*
        Attribution: See C07-6.

C08-17 "Concerning Us All," Delineator, 72 (Oct.), 537-38.*
        Attribution: See C07-6.

C08-18 "Just You and the Editor," Delineator, 72 (Nov.), 659-61.*
        Attribution: See C07-6.

C08-19 "Concerning Us All," Delineator, 72 (Nov.), 739-40.*
        Attribution: See C07-6.

C08-20 "Just You and the Editor," Delineator, 72 (Dec.), 881-83.*
        Attribution: See C07-6.

                          1909

C09-1   "Just You and the Editor," Delineator, 73 (Jan.), 6-7.*
        Attribution: See C07-6.

C09-2   "Concerning Us All," Delineator, 73 (Jan.), 69-70.*
        Attribution: See C07-6.

C09-3   "Just You and the Editor," Delineator, 73 (Feb.), 152-53.*
        Attribution: See C07-6.

C09-4   "Concerning Us All," Delineator, 73 (Feb.), 211-12.*
        Attribution: See C07-6.

C09-5   "Just You and the Editor," Delineator, 73 (Mar.), 318-19.*
        Attribution: See C07-6.

C09-6   "Concerning Us All," Delineator, 73 (Mar.), 391-92.*
        Attribution: See C07-6.

C09-7   "Concerning Us All," Delineator, 73 (Apr.), 556.*
        Attribution: See C07-6.

C09-8 "Concerning Us All," Delineator, 73 (May), 672.*
       Attribution: See C07-6.

C09-9 "Concerning Us All," Delineator, 73 (June), 766.*
       Attribution: See C07-6.

C09-10 "Concerning Us All," Delineator, 74 (July), 33.*
       Attribution: See C07-6.

C09-11 "Concerning Us All," Delineator, 74 (Aug.), 113.*
       Attribution: See C07-6.

C09-12 "Concerning Us All," Delineator, 74 (Sept.), 193.*
       Attribution: See C07-6.

C09-13 "At the Sign of the Lead Pencil: The Man on the Sidewalk,"
       Bohemian, 17 (Oct.), 422-23.*
           Attribution: Dreiser gained financial control of the
       Bohemian Magazine in the fall of 1909; for the three is-
       sues of October, November, and December, 1909, he directed
       the editorial policies of the magazine as well as con-
       tributed to it anonymously, pseudonymously, and in his
       own name. "At the Sign of the Lead Pencil" was an intro-
       ductory column of unsigned editorial and descriptive
       essays. In a letter to Dreiser on 21 September 1909 (in
       the Dreiser Collection), Fritz Krog--the nominal editor
       of the magazine--listed by title and author those essays
       which he had on hand. And in a letter to Robert H. Elias
       on 22 February 1945 (in the Cornell University Library),
       H. L. Mencken identified the essays which he had written
       for the column at Dreiser's request. I have therefore
       attributed to Dreiser essays in the "At the Sign of the
       Lead Pencil" column on the following bases: Krog does
       not attribute to another author; Mencken does not claim;
       subject matter and style are characteristically Dreiser's.

C09-14 "At the Sign of the Lead Pencil: In the Matter of Spiritual-
       ism," Bohemian, 17 (Oct.), 424-25.*
       Attribution: See C09-13.

C09-15 "At the Sign of the Lead Pencil: The Day of the Great
       Writer," Bohemian, 17 (Oct.), 426-27.*
       Attribution: See C09-13.

C09-16 "At the Sign of the Lead Pencil: The Defects of Organized
       Charity," Bohemian, 17 (Oct.), 429-31.*
       Attribution: See C09-13.

WORKS BY

C09-17 "The Cruise of the Idlewild," Bohemian, 17 (Oct.), 441-47.
         Repub: Free (1918).

C09-18 "The Flight of Pigeons," Bohemian, 17 (Oct.), 494-96.*
         Attribution: Signed "Edward Al"; See C95-4.
         Repub: The Color of a Great City (1923).

C09-19 "Concerning Us All," Delineator, 74 (Oct.), 292.*
         Attribution: See C07-6.

C09-20 "The Waterfront," Bohemian, 17 (Nov.), 633-36.*
         Attribution: Signed "Edward Al"; See C95-4.
         Repub: The Color of a Great City (1923).

C09-21 "Concerning Us All," Delineator, 74 (Nov.), 400.*
         Attribution: See C07-6.

C09-22 "At the Sign of the Lead Pencil: Our National Literary
         Debt," Bohemian, 17 (Dec.), 705-707.*
         Attribution: See C09-13.

C09-23 "At the Sign of the Lead Pencil: Pittsburgh," Bohemian, 17
         (Dec.), 712-14.*
         Attribution: See C09-13.

C09-24 "The Red Slayer," Bohemian, 17 (Dec.), 793-95.*
         Attribution: Signed "Edward Al"; See C95-4.
         Repub: The Color of a Great City (1923).

C09-25 "Concerning Us All," Delineator, 74 (Dec.), 494.*
         Attribution: See C07-6.

                            1910

C10-1   "Six O'Clock," 1910, no. 4 (no date), unpaginated, 2 pp.
         Repub: The Color of a Great City (1923).

C10-2   "The Factory," 1910, no. 5 (no date), unpaginated, 2 pp.

                            1911

C11-1   "The Mighty Burke," McClure's, 37 (May), 40-50.
         Repub: Twelve Men (1919) (as "The Mighty Rourke").

1912

C12-1   "The Men in the Dark," American Magazine, 73 (Feb.), 465-68.
Repub: The Color of a Great City (1923).

C12-2   "Deeper Than Man-Made Laws," Hearst's Magazine, 21 (June),
2395.
Contribution to a symposium entitled "How Shall We
Solve the Divorce Problem?"

1913

C13-1   "Lilly Edwards: An Episode," Smart Set, 40 (June), 81-86.
Repub: A Traveler at Forty (1913) (Chapter XIII).

C13-2   "Authors Dreiser and Brady Join in Hawthorne Plea," St. Louis
Star, 11 July, p. 2.
Contains a letter by Dreiser, dated 3 July 1913, to
a Mr. Warren of the Star.

C13-3   "The Toil of the Laborer," New York Call, 13 July, p. 11.
Repub: Reconstruction, 1 (Oct. 1919), 310-13.
Hey Rub-a-Dub-Dub (1920).

C13-4   "The First Voyage Over," Century, 86 (Aug.), 586-95.
Repub: A Traveler at Forty (1913) (Chapters I-III, V).

C13-5   "An Uncommercial Traveler in London," Century, 86 (Sept.),
736-49.
Repub: A Traveler at Forty (1913) (Chapters VII-XI).

C13-6   "Paris," Century, 86 (Oct.), 904-915.
Repub: A Traveler at Forty (1913) (Chapters XXI-XXIV).

C13-7   "The Girl in the Coffin," Smart Set, 41 (Oct.), 127-40.
Repub: Plays (1916).

C13-8   "The Man on the Bench," New York Call, 16 Nov., p. 9.
Repub: The Color of a Great City (1923).

C13-9   "Three Sketches of the Poor," New York Call, 23 Nov., p. 10.
"The Man Who Bakes Your Bread," "The Men in the Snow,"
and "The Silent Worker."
Repub: "The Man Who Bakes Your Bread," New York Call,
13 Apr. 1919, Call Magazine, pp. 1, 6.
"The Men in the Snow," The Color of a Great City (1923).

WORKS BY

1914

C14-1   "My Uncompleted Trilogy," New York Evening Sun, 30 May, p. 6.

C14-2   "The Blue Sphere," Smart Set, 44 (Dec.), 245-52.
         Repub: Plays (1916).

1915

C15-1   "In the Dark," Smart Set, 45 (Jan.), 419-25.
         Repub: Plays (1916).

C15-2   "Laughing Gas," Smart Set, 45 (Feb.), 85-94.
         Repub: Plays (1916).

C15-3   "The Saddest Story," New Republic, 3 (12 June), 155-56.
         Review of The Good Soldier by Ford Madox Ford.

C15-4   "Neither Devil Nor Angel," New Republic, 3 (10 July), 262-63.
         Review of One Man by Robert Steele.

C15-5   "'The Genius' Not of a Trilogy," Reedy's Mirror, 24 (15 Oct.),
         265.
              Letter to William Marion Reedy, dated 9 October 1915.

C15-6   "The Spring Recital," Little Review, 2 (Dec.), 28-35.
         Repub: Plays (1916).

C15-7   "As a Realist Sees It," New Republic, 5 (25 Dec.), 202-204.
         Review of Of Human Bondage by W. Somerset Maugham.

1916

C16-1   "The Light in the Window," International, 10 (Jan.), 6-8, 32.
         Repub: Plays (1916).

C16-2   "Freedom for the Honest Writer," Cleveland Leader, 12 Mar.,
         p. 7.
              Contribution to a symposium entitled "Literature and
         Art from the Point of View of American Ideals," syndicated
         by Newspaper Enterprise Associates.

C16-3   "The Lost Phoebe," Century, 91 (Apr.), 885-96.
         Repub: Free (1918).

C16-4   "Four Poems," Smart Set, 49 (May), 277-78.
       "Wood Note," "For a Moment the Wind Died," "They Shall
      Fall as Stripped Garments," and "Ye Ages, Ye Tribes!"
      Repub: "For the Moment the Wind Died" in "Four Poems,"
      American Mercury, 1 (Jan. 1924), 8-10 and For a Moment
      the Wind Died: Song, Words by Theodore Dreiser, Music by
      Carl E. Gehring, London: Dolart, 1925.
      All four poems are republished in Moods (1926).

C16-5   "Change," Pagan, 1 (Sept.), 27-28.
      Repub: New York Call, 26 Jan. 1918, Call Magazine,
      p. 1.
      Chicago Examiner, 30 Mar. 1918, Fine Arts Supplement,
      pp. 1, 7 (as "Dreiser Sees World-Hope in Change").
      Hey Rub-a-Dub-Dub (1920).

C16-6   "America's Foremost Author Protests Against Suppression of
      Great Books and Art by Self-Constituted Moral Censors,"
      Los Angeles Record, 7 Nov., p. 4.
      Syndicated by Newspaper Enterprise Associates.

1917

C17-1   Medical Review of Reviews, 23 (Jan.), 8-9.
      Contribution to a "Symposium on the Medical Profession."

C17-2   "Life, Art and America," Seven Arts, 1 (Feb.), 363-89.
      Repub: Life, Art and America (1917).
      Hey Rub-a-Dub-Dub (1920.

C17-3   "Mister Bottom," The Social War, 1 (Apr.), 2.

C17-4   "A Man and His House," Hoggson Magazine, 3 (June), 107.

C17-5   "Our Greatest Writer Tells What's Wrong with Our Newspapers,"
      Pep, 2 (July), 8-9.
      Syndicated by Newspaper Enterprise Associates.
      Repub: New York Call, 16 Dec. 1917, Call Magazine,
      p. 3 (as "Our Amazing Illusioned Press").

C17-6   "The Dream," Seven Arts, 2 (July), 319-33.
      Repub: Hey Rub-a-Dub-Dub (1920).

C17-7   "Married," Cosmopolitan, 63 (Sept.), 31-35, 112-15.
      Repub: Free (1918).

WORKS BY

1918

C18-1   "The Second Choice," Cosmopolitan, 64 (Feb.), 53-58, 104,
         106-107.
         Repub: Free (1918).

C18-2   "Free," Saturday Evening Post, 190 (16 Mar.), 13-15, 81-89.
         Repub: Free (1918).

C18-3   "The Right to Kill," New York Call, 16 Mar., Call Magazine,
         pp. 1, 12-13.

C18-4   "I Hope the War Will Blow Our Minds Clear of the Miasma of
         Puritanism," Philadelphia Press, 13 Apr., p. 12.

C18-5   "The Country Doctor," Harper's Monthly, 137 (July), 193-202.
         Repub: Twelve Men (1919).

C18-6   "The Old Neighborhood," Metropolitan, 49 (Dec.), 27-30, 46,
         48-50.
         Repub: Chains (1927).

C18-7   "Rural America in War-Time," Scribner's, 64 (Dec.), 734-46.

1919

C19-1   William Marion Reedy, "To Make It Safe for Art," Reedy's
         Mirror, 28 (21 Feb.), 101-102.
         Contains a statement by an unidentified "well-known
         writer" concerning a proposal for a society of artists;
         attributed to Dreiser on the basis of a letter by Reedy
         to Dreiser, 17 February 1919 (in the Dreiser Collection).

C19-2   "The Standard Oil Works at Bayonne," New York Call, 16 Mar.,
         Call Magazine, pp. 3, 5.
         Repub: The Color of a Great City (1923) (as "A Cer-
         tain Oil Refinery").

C19-3   "The Pushcart Man," New York Call, 30 Mar., Call Magazine,
         pp. 1, 7.
         Repub: The Color of a Great City (1923).

C19-4   "The Hand," Munsey's, 66 (May), 679-88.
         Repub: Chains (1927).

C19-5   "Love," New York Tribune, 18 May, Part 7, pp. 2-3.
         Repub: Live Stories, 25 (Dec. 1920), 3-19.
         Chains (1927) (as "Chains").

Contributions to Periodicals

C19-6   "Ashtoreth," Reedy's Mirror, 28 (10 July), 456-57.
         Repub: Hey Rub-a-Dub-Dub (1920).

C19-7   "Man and Romance," Reedy's Mirror, 28 (28 Aug.), 585.
         Repub: New York Call, 14 Sept. 1919, Call Magazine,
         p. 9.

C19-8   "Hey, Rub-a-Dub-Dub," Nation, 109 (30 Aug.), 278-81.
         Repub: Hey Rub-a-Dub-Dub (1920).

C19-9   "Sanctuary," Smart Set, 60 (Oct.), 35-52.
         Repub: Chains (1927).

C19-10   "More Democracy, or Less? An Inquiry," Reconstruction, 1
         (Dec.), 338-42.
         Repub: New York Call, 30 Nov. 1919, Call Magazine,
         pp. 5-7 (initial publication attributed to Reconstruction
         by the Call).
         Hey Rub-a-Dub-Dub (1920).

1920

C20-1   "Mr. Dreiser and the Broadway Magazine," The Review, 2
         (5 June), 597.
         Letter to the Editor, dated 16 May 1920.
         Repub: Notice (1920).

1921

C21-1   Frank Harris, "Dreiser vs. Harris," Pearson's, 46 (Jan.),
         234.
         Contains a letter to Harris, dated 3 November 1920.
         Repub: Letters of Theodore Dreiser (1959), I, 294-95.

C21-2   "Phantom Gold," Live Stories, 26 (Feb.), 3-23.
         Repub: Chains (1927).

C21-3   "Dreiser Sees No Progress," New York Globe and Commercial
         Advertiser, 22 Feb., p. 6.
         Letter to the Editor, dated 14 February 1921.

C21-4   "Americans Are Still Interested in Ten Commandments--For the
         Other Fellow, Says Dreiser," New York Call, 13 Mar., Call
         Magazine, p. 7.

WORKS BY

C21-5   "A Word Concerning Birth Control," <u>Birth Control Review</u>, 5
        (Apr.), 5-6, 12-13.
            Repub: New York <u>Call</u>, 1 May 1921, Call Magazine, p. 4.

C21-6   "Hollywood Now," <u>McCall's</u>, 48 (Sept.), 8, 18, 54.

C21-7   "Why Not Tell Europe About Bertha M. Clay?", St. Paul <u>Daily
        News</u>, 11 Sept., Section 2, p. 6.
            Letter to Thomas A. Boyd, dated 25 August 1921.
            Repub: New York <u>Call</u>, 24 Oct. 1921, p. 6.

C21-8   "I. Chicago. Out of My Newspaper Days," <u>Bookman</u>, 54 (Nov.),
        208-17.
            Repub: <u>A Book About Myself</u> (1922) (Chapters I, XIV).

C21-9   "Hollywood: Its Morals and Manners," <u>Shadowland</u>, 5 (Nov.),
        37, 61-63.

C21-10 "A Letter About Stephen Crane," <u>Michigan Daily</u> (Ann Arbor),
        27 Nov., Sunday Magazine Section, p. 1.
            Contains a letter to Max J. Herzberg, dated 2 November
        1921.

C21-11 "Hollywood: Its Morals and Manners," <u>Shadowland</u>, 5 (Dec.),
        51, 61.

                                1922

C22-1   "II. St. Louis. Out of My Newspaper Days," <u>Bookman</u>, 54
        (Jan.), 427-33.
            Repub: <u>A Book About Myself</u> (1922) (Chapters XX, XXIV-
        XXV).

C22-2   "Hollywood: Its Morals and Manners," <u>Shadowland</u>, 5 (Jan.),
        43, 67.

C22-3   "III. 'Red' Galvin. Out of My Newspaper Days," <u>Bookman</u>, 54
        (Feb.), 542-50.
            Repub: <u>A Book About Myself</u> (1922) (Chapters XLIV-XLV).

C22-4   "Hollywood: Its Morals and Manners," <u>Shadowland</u>, 5 (Feb.),
        53, 66.

C22-5   "IV. The Bandit. Out of My Newspaper Days," <u>Bookman</u>, 55
        (Mar.), 12-20.
            Repub: <u>A Book About Myself</u> (1922) (Chapter XLVI).

Contributions to Periodicals

C22-6   "V. I Quit the Game. Out of My Newspaper Days," Bookman, 55 (Apr.), 118-25.
      Repub: A Book About Myself (1922) (Chapters LXXV-LXXVII).

C22-7   "The Scope of Fiction," New Republic, 30 (12 Apr.), Spring Literary Supplement, 8-9.

1923

C23-1   "A Letter from Vienna to Theo. Dreiser--And His Reply," Tempest (Ann Arbor), 1 (2 Apr.), 3.
      Dreiser's reply to a series of questions asked by the editors of the Hungarian magazine Tuz.

C23-2   "Applied Religion--Applied Art," Survey, 50 (1 May), 175.
      Contribution to a symposium entitled "Who Challenges to Social Order?"

C23-3   Percy Hammond, "Oddments and Remainders," New York Tribune, 14 May, p. 8.
      Contains an undated letter to Sidney Kirkpatrick.

C23-4   "Dreiser Refuses to Help Films Reach 'Higher Level,'" New York Globe and Commercial Advertiser, 16 May, p. 5.
      Contains an undated letter to Rex Beach; the letter was widely reprinted, in whole or in part, in various newspapers throughout the country.
      Repub: Letters of Theodore Dreiser (1959), II, 408-410.

C23-5   "Ida Hauchawout," Century, 106 (July), 335-48.
      Repub: A Gallery of Women (1929).

C23-6   "Reina," Century, 106 (Sept.), 695-716.
      Repub: A Gallery of Women (1929).

C23-7   "These United States--XXXIX. Indiana: Her Soil and Light," Nation, 117 (3 Oct.), 348-50.
      Repub: These United States: A Symposium, Second Series, ed. Ernest Gruening, New York: Boni and Liveright, 1924.

C23-8   "Sombre Annals," New York Evening Post Literary Review, 17 Nov., p. 255.
      Review of Undertow by Henry K. Marks.

WORKS BY

1924

C24-1   "Four Poems," American Mercury, 1 (Jan.), 8-10.
"The Little Flowers of Love and Wonder," "Proteus,"
"For a Moment the Wind Died," and "Take Hands."
Repub: The first poem in Little Flowers of Love and
Wonder: Song, Words by Theodore Dreiser, Music by Carl E.
Gehring, London: Dolart, 1925, and in "Recent Poems of
Love and Sorrow," Vanity Fair, 27 (Sept. 1926), 54.
All four poems are republished in Moods (1926).

C24-2   "Fulfillment," Holland's Magazine, 43 (Feb.), 7-9, 31.
Repub: Chains (1927).

C24-3   "The Mercy of God," American Mercury, 2 (Aug.), 457-64.
Repub: Chains (1927) (as "The 'Mercy' of God").

C24-4   "Jealousy: Nine Women Out of Ten," Harper's Bazar, 59
(Aug.), 84-85, 92, 94, 96.
Repub: Chains (1927) (as "The Shadow").

C24-5   "The Irish Section Foreman Who Taught Me How to Live,"
Hearst's International, 46 (Aug.), 20-21, 118-21.

C24-6   "Five Poems," New York Evening Post Literary Review, 20 Dec.,
p. 8.
"Tall Towers," "The Poet," "In a Country Graveyard,"
"The Hidden God," and "The New Day."
Repub: Moods (1926).

1925

C25-1   "The Great Blossom," Leonardo, Annual Magazine of the
Leonardo da Vinci Art School, 1924-25 (New York), p. 54.
Repub: Moods (1926).

C25-2   "Glory Be! McGlathery," Pictorial Review, 26 (Jan.), 5-7,
51-52, 54, 71.
Repub: Chains (1927) (as "St. Columba and the River").

C25-3   "The Most Successful Ball-Player of Them All," Hearst's
International, 47 (Feb.), 82-83, 102-106.
Ty Cobb.

C25-4   "America and the Artist," Nation, 120 (15 Apr.), 423-25.

C25-5   "Chauncey M. Depew," Hearst's International-Cosmopolitan, 79
(July), 86-87, 183-85.

Theodore Dreiser: A Bibliography

C25-6   "Convention," American Mercury, 6 (Dec.), 398-408.
        Repub: Chains (1927).

C25-7   "'The Cliff Dwellers': A Painting by George Bellows, A Note
        by Theodore Dreiser," Vanity Fair, 25 (Dec.), 55, 118.

1926

C26-1   "My Favorite Fiction Character," Bookman, 63 (Apr.), 175.

C26-2   "This Florida Scene," Vanity Fair, 26 (May), 51, 100, 110.

C26-3   "Music," Vanity Fair, 26 (June), 68.
        Repub: Moods (1926).

C26-4   "This Florida Scene," Vanity Fair, 26 (June), 43, 98, 100.

C26-5   "This Florida Scene," Vanity Fair, 26 (July), 63, 94, 96.

C26-6   "Recent Poems of Life and Labour," Vanity Fair, 26 (Aug.),
        61.
            "The Factory," "The 'Bad' House," "The Stream," and
        "Geddo Street."
            Repub: Moods (1926).
C26-7   "Recent Poems of Love and Sorrow," Vanity Fair, 27 (Sept.),
        54.
            "Love Plaint," "Love and Wonder," "The Last Tryst,"
        and "The Beautiful."
            Repub: Moods (1926) ("Love and Wonder" as "The Little
        Flowers of Love and Wonder").
C26-8   "The Wages of Sin," Hearst's International-Cosmopolitan, 81
        (Oct.), 42-45, 175-81.
            Repub: Chains (1927) (as "Typhoon").

C26-9   "Recent Poems of Youth and Age," Vanity Fair, 27 (Oct.), 70.
            "The Far Country," "Youth," "Little Moonlight Things,"
        and "Where?"
            Repub: Moods (1926) ("Little Moonlight Things" as
        "Little Moonlight Things of Song").

C26-10 "Paris--1926," Vanity Fair, 27 (Dec.), 64, 136, 147-50.

1927

C27-1   "The Victim Speaks," Vanity Fair, 27 (Feb.), 40.
        Repub: Moods (1926).

WORKS BY

C27-2   "America's Restlessness Is Symbol of Our Hidden Power,"
        New York American, 10 Apr., Section E, p. 3.
            The first of six articles syndicated by Metropolitan
        Newspaper Service. The articles appeared in various news-
        papers under differing titles but on the same days from
        10 April 1927 to 11 March 1928. The other articles in
        the series are C27-5, C27-6, C27-8, C28-1, and C28-4.

C27-3   "Victory," Jewish Daily Forward (New York), 24 Apr., English
        Section, pp. 12-13, 23.
            Repub: Chains (1927).

C27-4   "Can a Criminal Come Back to Society? No!" Smoker's Com-
        panion, 1 (May), 19, 82.

C27-5   "Are We in America Leading Way Toward a Golden Age in
        the World?" New York American, 22 May, Section E, p. 3.
            See C27-2.

C27-6   "Fools of Success," New York American, 31 July, Section E,
        p. 4.
            See C27-2.

C27-7   "You Pays Your Money and You Takes Your Choice," Theatre
        Magazine, 46 (Aug.), 7.
            Contribution to a symposium entitled "What Makes a
        Play Great."

C27-8   "Fools for Love," New York American, 28 Aug., Section E,
        p. 4.
            See C27-2.

C27-9   "Portrait of a Woman," Bookman, 66 (Sept.), 2-14.
            Repub: A Gallery of Women (1929) (as "Ernestine").

C27-10 "The Romance of Power," Vanity Fair, 29 (Sept.), 49, 94, 96,
        98.

1928

C28-1   "Dreiser Analyzes the Rebellion of Women," New York American,
        5 Feb., Section E, p. 3.
            See C27-2.

C28-2   "Theodore Dreiser Finds Both Hope and Failure in Russian
        Soviet Drama," Chicago Daily News, 6 Feb., pp. 1-2.
            Dispatch datelined Odessa, 3 January 1928.

C28-3   "Stalin's Apartment in the Kremlin," New York Times, 28 Feb.,
             p. 24.
             Letter to the Editor, dated 22 February 1928.

C28-4   "Dreiser on Matrimonial Hoboes," New York American, 11 Mar.,
             Section E, p. 4.
             See C27-2.

C28-5   "Mr. Dreiser Excepts," New York Times, 15 Mar., p. 24.
             Letter to the Editor, dated 11 March 1928.

C28-6   "Soviet Plan to Spread to U. S., Dreiser Thinks," New York
             World, 18 Mar., pp. 1, 8.
             The first of 11 articles on Russia syndicated by the
             North American Newspaper Alliance.
             Repub: Dreiser Looks at Russia (1928) (Chapter I,
             pp. 9-15).

C28-7   "Dreiser Looks at Russia," New York World, 19 Mar., p. 13.
             Repub: Dreiser Looks at Russia (1928) (Chapter I,
             pp. 15-21).

C28-8   "Dreiser Looks at Russia," New York World, 20 Mar., p. 15.
             Repub: Dreiser Looks at Russia (1928) (Chapter VI,
             pp. 74-81).

C28-9   "Dreiser Looks at Russia," New York World, 21 Mar., p. 15.
             Repub: Dreiser Looks at Russia (1928) (Chapter VI,
             pp. 81-88).

C28-10   "Dreiser Looks at Russia," New York World, 22 Mar., p. 15.
             Repub: Dreiser Looks at Russia (1928) (Chapter XVIII,
             pp. 245-54).

C28-11   "Dreiser Looks at Russia," New York World, 23 Mar., p. 15.
             Repub: Dreiser Looks at Russia (1928) (Chapter VII,
             pp. 89-92).

C28-12   "Dreiser Looks at Russia," New York World, 24 Mar., p. 17.
             Repub: Dreiser Looks at Russia (1928) (Chapter VII,
             pp. 97-99; Chapter IX, pp. 120-21).

C28-13   "Dreiser Looks at Russia," New York World, 25 Mar., p. 6.
             Repub: Dreiser Looks at Russia (1928) (Chapter IX,
             pp. 121-23).

C28-14   "Dreiser Looks at Russia," New York World, 26 Mar., p. 15.
             Repub: Dreiser Looks at Russia (1928) (Chapter VII,
             pp. 99-101).

WORKS BY

C28-15 "Dreiser Looks at Russia," New York World, 27 Mar., p. 15.

C28-16 "Dreiser Looks at Russia," New York World, 28 Mar., p. 17.
        Repub: Dreiser Looks at Russia (1928) (Chapter XVIII,
        pp. 254-59).

C28-17 "Rella," Hearst's International-Cosmopolitan, 84 (Apr.),
        36-39, 199-204.
        Repub: A Gallery of Women (1929).

C28-18 "Russian Vignettes," Saturday Evening Post, 200 (28 Apr.),
        18-19, 80-82.
        Repub: London Times, 8 May 1928 (excerpted, as
        "Glimpses of Russia").
        Dreiser Looks at Russia (1928) (Chapter XVII).

C28-19 "Olive Brand," Hearst's International-Cosmopolitan, 84 (May),
        47-49, 130-34.
        Repub: A Gallery of Women (1929).

C28-20 Nation, 126 (30 May), 608.
        Contribution to "The Rights of a Columnist: A Sym-
        posium on the Case of Heywood Broun versus the New York
        World."

C28-21 "Regina C---," Hearst's International-Cosmopolitan, 84
        (June), 56-58, 144-49.
        Repub: A Gallery of Women (1929).

C28-22 "Russia: The Great Experiment," Vanity Fair, 30 (June),
        47-48, 102.
        Repub: Dreiser Looks at Russia (1928) (Chapter III).

C28-23 "American Tragedies," New York Herald-Tribune Books, 10 June,
        pp. 1-2.
        Review of The New Criminology by Max Schlapp and
        Edward H. Smith.

C28-24 "Woods Hole and the Marine Biological Laboratory," Collecting
        Net (Woods Hole, Mass.), 3 (21 July), 1-2.

C28-25 "The Best Motion Picture Interview Ever Written," Photoplay,
        34 (Aug.), 32-35, 124-29.
        Mack Sennett.

C28-26 Bookman, 68 (Sept.), 25.
        Contribution to a symposium entitled "Statements of
        Belief."

Contributions to Periodicals

C28-27 Harry Hansen, "The First Reader: Dreiser's Humanity," New
        York World, 5 Sept., p. 13.
            Contains Dreiser's replies to a series of questions
        asked by the French journal Le Monde.

C28-28 "Dreiser on Tolstoy," San Francisco Bulletin, 29 Sept., p. 12.
            Dreiser's reply to a request for an estimate of Tolstoy.

C28-29 "Citizens of Moscow," Vanity Fair, 31 (Oct.), 55-56, 102, 104.
            Repub: Dreiser Looks at Russia (1928) (Chapter XVI).

C28-30 "Theodore Dreiser on the Elections," New Masses, 4 (Nov.), 17.
            Contains an undated letter to Bruce Bliven.

C28-31 "My City," New York Herald-Tribune, 23 Dec., Section 3, p. 1.
            Consists of the poem "Tall Towers" and a prose poem.
            Repub: My City (1929).

                                1929

C29-1   "Dreiser on Hollywood," New Masses, 4 (Jan.), 16-17.

C29-2   "This Madness--An Honest Novel About Love. Part One--Aglaia,"
            Hearst's International-Cosmopolitan, 86 (Feb.), 22-27,
            192-203.

C29-3   "Comments on Film Arts Guild," W 8 Street Film Guild Cinema...
            Inaugural Program, 1 Feb., pp. 6-9.

C29-4   "The Muffled Oar," Nation, 128 (27 Feb.), 258.
            Repub: Moods (1935).

C29-5   "Another American Tragedy," Forum, 81 (Mar.), xlviii-li.
            Letter to the Editor.

C29-6   "This Madness. Part Two--Aglaia," Hearst's International-
            Cosmopolitan, 86 (Mar.), 44-47, 160-66.

C29-7   "This Madness. The Story of Elizabeth," Hearst's Inter-
            national-Cosmopolitan, 86 (Apr.), 81-85, 117-20.

C29-8   "Portrait of an Artist," Vanity Fair, 32 (Apr.), 70, 108,
            110.
            Jerome Blum.

C29-9   "This Madness," Hearst's International-Cosmopolitan, 86
            (May), 80-83, 146-54.
            "Elizabeth."

WORKS BY

C29-10 "The Meddlesome Decade," Theatre Guild Magazine, 6 (May),
        11-13, 61-62.

C29-11 "This Madness. The Book of Sidonie," Hearst's International-
        Cosmopolitan, 86 (June), 83-87, 156-68.

C29-12 "Theodore Dreiser Says," W 8 Street Film Guide Cinema...
        Fifteenth Program, June 29th to July 5th, p. 3.

C29-13 "This Madness," Hearst's International-Cosmopolitan, 87
        (July), 86-87, 179-86.
          "Sidonie."

C29-14 "Deutschland von 'Drüben' Gesehen," Deutsche Allgemeine
        Zeitung (Berlin), Aug., America-Germany Supplement, p. 1.
          In German.

C29-15 "Dreiser Discusses Dewey Plan," New York Telegram, 28 Sept.,
        p. 4.
          Letter to the Editor.

C29-16 "What I Believe: Living Philosophies--III," Forum, 82 (Nov.),
        279-81, 317-20.
          Also contains Dreiser's poems: "All in All," "Suns and
        Flowers, and Rats, and Kings," "For Answer," and "Related".
          Repub: Living Philosophies, New York: Simon and
        Schuster, 1931.

C29-17 "Fine Furniture," Household Magazine, 29 (Nov.), 5-7.
          Repub: Fine Furniture (1930).

C29-18 Tambour (Paris), no. 5 (Nov.), 25-26.
          Contribution to a symposium entitled "Anatole France:
        A Post-Mortem Five Years Later."

C29-19 "Fine Furniture," Household Magazine, 29 (Dec.), 4-5, 29-32.
          Repub: Fine Furniture (1930).

1930

C30-1   "Divorce as I See It," London Daily Express, 23 Jan., p. 8.
          Repub: Divorce as I See It, London: Douglas, 1930
        (as "Modern Marriage Is a Farce").

C30-2   "Group Here Scores Anti-Soviet Drive," New York Times,
        16 Mar., p. 7.
          Contains an undated letter, recipient unnamed.

Contributions to Periodicals

C30-3 "Whom God Hath Joined Together," Plain Talk, 6 (Apr.), 401-404.

C30-4 Harry Hansen, "The First Reader," New York World, 9 May, p. 11.
Contains an undated telegram to the Discussion Guild of New York.

C30-5 "The New Humanism," Thinker, 2 (July), 8-12.

C30-6 "Mooney and America," Hesperian (San Francisco), 1 (Winter), 2-4.

1931

C31-1 "Prosperity for Only One Percent of the People," Daily Worker (New York), 28 Jan., p. 4.

C31-2 "The Early Adventures of Sister Carrie," Colophon, Part 5 (Mar.), unpaginated, 4 pp.
Repub: Sister Carrie, New York: Random House, 1932 (Modern Library Edition).

C31-3 "Intellectual Unemployment," New Freeman, 2 (11 Mar.), 616-17.
Letter to the Editor.

C31-4 "'Free the Class War Prisoners in Boss Jails'--Dreiser," Daily Worker (New York), 9 May, p. 6.

C31-5 "Where Is Labor's Share?" New York Times, 13 May, p. 24.
Letter to the Editor, dated 9 May 1931.
Repub: Progressive (Madison, Wisc.), 2 (30 May 1931), 1-2 (as "Dreiser Raps Industry for Failure to Allow Worker Fair Share of Profits").

C31-6 "Silencing of Press by Gag Laws Flayed by Dreiser," Progressive (Madison, Wisc.), 2 (23 May), 1.

C31-7 "Dreiser on Scottsboro," Labor Defender, 6 (June), 108.

C31-8 "An Open Letter to the Governor of Alabama," Labor Defender, 6 (June), 109.
Signed by Dreiser as Chairman of the National Committee for the Defense of Political Prisoners.

C31-9 "Why I Believe the Daily Worker Should Live," Daily Worker (New York), 24 June, p. 4.

Theodore Dreiser: A Bibliography

C31-10   "Miners in Strike Zones Live Like Slaves, Theodore Dreiser
         Writes After a Visit," New York World-Telegram, 26 June,
         pp. 1, 10.

C31-11   "Remarks," Psychoanalytic Review, 18 (July), 250.
         On the occasion of a dinner honoring Freud.

C31-12   "Dreiser Defends Norris on Power," New York Times, 2 July,
         p. 16.
         Contains passages from an undated letter to Paul S.
         Clapp.

C31-13   "Dreiser Warns Films on 'American Tragedy'," New York Times,
         8 July, p. 20.
         Contains a letter to Paramount Publix Corporation,
         dated 26 June 1931.

C31-14   "Humanitarianism in the Scottsboro Case," Contempo (Chapel
         Hill, N. C.), 1 (Mid-July), 1.

C31-15   "Theodore Dreiser Denounces Campaign Against Communists,"
         Progressive (Madison, Wisc.), 2 (5 Sept.), 1-2.

C31-16   "America and Her Communists," Time and Tide, 12 (31 Oct.),
         1247-48.

C31-17   "Take a Look at Our Railroads," Liberty, 8 (7 Nov.), 24-27.

C31-18   "Dreiser Says Judge Evades Mine Issue," New York Times,
         12 Nov., p. 13.
         Quotes from a statement released by Dreiser.

C31-19   "Mankind's Future Hangs on Russia--Theodore Dreiser," Pro-
         gressive (Madison, Wisc.), 2 (21 Nov.), 1.

C31-20   "I Go to Harlan," Labor Defender, 7 (Dec.), 233.

C31-21   "Dreiser Charges Tyranny in Musicians' Union," New York
         World-Telegram, 15 Dec., p. 23.

1932

C32-1   "Individualism and the Jungle," New Masses, 7 (Jan.), 1-2.
         Given initially as an address before the Group Forum
         of New York, 15 December 1931.
         Repub: Crawford's Weekly (Norton, Va.), 2 Jan. 1932,
         p. 6.
         Harlan Miners Speak (1932) (Introduction).

Contributions to Periodicals

C32-2   "Theodore Dreiser Picks the Six Worst Pictures of the Year,"
        New Movie Magazine, 5 (Jan.), 25-27, 98.

C32-3   "Mr. Dreiser Replies," New York Herald-Tribune Books, 14 Feb.,
        p. 18.
            Letter to the Editor, replying to Stuart Chase's re-
        view of Tragic America in the 24 January 1932 New York
        Herald-Tribune Books.

C32-4   Monatshefte für Deutschen Unterricht, 24 (Mar.-Apr.), 78-79.
            Contribution to "Goethe as Viewed by American Writers
        and Scholars: A Symposium."

C32-5   "Greetings to the Canadian Workers in Their Struggle for
        Freedom," The Worker (Toronto), 26 Mar., p. 1.

C32-6   "War and America," International Literature, nos. 2-3 (Apr.-
        June), pp. 110-11.
            Repub: Labor Defender, 8 (Aug.), 143, 157; 8 (Sept.),
        169, 175 (as "America--And War").

C32-7   "The Seventh Commandment," Liberty, 9 (2 Apr.), 7-11.

C32-8   "The Seventh Commandment," Liberty, 9 (9 Apr.), 34-38.

C32-9   New York Times, 10 Apr., Section 8, p. 3.
            Contribution to an article entitled "A New Group
        Would Like to Know," concerning the Group Theatre.

C32-10 "At Boulder Dam," New York Times, 11 Apr., p. 14.
            Letter to the Editor, dated 8 April 1932.

C32-11 "A Statement by Theodore Dreiser," Experimental Cinema,
        no. 4 (May), p. 3.

C32-12 "The Real Sins of Hollywood," Liberty, 9 (11 June), 6-11.

C32-13 "Capitalism Fails, Says Dreiser," New York Times, 5 July,
        p. 18.
            Contains a passage from a statement released by
        Dreiser.

C32-14 "The Day of Surfeit," American Spectator, 1 (Nov.), 2-3.

C32-15 "The Great American Novel," American Spectator, 1 (Dec.),
        1-2.
            Repub: The American Spectator Yearbook, ed. George
        Jean Nathan, New York: Stokes, 1934.

WORKS BY

1933

C33-1   "Cattails--November," American Spectator, 1 (Jan.), 3.
            Repub: Moods (1935).

C33-2   International Literature, no. 1 (Jan.), 126.
            Contains a letter dated 11 October 1932, recipient un-
            named.

C33-3   "Dreiser Makes Stirring Appeal for Aid to Save 'Daily' from
            Suspension," Daily Worker (New York), 26 Jan., p. 1.

C33-4   "Appearance and Reality," American Spectator, 1 (Feb.), 4.
            Repub: The American Spectator Yearbook, ed. George
            Jean Nathan, New York: Stokes, 1934.
            The untitled poem in the article is republished in
            Moods (1935) (as "The Process").

C33-5   "A Writer Looks at the Railroads," American Spectator, 1
            (Mar.), 4.

C33-6   "A Letter to the Outlander," Outlander (Portland, Ore.), 1
            (Spring), 50.

C33-7   "The Child and the School," American Spectator, 1 (Apr.), 2.

C33-8   "Townsend," American Spectator, 1 (June), 2.
            Sketch.

C33-9   "A Tribute," Greenwich Villager, 1 (1 June), 1.
            Hubert Davis.

C33-10   "The Martyr," American Spectator, 1 (July), 4.
            Repub: Moods (1935).

C33-11   "Flies and Locusts," New York Daily Mirror, 1 Aug., pp. 19,
            31.
            Repub: Common Sense, 2 (Dec. 1933), 20-22 (as "The
            Profit-Makers Are Thieves").

C33-12   "Editorial Conference," American Spectator, 1 (Sept.), 1.
            With George Jean Nathan, James Branch Cabell, Eugene
            O'Neill, and Ernest Boyd.
            Repub: The American Spectator Yearbook, ed. George
            Jean Nathan, New York: Stokes, 1934.

C33-13   International Literature, no. 4 (Oct.), 123.
            Letter dated 4 July 1933, recipient unnamed.

C33-14 "Query," American Spectator, 2 (Nov.), 2.
        A brief rhetorical question.

C33-15 "Challenge to the Creative Man," Common Sense, 2 (Nov.), 6-8.
        Repub: Artists' and Writers' Chapbook, ed. J. George
        Frederick ("Issued on the Occasion of the Costume Ball of
        the Artists' and Writers' Dinner Club, December 15,
        1933... New York"), pp. 9-10, 45.

C33-16 "Solution," Woman's Home Companion, 60 (Nov.), 18-20, 132-35.
        Story.

C33-17 "Birth Control," American Spectator, 2 (Dec.), 1.

C33-18 "Winterton," American Spectator, 2 (Dec.), 3-4.
        Sketch.

C33-19 "Tabloid Tragedy," Hearst's International-Cosmopolitan, 95
        (Dec.), 22-25, 115-16, 119-21.

1934

C34-1   "Editorial Note," American Spectator, 2 (Feb.), 1.

C34-2   "Three Poems," American Spectator, 2 (Feb.), 4.
        "Evening--Mountains," "Chief Strong Bow Speaks," and
        "Love."
        Repub: Moods (1935) ("Love" as "The Unterrified").
C34-3   "The Myth of Individuality," American Mercury, 31 (Mar.),
        337-42.
        Repub: Molders of American Thought, 1933-34, ed.
        William H. Cordell, Garden City, N. Y.: Doubleday,
        Doran, 1934.

C34-4   "Keep Moving or Starve," Today, 1 (3 Mar.), 6-7, 22-23.

C34-5   "'They Shall Not Die' Indicts North as Well as the South,"
        New York Post, 24 Mar., p. 8.
        On the play They Shall Not Die by John Wexley.

C34-6   "Rally Around the Flag!" Common Sense, 3 (May), 23.

C34-7   "Mathewson," Esquire, 1 (May), 20-21, 125.
        Sketch.

C34-8   "Mathewson," Esquire, 2 (June), 24-25, 114.

WORKS BY

C34-9 "Temperaments--Artistic and Otherwise," Golden Book, 19
       (June), 650-54.

C34-10 "Why Capitalists Praise Democracy," Common Sense, 3 (July),
        19-20.

C34-11 International Literature, no. 3 (July), 80-82.
             Contribution to a symposium entitled "Where We Stand."

C34-12 "What Has the Great War Taught Me?" New Masses, 11 (7 Aug.),
        15.

C34-13 "Mr. Dreiser Denies Report," New York Times, 15 Aug., p. 16.
             Letter to the Editor, dated 13 August 1934.

C34-14 "An Address to Caliban," Esquire, 2 (Sept.), 20-21, 158D.
             Repub: 1935 Essay Annual, ed. Erich A. Walter, New
        York: Scott, Foresman, 1935.

C34-15 Modern Monthly, 8 (Sept.), 459-61.
             Contribution to a symposium entitled "Will Fascism
        Come to America?"

C34-16 "A Start in Life," Scribner's, 96 (Oct.), 211-17.
             Sketch.

C34-17 "Theodore Dreiser Describes 'American Tragedy' in Special
        Series for the Post," New York Post, 2 Oct., pp. 1, 6.
             The first in a series of five articles on the Robert
        Edwards murder case.

C34-18 "Dreiser on 'Tragedy'," New York Post, 3 Oct., p. 3.

C34-19 "Dreiser on 'Tragedy'," New York Post, 4 Oct., p. 23.

C34-20 "Dreiser Sees Error in Edwards Defense," New York Post,
        5 Oct., p. 12.

C34-21 "Dreiser Says Medical Testimony Would Have Helped Edwards,"
        New York Post, 6 Oct., p. 3.

C34-22 "You, the Phantom," Esquire, 2 (Nov.), 25-26.
             Repub: The Bedside Esquire, ed. Arnold Gingrich,
        New York: McBride, 1940.

C34-23 Herman Bernstein, "Can We Abolish War?" Liberty, 2 (17 Nov.),
        22.
             Contains a statement by Dreiser.

Contributions to Periodicals

Repub: Herman Bernstein, <u>Can We Abolish War?</u>, New York: Broadview, 1935.

C34-24 "The Epic Sinclair," <u>Esquire</u>, 2 (Dec.), 32-33, 178B-79. Upton Sinclair.

1935

C35-1 "Kismet," <u>Esquire</u>, 3 (Jan.), 29, 175-76.

C35-2 "I Find the Real American Tragedy," <u>Mystery Magazine</u>, 11 (Feb.), 9-11, 88-90.
The first of five articles on the Robert Edwards murder case.
Repub: <u>Resources for American Literary Study</u>, 2 (Spring 1972), 5-17.

C35-3 "Five Moods in Minor Key," Esquire, 2 (Mar.), 25.
"Tribute," "Improvisation," "The Loafer," "Escape," and "Machine."
Repub: <u>Moods</u> (1935).

C35-4 "I Find the Real American Tragedy," <u>Mystery Magazine</u>, 11 (Mar.), 22-23, 77-79.
Repub: <u>Resources for American Literary Study</u>, 2 (Spring 1972), 17-26.

C35-5 "I Find the Real American Tragedy," <u>Mystery Magazine</u>, 11 (Apr.), 24-26, 91-92.
Repub: <u>Resources for American Literary Study</u>, 2 (Spring 1972), 26-40.

C35-6 Hutchins Hapgood, "Is Dreiser Anti-Semitic?" <u>Nation</u>, 140 (17 Apr.), 436-38.
Contains letters to Hapgood, dated 10 October 1933 and 28 December 1933.
Repub: <u>Letters of Theodore Dreiser</u> (1959), II, 649-53, 658-64.

C35-7 "Dreiser Denies He Is Anti-Semitic," <u>New Masses</u>, 15 (30 Apr.), 10-11.
Contains a statement by Dreiser, dated 22 April 1935.

C35-8 "I Find the Real American Tragedy," <u>Mystery Magazine</u>, 11 (May), 22-24, 83-86.
Repub: <u>Resources for American Literary Study</u>, 2 (Spring 1972), 40-55.

WORKS BY

C35-9   "I Find the Real American Tragedy," <u>Mystery Magazine</u>, 11
        (June), 20-21, 68-73.
            Repub: <u>Resources for American Literary Study</u>, 2
        (Spring 1972), 55-74.

C35-10 "Crime Analyzed by Dreiser," Los Angeles <u>Examiner</u>, 23 July,
        pp. 1-2.

C35-11 "Overland Journey," <u>Esquire</u>, 4 (Sept.), 24, 97.

C35-12 "Mark the Double Twain," <u>English Journal</u>, 24 (Oct.), 615-27.
        Mark Twain.

C35-13 "Mark Twain: Three Contacts," <u>Esquire</u>, 4 (Oct.), 22, 162,
        162A-B.

                            1936

C36-1   "Four Cases of Clyde Griffiths," New York <u>Times</u>, 8 Mar.,
        Section 9, pp. 1-2.
            Four theatrical versions of <u>An American Tragedy</u>.
            Repub: <u>National EPIC</u>, 1 (June), 9 (as "An American
        Tragedy").

C36-2   "Theodore Dreiser Defends His Brother's Memory," New York
        <u>Post</u>, 27 Mar., p. 14.
            Letter to the Editor.

C36-3   <u>Partisan Review and Anvil</u>, 3 (Apr.), 3-4.
            Contribution to a symposium entitled "What Is Ameri-
        canism?"

C36-4   <u>Soviet Russia Today</u>, 5 (July), 7.
            Contribution to a collection of "Tributes to Gorky."

C36-5   "Mea Culpa!" <u>Nation</u>, 143 (4 July), 25-26.
            Letter to the Editor, dated 17 June 1936.

C36-6   Carolyn Marx, "Book Marks," New York <u>World-Telegram</u>, 25
        Sept., p. 23.
            Contains a letter to Mike Gold, dated 7 August 1928.
            Repub: <u>Letters of Theodore Dreiser</u> (1959), II, 472.

C36-7   "How They Are Voting: II," <u>New Republic</u>, 88 (7 Oct.), 249.
            Contains a statement by Dreiser.

C36-8   "Like the Good Deed," <u>New Masses</u>, 21 (15 Dec.), 9.

Contributions to Periodicals

1937

C37-1   Modern Monthly, 10 (Mar.), 5.
             Contribution to a symposium entitled "Is Leon Trotsky
         Guilty?"

C37-2   "Legalizing Games of Chance," New York Times, 4 May, p. 24.
             Letter to the Editor, dated 30 April 1937.

C37-3   "I Am Grateful to Soviet Russia," Soviet Russia Today, 6
         (Nov.), 11.
             Repub: International Literature, no. 12 (Dec.), 107-
         108.

C37-4   "Foreword," Direction, 1 (Dec.), 2.

C37-5   "II. If Man Is Free, So Is All Matter," Forum, 98 (Dec.),
         301-304.
             Contribution to a symposium entitled "Have We Free
         Will?"

1938

C38-1   "A Conversation," Direction, 1 (Jan.), 2-3, 28.
             Between Dreiser and John Dos Passos.

C38-2   "Lessons I Learned from an Old Man," Your Life, 2 (Jan.),
         6-10.

C38-3   "Is College Worth-While? No!" Your Life, 2 (Mar.), 8-12.

C38-4   "The Tithe of the Lord," Esquire, 10 (July), 36-37, 150,
         155-58.
             Story.
             Repub: The Armchair Esquire, ed. Arnold Gingrich and
         L. Rust Hills, New York: Putnam, 1958.

C38-5   "Equity Between Nations," Direction, 1 (Sept.-Oct.), 5-6, 11.
             Dreiser's speech before the International Association
         of Writers in Paris on 25 July 1938.
             Repub: Collection de L'Association Internationale des
         Ecrivains pour la Défense de la Culture... Conférence
         Extraordinaire Tenue à Paris le 25 Juillet, Paris: Denöel,
         1938 (as M. Théodore Dreiser prend la parole: in French).

C38-6   "Dreiser Gives Vivid Picture of Conditions in Spain,"
         Philadelphia Evening Bulletin, 10 Sept., p. 7.

WORKS BY

C38-7   "Dreiser Recounts Loyalist Tension," New York <u>Times</u>, 11
        Sept., Section 1, p. 30.
            Syndicated by the North American Newspaper Alliance.

C38-8   "Barcelona's Modernity Shines Through Battle Damage,"
        Philadelphia <u>Evening Bulletin</u>, 12 Sept., p. 9.

C38-9   "Good and Evil," <u>North American Review</u>, 246 (Autumn), 67-86.

C38-10 "Barcelona in August," <u>Direction</u>, 1 (Nov.-Dec.), 4-5.

1939

C39-1   "Dreiser Answers French Labor," <u>Direction</u>, 2 (Jan.-Feb.), 19.
            Contains an undated telegram to <u>Messidor</u>, a French
        labor publication.

C39-2   "To the Third Annual Congress," <u>Direction</u>, 2 (May-June), 2.

C39-3   "Life at Sixty-Seven," <u>Rotarian</u>, 55 (Aug.), 8-10.

C39-4   "Women Are the Realists," <u>You</u>, 2 (Fall), 5, 48-49.
            Repub: New York <u>Journal-American</u>, 13 Apr. 1946,
        Saturday Home Magazine, p. 10; 20 Apr. 1946, Saturday
        Home Magazine, pp. 10-11; 27 Apr. 1946, Saturday Home
        Magazine, pp. 5-6 (as "Women Can Take It!").

C39-5   "The Dawn Is in the East," <u>International Literature</u>, no. 11
        (Nov.), pp. 109-111.
            Repub: <u>Common Sense</u>, 8 (Dec.), 6-7.
        <u>The Dawn Is in the East</u> (1939).

C39-6   "Daily News Ears Batted Down by Dreiser," Los Angeles
        <u>Daily News</u>, 27 Nov., p. 6.

1940

C40-1   "Theodore Dreiser Snubs Hoover," <u>People's World</u> (San Fran-
        cisco), 12 Jan., pp. 1, 6.
            Contains a letter to Fred Smith, dated 9 January 1940.
            Repub: <u>Letters of Theodore Dreiser</u> (1959), III, 864-
        65.

Contributions to Periodicals

C40-2 "The Soviet-Finnish Treaty and World Peace," Soviet Russia
       Today, 8 (Apr.), 8-9.
       Repub: Concerning Dives and Lazarus (1940).

C40-3 "Lenin," International Literature, nos. 4-5 (Apr.-May), p. 82.

C40-4 "Theodore Dreiser Condemns War," People's World (San Fran-
       cisco), 6 Apr., p. 7.
       Repub: War (1940).

C40-5 "Tribute to Lenin," People's World (San Francisco), 20 Apr.,
       p. 5.
       Repub: New Masses, 35 (23 Apr.), 16 (as "V. I.
       Lenin").

C40-6 "Upton Sinclair," Clipper, 1 (Sept.), 3-4.

C40-7 "Theodore Dreiser and the Free Press," People's World (San
       Francisco), 2 Oct., p. 5.
       Repub: Editor & Publisher (1940).

C40-8 "The Story of Harry Bridges," Friday, 1 (4 Oct.), 1-8, 28.

C40-9 "The Story of Harry Bridges," Friday, 1 (11 Oct.), 14-17.

C40-10 "The Meaning of the USSR in the World Today," Soviet Russia
       Today, 9 (Nov.), 23, 47.
       Repub: Current History, 52 (10 Dec.), 28-30 (as "The
       USSR Today").

C40-11 "U. S. Must Not Be Bled for Imperial Britain," People's
       World (San Francisco), 12 Nov., p. 6.
       An address given over CBS on 9 November 1940.
       Repub: U. S. Must Not Be Bled for Imperial Britain
       (1940).

C40-12 "What Is Democracy?" Clipper, 1 (Dec.), 3-7.
       Repub: America Is Worth Saving (1941) (Chapter 11).

1941

C41-1 "Our Democracy: Will It Endure?" New Masses, 38 (21 Jan.),
       8-9.
       Repub: America Is Worth Saving (1941) (Chapter 16).

WORKS BY

C41-2   "This Is Churchill's 'Democracy'," New Masses, 38 (18 Feb.),
         35-36.
             Repub: Concerning Our Helping England Again (1941).

C41-3   "Sherwood Anderson," Clipper, 2 (May), 5.
             Repub: Story, 19 (Sept.-Oct.), 4.

C41-4   "Nothing So Important to American People Now as Aiding USSR--
         Dreiser," People's World (San Francisco), 2 July, p. 1.
             Contains an undated telegram to Dr. John A. Kingbury.

C41-5   "Freedom of the Press," In Fact, 3 (29 Sept.), 1.

C41-6   Daily Worker (New York), 21 Dec., Section 2, p. 6.
             Contains a statement in an article entitled "Writers
         Declare: 'We Have a War to Win.'"

                              1942

C42-1   "Lion and the Mange," Portland Oregonian, 21 Oct., p. 12.
             Letter to the Editor.

C42-2   "The Harlot Press," In Fact, 6 (7 Dec.), 4.
             Repub: In Fact, 12 (14 Jan. 1946), 1.

C42-3   "A Statement from Dreiser," New Republic, 107 (14 Dec.), 795.

                              1943

C43-1   "Myself and the Movies," Esquire, 20 (July), 50, 159.

                              1944

C44-1   "Broadcast by Theodore Dreiser to the People of Europe,"
         Direction, 7 (July), 4.
             Text of Dreiser's broadcast, under the auspices of the
         Office of War Information, in May 1944.

C44-2   "The Russian Advance," Soviet Russia Today, 13 (July), 9.

C44-3   "Black Sheep Number One: Johnny," Esquire, 22 (Oct.), 39,
         156-60.
             The first in a series of six sketches. Although all
         are signed by Dreiser, it is clear from correspondence in
         the Dreiser Collection that at least two were written by

friends: number three by Sylvia Bradshaw and number four
by Louise Campbell. Of the other four sketches, the prose
style of numbers one, five, and six resembles Dreiser's
while that of number two does not.

C44-4   The Magazine of Sigma Chi, 63 (Oct.-Nov.), 39-40.
       Contribution to a symposium on George Ade.

C44-5   New Masses, 53 (3 Oct.), 6.
       Contribution to a symposium entitled "My Vote--And
Why."

C44-6   "Black Sheep Number Two: Otie," Esquire, 22 (Nov.), 65.
       See C44-3.

1945

C45-1   "Black Sheep Number Five: Clarence," Esquire, 23 (Feb.),
49, 129-30.
       See C44-3.

C45-2   "Black Sheep Number Six: Harrison Barr," Esquire, 23 (Mar.),
49, 131.
       See C44-3.

C45-3   "What to Do," Free World, 9 (Mar.), 10.
       Poem.

C45-4   "Theodore Dreiser Joins Communist Party," Daily Worker
(New York), 30 July, p. 5.
       Contains a letter to William Z. Foster, dated 20 July
1945.
       Repub: Daily Worker (New York), 28 Dec. 1947, Magazine
Section, p. 11 (as "Why I Joined the Communist Party").
       Theodore Dreiser. Essays and Articles, Moscow: Foreign
Languages Publishing House, 1951 (as "The Logic of my
Life....").

C45-5   "Interdependence," Free World, 10 (Sept.), 69-70.

Posthumous

C50-1   "Theodore Dreiser on 'Road to Life'," Daily Worker
(New York), 16 Apr., Section 1, p. 9.
       Review of the Soviet film; previous publication un-
known.

C51-1   "To Him I Owe Very Much," Political Affairs, 30 (Mar.), 95-
96.

WORKS BY

Tribute to William Z. Foster; previous publication
unknown.

C58-1   "Background for 'An American Tragedy'," Esquire, 50 (Oct.),
155-57.
Chapter VIII of a discarded early draft of the novel.

CA.

PITTSBURG DISPATCH ARTICLES POSSIBLY BY DREISER

Dreiser arrived in Pittsburgh in early May 1894 and within a few days got a job on the Dispatch. He began as a reporter, but soon, as he recalled in A Book About Myself (pp. 395-96), began to contribute a regular semi-humorous column on topics of local interest. A number of these unsigned columns are preserved as clippings in the Dreiser Collection and are therefore attributed to Dreiser in Section C. The articles which follow cannot be conclusively attributed to Dreiser. However, these articles appeared during the period he worked for the Dispatch, they occur in the same location as the articles which he preserved, and they resemble his preserved articles in contents and tone. The articles are arranged chronologically by month.

May 1894

"Two Comets Are In Sight," 14th, p. 2.

"A Little Mixed on Dates," 16th, p. 2.

"A Chamber of Horrors," 17th, p. 2.

"The Annual Hailstorm," 18th, p. 2.

"A Tale About Two Cats," 20th, p. 2.

"An Hour Among Sinners," 21st, p. 2.

"Funny Man's Gala Day," 23rd, p. 2.

"Is Not Down on the List," 25th, p. 2.

"Gathered the Shekels In," 27th, p. 2.

"James Treacy's New Job," 30th, p. 2.

"The Weather Man's Woes," 31st, p. 2.

WORKS BY

June 1894

"Belfour's Slick Game," 1st, p. 2.

"Must Climb the Stairs," 2nd, p. 2.

"How It All Came About," 3rd, p. 2.

"Frank Bruin Is a Pig," 4th, p. 3.

"An Emblem of Socialism," 7th, p. 3.

"A Novelty of Its Kind," 8th, p. 3.

"Swearing as a Fine Art," 9th, p. 2.

"Where Humility Fails," 10th, p. 2.

"Cool Spots Were Found," 12th, p. 2.

"Wheels Went 'Round," 13th, p. 2.

"Hoodwinking Uncle Sam," 16th, p. 2.

"Some of Baby's Spheres," 17th, p. 2.

"Killed by a Thunder Clap," 18th, p. 3.

"Three Ways to Get Rain," 19th, p. 2.

"Cupid's Bargain Day," 21st, p. 2.

"Many Children in Line," 22nd, p. 2.

"A New Comedy of Errors," 23rd, p. 2.

"River Alive with Fish," 24th, p. 2.

"A Midsummer Mania," 25th, p. 2.

"The Fresh Air Funders," 26th, p. 2.

"Fooled Him Every Time," 27th, p. 2.

"Lemonade 1 Cent a Glass," 29th, p. 2.

"Bade Defiance to Law," 30th, p. 2.

Theodore Dreiser: A Bibliography

July 1894

"Along the River Shore," 2nd, p. 9.

"Triumph for the Toby," 8th, p. 3.

"This Girl Is a Puzzle," 11th, p. 3.

"Charity in the Woods," 12th, p. 3.

"The Spirit of the Spire," 13th, p. 3.

"See the Graphomaniac," 14th, p. 3.

"Patrons of the Springs," 16th, p. 3.

"Views the Passing Show," 17th, p. 3.

"In Old Hancock Street," 18th, p. 3.

"The Cat Became Woolly," 20th, p. 3.

"Billy Boy's Bad Blunder," 21st, p. 3.

"No Doting on the Lodge," 24th, p. 3.

"It Was Hoax All Around," 27th, p. 3.

"Confound the Mosquito!" 28th, p. 3.

"Secret Service Agents," 30th, p. 3.

"Sleep During Hot Nights," 31st, p. 3.

August 1894

"This Settles the Japs," 1st, p. 3.

"Woes of Dog Catchers," 2nd, p. 3.

"Isobars and Isotherms," 3rd, p. 3.

"Spoiled by a Meek Cow," 6th, p. 3.

"Relics of a Bygone Age," 7th, p. 3.

"Midsummer's Day Dream," 9th, p. 3.

WORKS BY

"Fishy Record Beaten," 13th, p. 3.

"Here's to the Sadder Men," 16th, p. 3.

"They Are Passing Away," 17th, p. 2.

"Fates Were Against Him," 19th, p. 3.

"The Baby Autographer," 23rd, p. 3.

"Survival of Unfittest," 24th, p. 3.

"Sweet Corn on the Cob," 27th, p. 3.

September 1894

"Tramps in Convention," 3rd, p. 3.

"In a Rambling Sort o' Way," 13th, p. 3.

"Telepathy Now Upon Us," 23rd, p. 3.

"September in the Park," 24th, p. 3.

"The Last of the Season," 28th, p. 3.

October 1894

"Mushrooms in Season," 1st, p. 3.

"The Last Fly of Fly Time," 3rd, p. 3.

"Uncle Simon Sees Frost," 7th, p. 3.

"Study of Spider Webs," 13th, p. 3.

D

This section contains books and pamphlets, principally posthumous and including translations, which are devoted entirely to miscellaneous material previously published by Dreiser.

D23-1   Little Blue Books 659, 660, 661, Girard, Kansas: Haldeman-Julius,   [1923].

      659.   The Lost Phoebe and Old Rogaum and His Theresa (Free).
      660.   My Brother Paul and W. L. S. (Twelve Men).
      661.   Neurotic America and the Sex Impulse and Some Aspects of Our National Character (Hey Rub-a-Dub-Dub).

D28-1   Dreiser's Russia: An 11 Week Personal Investigation. Melbourne, Australia: H. E. Langridge, 1928.
      A 40 page pamphlet republication of Dreiser's "Dreiser Looks at Russia" articles, republished from the syndication of the articles in the Sydney Sun.

D47-1   The Best Short Stories of Theodore Dreiser, edited with an introduction by Howard Fast, Cleveland: World, 1947.

      Published in German as Die Besten Novellen, trans. Marianne Schön, Vienna: Paul Zsolnay, 1950.

      Republished with a new introduction by James T. Farrell, Cleveland: World, 1956; this edition republished, Greenwich, Conn.:   Fawcett, 1961 (Premier Book).

      Selections published in Italian with an introduction by Rolando Anzilotti as Racconti, trans. Diana Bonaccossa, Bari: De Donato, 1971.

WORKS BY

Contains: "Free," "McEwen of the Shining Slave
Makers," "Nigger Jeff," "The Lost Phoebe" (Free); "Khat,"
"St. Columba and the River," "The Shadow," "The Old
Neighborhood," "Phantom Gold," "Convention," "Marriage
for One," "The Prince Who Was a Thief" (Chains); "A Doer
of the Word" and "My Brother Paul" (Twelve Men).

D51-1 Theodore Dreiser. Essays and Articles, with a foreword and
commentary by Y. Zasurskii, Moscow: Foreign Languages
Publishing House, 1951.
Contains: "Los Angeles Communists to Honor Dreiser's
Memory"; selections from Tragic America (chapters 1, 2,
10, 11, 17, 20); selections from America Is Worth Saving
(chapters 1, 5, 10, 14, 16, 17); "This Is Churchill's
Democracy" (New Masses, 18 Feb. 1941); "War and America"
(International Literature, Apr.-June 1932); "The Russian
Advance" (Soviet Russia Today, July 1944); "The Meaning
of the U.S.S.R. in the World Today" (Soviet Russia Today,
Nov. 1940); "The Logic of My Life..." (Daily Worker,
30 July 1945).

D52-1 Americké Osudy, trans. Zdeněk Urbánek, afterword Vladimír
Smrž, Prague: Vydavatelstvo Roh, 1952 (Selections in
Czech from Chains, Twelve Men, Free, and The Color of
a Great City).

D62-1 Theodore Dreiser, edited with an introduction by James T.
Farrell, New York: Dell (Laurel Reader), 1962.
Contains: Letters to H. L. Mencken, 8 March 1943,
and James T. Farrell, 5 November 1943 (Letters of Theodore
Dreiser); selections from Dawn and Newspaper Days; "De
Maupassant, Jr." (Twelve Men); "Ernestine" (A Gallery
of Women); "Lilly: A Girl of the Street" (A Traveler
at Forty); "The Log of a Harbor Pilot" (The Color of a
Great City); "Hey Rub-a-Dub-Dub" (Hey Rub-a-Dub-Dub);
"Tall Towers," "The Young God," "The Road I Came," "The
Dole," "Requiem" (Moods, 1935); "Will You Walk into My
Parlor?" "The Cruise of the 'Idlewild'," "When the Old
Century Was New" (Free); "Chains" and "The 'Mercy' of
God" (Chains).

D66-1 Iró Lettem Amerikában, selected by Sarolta Valkay, trans.
György Déri, Béla Korponay, György Raáb, preface Lenke
Bizám, Budapest: Gondolat, 1966 (Selections in Hungarian
from Dawn, A Book About Myself, and Letters of Theodore
Dreiser).

D69-1   <u>Selected Poems (from Moods) by Theodore Dreiser</u>, with an
        introduction and notes by Robert P. Saalbach, Jericho,
        New York: Exposition Press, 1969.
        Contains: 160 poems.

E

PUBLISHED LETTERS

Omitted are letters published in critical and biographical studies; such letters are noted in the annotation accompanying relevant items in Part II: Works on Dreiser.

Letters published during Dreiser's lifetime are presumed to have been intended for publication or to have had their publication approved by Dreiser and are therefore listed in section C. This presumption is of course self-evident for letters addressed to magazines and newspapers. For other letters, evidence bearing on Dreiser's intent is usually unavailable or ambiguous. It therefore appeared to be best, in the sense of organizational convenience, to consider letters published during Dreiser's lifetime as Contributions to Periodicals (Newspapers and Journals) and to consider posthumously published letters as Published Letters.

E51-1   FARRELL, JAMES T. "Some Correspondence with Theodore Dreiser," General Magazine and Historical Chronicle (University of Pennsylvania), 53 (Summer), 237-52. Republished in James T. Farrell, Reflections at Fifty, and Other Essays, New York: Vanguard, 1954, pp. 124-41.
   Correspondence with Farrell, 1943-45.

E55-1   "Dreiser Discusses Sister Carrie," Masses and Mainstream, 8 (Dec.), 20-22.
   Correspondence with John Howard Lawson, 10 August and 10 October, 1928.

E57-1   FRIEDRICH, GERHARD. "The Dreiser-Jones Correspondence." Bulletin of Friends Historical Association, 5 (Spring), 23-24.
   Correspondence with Rufus Jones, 1938-45.

E59-1   ELIAS, ROBERT H., ed. Letters of Theodore Dreiser, 3 vols., Philadelphia: University of Pennsylvania Press.

THEODORE DREISER: A BIBLIOGRAPHY

Published Letters

E59-2   CAMPBELL, LOUISE, ed. Letters to Louise, Philadelphia:
         University of Pennsylvania Press.

E68-1   WHITE, WILLIAM. "Dreiser on Hardy, Henley, and Whitman: An
         Unpublished Letter," English Language Notes, 6 (Dec.),
         122-24.
            Correspondence with Richard Duffy, 2 February 1902.

E70-1   DOWELL, RICHARD W. "'You Will Not Like Me, Im Sure':
         Dreiser to Miss Emma Rector, November 28, 1893, to
         April 4, 1894," American Literary Realism, 3 (Summer),
         259-70.

E73-1   "Dreiser on An American Tragedy in Prague," Dreiser News-
         letter, 4 (Spring), pp. 21-22.
            Correspondence with a Mr. Kohl, 8 February 1927.

F

INTERVIEWS AND SPEECHES

In addition to formal interviews and news stories on Dreiser's speeches, this section cites news stories that include comments Dreiser made to the press. Omitted are prepared statements given to the press for publication and published texts of speeches; these items appear in section C.

Because news stories of an event frequently vary in content and emphasis in different newspapers and journals, all stories based on public interviews, such as those Dreiser held on his birthdays, and all stories reporting on a particular speech are cited. Only one appearance of a syndicated piece is presented, however.

The first book republication of an item is noted plus any additional republication in books included in section I. Textual changes in connection with republication are not indicated.

An asterisk at the end of an entry based on a clipping (See F19-3) indicates that we were unable to locate the work in the place cited. In these instances, the asterisk signifies that the item does exist, but the bibliographical information may not be accurate.

1902

F02-1   ANON. "Author of 'Sister Carrie' Formerly Was a St. Louisan," St. Louis Post-Dispatch, 26 Jan., p. 4. Repub: Pizer, pp. 456-58; See I70-1.

1907

F07-1   NOTMAN, OTIS. "Talks with Four Novelists: Mr. Dreiser," New York Times Saturday Review of Books, 15 June, p. 393. Repub: Kazin and Shapiro, pp. 59-60, under incorrect date; See I55-1. Repub: Pizer, pp. 474-75; See I70-1.

Interviews and Speeches

FO7-2   ANON. "'Sister Carrie' Theodore Dreiser," New York Herald,
         7 July, Literary and Art Section, p. 2. Repub: Pizer,
         p. 432; See I70-1.

                              1908

FO8-1   ANON. "President Orphans' Friend," Washington Evening Star,
         10 Oct., p. 9.

FO8-2   ANON. "President Told of Babies," Washington Herald, 11 Oct.
         [PU].

                              1911

F11-1   [SANBORN, ALMER C.] "Author Theodore Dreiser Tells of
         100,000 Jennie Gerhardts," Cleveland Leader, 12 Nov.,
         Cosmopolitan Section, p. 5.

F11-2   ANON. "Theodore Dreiser," New York Evening Post, 15 Nov.,
         pp. 6-7.

F11-3   ANON. "Realistic Novelists," New York Daily People, 20 Nov.,
         p. 3.

F11-4   ANON. "Novels to Reflect Real Life," New York Sun, 21 Nov.,
         p. 9.

F11-5   MACY, BALDWIN. "New York Letter," Chicago Evening Post
         Friday Literary Review, 24 Nov., p. 6.

                              1912

F12-1   MOSES, MONTROSE J. "Theodore Dreiser," New York Times Review
         of Books, 23 June, pp. 377-78.

F12-2   ANON. "Theodore Dreiser on the Novel," New York Evening Sun,
         28 Sept., p. 7.

F12-3   ANON. "Theodore Dreiser Now Turns to High Finance," New York
         Sun, 19 Oct., Part 2, p. 3.

                              1913

F13-1   ANON. "Calls American Mothers Unfit," Chicago Examiner,
         13 Jan., p. 8.

WORKS BY

F13-2   ANON. "The Londoner and His 'Rather Dreary Situation,'"
         London Evening Standard, 6 Sept. [PU].

F13-3   ANON. "Dreiser on Need of Liberty in Writing," New York Sun,
         29 Nov., Literary Section, p. 4.

F13-4   ANON. "An Author 'Personally Conducted,'" New York Times
         Review of Books, 30 Nov., p. 696.

F13-5   MORDELL, ALBERT. "Theo. Dreiser--Radical," Philadelphia
         Record, 7 Dec., Part 3, p. 8.

                              1914

F14-1   ANON. "Dreiser Plays Role of Van Winkle Here," Chicago
         Daily News, 17 Mar., p. 3.

F14-2   ANON. "Theo. Dreiser Cries City Is Backsliding," Chicago
         Daily Journal, 18 Mar., p. 1.

F14-3   ANON. "Civic Torpidity Retards City, Says Dreiser," Chicago
         Daily Journal, 20 Mar., Section 2, p. 1.

F14-4   ANON. "Author Criticises Orthodox Editors," Philadelphia
         Public Ledger, 26 Apr., p. 7.

F14-5   MARSHALL, MARGUERITE MOOERS. "Business Overlords of America
         Greatest, Most Powerful Men Since Days of Old Rome,"
         New York Evening World, 18 June, p. 3.

F14-6   ANON. "Business and Morality Are To Be Separate," Rochester
         Union and Advertiser, 10 July, p. 2.

                              1915

F15-1   McDONALD, BENNETT. "Genius Is a Merciless Obsession, Says
         Dreiser," New York Tribune, 5 Dec., Part 5, p. 3.

                              1916

F16-1   ANON. "No More Free Ads for Racy Novels," New York Tribune,
         20 Aug., pp. 1, 3.

F16-2   ANON. "Vice Society Assails Book," New York Times, 21 Aug.,
         p. 20.

Interviews and Speeches

F16-3   ANON. "Sees Literary Reign of Terror," New York Tribune,
        9 Sept., p. 9.

1917

F17-1   H[OLMES], R[ALPH] F. "Musings with the Muses," Detroit
        Journal, 1 Dec., p. 4.

F17-2   H[OLMES], R[ALPH] F. "Musings with the Muses," Detroit
        Journal, 5 Dec., p. 4.

1918

F18-1   KITCHEN, KARL K. "To Batter Down Gates of Fame," Cleveland
        Plain Dealer, 24 Jan., p. 8.

F18-2   KARSNER, DAVID. "Theodore Dreiser," New York Call, 3 Mar.,
        Call Magazine, pp. 20, 16.

F18-3   SKIDELSKY, BERENICE C. "Theodore Dreiser Deplores Suppres-
        sion of His Novel 'The Genius,' by Vice Agent," Brooklyn
        Daily Eagle, 26 May [Section 3], pp. 2, 5.

1919

F19-1   HARRIS, FRANK. "Theodore Dreiser," Contemporary Portraits:
        Second Series. New York: Frank Harris. Pp. 81-106.

F19-2   ANON. "Dreiser Favors Federal Control; Hits Financiers,"
        Huntington [IN] Press, 18 June, p. 1.

F19-3   "Noted Novelist Visits in City," Indianapolis Star, 27 June*
        [PU].

F19-4   ANON. "Labor Union of Authors? They Need Protection, Says
        Theodore Dreiser," Brooklyn Daily Eagle, 11 Oct., p. 9.

1921

F21-1   SMITH, EDWARD H. "Dreiser--After Twenty Years," Bookman, 53
        (Mar.), 27-39.

Theodore Dreiser: A Bibliography

WORKS BY

1922

F22-1 RYAN, EDITH MILLICENT. "Cruel Words, Theodore Dreiser!"
Los Angeles Sunday Times, 17 Sept., Part 3, pp. 13, 15.

F22-2 RASCOE, BURTON. "A Bookman's Day Book," New York Tribune,
24 Dec., Section 6, p. 22. Repub: Burton Rascoe, A
Bookman's Daybook. Ed. C. Hartley Grattan. New York:
Liveright, 1929. Pp. 53-56 (as "First Visit to Dreiser").

1923

F23-1 SMITH, ELIZABETH. "Literary Censorship Bunk and Hokum, Says
Theodore Dreiser," New York Telegram, 4 Mar., p. 5.

F23-2 [STARK, HAROLD]. "Young Boswell Interviews Theodore Dreiser,"
New York Tribune, 7 Apr., p. 11. Repub: Young Boswell,
pseud. [Harold Stark]. People You Know. New York: Boni
and Liveright, 1924. Pp. 68-70.

F23-3 EATON, G. D. "A Talk with Theodore Dreiser in His New York
Studio," Detroit Free Press, 10 June, Magazine Section,
p. 4.

F23-4 FELD, ROSE C. "Mr. Dreiser Passes Judgement on American
Literature," New York Times Book Review, 23 Dec., p. 7.

1924

F24-1 RICE, DIANA. "Terrible Typewriter on Parnassus," New York
Times Magazine, 27 Apr., pp. 11, 14.

F24-2 "QUIZ," pseud. "Fixing the Fate of American Letters:
Literary Lunch," New York Evening Post Literary Review,
2 Aug., pp. 936-37.

1925

F25-1 ANON. "Clean Book Bill Slays Freedom, Insists Dreiser,"
New York Herald Tribune, 27 Jan., p. 4.

F25-2 HUNTER, SUSAN FRANCIS. "See America, Says Dreiser," New York
World, 5 Apr., Third Section, pp. 1, 9.

172

Theodore Dreiser: A Bibliography

F25-3   TITTLE, WALTER. "Glimpses of Interesting Americans: Theodore Dreiser," Century, 110 (Aug.), 441-47.

F25-4   GOLDBERG, ISAAC. "A Visit with Theodore Dreiser," Haldeman-Julius Monthly, 5 (Oct.), 448-52.

F25-5   MERRILL, FLORA. "Master of Creative Art Discusses Modern Problems," Success, 9 (Nov.), 21, 109.

F25-6   ANON. "Dreiser Interviews Pantano in Death House: Doomed Man Avows Faith in a Hereafter," New York World, 30 Nov., pp. 1, 14.

1926

F26-1   MAURY, JEAN WEST. "In the Workshop of an American Realist," Literary Digest International Book Review, 4 (Mar.), 223-24.

F26-2   NICHOLS, DUDLEY. "An American Comedy--The Long-Delayed Golden Shower Falls on Dreiser," New York World, 11 Apr., Metropolitan Section, pp. 1, 12.

F26-3   ANON. "'England Gone America Mad,' Dreiser Says on Return Here," New York Herald Tribune, 23 Oct., p. 7.

F26-4   STONG, PHIL D. "Dreiser Says Jury Systems Fail in 'Knife Edge' Criminal Cases," Denver Post, 28 Nov., p. [24].

1927

F27-1   MOUNT, LAURA. "Theodore Dreiser Defends Heavy Baumes Law Penalty," New York Evening Post, 11 Jan., p. 9.

F27-2   MAURY, JEAN WEST. "A Neighborly Call on Theodore Dreiser," Boston Evening Transcript, 29 Jan., Book Section, p. 1.

F27-3   ANON. "Censor Coming to Stop Sex Wave, Says Dreiser," New Orleans Morning Tribune, 3 Feb., p. 1.

F27-4   HARVEY, ALEXANDER. "New York Vicious? 'No, Just Dull,' Says Dreiser," New York World, 16 Oct., Metropolitan Section, pp. 1, 14.

F27-5   ANON. "Dreiser Sails Tonight for Red Celebration," New York Times, 19 Oct., p. 3.

WORKS BY

F27-6   ANON. "Theodore Dreiser Sails for Russia," New York Evening
         Post, 20 Oct., p. 5.

F27-7   "Theodore Dreiser Here on Way to Study Results of Sovietism,"
         New York Herald Tribune, Paris ed., 27 Oct., pp. 1, 10
         [PU].

                              1928

F28-1   WOOD, JUNIUS B. "Theodore Dreiser Reveals His Views on
         Russia in Interview," Huntington [W.Va.] Advertiser, 12 Feb.
         [PU].

F28-2   ANON. "No Bread Line, Says Dreiser, Back," New York Evening
         Post, 21 Feb., p. 2.

F28-3   ANON. "Dreiser Back from Russia; Praises Soviet," New York
         Herald Tribune, 22 Feb., p. 6.

F28-4   ANON. "Dreiser Home, Sees Soviet Aims Gaining," New York
         Times, 22 Feb., p. 9.

F28-5   BERCOVICI, H. L. B. "Newspaper Soulless, Dreiser Says,"
         American Press, 47 (Oct.), 3 [PU].

                              1929

F29-1   ISH-KISHOR, SULAMITH. "Dreiser Looks at the Russian Jews,"
         New York Day, 10 Feb. [PU].

F29-2   WOLLSTEIN, R. H. "You Know Mr. Dreiser; the American Tra-
         gedian Turns His Freudian Eyes on Music," Musical America,
         49 (25 Feb.), 36-37, 55-56.

F29-3   BIRD, CAROL. "Theodore Dreiser Speaks," Writer's Monthly,
         33 (May), 392-98.

F29-4   WORDEN, HELEN. "How Would You Spend $10,000,000 to Aid Man-
         kind? Prize of $1,000 Will Be Given Best Answer,"
         New York Evening World, 3 May, p. 23.

                              1930

F30-1   DAVIS, FORREST. "'1980': Theodore Dreiser Foresees a Ban
         on Babies," New York Telegram, 24 Jan., p. 7.

Interviews and Speeches

F30-2   COSULICH, GILBERT. "Next 25 Years Will Find 'Folks' Happier
        Famous Author Says," Tucson Daily Citizen, 6 Apr., pp. 1,
        4.

F30-3   ANON. "Theo. Dreiser Thinks People Over-Regulated," Albu-
        querque Journal, 19 Apr., p. 7.

F30-4   "Sock, Sock, Sock. Theodore Dreiser in Town: 'Too Many
        Potato Minds in U. S.,' He States; Lams Reformers, Y Sec-
        retaries, Newspapers," Albuquerque New Mexico State
        Tribune, 19 Apr., pp. 1, 3 [PU].

F30-5   "Dreiser Says Religion Total Loss in America," El Paso
        Evening Post, 26 Apr., pp. 1, 8 [PU].

F30-6   COSULICH, GILBERT. "Theodore Dreiser Asserts Religion Is
        Total Loss and Its Dogma Worn Out," Tucson Daily Citizen,
        30 Apr., p. 7.

F30-7   ANON. "Dreiser Ired at Censoring by Humanists," Dallas
        Morning News, 6 May, pp. 1, 16.

F30-8   RICHARDSON, VIVIAN. "Dreiser Talks About Women and Russia,"
        Dallas Morning News, 18 May, Feature Section, p. 2.

F30-9   BENNETT, MILLY. "Dreiser Goes to See Mooney in Quentin,"
        San Francisco Daily News, 30 May [PU].

F30-10 ANON. "Author Laughs at Democracy of Americans," San Fran-
        cisco Chronicle, 31 May, p. 3.

F30-11 DANNENBAUM, RAYMOND. "Theodore Dreiser Discounts Inter-
        marriage," Jewish Journal, 3 (4 June), 3, 16.

F30-12 HAZEN, DAVID W. "Dreiser Asserts His Books Never Will Sell
        for $1.50," Portland Morning Oregonian, 13 June, p. 9.

F30-13 FLEXNER, JAMES. "Dreiser Brings Pessimism Back from U. S.
        Tour," New York Herald Tribune, 8 July, p. 14.

F30-14 DAVIS, FORREST. "Dreiser Now Rediscovers America," New York
        Telegram, 9 July, p. 9.

F30-15 SEBESTYÉN, KARL. "Theodore Dreiser at Home," Living Age,
        339 (Dec.), 375-78. Trans. from the Pester Lloyd, a
        Budapest German Language Daily.

WORKS BY

1931

F31-1   ANON. "Slapping Lewis Proves Nothing, Dreiser Admits,"
         New York Herald Tribune, 22 Mar., p. 3.

F31-2   ANON. "Lewis Calls Witness to Challenge Dreiser," New York
         Times, 25 Mar., p. 27.

F31-3   ANON. "Dreiser Threatens Suit," New York Times, 9 Apr.,
         p. 28.

F31-4   ANON. "Dreiser Scorns Movies," New York Times, 11 Apr.,
         p. 17.

F31-5   ANON. "Call It 'Hooeyland,' Cries Dreiser Just Back from
         Movie Capital," New York American, 12 Apr., p. 22-L.

F31-6   ANON. "Dreiser on the Sins of Hollywood," Literary Digest,
         109 (2 May), 21. Excerpts from interview with Elenore
         Kellogg in New York Herald Tribune, date unknown.

F31-7   ANON. "Dreiser, 60, Glad He's Rich, but Doubts He's Happier,"
         New York World-Telegram, 27 Aug., p. 3.

F31-8   KELLOGG, ELENORE. "Dreiser Carries His Pessimism Lightly at
         Sixty," New York Herald Tribune, 28 Aug., p. 11.

F31-9   KROPOTKIN, ALEXANDRA. "To the Ladies," Liberty, 8 (26 Sept.),
         63-64.

F31-10   ANON. "Writers Are to Test Harlan 'Free Speech' for Miners
         on Nov. 8," Knoxville News-Sentinel, 3 Nov., p. 3.

F31-11   ANON. "Dreiser Group in Mine War Area," New York Times,
         6 Nov., p. 9.

F31-12   SMITH, EDWARD B. "Dreiser Demands Witnesses' Safety,"
         Knoxville News-Sentinel, 6 Nov., pp. 1, 12.

F31-13   ANON. "Kentucky Editor Questions Dreiser," New York Times,
         7 Nov., p. 19.

F31-14   SMITH, EDWARD B. "'Law' in Capitalists' Hands in Labor War,
         Says Dreiser," Knoxville News-Sentinel, 9 Nov., p. 11.

F31-15   ANON. "Dreiser Speaks His Mind Here," New York Sun, 12 Nov.,
         p. 9.

Interviews and Speeches

F31-16   ANON. "Public Blinded, Dreiser Avers," Knoxville News-Sentinel, 12 Nov., pp. 1, 18.

F31-17   WORTH, CEDRIC. "Angry Mr. Dreiser Speaks His Mind," New York Evening Post, 12 Nov.* [PU].

F31-18   ANON. "Dreiser Here Says Miners Will Rebel," New York Times, 13 Nov., p. 18.

F31-19   ANON. "Dreiser Ready to Come Back if Necessary," Knoxville News-Sentinel, 13 Nov., p. 24.

F31-20   JOHNSTON, ALVA. "Theodore Dreiser, Explaining His Political and Economic Views, Calls Himself an 'Equitist'; Novelist, Indicted in Kentucky, Coins Word to Describe Those Who Favor 'Fair Break for All,'" New York Herald Tribune, 22 Nov., Section 8, p. 2.

F31-21   TEED, DEXTER H. "Dreiser Case May Be Fight to Finish as John W. Davis Takes Writer's Defense," Knoxville News-Sentinel, 23 Nov., p. 2.

1932

F32-1   ANON. "Dreiser Promises Vote to Communist Ticket," New York Herald Tribune, 5 July, p. 4.

F32-2   ANON. "Dreiser at 61 Still Lost in Riot of Words," New York Herald Tribune, 26 Aug., p. 11.

F32-3   ANON. "Dreiser Here, Sees Hope for Tom Mooney," San Francisco Call-Bulletin, 5 Nov., p. 3.

F32-4   ESTCOURT, ZILFA. "Dreiser Holds Mooney Bomb Sympathy Act," San Francisco Chronicle, 6 Nov., p. 4.

F32-5   ANON. "Dreiser Plea for Mooney," San Francisco Call-Bulletin, 7 Nov., p. 2.

F32-6   RYAN, DON. "Parade Ground," Los Angeles Daily News, 12 Nov. [PU].

F32-7   BRITT, GEORGE. "Dreiser Overlooks His Former Experiences with Hollywood, for Things Will Be Different in the Filming of 'Jennie Gerhardt,'" New York World-Telegram, 15 Dec., p. 13.

WORKS BY

1933

F33-1   ANON. "News of Books: Dreiser Sees a Chance Lost," New York
        Times, 2 Mar., p. 15.

F33-2   ANON. "Dreiser Says NRA Is Training Public," New York Times,
        28 Aug., p. 19.

F33-3   ANON. "Dreiser in Court Action," New York Times, 11 Nov.,
        p. 12.

1934

F34-1   SMITS, JEANETTE. "'Tragedy' Case Fails to Stir Dreiser,"
        New York Evening Journal, 8 Aug., p. 4.

F34-2   WITT, BONITA. "Theodore Dreiser Isn't Surprised Over Parallel
        between His Novel and Real-Life Drama in News," Passaic
        [N.J.]Herald-News, 15 Aug., p. 2 [PU].

F34-3   ANON. "No 'Sitting in Shade' for Dreiser, at 63," New York
        Times, 28 Aug., p. 19.

F34-4   "Dreiser, at 63, Clings to Hope of Better World," New York
        Herald Tribune, 28 Aug.* [PU].

1935

F35-1   HAZEN, DAVID W. "Dreiser Laughs at Nursing Case," Portland
        Sunday Oregonian, 30 June, pp. 1, 3.

F35-2   ANON. "Rake Calls to Dreiser," Los Angeles Times, 29 July,
        Part 2, p. 1.

F35-3   PURDY, RICHARD. "A Visit with Dreiser," Fayette Review,
        7 Nov. [PU].

1936

F36-1   CAMERON, MAY. "Play Critics Wrong Again, Groans Theodore
        Dreiser," New York Post, 25 Mar.* [NN].

F36-2   GREENBERG, SELIG. "Dreiser Finds Journalism Has Improved
        Literature," Providence Evening Bulletin, 24 Apr. [PU].

Interviews and Speeches

F36-3   ANON. "Dreiser, at 65, May Quit Reds for Roosevelt,"
        New York Herald Tribune, 22 Aug., p. 9.

F36-4   ANON. "Dreiser, at 65, Hails Roosevelt on Peace," New York
        Times, 30 Aug., Section 2, p. 2.

F36-5   ANON. "Dreiser Explains Views," New York Times, 3 Sept.,
        p. 19.

                              1937

F37-1   ANON. "Dreiser Sees Lone Writer Doomed by Movie and Radio
        Specialists," New York World-Telegram, 24 Feb., p. 4.

F37-2   ANON. "Sad Dreiser Grows Gay in Scientific 'Monastery,'"
        New York Herald Tribune, 25 Aug., p. 13.

                              1938

F38-1   CRAWFORD, BRUCE. "Ere the Sun Sets," Bluefield [W.Va.] Sunset
        News, 18 Apr., pp. 1, 10. Interview rpt. from Real
        America magazine, date unknown.

F38-2   TINKLE, LON. "Theodore Dreiser Discusses Dallas and His
        Next Novel," Dallas Morning News, 14 Aug., Section Two,
        p. 8.

F38-3   ANON. "Says Roosevelt Uses Karl Marx's Ideas," New York
        Times, 22 Aug., p. 3.

F38-4   ANON. "Dreiser, Now 67, Is Critic of Critics," New York
        Times, 27 Aug., p. 16.

F38-5   ANON. "Loyalists Called Not Anti-Religious," New York Times,
        16 Sept., p. 10.

F38-6   NEISSEN, JOHN. "What Dreiser Seeks in a Test Tube," New York
        Journal-American, 25 Sept.* [PU].

F38-7   ANON. "Hughes Defends Scenarists Against Views of Dreiser,"
        Los Angeles Times, 15 Dec., Part 2, p. 7.

F38-8   SMITH, LORNA D. "Author Dreiser Stresses Need for Greater
        Political Understanding Among Youth," People's Daily
        World, 28 Dec., p. 5.

                              179

WORKS BY

1939

F39-1   HITT, NEIL. "Author and Destiny Reach a Compromise," San Francisco Chronicle, 10 Feb., p. 7.

F39-2   ESTCOURT, ZILFA. "Right Off the Chest," San Francisco Chronicle, 15 Feb., p. 13.

F39-3   ANON. "Flirting Powers Held in Danger," Portland Oregonian, 16 Feb., p. 1.

F39-4   ANON. "Dreiser, Here to Talk, Asks U. S. to Awake," Salt Lake City Deseret News, 20 Feb., p. 1.

F39-5   ANON. "Noted Author Predicts Another War," Salt Lake City Tribune, 20 Feb., p. 16.

F39-6   WILLIAMS, CLARENCE. "'Awake, Get Ready for War,' Dreiser Admonishes U. S.," Salt Lake City Telegram, 20 Feb., p. 11.

F39-7   ANON. "Dreiser Scores Sham Democracy," Salt Lake City Telegram, 21 Feb., p. 9.

F39-8   ANON. "Dreiser Views Challenge to Democracy," Salt Lake City Tribune, 21 Feb., p. 22.

F39-9   ANON. "Theodore Dreiser Warns of Anglo-French Duplicity," Salt Lake City Deseret News, 21 Feb., p. 3.

F39-10 MILLIER, ARTHUR. "American Literature's 'Gloomy Gus,'" Los Angeles Times, 12 Mar., Magazine Section, pp. 5, 8.

F39-11 "Theodore Dreiser: 'Gentleman for Lousy Reasons,'" Hollywood Tribune, 17 July [PU].

F39-12 BRUNSTEIN, MAX. "Hour with Dreiser," Huntington Park Signal, 18 Oct., pp. 1-2 [PU].

F39-13 SMITH, LORNA D. "Theodore Dreiser's Plan to Engligaten U. S. Workers," People's Daily World, 7 Nov., p. 5.

F39-14 BLAKE, CHARLES E. "Mr. Dreiser Says Earful to Clubwomen," Los Angeles Evening Herald, 22 Nov., pp. 2, 8 [PU].

1940

F40-1   ANON. "Theodore Dreiser Derides Discussion About Activities of Fifth Column," Portland Oregonian, 21 June, p. 7.

Interviews and Speeches

F40-2   SHIPPEN, W. H., JR. "Dreiser Says England Seeks to Drag
         U. S. in European War," Washington Evening Star, 10 Nov.,
         p. A-3.

1941

F41-1   YOUNG, JACK. "3000 Jam Biggest L. A. Peace Rally," People's
         Daily World, 15 Jan., p. 3.

F41-2   QUIN, MIKE, pseud. [Paul William Ryan]. "Double Check,"
         People's Daily World, 29 Jan., p. 5.

F41-3   ROBBIN, EDWARD. Radio Interview with Theodore Dreiser.
         n.p., [ca. 1 Feb.]. 5 pp. Text of interview on KMTR,
         Hollywood, aired on 1 Feb.

F41-4   ANON. "Dreiser Stresses Need to Spread Truth of U. S. S. R.,"
         Sunday Worker, 2 Mar., p. 3.

F41-5   ANON. "Theodore Dreiser Airs His Views," People's Daily
         World, 6 Mar., p. 5.

F41-6   VAN GELDER, ROBERT. "An Interview with Theodore Dreiser,"
         New York Times Book Review, 16 Mar., pp. 2, 16. Repub:
         Robert Van Gelder, Writers and Writing. New York:
         Scribner, 1946. Pp. 164-68.

F41-7   ANON. "Dreiser Asks End of Aid to British," Indianapolis
         News, 21 Nov., p. 5.

F41-8   TIERNAN, ARTHUR P. "Not a Communist, Dreiser Declares;
         Answers Chaillaux," Indianapolis Star, 21 Nov., pp. 1, 16.

1942

F42-1   OTHMAN, FREDERICK C. "Filmland Just Has Him Down," Boston
         Post, 15 May* [PU].

F42-2   SCHEUER, PHILLIP K. "Theodore Dreiser Goes All-Out for New
         Pictures," Los Angeles Times, 25 May, Part 2, p. 14.

F42-3   ANON. "Abuse for Britain Dreiser's Contribution to Anglo-
         U. S. Amity," Toronto Evening Telegram, 21 Sept., p. 2.

F42-4   ANON. "Dreiser Gibes at Canada," New York Times, 25 Sept.,
         p. 6.

WORKS BY

F42-5   ANON. "Dreiser Tells Friends Here of Speech Intended for
        Audience in Toronto," Indianapolis Star, 5 Oct.* [PU].

                              1944

F44-1   WILSON, EARL. "I Take In Some Saloons with Theodore Dreiser
        (Salted)," New York Post, 18 May, p. 32.

F44-2   NORMAN, DOROTHY. "The Eternally Youthful Theodore Dreiser,"
        New York Post, 10 July, Magazine and Comic Section, p. 1.

G

LIBRARY HOLDINGS

Only major Dreiser collections are listed. For a fuller list of libraries with Dreiser manuscript material, see American Literary Manuscripts, ed. Joseph Jones and others, Austin: University of Texas Press, 1960, and the National Union Catalogue of Manuscript Collections (1959-   ).

G-1   COLUMBIA UNIVERSITY LIBRARY, New York.
        MSS. of "Fulfilment" and "Some American Women Painters"; misc. correspondence, including 33 letters to Edna Kenton (1906-22) and 8 to Manuel Komroff (1926-31).

G-2   CORNELL UNIVERSITY LIBRARY, Ithaca, N. Y.
        Misc. correspondence of Robert Elias in connection with his critical biography and his edition of Dreiser's letters, including letters by Dreiser (1937-45), Helen Dreiser, H. L. Mencken, Donald Elder, James T. Farrell, and Louise Campbell; misc. Dreiser correspondence; Harold Hersey's scrapbooks on The "Genius" suppression; a collection of Dreiser first editions and of magazines containing contributions by him.

G-3   DARTMOUTH COLLEGE LIBRARY, Hanover, N. H.
        Misc. correspondence, including 29 letters to Grant Richards (1911-12).

G-4   HUNTINGTON LIBRARY, San Marino, Calif.
        Material collected by Mrs. Elizabeth Kearney Coakley, including 34 letters to Mrs. Coakley (1939-45), and misc. clippings, notes, and memorabilia.

G-5   LILLY LIBRARY, Indiana University, Bloomington.
        Flanagan Collection. Misc. correspondence about the Dreiser family.
        MSS. of Dawn, "The Day of the Coon Song," and "New York Fifty Years Ago and Today"; misc. notes and MS fragments

WORKS BY

of The Stoic; Dreiser's 1902-1903 diary; misc. correspondence, including 70 letters to Sallie White (1896-98),
29 to Upton Sinclair (1914-41), and 34 to Claude Bowers
(1923-44). (The letters to Sallie White are at present
sequestered.)

G-6   LOS ANGELES PUBLIC LIBRARY.
        Lorna Smith Collection. MSS. of "Nigger Jeff" and
        "The Blue Sphere," 18 letters to Lorna Smith (1939-41),
        and misc. magazine publications by Dreiser.

G-7   NEWBERRY LIBRARY, Chicago.
        Misc. correspondence, including 11 letters to Floyd
        Dell (1911-28) and 20 to Sherwood Anderson (1924-41).

G-8   THE NEW YORK PUBLIC LIBRARY.
        H. L. Mencken Collection. Ca. 600 letters to Mencken
        (1907-45).
        MS. of Sister Carrie; misc. correspondence, including
        7 letters to Robert H. Davis (1915-25).

G-9   UNIVERSITY OF CALIFORNIA AT LOS ANGELES LIBRARY.
        Will Donaldson Collection. MSS. of A Book About My-
        self and "The Lost Phoebe"; misc. correspondence; a col-
        lection of first editions and other publications by
        Dreiser.

G-10   UNIVERSITY OF ILLINOIS LIBRARY, Urbana.
        Grant Richards Collection. 31 letters to Grant Richards
        (1903-1923) and copies of Richards' letters to Dreiser.

G-11   UNIVERSITY OF PENNSYLVANIA LIBRARY, Philadelphia.
        Theodore Dreiser Collection. The principal collection
        of Dreiser's literary remains, consisting of approximately
        450 manuscript boxes, 300 books, and files of clippings.
        The basic contents are: MSS of Dreiser's books and of
        his uncollected and unpublished writings, including pre-
        liminary notes and drafts; letters by Dreiser, many of
        which are photo-copies of originals in other collections
        (ca. 44 boxes); letters to Dreiser (ca. 100 boxes);
        clippings and scrapbooks; and Dreiser's library. Also
        reprints and translations of Dreiser's works. A case file
        of the Collection is available for use at the Library.

G-12   UNIVERSITY OF TEXAS LIBRARY, Austin.
        Misc. correspondence, including 30 letters to George
        Douglas (1920-35) and 24 to Sulamith Ish-Kishor (1929-39).

G-13   UNIVERSITY OF VIRGINIA LIBRARY, Charlottesville.
Clifton Waller Barrett Collection. Second only to the
Dreiser Collection of the University of Pennsylvania
Library as a repository of Dreiser manuscripts. Contains
ca. 85 misc. MSS, including Jennie Gerhardt, "The Houses
of Longfellow," "The Philosophy of the Minor Note," "Pullman," "In the Haunts of Bayard Taylor," "The University
of Chicago," "A Victim of Justice," and "What the New
Century Offers the Young Man"; galley proof of Book I of
An American Tragedy; misc. correspondence, including 8
letters to Ernest Boyd (1923-31), 8 to Frank Harris (1918),
33 to Sally Kusell (1923-30), 37 to Albert Mordell (1913-
24), 7 to John Cowper Powys (1928-32), and 15 to Rosa
Vermonte (1930-32).

G-14   YALE UNIVERSITY LIBRARY, New Haven, Conn.
MS. of "The Prince Who Was a Thief"; misc. correspondence, including 11 letters to Ernest Boyd (1927-36),
13 to Arthur D. Ficke (1913-44), and 7 to Willard H.
Wright (1912-13).

H

BIBLIOGRAPHIES AND CHECKLISTS

All bibliographic publications devoted exclusively to works by and/or about Dreiser have been included, regardless of length or completeness. General checklists, as a rule, have been cited only when they contain twenty-five or more Dreiser items. Annual general bibliographies (i.e., PMLA, MHRA) and selected bibliographies appended to critical studies are not included. Bibliographical essays, and checklists, however, are frequently noted in the descriptive annotations of secondary works. Revisions and republications of the items cited are included in the entries. Also accompanying each entry is a descriptive annotation.

1923

H23-1   LANGE, W. W. "American First Editions: Theodore Dreiser 1871--," Publishers' Weekly, 104 (22 Dec.), 1925. Repub: Merle Johnson, American First Editions. New York: Bowker, 1929. Rev. eds. 1932, 1936, 1942 (1936, 1942 by Jacob Blanck).
    Lange lists the first publication of Dreiser's books and contributions to books through 1923; subsequent editions of American First Editions bring the listing to 1940. Brief annotations.

1928

H28-1   McDONALD, EDWARD D.   A Bibliography of the Writings of Theodore Dreiser.   Philadelphia: Centaur Book Shop. 130 pp. Repub: New York: Burt Franklin, 1968.
    Contains collations of the first and certain special editions of Dreiser's books and an annotated listing of Dreiser's major contributions to books and periodicals; also includes an annotated listing of studies and reviews of Dreiser's works; each section arranged chronologically through 1927.

WORKS ON

H28-2 ORTON, VREST. Notes to Add to a Bibliography of Theodore
       Dreiser. Perth Amboy: Mosquito Press. 21 pp.
       Lists errata and addenda to McDonald bibliography.

1929

H29-1 ORTON, VREST. Dreiserana: A Book About His Books.
       New York: Chocorua Bibliographies. 84 pp. Repub:
       New York: Haskell House, 1973.
       Expanded discussion and listing of errata and addenda
       to McDonald bibliography, bringing it into 1929; admit-
       tedly incomplete, however.

1931

H31-1 SCHWARTZ, JACOB. "Dreiser, (Theodore)," 1100 Obscure Points:
       The Bibliographies of 25 English and 21 American Authors.
       London: Ulysses Bookshop. Pp. 50-51.
       Descriptive listing of the first editions of Dreiser
       books and pamphlets through 1927, when, Schwartz asserted,
       Dreiser was finished.

1937

H37-1 FORD, EDWIN H. "Theodore Dreiser," A Bibliography of Literary
       Journalism in America. Minneapolis: Burgess. P. 22.
       Lists primary and secondary works dealing with Dreiser's
       career in journalism.

1940

H40-1 MILLETT, FRED B. "Theodore (Herman Albert) Dreiser, 1871--,"
       Contemporary American Authors: A Critical Survey and 219
       Bio-Bibliographies. New York: Harcourt. Pp. 332-37.
       Lists Dreiser's books and contributions to books and
       surveys books and articles about Dreiser to 1939.

1947

H47-1 ANON. "The Theodore Dresier Collection," Library Chronicle,
       14 (Oct.), 34.
       Describes correspondence obtained by University of
       Pennsylvania to supplement the Dreiser collection.

Bibliographies and Checklists

H47-2   MILLER, RALPH N. A Preliminary Checklist of Books and
        Articles on Theodore Dreiser. Kalamazoo: Western
        Michigan College Library. 11 pp. [Mimeograph].
        "The items in this preliminary checklist are biographi-
        cal, critical, and bibliographical studies of Dreiser and
        his fiction. Book reviews, except for unusual critical
        notices, are not included, nor are books and articles by
        continental scholars and critics, except for a few which
        are frequently cited in standard reference works"
        (Miller's note).

1948

H48-1   SPILLER, ROBERT E., et al., eds. "Theodore (Herman Albert)
        Dreiser," Literary History of the United States. New York:
        Macmillan. Vol. 3, 474-77. Repub: Literary History of
        the United States: Bibliography. 3rd ed. New York:
        Macmillan, 1963.
        Lists Dreiser books and reprints and surveys secondary
        sources to 1947.

1949

H49-1   ALDEN, JOHN. "Theodore Dreiser," Library Chronicle, 15
        (Summer), 68-69.
        Describes manuscripts added to the Dreiser Collection
        at the University of Pennsylvania.

1950

H50-1   ELIAS, ROBERT H. "The Library's Dreiser Collection," Library
        Chronicle, 17 (Fall), 78-80.
        Briefly outlines the scope and potential of the Dreiser
        Collection.

1954

H54-1   BROWN, GLENORA W., and DEMING B. BROWN. "Dreiser, Theodore,"
        A Guide to Soviet Russian Translations of American Litera-
        ture. New York: King's Crown. Pp. 73-76.
        Lists Russian translations of Dreiser's books and
        stories, 1917-1947; introductions included in citations.

WORKS ON

H54-2 LEARY, LEWIS. "Dreiser, Theodore," Articles on American
       Literature 1900-1950. Durham: Duke U. Press. Pp. 73-75.
       Cites 90 periodical articles.

                              1959

H59-1 SPILLER, ROBERT E., et al., eds. "Theodore (Herman Albert)
       Dreiser," Literary History of the United States: Biblio-
       graphy Supplement. New York: Macmillan. Pp. 108-09.
       Repub: Literary History of the United States: Biblio-
       graphy. 3rd ed. New York: Macmillan, 1963.
       Lists secondary sources 1947-1957.

H59-2 W[ESTLAKE], N[EDA] M. "Theodore Dreiser Collection--Addenda,"
       Library Chronicle, 25 (Summer), 55-57.
           Describes the contracts, publishing records, and cor-
       respondence with publishers and film makers added to the
       Dreiser Collection at the University of Pennsylvania.

                              1961

H61-1 GERSTENBERGER, DONNA, and GEORGE HENDRICK. "Dreiser, Theo-
       dore," The American Novel 1789-1959: A Checklist of
       Twentieth-Century Criticism. Denver: Swallow. Pp. 60-66.
           Lists 28 studies of individual novels, 89 general
       studies, and 5 bibliographies.

                              1963

H63-1 ANON. "Bibliographia: Theodore Dreiser," Booklover's
       Answer, 1 (Jan.-Feb.), 11.
           Descriptive bibliography of Dreiser books and pamphlets
       through 1918.

                              1969

H69-1 ATKINSON, HUGH C. The Merrill Checklist of Theodore Dreiser.
       Columbus, Ohio: Merrill. 43 pp.
           Highly selective checklist of primary and secondary
       works; no annotations.

H69-2 ELIAS, ROBERT H. "Theodore Dreiser," Fifteen Modern American
       Authors: A Survey of Research and Criticism. Ed. Jackson
       R. Bryer. Durham: Duke U. Press. Pp. 101-38. Repub:

Bibliographies and Checklists

Elias, emended ed., pp. 355-414; See I49-1. Repub. with
Supplement: Sixteen Modern American Authors: A Survey of
Research and Criticism. Ed. Jackson R. Bryer. Durham:
Duke U. Press, 1974. Pp. 123-79.
Essay describing and evaluating major secondary works.

H69-3   LIBMAN, VALENTINA. "Draizer, Teodor," Russian Studies of
American Literature: A Bibliography. Trans. Robert V.
Allen. Ed. Clarence Gohdes. Chapel Hill: U. North
Carolina Press. Pp. 65-76.
Chronological checklist of Russian scholarship, 1925-
1963.

H69-4   MOOKERJEE, R. N. "An Embarrassment of Riches: Dreiser Research: Materials and Problems," Indian Journal of American Studies, 1 (July), 91-96.
Brief survey of Dreiser materials and opportunities,
particularly at the University of Pennsylvania.

H69-5   SALZMAN, JACK. "Theodore Dreiser (1871-1945)," American
Literary Realism 1870-1910, 2 (Summer), 132-38.
A selective survey of Dreiser scholarship; descriptive
annotations.

1970

H70-1   DOWELL, RICHARD W. "Dreiser Holdings at the Lilly Library,"
Dreiser Newsletter, 1 (Spring), 13-15.
Survey of Dreiser manuscript holdings at Indiana Uni-
versity.

H70-2   DOWELL, RICHARD W. "Checklist: Dreiser Studies, 1969,"
Dreiser Newsletter, 1 (Fall), 14-18.
Annotated checklist of Dreiser scholarship published
in 1969.

H70-3   GERSTENBERGER, DONNA, and GEORGE HENDRICK. "Dreiser, Theodore," The American Novel: A Checklist of Twentieth
Century Criticism on Novels Written since 1789. Vol. 2:
Criticism Written 1960-1968. Chicago: Swallow. Pp. 74-
78.
Updates The American Novel 1789-1959, See H61-1; lists
55 studies of individual novels, 29 general studies, and
5 bibliographies.

H70-4   LEARY, LEWIS. "Dreiser, Theodore," Articles on American
Literature, 1950-1967. Durham: Duke U. Press. Pp. 116-
20.

WORKS ON

Updates Articles on American Literature, 1900-1950,
See H54-2; lists 110 items.

1971

H71-1   ATKINSON, HUGH C. Theodore Dreiser: A Checklist. Kent,Ohio:
Kent State U. Press. 104 pp.
Presented as "a guide for the student, rather than as
a definitive listing"; includes, without annotation,
Dreiser's major works, prefaces, published letters, and
miscellaneous pieces; also lists books, articles, selected
reviews, and dissertations about Dreiser and his works.

H71-2   COMBS, RICHARD E. "Theodore Dreiser," Authors: Critical and
Biographical References. Metuchen,N.J.: Scarecrow. P. 48.
Cites 25 general studies including Dreiser.

H71-3   PIZER, DONALD. "The Publications of Theodore Dreiser: A
Checklist," Proof: The Yearbook of American Bibliographical and Textual Studies. Ed. Joseph Katz. Vol. 1.
Columbia, S.C.: U. South Carolina Press. Pp. 247-92.
Chronological listing of Dreiser's separate publications and contributions to books, magazines, and newspapers.

H71-4   Theodore Dreiser: Centenary Exhibition. Philadelphia: U.
Pennsylvania Library. 27 pp.
Catalogue describing items on exhibition; preface by
Neda M. Westlake.

1972

H72-1   DOWELL, RICHARD W., and FREDERIC E. RUSCH. "A Dreiser Checklist, 1970," Dreiser Newsletter, 3 (Spring), 13-21.
Annotated listing of articles, books, dissertations,
and reprints appearing in 1970.

H72-2   RUSCH, FREDERIC E. "A Dreiser Checklist, 1971: Part One,"
Dreiser Newsletter, 3 (Fall), 12-19.
Annotated listing of publications about Dreiser and new
editions or reprints of his works appearing in 1971 or
omitted from the 1970 Dreiser Newsletter checklist.

H72-3   SPILLER, ROBERT E., et al., eds. "Theodore (Albert Herman)
Dreiser," Literary History of the United States: Biblio-
graphy Supplement II. New York: Macmillan. Pp. 146-47.
Lists primary and secondary works published 1958-1970.

THEODORE DREISER: A BIBLIOGRAPHY

Bibliographies and Checklists

1973

H73-1   POWNALL, DAVID E. "Dreiser, Theodore," Articles on Twentieth
        Century Literature: An Annotated Bibliography 1954-1970.
        New York: Kraus-Thomson. Vol. 2, 702-17.
        Includes 72 items.

H73-2   RUSCH, FREDERIC E. "A Dreiser Checklist, 1971: Part Two,"
        Dreiser Newsletter, 4 (Spring), 5-11.
        Annotated listing of studies including Dreiser, re-
        prints of earlier Dreiser studies, and items omitted from
        previous Dreiser Newsletter checklists.

H73-3   RUSCH, FREDERIC E. "A Dreiser Checklist, 1972," Dreiser
        Newsletter, 4 (Fall), 12-23.
        Listing of new editions or reprints of Dreiser's work,
        new studies or reprints of studies about or including
        Dreiser, and items omitted from previous Dreiser News-
        letter checklists; original scholarship annotated, ex-
        cluding dissertations.

H73-4   OLDANI, LOUIS JOSEPH. "Bibliographical Description of
        Dreiser's The 'Genius,'" Library Chronicle, 39 (Winter),
        40-55.
        A descriptive bibliography of copies of The "Genius"
        in the Charles Patterson Van Pelt Library of the Univer-
        sity of Pennsylvania.

I

BOOKS AND PAMPHLETS

Only books devoted exclusively or primarily to Dreiser are included in this section. With the exception of foreign publications, each entry is accompanied by an annotation describing the scope, uniqueness, or general focus of the work. Republication information is also included in the entries.

1916

I16-1   A Protest against the Suppression of Theodore Dreiser's The
        "Genius." n.p., [1916]. 4 pp. Text of protest repub.
        in McDonald, pp. 101-02; See H28-1.
            Statement issued by the Authors' League of America and
        endorsed by 130 writers whose names appear in the pamph-
        let. Unverified; citation from McDonald.

I16-2   ROSENTHAL, ELIAS. Theodore Dreiser's "Genius" Damned. n.p.,
        [1916]. 8 pp.
            Defense of The "Genius" by a member of the New York Bar
        Association. Unverified; citation from McDonald.

1917

I17-1   Theodore Dreiser: America's Foremost Novelist. New York:
        John Lane [ca. 1917]. 32 pp. Repub: Folcroft, Pa.:
        Folcroft Library Editions, 1973.
            Advertising brochure which republishes poems by Edgar
        Lee Masters and Arthur D. Ficke and essays by Harris
        Merton Lyon and John Cowper Powys.

1919

I19-1   The Hand of the Potter: A Tragedy in Four Acts. New York:
        Boni and Liveright [ca. 1919]. 12 pp.

194

Advertising brochure which republishes numerous excerpts from reviews of the book.

I19-2   Twelve Men. New York: Boni and Liveright [ca. 1919]. 20 pp.
Advertising brochure which republishes reviews of the book. Unverified; citation from McDonald.

1920

I20-1   Free and Other Stories. New York: Boni and Liveright [ca. 1920]. 8 pp.
Advertising brochure which republishes reviews of the book. Unverified; citation from Orton.

1925

I25-1   RASCOE, BURTON. Theodore Dreiser. New York: Robert M. McBride. 83 pp. Repub: New York: Haskell House, 1972.
Defends Dreiser and his work against the charges of hostile critics and assesses his achievement through 1922.

1926

I26-1   A Book About Theodore Dreiser and His Work. New York: Boni and Liveright [ca. 1926]. 24 pp.
Advertising brochure which republishes a poem by Edgar Lee Masters and essays by Sherwood Anderson and H. L. Mencken.

1927

I27-1   Theodore Dreiser and His Books. London: Constable [ca. 1927]. 16 pp.
Advertising brochure which republishes excerpts from the criticism of H. G. Wells, Thomas Burke, Gerald Gould, John Cowper Powys, Sarah Gertrude Millin, Harris Merton Lyon, and H. L. Mencken.

1932

I32-1   DUDLEY, DOROTHY. Forgotten Frontiers: Dreiser and the Land of the Free. New York: Harrison Smith. 485 pp. Repub:

WORKS ON

Dreiser and the Land of the Free. New York: Beechhurst, 1946.
Impressionistic biography which attempts to establish Dreiser's place in the intellectual and cultural milieu; draws upon conversations and correspondence with Dreiser and his friends as well as Dudley's free access to his files.

1949

I49-1   ELIAS, ROBERT H. Theodore Dreiser: Apostle of Nature.
New York: Knopf. 354 pp. Emended ed.: Ithaca, N.Y.: Cornell U. Press, 1970.
First carefully documented biography; focuses upon the relationship of Dreiser's personal experience to the philosophical concerns of his writing and draws upon Elias's eight-year acquaintance with Dreiser and an unrestricted use of his private papers. Emended edition includes a critical survey of Dreiser research and criticism to 1970.

1951

I51-1   DREISER, HELEN. My Life with Dreiser. Cleveland: World.
328 pp.
Memoirs of Dreiser's second wife, detailing their life together from 1919 until his death in 1945; includes previously unpublished Dreiser correspondence, primarily to Helen Dreiser.

I51-2   MATTHIESSEN, F. O. Theodore Dreiser. New York: William
Sloane Associates. 267 pp. Repub: Westport, Conn.: Greenwood Press, 1973.
Biography which gives particular attention to the structure, images, symbols, and language of the novels.

1952

I52-1   ZASURSKII, YASEN N., and ROMAN SAMARIN. Teodor Draĭzer v
Bor'be Protiv Amerikanskogo Imperializma. Moscow: Moscow U. Press. 108 pp.

THEODORE DREISER: A BIBLIOGRAPHY

Books and Pamphlets

1955

I55-1   KAZIN, ALFRED, and CHARLES SHAPIRO, eds. The Stature of Theodore Dreiser: A Critical Survey of the Man and His Work. Bloomington, Ind.: Indiana U. Press. 303 pp. Repub (paper): Bloomington, Ind.: Indiana U. Press, 1965.

Republishes reminiscences by Dreiser's contemporaries, newspaper reviews of Sister Carrie, and critical essays dating from 1915 to 1953; thirty-four items including one original essay by David Brion Davis (See J55-2) and a selected bibliography of Dreiser biography and criticism.

I55-2   WIRZBERGER, KARL-HEINZ. Die Romane Theodore Dreisers. Berlin: Deutscher Verlag der Wissenschaften. 300 pp.

1956

I56-1   ARNAVON, CYRILLE. Théodore Dreiser: Romancier Américain. Paris: U. Lille, Centre de Documentation Universitaire. 142 pp.

1957

I57-1   ZASURSKIĬ, YASEN N. Teodor Draĭzer: Pisatel i Publitsist. Moscow: Moscow U. Press. 220 pp.

1961

I61-1   STAAB, WOLFGANG. Das Deutschlandbild Theodore Dreisers. Mainz: U. Mainz Press. 104 pp.

1962

I62-1   SHAPIRO, CHARLES. Theodore Dreiser: Our Bitter Patriot. Carbondale, Ill.: Southern Illinois U. Press. 137 pp. Repub (paper): Carbondale, Ill.: Southern Illinois U. Press, 1964.

Analyzes Dreiser's treatment of the American Dream and its destructive influence on the individual, the family, art, business, and religion; focuses primarily on the novels.

WORKS ON

1963

I63-1   BIZÁM, LENKE. Theodore Dreiser. Budapest: Gondolat.
164 pp.

I63-2   BRODERICK, JOHN C. Theodore Dreiser's Sister Carrie: A
Study Guide. Bound Brook, N.J.: Shelley. 74 pp.
Contains a biographical sketch, excerpts of criticism,
character analyses, and study questions.

1964

I64-1   GERBER, PHILIP L. Theodore Dreiser. New York: Twayne.
220 pp.
A critical introduction to Dreiser and his novels;
chapter-length analysis of each novel.

I64-2   ZASURSKIĬ, YASEN N. Teodor Draĭzer. Moscow: Moscow U.
Press. 319 pp.

1965

I65-1   SWANBERG, W. A. Dreiser. New York: Scribners. 614 pp.
Repub (paper): New York: Bantam Books, 1967.
Biography; an exhaustive study drawing to a large extent on interviews with Dreiser's friends and associates
and on personal correspondence, much of which had not been
previously published; no attempt at in-depth literary
criticism.

I65-2   TJADER, MARGUERITE. Theodore Dreiser: A New Dimension.
Norwalk, Conn.: Silvermine. 244 pp.
Focuses on the philosophical and spiritual probings of
Dreiser's last seventeen years; draws upon the author's
personal association with Dreiser, particularly during his
struggle to complete The Bulwark.

1967

I67-1   SCHMIDT-VON BARDELEBEN, RENATE. Das Bild New Yorks im Erzähl-
werk von Dreiser und Dos Passos. Munich: Heuber. 206 pp.

Theodore Dreiser: A Bibliography

Books and Pamphlets

1968

I68-1   McALEER, JOHN J. Theodore Dreiser: An Introduction and Interpretation. New York: Holt. 180 pp.
Analyzes in chapter-length discussions of each novel the biographical implications in theme, structure, and imagery.

1969

I69-1   KENNELL, RUTH EPPERSON. Theodore Dreiser and the Soviet Union, 1927-1945: A First-Hand Chronicle. New York: International. 320 pp.
Part One provides an in-depth narration of Dreiser's tour of Russia in 1927-28; Part Two discusses the impact of that trip on his later life; quotes extensively from the diary Mrs. Kennell kept as his tour guide and from her correspondence with Dreiser during the years that followed.

I69-2   LEHAN, RICHARD. Theodore Dreiser: His World and His Novels. Carbondale, Ill.: Southern Illinois U. Press. 280 pp.
A critical biography, emphasizing Dreiser's evolution as an artist and thinker; analyzes and quotes from holograph versions of novels.

I69-3   MOERS, ELLEN. Two Dreisers. New York: Viking. 366 pp.
An in-depth analysis of the source material and influences contributing to the composition of Sister Carrie and An American Tragedy; included in the copious amount of material quoted are excerpts from numerous pieces of unpublished Dreiser correspondence.

I69-4   SHAPIRO, CHARLES. The Merrill Guide to Theodore Dreiser. Columbus, Ohio: Merrill. 44 pp.
Summarizes Dreiser's life, the themes of his novels, and the circumstances surrounding their publication.

1970

I70-1   PIZER, DONALD, ed. Sister Carrie: An Authoritative Text, Backgrounds and Sources, Criticism. New York: Norton. 591 pp.
In addition to an annotated text of the 1900 Doubleday, Page and Company first edition, Pizer republishes numerous newspaper articles, excerpts from Dreiser's autobiographies,

WORKS ON

and exchanges of correspondence to provide background
material on principal characters and publication history;
also republishes 14 critical essays.

1971

I71-1   LYDENBERG, JOHN, ed. Dreiser: A Collection of Critical
        Essays. Englewood Cliffs, N.J.: Prentice-Hall. 182 pp.
        Republishes fifteen polemical essays (1915 to 1964)
        which highlight the continuing controversy over Dreiser's
        work.

I71-2   MENDEL'SON, MORIS OSIPOVICH. Amerikanskaia Tragediia Teodora
        Draizera. Moscow: Khudozhestvennaia literatura. 103 pp.

I71-3   SALZMAN, JACK. The Merrill Studies in An American Tragedy.
        Columbus, Ohio: Merrill. 111 pp.
        Republishes five reviews and eight critical studies of
        An American Tragedy.

I71-4   WARREN, ROBERT PENN. Homage to Theodore Dreiser: On the
        Centennial of His Birth. New York: Random. 171 pp.
        Expanded version of an essay published under the same
        title in the Southern Review, 7 (Spring 1971), 345-410.
        Sees in Dreiser's novels the ambitions, frustrations,
        guilt, and ambivalence of their author.

I71-5   ZASURSKIĬ, YASEN N. Teodor Draĭzer. Moscow: Znanie. 32 pp.

1972

I72-1   FROHOCK, W[ILBUR] M[ERRILL]. Theodore Dreiser. Minneapolis:
        U. Minnesota Press. 48 pp.
        Analyzes Dreiser's novels, focusing on the poverty
        background that contributed to his grim interpretation of
        American life.

I72-2   SALZMAN, JACK. Theodore Dreiser: The Critical Reception.
        New York: Lewis. 741 pp.
        A collection of American reviews of all of Dreiser's
        books except those printed in limited editions. In his
        introduction Salzman gives a chronological summary of the
        reviews, showing how they reveal the development of
        Dreiser's critical reception.

1973

I73-1   PALEY, ALAN L. Theodore Dreiser: American Editor and
         Novelist. Charlotteville, N.Y.: SamHar. 32 pp.
            Surveys Dreiser's critical reception and summarizes
         the events of his life, frequently demonstrating how
         these events are reflected in the art and philosophy of
         his novels.

J

PARTS OF BOOKS

Included in this section are books containing material on Dreiser as part of a more inclusive study. As a general rule, we have restricted the citations to items published originally in book form; however, there are a few instances in which vaguely acknowledged or unacknowledged republication has precluded the location of the material in its original form and thus made inclusion in this section the only practical recourse. For items that have been frequently re-published, only the first republication and republication in books cited in section I are listed. We have made no attempt to describe the revision involved in such republication.

Also, we have made sparing use of annotations in this section. When references to Dreiser are brief or scattered, we have provided a note suggesting the scope or emphasis of the treatment. When the discussion of Dreiser is localized in a single chapter or unit, we have allowed the title of that section to serve as the annotation.

1902

J02-1 HENRY, ARTHUR. An Island Cabin. New York: McClure, Phillips. Pp. 159-236.
  Identifying him as "Tom," Henry describes Dreiser's irritation and despondency while roughing it on an island near Noank in the summer of 1901.

1905

J05-1 HENRY, ARTHUR. Lodgings in Town. New York: A. S. Barnes. Pp. 80-88.
  Recalls a visit with Dreiser at the Ev'ry Month office.

Parts of Books

1915

J15-1   MASTERS, EDGAR LEE. "Theodore the Poet," Spoon River Anthol-
         ogy. New York: Macmillan. P. 41.
         Poem; originally enclosed in a letter from Masters to
         Dreiser, dated April 1914.

1916

J16-1   POWYS, JOHN COWPER. "Theodore Dreiser. The Titan," One
         Hundred Best Books. New York: G. A. Shaw. P. 28.
         Repub: New York: American Library Service, 1922.

1917

J17-1   MENCKEN, H. L. "Theodore Dreiser," A Book of Prefaces.
         New York: Knopf. Pp. 67-148. Repub: The Shock of
         Recognition. Ed. Edmund Wilson. Garden City, N.Y.:
         Doubleday, 1943. Pp. 1160-1208.
         This essay is the combination and expansion of
         Mencken's essays for the Baltimore Evening Sun; See
         K16-7, K16-8, K16-9.

1918

J18-1   BROOKS, VAN WYCK. Letters and Leadership. New York:
         Heubsch. Pp. 13-14.
         Sees Dreiser as typifying the intellectual and cultural
         sterility of American life.

J18-2   FOLLETT, HELEN, and WILSON FOLLETT. Some Modern Novelists,
         Appreciations and Estimates. New York: Holt. Pp. 350-52.
         Dreiser briefly discussed as one who never went beyond
         the limited views of Naturalism.

1919

J19-1   DUNN, JACOB P. Indiana and Indianians. Chicago: American
         Historical Society. Pp. 1185-89.
         Negative evaluation of Dreiser and his work.

J19-2   FRANK, WALDO. Our America. New York: Boni and Liveright.
         Pp. 129-33.
         Sees Dreiser as an artist gripped by the American past.

WORKS ON

J19-3   GORDON, GEORGE, pseud. [Charles C. Baldwin]. "Theodore
         Dreiser," The Men Who Make Our Novels. New York: Moffat,
         Yard. Repub: Charles C. Baldwin. "Theodore Dreiser,"
         The Men Who Make Our Novels. New York: Dodd, Mead, 1924.
         Pp. 141-53.

                              1920

J20-1   MENCKEN, H. L. "The Human Face," Prejudices: Second Series.
         New York: Knopf. Pp. 206-08.

                              1921

J21-1   MacCOLLOUGH, MARTIN, pseud. [Samuel W. Tait, Jr.]. Letters
         on Contemporary American Authors. Boston: Four Seas.
         Pp. 81-87.
             Chooses Jennie Gerhardt and The Titan as Dreiser's
         greatest novels because determinism and the meaningless-
         ness of life are most dominant in those works.

                              1922

J22-1   GARNETT, EDWARD. Friday Nights. New York: Knopf. Pp. 297-
         303.
             Praises The Titan for its accurate portrayal of Ameri-
         can life and condemns it for its stultifying detail.

J22-2   MANLY, JOHN M., and EDITH RICKERT. "Theodore Dreiser," Con-
         temporary American Literature. New York: Harcourt.
         Pp. 42-44.
             Study guide to Dreiser and his work.

J22-3   MENCKEN, H. L. "Footnote on Criticism," Prejudices: Third
         Series. New York: Knopf. Pp. 84-104. Repub: Criticism
         in America: Its Function and Status. Ed. Irving Babbitt.
         New York: Harcourt, 1924. Pp. 261-86.
             Essay initially appeared as "The Motive of the Critic,"
         New Republic Literary Supplement, 28 (26 Oct. 1921), 249-
         51.
             Material on Dreiser added during revision for Preju-
         dices.

J22-4   SCHELLING, FELIX E. "The Greatest Play since Shakespeare,"
         Appraisements and Asperities. Philadelphia: Lippincott.
         Pp. 120-25.
             Lampoons Dreiser's introduction to Caius Gracchus.

Theodore Dreiser: A Bibliography

1923

J23-1   MARKEY, GENE. "Two Great Realists: Theodore Dreiser and E. Phillips Oppenheim," Literary Lights: A Book of Caricatures. New York: Knopf. P. [8].

J23-2   O'BRIEN, EDWARD J. The Advance of the American Short Story. New York: Dodd, Mead. See Index. Rev. ed.: Dodd, Mead, 1931.
Praises "The Lost Phoebe" but otherwise dismisses Dreiser as a short story writer whose works have power but read like "an inferior translation."

J23-3   [ROBERTS], CARL ERIC BECHHOFER. The Literary Renaissance in America. London: Heinemann. Pp. 92-99.
Views Dreiser's strength and crudeness as representative of the "young American of the Middle West."

J23-4   YEWDALE, MERTON S. "Foreword," The "Genius." New York: Boni and Liveright. Pp. v-x.

1924

J24-1   ANDERSON, SHERWOOD. "Introduction," Free and Other Stories. New York: Modern Library. Pp. v-x.

J24-2   BOYD, ERNEST A. "Theodore Dreiser," Portraits: Real and Imaginary. New York: Doran. Pp. 168-70. Repub: New York: AMS, 1970.

J24-3   BURKE, HARRY ROSECRANS. "Dreiser and the Riddle of the Sphinx," From the Day's Journey: A Book of By-Paths and Eddies about Saint Louis. St. Louis: Miner. Pp. 165-71.

1925

J25-1   BERG, RUBEN G. "Theodore Dreiser--Sherwood Anderson," Moderna Amerikaner. Stockholm: Geber. Pp. 100-25.

J25-2   GOLDBERG, ISAAC. The Man Mencken: A Biographical and Critical Survey. New York: Simon. See Index. Repub: New York: AMS, 1968.
Scattered references to Mencken's association with and evaluation of Dreiser.

WORKS ON

J25-3   GREEN, ELIZABETH, and PAUL GREEN. "Theodore Dreiser,"
         Contemporary American Literature. Chapel Hill, N.C.: U.
         North Carolina Press. Pp. 12-15.

J25-4   VAN DOREN, CARL, and MARK VAN DOREN. American and British
         Literature since 1890. New York: Century. Pp. 57-60.
         Rev. ed.: New York: Appleton-Century, 1939.
             Notes Dreiser's respect for individuality and indiffer-
         ence to conventional morality.

                              1926

J26-1   BEACH, JOSEPH WARREN. The Outlook for American Prose.
         Chicago: U. Chicago Press. Pp. 225-33.
             Analyzes the style of A Book About Myself.

J26-2   CESTRE, C., and B. GAGNOT. "Theodore Dreiser," Anthologie de
         la Littérature Américaine. Paris: Delagrave. Pp. 143-48.
             Biographical sketch accompanying a French translation
         of chapter 26 of The "Genius."

J26-3   DREW, ELIZABETH A. The Modern Novel: Some Aspects of Con-
         temporary Fiction. New York: Harcourt. Pp. 146-47.
             Briefly dismisses Dreiser as one whose "ugly solidity
         of craftsmanship" is made bearable by a "terrific de-
         termination to express . . . forces of life . . . ."

J26-4   MICHAUD, RÉGIS. "Theodore Dreiser: L'homme et sa philo-
         sophie," Le roman américain d'aujourd'hui: Critique d'une
         civilisation. Paris: Boivin. Pp. 55-79. Repub. in
         translation: The American Novel of Today: A Social and
         Psychological Study. Boston: Little, 1928.

J26-5   MUMFORD, LEWIS. The Golden Day. New York: Boni and
         Liveright. Pp. 250-54. Repub: New York: Norton, 1934.
             Sees Dreiser as one who stood apart from the muckrakers
         to revolt from conventional morality and celebrate power.

J26-6   POWYS, LLEWELYN. "Good Friends," The Verdict of Bridlegoose.
         New York: Harcourt. Pp. 60-70.

J26-7   TOWNE, CHARLES HANSON. Adventures in Editing. New York:
         Appleton. Pp. 121-53.
             Recalls working under Dreiser at the Delineator.

THEODORE DREISER: A BIBLIOGRAPHY

1927

J27-1 BENCHLEY, ROBERT. "Compiling an American Tragedy," The
       Early Worm. New York: Holt. Pp. 246-50. Repub: Robert
       Benchley, The Benchley Roundup. Ed. Nathaniel Benchley.
       New York: Harper, 1954. [Parody].

J27-2 COBLENTZ, STANTON A. The Literary Revolution. New York:
       Frank Maurice. Pp. 151-52. Repub: New York: Johnson
       Reprint Corp., 1969.
          Dreiser's style termed "a devotion to the creed of
       confusion and chaos."

J27-3 HAZARD, LUCY L. "Theodore Dreiser: Cowperwood, the Creature
       of Chemistry," The Frontier in American Literature.
       New York: Crowell. Pp. 235-42.

J27-4 LEWISOHN, LUDWIG. "Culture and Barbarism," Cities and Men.
       New York: Harper. Pp. 3-18.
          Defends subjective writers, including Dreiser.

J27-5 RIDDELL, JOHN, pseud. [Corey Ford]. "Blue-prints for Another
       American Tragedy," Meaning No Offense. New York: John
       Day. Pp. 65-72. [Parody].

J27-6 SINCLAIR, UPTON. "An American Victory," Money Writes.
       New York: Boni. Pp. 124-28.

1928

J28-1 ADCOCK, ARTHUR ST. JOHN. "Theodore Dreiser," The Glory That
       Was Grub Street. London: Marston. Pp. 43-52. Repub:
       Freeport, N.Y.: Books for Libraries Press, 1969.

J28-2 BALLOU, ROBERT. "Introduction," Twelve Men. New York:
       Modern Library. Pp. v-ix.

J28-3 BENNETT, ARNOLD. The Savour of Life: Essays in Gusto.
       New York: Doubleday, Doran. Pp. 303-05.
          Sees An American Tragedy as a powerful book despite
       its stylistic vulgarity.

J28-4 ERNST, MORRIS, and WILLIAM SEAGLE. To the Pure . . . A Study
       of Obscenity and the Censor. New York: Viking. See
       Index.
          Numerous references to Dreiser's legal difficulties.

THEODORE DREISER: A BIBLIOGRAPHY

WORKS ON

J28-5   GRABO, CARL H.   The Technique of the Novel.   New York:
        Scribner.   Pp. 258-63.   Repub: New York: Gordian, 1964.
        Discussion of Dreiser's Naturalistic method.

J28-6   HALDEMAN-JULIUS, EMANUEL.   The First Hundred Million.
        New York: Simon.   No Index.
            A few brief and scattered references to Dreiser's popu-
        larity as a contributor to Haldeman-Julius's Little Blue
        Books.

J28-7   KARSNER, DAVID.   "Theodore Dreiser," Sixteen Authors to One:
        Intimate Sketches of Leading American Story Tellers.
        New York: Copeland.   Pp. 3-24.

J28-8   MARBLE, ANNIE R.   A Study of the Modern Novel, British and
        American, since 1900.   New York: Appleton.   Pp. 366-72.
            Discusses Dreiser's revolt from the genteel tradition.

J28-9   MICHAUD, RÉGIS.   "Theodore Dreiser," Panorama de la Littéra-
        ture Américaine Contemporaine.   Paris: Kra.   Pp. 165-70.

J28-10 MORE, PAUL ELMER.   The Demon of the Absolute.   Princeton:
        Princeton U. Press.   Pp. 64-69.
            Sees Dreiser's work as typical of the "noisy realism"
        that had invaded American literature.

J28-11 MUNSON, GORHAM B.   "The Motivation of Theodore Dreiser,"
        Destinations: A Canvass of American Literature since
        1900.   New York: Sears.   Pp. 41-56.   Repub: New York:
        AMS, 1970.

J28-12 OPPENHEIM, JAMES.   Behind Your Front.   New York: Harper.
        Pp. 59-63.
            Psychoanalytic contrast of Dreiser and Edison.

J28-13 PARRINGTON, VERNON L.   "The Development of Realism," The Re-
        interpretation of American Literature.   Ed. Norman
        Foerster.   New York: Harcourt.   Pp. 139-59.

J28-14 WHIPPLE, THOMAS K.   "Theodore Dreiser," Spokesmen: Modern
        Writers and American Life.   New York: Appleton.   Pp. 70-
        93.   Repub: Kazin and Shapiro, pp. 96-110 (as "Aspects
        of a Pathfinder"; See I55-1).

1929

J29-1   BENÉT, WILLIAM ROSE.   "Dreiser, Theodore," Encyclopedia Bri-
        tannica.   14th edition.   Chicago: Encyclopedia Britannica.

J29-2   LEISY, ERNEST E. American Literature: An Interpretive
Survey. New York: Crowell. Pp. 209-10.
Sees Dreiser as the "Nestor" of American Naturalists.

J29-3   LEVINSON, ANDRÉ. "Avant-Propos," Une Tragédie Américaine.
Trans. Victor Llona. Paris: Fayard. Pp. 7-16.

J29-4   MUNSON, GORHAM B. "Prose for the Drama: William Vaughn
Moody, Theodore Dreiser, and Eugene O'Neill," Style and
Form in American Prose. Garden City, N.Y.: Doubleday,
Doran. Pp. 234-55.

J29-5   OVERTON, GRANT M. "Dreiser," An Hour of the American Novel.
Philadelphia: Lippincott. Pp. 104-08.

1930

J30-1   ANDERSON, MARGARET. My Thirty Years' War. New York:
Covici, Friede. Pp. 33-34, 39.
Recalls the outrage she created by calling Sister
Carrie "a fine piece of work" and expresses her personal
aversion to Dreiser.

J30-2   BRUNS, FRIEDRICH. "Theodore Dreiser," Die Amerikanische
Dichtung der Gegenwart. Leipzig: Teubner. Pp. 22-33.

J30-3   CABELL, JAMES BRANCH. "Protégés of the Censor," Some of Us.
New York: McBride. Pp. 77-88.

J30-4   CAIRNS, WILLIAM B. A History of American Literature. Rev.
ed. New York: Oxford U. Press. See Index.
Brief consideration of Dreiser's role in the movement
toward Naturalism.

J30-5   PARRINGTON, VERNON L. "Theodore Dreiser: Chief of American
Naturalists," Main Currents of American Thought. New York:
Harcourt. Vol. 3, 354-59.

J30-6   PATTEE, FRED L. "Theodore Dreiser," The New American Literature, 1890-1930. New York: Century. Pp. 180-93.

J30-7   SCHYBERG, FREDERIK. Moderne Amerikansk Litteratur, 1900-1930.
Copenhagen: Gyldendalske. See Index.

J30-8   SHAFER, ROBERT. "An American Tragedy," Humanism and America:
Essays on the Outlook of Modern Civilization. Ed. Norman
Foerster. New York: Farrar, Rinehart. Pp. 149-69.

WORKS ON

> Repub: Kazin and Shapiro, pp. 113-26 (as "An American
> Tragedy: A Humanistic Demurrer"; See I55-1). Salzman,
> Merrill Studies, pp. 92-98; See I71-3.

1931

J31-1   BLANKENSHIP, RUSSELL. "Theodore Dreiser," American Literature as an Expression of the National Mind. New York:
Holt. Pp. 532-41.

J31-2   EASTMAN, MAX. The Literary Mind: Its Place in an Age of
Science. New York: Scribners. Pp. 231-33.
     Describes Dreiser as one who "did not join the march
of science."

J31-3   JONES, LLEWELLYN. "Contemporary Fiction," American Writers
on American Literature. Ed. John Macy. New York:
Liveright. Pp. 488-502.
     In the course of this chapter, Jones reviews the con-
fusion and inconsistencies in Dreiser's mechanistic
philosophy.

J31-4   KNIGHT, GRANT C. "The Triumph of Realism: Theodore Dreiser,"
The Novel in English. New York: R. R. Smith. Pp. 338-46.

J31-5   KUNITZ, STANLEY J. "Theodore Dreiser," Living Authors: A
Book of Biographies. New York: Wilson. Pp. 109-11.

J31-6   SALZMAN, MAURICE. Plagiarism: The "Art" of Stealing Literary
Material. Los Angeles: Parker. Pp. 202-05.
     Concerns the Dreiser-Dorothy Thompson controversy.

1932

J32-1   BEACH, JOSEPH WARREN. "The Realist Reaction: Dreiser,"
The Twentieth Century Novel. New York: Century. Pp. 321-
31.

J32-2   BENNETT, ARNOLD. The Journal of Arnold Bennett. New York:
Viking. Vol. 3, 153-58, 184, 186.
     Daily entries during the reading of An American Tragedy
demonstrate Bennett's growing appreciation of the novel's
power and waning annoyance with its stylistic deficiencies.

J32-3   CALVERTON, VICTOR F. The Liberation of American Literature.
New York: Scribner. See Index.
     Calls Dreiser the "father of candid realism."

J32-4   CHAMBERLAIN, JOHN. Farewell to Reform: The Rise, Life, and Decay of the Progressive Mind in America. New York: John Day. See Index. Repub: Chicago: Quadrangle Books, 1965.
Focuses on The Financier and The Titan to demonstrate Dreiser's grasp of late-19th-Century America.

J32-5   KNIGHT, GRANT C. "Literature of Realism: Theodore Dreiser," American Literature and Culture. New York: Long. Pp. 400-13.

J32-6   LEWISOHN, LUDWIG. Expression in America. New York: Harper. Pp. 473-82; See also Index.
Demonstrates Dreiser's power in transmuting experience into expression and sees the correlation between Dreiser's stylistic crudity and the hostility of conservative critics.

J32-7   NATHAN, GEORGE JEAN. "Theodore Dreiser," The Intimate Notebooks of George Jean Nathan. New York: Knopf. Pp. 38-53. Repub: George Jean Nathan, The World of George Jean Nathan. Ed. Charles Angoff. New York: Knopf, 1952. Pp. 66-79.

J32-8   RIDDELL, JOHN, pseud. [Corey Ford]. "Dawn Jawn," In the Worst Possible Taste. New York: Scribners. Pp. 17-27. [Parody].

J32-9   WARD, ALFRED C. American Literature, 1880-1930. New York: Dial. Pp. 111-17.
Demonstrates Dreiser's "determined facing away from romantic idealism."

1933

J33-1   COMBS, GEORGE H. "Theodore Dreiser and James Branch Cabell-- The Unheavenly Twins," These Amazing Moderns. St. Louis: Bethany. Pp. 75-95.

J33-2   DE FABREQUES, JEAN. "Introduction," Jenny Gerhardt. Paris: Catalogne. Pp. v-xii.

J33-3   DELL, FLOYD. Homecoming. New York: Farrar, Rinehart. Pp. 268-70.
Recounts Dell's association with Dreiser in Greenwich Village, particularly during the writing of The "Genius."

WORKS ON

J33-4   EDGAR, PELHAM. "American Realism, Sex, and Theodore
Dreiser," The Art of the Novel. New York: Macmillan.
Pp. 244-54.

J33-5   HICKS, GRANVILLE. The Great Tradition. New York: Macmillan.
See Index. Rev. ed.: New York: Biblo, 1967.
Comments on Dreiser's confusion and ambivalence in
facing the problems and complexities of American life.

J33-6   LEAVIS, FRANK R. "Arnold Bennett: American Version," For
Continuity. Cambridge, England: Fraser. Pp. 97-101.
Repub: Freeport, N.Y.: Books for Libraries, 1968.

J33-7   RASCOE, BURTON. "Theodore Dreiser," Prometheans, Ancient
and Modern. New York: Putnam. Pp. 241-69.

1934

J34-1   ANDERSON, SHERWOOD. "The Dreiser," No Swank. Philadelphia:
Centaur. Pp. 13-16.

J34-2   HALLECK, REUBEN P. "The Novel: Theodore Dreiser 1871-   ,"
The Romance of American Literature. New York: American
Book. Pp. 309-14.

J34-3   HARTWICK, HARRY. "Hindenburg of the Novel," The Foreground
of American Fiction. New York: American Book. Pp. 85-
110.

J34-4   LUCCOCK, HALFORD E. Contemporary American Literature and
Religion. Chicago: Willett, Clark. Pp. 62-67.
Sees Dreiser's as "the most thoroughgoing mechanistic
point of view" in modern American literature.

J34-5   POWYS, JOHN COWPER. Autobiography. New York: Simon. No
Index. Repub: New York: New Directions, 1960.
Scattered references to Dreiser as a supporter and
kindred spirit.

J34-6   RICHARDS, GRANT. Author Hunting: Memories of Years Spent
Mainly in Publishing. New York: Coward-McCann. See
Index. Repub: London: Unicorn, 1960.
Two chapters devoted to Dreiser.

J34-7   VOČADLO, OTAKAR. "Theodore Dreiser," Současná Literatura
Spojených Států. Prague: Laichter. Pp. 144-50.

Parts of Books

1935

J35-1   HAIGHT, ANNE LYON. Banned Books: Informal Notes on Some
        Books Banned for Various Reasons at Various Times and in
        Various Places. New York: Bowker. Pp. 63-64. Rev. ed.:
        New York: Bowker, 1955.
           Brief review of Dreiser censorship.

J35-2   HATCHER, HARLAN. "Theodore Dreiser," Creating the Modern
        American Novel. New York: Farrar, Rinehart. Pp. 34-57.

J35-3   ISH-KISHOR, SULAMITH. "Introduction," Moods: Philosophical
        and Emotional (Cadenced and Declaimed). New York: Simon.
        Pp. v-viii.

J35-4   VAN DOREN, CARL. What Is American Literature? New York:
        Morrow. Pp. 114-18.
           Sees Dreiser's uncompromising view of life as the first
        challenge to Howellsian Realism.

1936

J36-1   BOYNTON, PERCY H. Literature and American Life. Boston:
        Ginn. Pp. 789-92.
           Briefly traces Dreiser's philosophical probings.

J36-2   FREEMAN, JOSEPH. An American Testament: A Narrative of
        Rebels and Romantics. New York: Farrar, Rinehart. See
        Index.
           Briefly discusses Dell's criticism of Dreiser's works.

J36-3   MASTERS, EDGAR LEE. Across Spoon River. New York: Farrar,
        Rinehart. See Index.
           Reminisces about Dreiser as a friend and writer.

J36-4   NATHAN, GEORGE JEAN. "Three Friends: Lewis, O'Neill,
        Dreiser," The Borzoi Reader. Ed. Carl Van Doren. New
        York: Knopf. Pp. 579-615. Repub: Garden City, N.Y.:
        Garden City Publishing Co., 1938.

J36-5   QUINN, ARTHUR H. American Fiction. New York: Appleton-
        Century. Pp. 645-52.
           Sees Dreiser as a writer who could neither think
        clearly nor stir sympathy for characters.

J36-6   TAYLOR, WALTER F. "The Maturity of Naturalism: Theodore
        Dreiser (1871-   ) and Sherwood Anderson (1876-   ),"

A History of American Letters. Boston: American Book.
Pp. 365-80.

1937

J37-1   ADLER, ELMER. Breaking Into Print. New York: Simon.
Pp. 67-71.
Includes a letter from Dreiser's secretary, Harriet
Bissell, describing his manuscript preparation and re-
vision.

J37-2   CARNEGIE, DALE. "God's Mercy and Three Gin Rickeys Brought
a Titan to American Literature," Five-Minute Biographies.
New York: Greenberg. Pp. 235-38.

J37-3   CLEATON, IRENE, and ALLEN CLEATON. Books and Battles:
American Literature, 1920-1930. Boston: Houghton. See
Index.
Numerous references to Dreiser's battles with censors.

J37-4   JOHNS, ORRICK. The Time of Our Lives. New York: Stockpole.
Pp. 325-29.
Recalls the details of Dreiser's visiting Tom Mooney
in prison in 1932.

J37-5   LOGGINS, VERNON. "Dominant Primordial: Theodore Dreiser,"
I Hear America . . . Literature in the United States since
1900. New York: Crowell. Pp. 125-34.

J37-6   McCOLE, C[AMILLE] JOHN. "Theodore Dreiser and the Rise of
American Realism," Lucifer at Large. New York: Longmans.
Pp. 17-54.

J37-7   MULLER, HERBERT J. "Naturalism in America: Theodore Dreiser
and Proletarian Fiction," Modern Fiction: A Study of
Values. New York: Funk. Pp. 199-222; See also Index.

1938

J38-1   ADAMIC, LOUIS. My America: 1928-1938. New York: Harper.
Pp. 109-10.
Undated diary entry for 1931 describing a meeting of
approximately 50 artists and writers at Dreiser's apart-
ment to discuss the state of the nation. Paraphrases
Dreiser's comments to open the meeting.

THEODORE DREISER: A BIBLIOGRAPHY

Parts of Books

1939

J39-1 HANEY, JOHN LOUIS. "Theodore Dreiser," The Story of Our Literature: An Interpretation of the American Spirit, rev. ed. New York: Scribners. Pp. 264-65.

J39-2 HAPGOOD, HUTCHINS. A Victorian in the Modern World. New York: Harcourt. See Index. Repub: Seattle: U. Washington Press, 1972.
Recalls Hapgood's various associations with Dreiser.

J39-3 LUNDKVIST, ARTUR. Tre Amerikaner: Dreiser-Lewis-Anderson. Stockholm: Bonnier. See Index.

J39-4 RASCOE, BURTON. "Introduction," Sister Carrie. New York: Heritage. Pp. v-xii.

J39-5 SMITH, BERNARD. Forces in American Criticism. New York: Harcourt. See Index.
Quotes Floyd Dell and H. L. Mencken on Dreiser.

1940

J40-1 BOYNTON, PERCY H. "Theodore Dreiser," America in Contemporary Fiction. Chicago: U. Chicago Press. Pp. 131-44.

J40-2 VAN DOREN, CARL. "Theodore Dreiser," The American Novel, 1789-1939, rev. ed. New York: Macmillan. Pp. 245-59.

J40-3 WILSON, WILLIAM E. The Wabash. New York: Rinehart. Pp. 312-14.
Describes Dreiser as an atypical Hoosier writer but one who retained his nostalgia for Indiana.

1941

J41-1 CARGILL, OSCAR. Intellectual America. New York: Macmillan. See Index. Repub: New York: Macmillan, 1948.
Discusses Dreiser's works as "the very quintessence of Naturalism."

J41-2 HART, JAMES D. "Dreiser, Theodore," Oxford Companion to American Literature. New York: Oxford U. Press. Pp. 205-06. Repub: New York: Oxford U. Press, 1944.

215

WORKS ON

J41-3   LYONS, EUGENE. The Red Decade: The Stalinist Penetration
        of America. Indianapolis: Bobbs-Merrill. See Index.
        Several brief references to Dreiser's Communistic
        sympathies.

J41-4   QUIN, MIKE, pseud. [Paul William Ryan]. "Dreiser Tells 'Em,"
        More Dangerous Thoughts. San Francisco: People's World.
        Pp. 97-99.

                              1942

J42-1   ANDERSON, SHERWOOD. Sherwood Anderson's Memoirs. New York:
        Harcourt. Pp. 333-40; See also Index.
        Scattered references to Anderson's associations with
        Dreiser, including "Dreiser's Party."

J42-2   KUNITZ, STANLEY J., and HOWARD HAYCRAFT. "Dreiser, Theodore,"
        Twentieth Century Authors. New York: Wilson. Pp. 398-99.

                              1943

J43-1   CROY, HOMER. Country Cured. New York: Harper. Pp. 142-45.
        Recalls working under Dreiser on the Delineator.

J43-2   SCULLY, FRANK. "Theodore Dreiser," Rogues' Gallery: Pro-
        files of My Eminent Contemporaries. Hollywood: Murray.
        Pp. 108-24. Repub: Freeport, N.Y.: Books for Libraries,
        1972.

J43-3   STOVALL, FLOYD. American Idealism. Norman, Okla.: U.
        Oklahoma Press. Pp. 131-36.
        Places Dreiser's literature at the final point of
        decline from idealism.

                              1944

J44-1   ADAMS, J[AMES] DONALD. "The Heavy Hand of Dreiser," The
        Shape of Books to Come. New York: Viking. Pp. 54-83.
        Repub: J. Donald Adams, The Writer's Responsibility.
        London: Secker, Warburg, 1946. Pp. 62-88.

Parts of Books

1946

J46-1   MENCKEN, H. L. "Introduction," An American Tragedy.
         Cleveland: World. Pp. ix-xvi. Repub: Cleveland:
         World, 1948.

J46-2   VAN GELDER, ROBERT. "Notes on the Literary Life," Writers
         and Writing. New York: Scribners. Pp. 1-19.

1947

J47-1   BRODIN, PIERRE. "Theodore Dreiser," Les Écrivains Américains
         du Vingtième Siècle. Paris: Horizons de France. Pp. 11-
         24.

J47-2   FAST, HOWARD. "Introduction," The Best Short Stories of
         Theodore Dreiser. Cleveland: World. Pp. 7-11.

J47-3   MORRIS, LLOYD. "Skepticism of the Young: Puzzled Icono-
         clast," Postscript to Yesterday. New York: Random.
         Pp. 121-30.

J47-4   RASCOE, BURTON. We Were Interrupted. Garden City, N.Y.:
         Doubleday. No Index.
              Scattered references to Rascoe's association with and
         critical attitudes toward Dreiser between 1920 and 1930;
         republishes two Rascoe essays on Dreiser.

J47-5   SNELL, GEORGE. "Theodore Dreiser: Philosopher," The Shapers
         of American Fiction, 1798-1947. New York: Dutton.
         Pp. 233-48.

J47-6   WITHAM, W. TASKER. "The Rise of Realism: Theodore Dreiser,"
         Panorama of American Literature. New York: Daye.
         Pp. 219-23.

J47-7   WOODWARD, WILLIAM E. The Gift of Life: An Autobiography.
         New York: Dutton. See Index.
              Several anecdotes revealing Dreiser's mysticism, in-
         terest in Communism, and publishing problems with Sister
         Carrie.

1948

J48-1   FRIEDE, DONALD. The Mechanical Angel: His Adventures and
         Enterprises in the Glittering 1920's. New York: Knopf.
         See Index.

WORKS ON

Recalls experiences with Dreiser, both as friend and
publisher, particularly the legal entanglements surrounding An American Tragedy.

J48-2   SPILLER, ROBERT E., et al., eds. "Theodore Dreiser,"
         Literary History of the United States. New York: Mac-
         millan. Vol. 2, 1197-1207. Rev. ed.: New York: Mac-
         millan, 1953.

                              1949

J49-1   BANTA, RICHARD E. "Dreiser, Theodore: 1871-1945," Indiana
         Authors and Their Books, 1816-1916. Scranton, Pa.:
         Haddon Craftsmen. Pp. 90-92.

J49-2   FOWLER, GENE. Beau James: The Life and Times of Jimmy
         Walker. New York: Viking. Pp. 36-38.
            Brief but revealing quotations from Sara White
         Dreiser concerning "Theo."

J49-3   GEISMAR, MAXWELL. "Introduction," Sister Carrie. New York:
         Pocket Books. Pp. [7-12]. Repub: Maxwell Geismar,
         American Moderns. New York: Hill, 1958. Pp. 49-53 (as
         "Theodore Dreiser").

J49-4   MAYBERRY, GEORGE. "Introduction," An American Tragedy
         [abridged]. New York: NAL. Pp. [5-6].

                              1950

         o
J50-1   AHNEBRINK, LARS. The Beginnings of Naturalism in American
         Fiction. Uppsala: Lundequistska Bokhendeln. See Index.
         Repub: New York: Russell, 1961.
            Scattered references to Dreiser's relationship with
         Norris, Crane, and Garland.

J50-2   BUDENZ, LOUIS FRANCIS. Men Without Faces: The Communist
         Conspiracy in the U. S. A. New York: Harper. Pp. 242-45.
            Includes Dreiser among those used by the Communists.

J50-3   COMMAGER, HENRY STEELE. "Determinism in Literature," The
         American Mind. New Haven: Yale U. Press. Pp. 108-19.

J50-4   KAZIN, ALFRED. "American Naturalism: Reflections from
         Another Era," The American Writer and the European Tradi-
         tion. Eds. Margaret Denny and William H. Gilman. Min-
         neapolis: U. Minnesota Press. Pp. 121-31.

                              218

THEODORE DREISER: A BIBLIOGRAPHY

J50-5   KEMLER, EDGAR. "How Dreiser Was Managed," The Irreverent
         Mr. Mencken. Boston: Little. Pp. 70-84; See also Index.

J50-6   SIMON, JEAN. "La Génération de 1900: Theodore Dreiser,"
         Le Roman Américain au XXe Siecle. Paris: Boivin.
         Pp. 19-37.

J50-7   TRILLING, LIONEL. "Reality in America," The Liberal Imagina-
         tion. New York: Viking. Pp. 3-21. Repub: Literary
         Opinion in America, rev. ed. Ed. Morton D. Zabel.
         New York: Harper, 1951. Pp. 404-16; Kazin and Shapiro,
         pp. 132-45; See I55-1. Lydenberg, pp. 87-95; See I71-1.
         Second half of this essay a revision of Trilling's
         review of The Bulwark, Nation, 20 Apr. 1946.

                              1951

J51-1   DEEGAN, DOROTHY YOST. The Stereotype of the Single Woman in
         American Novels. New York: King's Crown. Pp. 49-56.
            Praises Dreiser's tolerant handling of the "fallen"
         woman in Jennie Gerhardt.

J51-2   DRUMMOND, EDWARD J. "Theodore Dreiser: Shifting Naturalism,"
         Fifty Years of the American Novel: A Christian Appraisal.
         Ed. Harold C. Gardiner. New York: Scribners. Pp. 33-47.

J51-3   EHRMANN, BERTHA K. Max Ehrmann: A Poet's Life. Boston:
         Humphries. Pp. 37-39.
            Quotes Terre Haute poet's praise of Dreiser's courage
         and disappointment at his personality.

J51-4   HOFFMAN, FREDERICK J. The Modern Novel in America. Chicago:
         Regnery. Pp. 41-51. Repub: Chicago: Gateway Editions,
         1956.
            Dreiser's novels analyzed as part of "pre-war Natural-
         ism."

J51-5   MANCHESTER, WILLIAM R. Disturber of the Peace: The Life of
         H. L. Mencken. New York: Harper. See Index.
            Frequent references to Mencken's association with and
         defense of Dreiser.

J51-6   MORDELL, ALBERT. "My Relations with Theodore Dreiser," My
         Relations with Theodore Dreiser; Haldeman-Julius as a
         Writer on Freethought; Some Reflections on Freethought;
         And Haldeman-Julius Publications in Freethought. Ed.
         Emanuel Haldeman-Julius. Girard, Kans.: Haldeman-Julius.
         Pp. 3-18.

WORKS ON

J51-7   STRAUMANN, HEINRICH. American Literature in the Twentieth
         Century. London: Hutchinson. Pp. 43-45.
              Notes the complexity and inconsistency of Dreiser's
         determinism.

J51-8   WHICHER, GEORGE F. "Respectability Defied," The Literature
         of the American People: A Historical and Critical Survey.
         Ed. Arthur Hobson Quinn. New York: Appleton. Pp. 847-51.

J51-9   ZASURSKIĬ, YASEN N. "Forward," Essays and Articles by Theo-
         dore Dreiser. Moscow: Foreign Languages Publishing
         House. Pp. 5-16.

                              1952

J52-1   BROOKS, VAN WYCK. "Theodore Dreiser," The Confident Years:
         1885-1915. New York: Dutton. Pp. 301-20. See also
         Index. Repub: New York: Dutton, 1955.

J52-2   MILLER, HENRY. The Books of My Life. London: Owens.
         Pp. 217-20. Repub: New York: New Directions, 1957.
              Comments on the influence of Dreiser's honesty and
         fullness.

J52-3   SCHERMAN, DAVID E., and ROSEMARIE REDLICH. "Theodore
         Dreiser," Literary America. New York: Dodd. Pp. 134-35.

J52-4   WAGENKNECHT, EDWARD. "Theodore Dreiser, The Mystic Natural-
         ist," Cavalcade of the American Novel. New York: Holt.
         Pp. 281-93.

J52-5   WEST, RAY B., JR. The Short Story in America, 1900-1950.
         Chicago: Regnery. Pp. 33-44.
              Discusses Dreiser's general lack of facility with the
         short story.

                              1953

J53-1   BLACKSTOCK, WALTER. "Theodore Dreiser's Literary Style,"
         Florida State University Studies. Ed. Weymouth T. Jordon.
         Tallahassee: Florida State U. Pp. 95-116.

J53-2   GEISMAR, MAXWELL. "Theodore Dreiser: The Double Soul,"
         Rebels and Ancestors: The American Novel, 1890-1915.
         Boston: Houghton. Pp. 287-379.

THEODORE DREISER: A BIBLIOGRAPHY

J53-3   JONES, HOWARD MUMFORD, and WALTER RIDEOUT, eds. Letters of
         Sherwood Anderson. Boston: Little. See Index.
         Eight letters to Dreiser and numerous other references.

                                1954

J54-1   BLACKSTOCK, WALTER. "Dreiser's Dramatization of American
         Success," Florida State University Studies. Ed. Weymouth
         T. Jordon. Tallahassee: Florida State U. Pp. 107-30.

J54-2   COWLEY, MALCOLM. The Literary Situation. New York: Viking.
         See Index.
            Frequently uses Dreiser to typify the 1920's and
         1930's.

J54-3   CUNLIFFE, MARCUS. "Realism in American Prose: From Howells
         to Dreiser," The Literature of the United States. Balti-
         more: Penguin. See Index.

J54-4   DUFFEY, BERNARD I. The Chicago Renaissance in American
         Letters. East Lansing: Michigan State U. Press. See
         Index.
            Frequent references to Dreiser's participation.

J54-5   GELFANT, BLANCHE H. "Theodore Dreiser: The Portrait Novel,"
         The American City Novel. Norman: U. Oklahoma Press.
         Pp. 42-94; See also Index.

J54-6   GOLD, MICHAEL. "The Dreiser I Knew," The Mike Gold Reader.
         Ed. Samuel Sillen. New York: International. Pp. 159-64.

J54-7   HANSON, HARRY. "Introduction," An American Tragedy. New
         York: Limited Editions Club. Pp. vii-x.

J54-8   KNIGHT, GRANT C. The Strenuous Age in American Literature.
         Chapel Hill: U. North Carolina Press. Pp. 36-39.
         Analyzes the historical significance of Sister Carrie.

                                1955

J55-1   BROOKS, VAN WYCK. John Sloan: A Painter's Life. New York:
         Dutton. See Index.
            Demonstrates Sloan's annoyance with Dreiser and The
         "Genius."

WORKS ON

J55-2   DAVIS, DAVID BRION. "Dreiser and Naturalism Revisited,"
         The Stature of Theodore Dreiser. Eds. Alfred Kazin and
         Charles Shapiro. Bloomington, Ind.: Indiana U. Press.
         Pp. 225-36.

J55-3   KAZIN, ALFRED. "Introduction," The Stature of Theodore
         Dreiser. Eds. Alfred Kazin and Charles Shapiro. Bloom-
         ington, Ind.: Indiana U. Press. Pp. 3-12. Repub:
         Literature in America. Ed. Philip Rahv. New York:
         Meridian, 1957. Pp. 323-33 (as "Theodore Dreiser and His
         Critics"); Lydenberg, pp. 11-21 (as "The Stature of Theo-
         dore Dreiser"; See I71-1).

J55-4   LYNN, KENNETH. "Theodore Dreiser: The Man of Ice," The
         Dream of Success. Boston: Little. Pp. 13-74. Repub:
         Lydenberg, pp. 37-44 (as "Dreiser and the Success Dream";
         See I71-1).

J55-5   REYNOLDS, QUENTIN. The Fiction Factory. New York: Random.
         Pp. 147-51.
             Comments on Dreiser's association with Street and
         Smith.

J55-6   RICHARDS, ROBERT FULTON. "Dreiser, Theodore," Concise Dic-
         tionary of American Literature. New York: Philosophical
         Library. Pp. 69-71.

J55-7   SIEVERS, WIEDER DAVID. "The Post-War Era--Transition: Theo-
         dore Dreiser," Freud on Broadway: A History of Psycho-
         analysis and the American Dream. New York: Hermitage
         House. Pp. 66-68.

J55-8   SPILLER, ROBERT. "Second Renaissance: Dreiser, Frost,"
         The Cycle of American Literature. New York: Macmillan.
         Pp. 211-42.

J55-9   UNTERMEYER, LOUIS. "Theodore Dreiser," The Makers of the
         Modern World. New York: Simon. Pp. 434-43.

1956

J56-1   ANGOFF, CHARLES. H. L. Mencken: A Portrait from Memory.
         New York: Yoseloff. Pp. 99-101.
             Recalls Dreiser's annoyance with Mencken's insensi-
         tivity to his novels, particularly An American Tragedy.

J56-2   BROOKS, VAN WYCK, and OTTO L. BETTMANN. "The Confident
        Years: Theodore Dreiser," A Pictorial History of Ameri-
        can Literature. London: Dent. Pp. 201-05.

J56-3   DOS PASSOS, JOHN. The Theme Is Freedom. New York: Dodd.
        Pp. 73-88.
        Narrates the experiences in Harlan County and their
        aftermath.

J56-4   FARRELL, JAMES T. "Introduction," The Best Short Stories of
        Theodore Dreiser. Cleveland: World. Pp. 9-12. Repub:
        Greenwich, Conn.: Fawcett, 1961. Pp. vii-x.

J56-5   KWIAT, JOSEPH J. "Theodore Dreiser; The Writer and Early
        Twentieth-Century American Society," Sprache und Literatur
        Englands und Amerikas: Lehrgangsvortrage der Akademie
        Comburg, II. Ed. Carl A. Weber. Tubingen: Niemeyer.
        Pp. 135-50.

J56-6   RIDEOUT, WALTER B. The Radical Novel in the United States,
        1900-1954. Cambridge: Harvard U. Press. See Index.
        Brief references and comparisons but no sustained
        discussion.

J56-7   SINCLAIR, UPTON. The Cup of Fury. Great Neck, N.Y.:
        Channel. Pp. 116-23.
        Anecdotes and impressions of Dreiser as friend and
        writer.

1957

J57-1   ANDERSON, CARL L. The Swedish Acceptance of American
        Literature. Philadelphia: U. Pennsylvania Press. See
        Index.

J57-2   FARRELL, JAMES T. "Introduction," Sister Carrie. New York:
        Sagamore. Pp. vii-xv.

J57-3   LYNN, KENNETH S. "Introduction," Sister Carrie. New York:
        Holt. Pp. v-xvi. Repub: Pizer, pp. 509-18; See 170-1.

J57-4   WOLFE, DON M. "Theodore Dreiser and the Human Enigma," The
        Image of Man in America. Dallas: Southern Methodist U.
        Press. Pp. 317-37. Repub: New York: Crowell, 1970.

WORKS ON

1958

J58-1   SHAPIRO, CHARLES. "Jennie Gerhardt: The American Family and
         the American Dream," Twelve Original Essays on Great
         American Novels. Ed. Charles Shapiro. Detroit: Wayne
         State U. Press. Pp. 177-95.

J58-2   SKARD, SIGMUND. American Studies in Europe. 2 Vols. Phila-
         delphia: U. Pennsylvania Press. See Index.
         Assesses Dreiser's popularity abroad.

J58-3   STEWART, RANDALL. American Literature and Christian Doctrine.
         Baton Route: Louisiana State U. Pp. 113-20.
         Sees An American Tragedy as a touchstone of naturalis-
         tic amorality.

1959

J59-1   ELIAS, ROBERT H. "Preface," Letters of Theodore Dreiser:
         A Selection. Ed. Robert H. Elias. Philadelphia: U.
         Pennsylvania Press. Vol. 1, 5-9.

J59-2   GOODFELLOW, DONALD M. "Theodore Dreiser and the American
         Dream," Six Novelists: Stendahl, Dostoevski, Tolstoy,
         Hardy, Dreiser, and Proust. Eds. William M. Schulte et
         al. Pittsburg: Carnegie Institute of Technology Press.
         Pp. 53-66. Repub: Freeport, N.Y.: Books for Libraries,
         1972.

J59-3   MAY, HENRY F. The End of American Innocence: A Study of
         the First Years of Our Own Time, 1912-1917. New York:
         Knopf. See Index.
         Calls Dreiser "in a sense the only real naturalist in
         our literature."

J59-4   TAYLOR, DWIGHT. "The Life of the Party," Joy Ride. New York:
         Putnam's. Pp. 221-33.

J59-5   WASSERSTROM, WILLIAM. Heiress of All the Ages: Sex and
         Sentiment in the Genteel Tradition. Minneapolis: U.
         Minnesota Press. Pp. 82-84.
         Sees Sister Carrie's uniqueness in Dreiser's disregard
         for the past and family ties.

Parts of Books

1960

J60-1 FIEDLER, LESLIE A. Love and Death in the American Novel.
New York: Criterion. Pp. 241-48. Repub: Cleveland:
World, 1962; Lydenberg, pp. 45-51 (as "Dreiser and the
Sentimental Novel"; See I71-1).

J60-2 FOSTER, CHARLES H. "The 'Theonomous Analysis' in American
Culture," Studies in American Culture: Dominant Ideas
and Images. Eds. Joseph J. Kwiat and Mary C. Turpie.
Minneapolis: U. Minnesota Press. Pp. 189-206.

J60-3 HOWARD, LEON. Literature and the American Tradition.
Garden City, N.Y.: Doubleday. Pp. 242-46.
Examines the tension between Dreiser's belief in
social evolution and his pity for life's victims.

J60-4 KAZIN, ALFRED. "General Introduction," Sister Carrie.
New York: Dell. Pp. 9-21. Repub: Alfred Kazin, Con-
temporaries. Boston: Little, 1962. Pp. 87-99 (as
"Dreiser: The Esthetic of Realism").
This introduction also appears in Dell editions of
The Financier, The Titan, and An American Tragedy.

J60-5 NYREN, DOROTHY, ed. "Dreiser, Theodore (1871-1945)," A
Library of Literary Criticism. New York: Ungar.
Pp. 145-50. Repub: New York: Ungar, 1961.
Contains excerpts from fifteen of the foremost articles
and books on Dreiser and his work.

J60-6 SPRINGER, ANNE M. "Theodore Dreiser," The American Novel in
Germany: A Study of the Critical Reception of Eight
American Novelists Between the Two World Wars. Hamburg:
Cram, De Gruyter. Pp. 60-74.

J60-7 THORP, WILLARD. American Writing in the Twentieth Century.
Cambridge, Mass.: Harvard U. Press. Pp. 164-68.
Comments on the shifts in Dreiser's Naturalistic
philosophy.

1961

J61-1 AARON, DANIEL. Writers on the Left. New York: Harcourt.
See Index.
Focuses on Dreiser's involvement in Communist causes.

THEODORE DREISER: A BIBLIOGRAPHY

J61-2 ASSELINEAU, ROGER. "Theodore Dreiser's Transcendentalism,"
       English Studies Today. Ed. G. A. Bonnard. Bern: Francke
       Verlag. Pp. 233-43.

J61-3 FORGUE, GUY J., ed. Letters of H. L. Mencken. New York:
       Knopf. See Index.
       Includes eighty-four letters to Dreiser.

J61-4 FROHOCK, WILBUR M. "Lionel Trilling and the American Real-
       ity," Strangers to This Ground. Dallas: Southern Metho-
       dist U. Press. Pp. 31-34.

J61-5 LOMBARDO, AGOSTINO. "Lettere di Dreiser," La Ricerca del
       Vero: Saggi sulla Tradizione Letteraria Americana. Rome:
       Edizioni di Storia e Letteratura. Pp. 309-15.

J61-6 ROSS, DANFORTH. The American Short Story. Minneapolis: U.
       Minnesota Press. Pp. 28-29.
       Briefly discusses Dreiser's achievement in terms of
       "The Lost Phoebe" and "Typhoon."

J61-7 SCHORER, MARK. Sinclair Lewis: An American Life. New York:
       McGraw-Hill. See Index.
       Numerous references to Lewis's attitudes toward and
       entanglements with Dreiser.

J61-8 THORP, WILLARD. "Afterword," Sister Carrie. New York: NAL.
       Pp. 467-75.

J61-9 WRIGHT, AUSTIN McGIFFERT. The American Short Story in the
       Twenties. Chicago: U. Chicago Press. See Index.

                              1962

J62-1 BOWERS, CLAUDE G. "Memories of Theodore Dreiser," My Life:
       The Memoirs of Claude Bowers. New York: Simon. Pp. 153-
       72.

J62-2 BROWN, DEMING B. "Sinclair Lewis and Theodore Dreiser,"
       Soviet Attitudes Toward American Writing. Princeton:
       Princeton U. Press. Pp. 239-71.

J62-3 FARRELL, JAMES T. "Introduction," Theodore Dreiser. Ed.
       James T. Farrell. New York: Dell. Pp. 7-15.

J62-4 GEISMAR, MAXWELL. "Society and the Novel," A Time of Harvest:
       American Literature 1910-1960. Ed. Robert E. Spiller.
       New York: Hill. Pp. 33-41.

THEODORE DREISER: A BIBLIOGRAPHY

J62-5   KAZIN, ALFRED. "Theodore Dreiser, 1871-1945: Introduction," Major American Writers. Gen. ed. Perry Miller. New York: Harcourt. Vol. 2, 461-72.

J62-6   LENGEL, WILLIAM C. "Introduction," A Gallery of Women. Greenwich, Conn.: Fawcett. Pp. vii-x.

J62-7   LENGEL, WILLIAM C. "The Thirteenth Man," Twelve Men. Greenwich, Conn.: Fawcett. Pp. vii-x.

J62-8   WARREN, ROBERT PENN. "Introduction," An American Tragedy. Cleveland: World. Pp. 7-12.

J62-9   WHITE, MORTON G., and LUCIA WHITE. "Disappointment in New York: Frank Norris and Theodore Dreiser," The Intellectual Versus the City. Cambridge, Mass: Harvard U. Press. Pp. 117-38.

1963

J63-1   KAZIN, ALFRED. "Introduction," Jennie Gerhardt. New York: Dell. Pp. 5-12.

J63-2   PUTZEL, MAX. The Man in the Mirror: William Marion Reedy and His Magazine. Cambridge, Mass.: Harvard U. Press. See Index.
        Frequent references and two chapters devoted to Reedy's and Lyon's friendship for and support of Dreiser.

J63-3   SCHWAB, ARNOLD T. James Gibbons Huneker: Critic of the Seven Arts. Stanford: Stanford U. Press. Pp. 199-201.
        Discusses Huneker's reaction to Jennie Gerhardt in manuscript and prints a detailed letter from Huneker to Dreiser suggesting revisions.

J63-4   SHEEAN, VINCENT. Dorothy and Red. Boston: Houghton. See Index.
        Develops through analysis and correspondence Dorothy Thompson's and Sinclair Lewis's attitude toward Dreiser during the trip to Russia and the plagiarism incident that followed.

1964

J64-1   ALLEN, WALTER. The Modern Novel. New York: Dutton. Pp. 81-86.

Sees Dreiser's virtue in his "painful, almost agonized fidelity to the grain of life."

J64-2　BURBANK, REX. Anderson. New York: Twayne. Pp. 49-51.
Contrasts Cowperwood and McPherson.

J64-3　DAHLBERG, EDWARD. "My Friends: Stieglitz, Anderson, and Dreiser," Alms for Oblivion. Minneapolis: U. Minnesota Press. Pp. 3-15.

J64-4　MIZENER, ARTHUR. The Sense of Life in the Modern Novel. Boston: Houghton. Pp. 9-12.
Notes the importance of Dreiser's "incredibly silly" philosophies in releasing his creative imagination.

J64-5　SMITH, HENRY NASH. "The Search for a Capitalist Hero: Businessmen in American Fiction," The Business Establishment. Ed. Earl F. Cheit. New York: Wiley. Pp. 77-112.

J64-6　WITHAM, W. TASKER. The Adolescent in the American Novel: 1920-1960. New York: Ungar. See Index.
Frequent analyses of Dreiser's treatment of adolescent behavior, focusing primarily on Clyde Griffiths.

1965

J65-1　BERRYMAN, JOHN. "Afterword," The Titan. New York: NAL. Pp. 503-11.

J65-2　BERTHOFF, WARNER. "Lives of the Americans: Theodore Dreiser," The Ferment of Realism: American Literature 1884-1919. New York: Free Press. Pp. 235-44.

J65-3　CAWELTI, JOHN G. "Dream or Rat Race: The Failure of Success," Apostles of the Self-Made Man. Chicago: U. Chicago Press. Pp. 227-36.

J65-4　EDELSTEIN, ARTHUR. "Introduction," Sister Carrie. New York: Harper. Pp. xv-xix.

J65-5　KRAFT, HY. "Foreword," The Tobacco Men, by Borden Deal. New York: Holt. Pp. 11-13.

J65-6　MILLGATE, MICHAEL. "Introduction," Sister Carrie. London: Oxford U. Press. Pp. ix-xxiv.

THEODORE DREISER: A BIBLIOGRAPHY

J65-7   MORGAN, H. WAYNE. "Theodore Dreiser: The Naturalist as Humanist," _American Writers in Rebellion from Mark Twain to Dreiser._ New York: Hill. Pp. 146-89.

J65-8   SCHNEIDER, ROBERT W. "Theodore Dreiser: The Cry of Despair," _Five Novelists of the Progressive Era._ New York: Columbia U. Press. Pp. 153-204.

J65-9   SIMPSON, CLAUDE M., JR. "Theodore Dreiser, _Sister Carrie_," _The American Novel from James Fenimore Cooper to William Faulkner._ Ed. Wallace Stegner. New York: Basic Books. Pp. 106-16.

J65-10   SPILLER, ROBERT E. _The Third Dimension._ New York: Macmillan. _See_ Index.
Sees Dreiser's work as the beginning of a "new process of symbolization of actual life."

1966

J66-1   CHAPMAN, ARNOLD. "Theodore Dreiser: Triumph of the Trivial," _The Spanish-American Reception of United States Fiction, 1920-1940._ Los Angeles: U. California Press. Pp. 112-17.

J66-2   FILLER, LOUIS. "A Tale of Two Authors: Theodore Dreiser and David Graham Phillips," _New Voices in American Studies._ Eds. Ray B. Browne et al. Lafayette, Ind.: Purdue U. Press. Pp. 35-48.

J66-3   FRENCH, WARREN. _The Social Novel at the End of an Era._ Carbondale: Southern Illinois U. Press. Pp. 173-74. Contrasts _An American Tragedy_ and _Native Son._

J66-4   GREBSTEIN, SHELDON N. "_An American Tragedy_: Theme and Structure," _The Twenties, Poetry and Prose: Twenty Critical Essays._ Eds. Richard Langford and William E. Taylor. Deland, Fla.: Everett/Edwards. Pp. 62-66.

J66-5   KRAMER, DALE. _Chicago Rennaissance._ New York: Appleton. _See_ Index.
Three chapters devoted to or significantly involving Dreiser.

J66-6   LIPTZIN, SOL. _The Jew in American Literature._ New York: Bloch. Pp. 159-66.
Discusses Dreiser's anti-Semitism.

Theodore Dreiser: A Bibliography

J66-7 NOLTE, WILLIAM H. H. L. Mencken: Literary Critic. Middleton, Conn.: Wesleyan U. Press. See Index.
Frequent analyses of Mencken's role in Dreiser's career.

J66-8 POIRIER, RICHARD. "Panoramic Environment and the Anonymity of the Self," A World Elsewhere: The Place of Style in American Literature. New York: Oxford U. Press. Pp. 208-52. Repub: London: Chatto, 1967. Pizer, pp. 574-83; See 170-1.

J66-9 PRICE, LAWRENCE MARSDEN. The Reception of United States Literature in Germany. Chapel Hill: U. North Carolina Press. See Index.

J66-10 STONE, EDWARD. Voices of Despair. Athens, Ohio: Ohio U. Press. See Index.
Frequent references to Dreiser's Naturalistic concepts.

J66-11 WEIMER, DAVID R. "Heathen Catacombs: Theodore Dreiser," The City as Metaphor. New York: Random. Pp. 65-77.

J66-12 WILSON, WILLIAM E. Indiana: A History. Bloomington, Ind.: Indiana U. Press. See Index.
Extensive comparison of the careers of Dreiser and Tarkington.

J66-13 ZIFF, LARZER. "A Decade's Delay: Theodore Dreiser," The American 1890s. New York: Viking. Pp. 334-48.

1967

J67-1 ANDREWS, CLARENCE A. "Introduction," Sister Carrie. New York: Airmont. Pp. 3-9.

J67-2 HANSEN, ERIK A. "Theodore Dreiser," Fremmede Digtere i det 20 Arhundrede. Ed. Sven M. Kristensen. Copenhagen: Gad. Vol. 1, 217-28.

J67-3 MARTIN, JAY. "The Visible and Invisible Cities," Harvests of Change: American Literature, 1865-1914. Englewood Cliffs, N.J.: Prentice-Hall. Pp. 252-63.

J67-4 RULAND, RICHARD. The Rediscovery of American Literature: Premises of Critical Taste, 1900-1940. Cambridge, Mass.: Harvard U. Press. See Index.
Analyzes the critical reactions to Dreiser's work.

THEODORE DREISER: A BIBLIOGRAPHY

Parts of Books

J67-5   ZIFF, LARZER. "Afterword," The Financier. New York: NAL.
         Pp. 451-60.

J67-6   ZIFF, LARZER. "Afterword," The "Genius." New York: NAL.
         Pp. 719-28.

1968

J68-1   ANISIMOV, IVAN I. Mastera Kul'tury. Moscow: Khudozhest-
         vennaĭa literatura. See Index. Repub: Moscow:
         Khudozhestvennaĭa literatura, 1971.

J68-2   ANZILOTTI, ROLANDO. "Theodore Dreiser: Le Fonti e il
         Metodo del Romanziere," Studi e Ricerche di Letteratura
         Americana. Firenze: La Nuova Italia. Pp. 183-210.

J68-3   DEBOUZY, MARIANNA. La Genèse de l'Esprit de Révolte dans le
         Roman Américain, 1875-1915. Paris: Lettres Modernes.
         See Index.

J68-4   NOBLE, DAVID W. "The Naturalists: Frank Norris, Stephen
         Crane, Theodore Dreiser," The Eternal Adam and the New
         World Garden. New York: Braziller. Pp. 124-32.

J68-5   PIZER, DONALD, ed. "Theodore Dreiser," Hamlin Garland's
         Diaries. San Marino, Calif.: Huntington Library.
         Pp. 123-24.

J68-6   ROSENTHAL, T. G. "Introduction," The Financier. London:
         Panther. Pp. [xi-xix]. Repub: The Titan. London:
         Panther, 1968. Pp. [ix-xvii].

J68-7   WAGER, WILLIS. American Literature: A World View.
         New York: New York U. Press. Pp. 223-35.
         Brief summary of Dreiser's career and neglect in
         America.

1969

J69-1   ALLEN, WALTER. The Urgent West: The American Dream and
         Modern Man. New York: Dutton. Pp. 193-95.
         Considers the influence of the Midwest on Dreiser.

J69-2   AUCHINCLOSS, LOUIS. "Introduction," Sister Carrie.
         Columbus, Ohio: Merrill. Pp. v-xi.

231

WORKS ON

J69-3   BODE, CARL. Mencken. Carbondale: Southern Illinois U.
        Press. See Index.
        Frequent references to the Dreiser-Mencken relation-
        ship.

J69-4   CLAYTON, CHARLES C. Little Mack: Joseph B. McCullagh of
        The St. Louis Globe-Democrat. Carbondale: Southern
        Illinois U. Press. See Index.
        Relies on and generally verifies Dreiser's evaluations
        of McCullagh in A Book About Myself.

J69-5   DEKLE, BERNARD. "Theodore Dreiser: A Tortured Life," Pro-
        files of Modern American Authors. Rutland, Vt.: Tuttle.
        Pp. 38-43.

J69-6   HILFER, ANTHONY CHANNELL. The Revolt from the Village:
        1915-1930. Chapel Hill: U. North Carolina. Pp. 24-27.
        Uses Dreiser's autobiographical writings to demonstrate
        the charm and danger of the small town.

J69-7   ROSENBLATT, PAUL. "Woolman and Dreiser," John Woolman.
        New York: Twayne. Pp. 122-25.

J69-8   SAALBACH, ROBERT PALMER. "Introduction," Selected Poems
        from Moods. New York: Exposition. Pp. 9-22.

J69-9   SALZMAN, JACK. "Introduction," Sister Carrie. New York:
        Johnson Reprint. Pp. v-x.

J69-10 SPATZ, JONAS. "Dreiser's Bulwark: An Archaic Masterpiece,"
        The Forties: Fiction, Poetry, Drama. Ed. Warren French.
        Deland, Fla.: Everett/Edwards. Pp. 155-62.

J69-11 TAYLOR, GORDON O. "The Voice of Want: Frank Norris and
        Theodore Dreiser," The Passages of Thought: Psychological
        Representation in the American Novel, 1870-1900. New
        York: Oxford U. Press. Pp. 136-57.

J69-12 WHITE, RAY LEWIS, ed. Sherwood Anderson's Memoirs: A
        Critical Edition. Chapel Hill: U. North Carolina Press.
        See Index.
        Numerous references to Dreiser and his work.

J69-13 ZASURSKIĬ, YASEN. [Introduction], Amerikanskaĩa Tragediĩa.
        Moscow: Khudozhestvennaĩa literatura.

THEODORE DREISER: A BIBLIOGRAPHY

1970

J70-1   BERRY, THOMAS ELLIOTT. The Newspaper in the American Novel,
        1900-1969. Metuchen, N.J.: Scarecrow. See Index.
        Frequent references to Dreiser's treatment of news-
        papers in his fiction and autobiographies.

J70-2   BLOCK, HASKELL. "Dreiser's An American Tragedy," Naturalis-
        tic Triptych: The Fictive and the Real in Zola, Mann,
        and Dreiser. New York: Random. Pp. 54-77.

J70-3   EARNEST, ERNEST. The Single Vision: The Alienation of
        American Intellectuals. New York: New York U. Press.
        See Index.
        Traces Dreiser's role in the anti-puritanism crusade
        between 1910 and 1930.

J70-4   GEISMAR, MAXWELL. "The Shifting Illusion: Dream and Fact,"
        American Dreams, American Nightmares. Ed. David Madden.
        Carbondale: Southern Illinois U. Press. Pp. 45-57.

J70-5   GILMER, WALKER. Horace Liveright: Publisher of the
        Twenties. New York: Lewis. See Index.
        Two chapters and frequent references reveal Dreiser's
        association with Liveright.

J70-6   HENSLEY, DONALD M. Burton Rascoe. New York: Twayne. See
        Index.
        Reveals Rascoe's opinion and frequent support of
        Dreiser.

J70-7   GARRATY, JOHN A. "A Century of Realism in American Litera-
        ture," Interpreting American History: Conversations with
        Historians. New York: Macmillan. Vol. 2, 289-311.
        Repub: American Heritage, 21 (June 1970), 12-15, 86-90
        (as "A Century of American Realism").
        Interview with Alfred Kazin.

J70-8   LEONARD, NEIL. "Theodore Dreiser and Music," Challenges in
        American Culture. Eds. Ray B. Browne et al. Bowling
        Green, Ohio: Bowling Green U. Popular Press. Pp. 242-50.

J70-9   SALZMAN, JACK. "Introduction," Sister Carrie. Indianapolis:
        Bobbs-Merrill. Pp. ix-xxiii.

J70-10 SAPORTA, MARC. "Theodore Dreiser (1871-1945)," Histoire du
        Roman Américain. Paris: Seghers. Pp. 130-34.

WORKS ON

1971

J71-1   ANZILOTTI, ROLANDO. "Introduzione," Racconti. Trans. Diana
        Bonaccossa. Bari, Italy: De Donato. Pp. vii-xxii.

J71-2   BORGES, JORGE LUIS. An Introduction to American Literature.
        Eds. and trans. L. Clark Keating and Robert O. Evans.
        Lexington: U. Kentucky Press. P. 46.
        Classifies Dreiser a Romantic "at heart."

J71-3   CHURCHILL, ALLEN. The Literary Decade. Englewood Cliffs,
        N.J.: Prentice-Hall. See Index.
        Numerous references and three chapters in which
        Dreiser figures prominently.

J71-4   COHN, RUBY. Dialogue in American Drama. Bloomington:
        Indiana U. Press. Pp. 272-76.
        Comments on Dreiser's weaknesses as a playwright,
        specifically in his use of dialogue.

J71-5   DE JOVINE, F. ANTHONY. The Young Hero in American Fiction.
        New York: Appleton. See Index.
        An American Tragedy used to demonstrate characteriza-
        tion, theme, and style.

J71-6   DENISOVA, T. [Afterword], Sestra Kerri. Kiev: Dnipro.

J71-7   GINGRICH, ARNOLD. Nothing But People. New York: Crown.
        See Index.
        Recalls his attempt to patch up a feud between Mencken
        and Dreiser.

J71-8   GLICKSBERG, CHARLES I. "Dreiser and Sexual Freedom," The
        Sexual Revolution in Modern American Literature. The
        Hague: Martinus Nijhoff. Pp. 33-46.

J71-9   GREBSTEIN, SHELDON NORMAN. "Theodore Dreiser (1871-1945),"
        The Politics of Twentieth Century Novelists. Ed. George
        A. Panichas. New York: Hawthorn. Pp. 231-50.

J71-10 KATZ, JOSEPH. "Dummy: The 'Genius,' by Theodore Dreiser,"
        Proof: The Yearbook of American Bibliographical and
        Textual Studies. Ed. Joseph Katz. Vol. 1. Columbia:
        U. South Carolina Press. Pp. 330-57.

J71-11 KRAFT, HY. "Inside Dreiser," On My Way to the Theater.
        New York: Macmillan. Pp. 59-103.

THEODORE DREISER: A BIBLIOGRAPHY

J71-12 MOTTRAM, ERIC. "The Hostile Environment and the Survival
Artist," The American Novel and the Nineteen Twenties.
Eds. Malcolm Bradbury and David Palmer. Stratford-Upon-
Avon Studies 13. London: Arnold. Pp. 233-62.

J71-13 PIPER, HENRY DAN. "Social Criticism in the American Novel of
the Nineteen Twenties," The American Novel and the Nineteen Twenties. Eds. Malcolm Bardbury and David Palmer.
Stratford-Upon-Avon Studies 13. London: Arnold. Pp. 59-
83.

J71-14 PIRINSKA, PAVLINA. "Theodore Dreiser 1871-1945," Six Writers
and Their Themes: Theodore Dreiser, Sinclair Lewis, F.
Scott Fitzgerald, Ernest Hemingway, John Steinbeck, William
Faulkner. Sofia. Pp. 1-23.

J71-15 STENERSON, DOUGLAS C. H. L. Mencken: Iconoclast from
Baltimore. Chicago: U. Chicago Press. See Index.
Discusses Mencken's admiration for Dreiser and his
many literary battles in Dreiser's behalf.

1972

J72-1 BENARDETE, JANE. "Theodore Dreiser: Native American
Naturalist," American Realism. New York: Putnam's.
Pp. 313-17.

J72-2 BLAKE, FAY M. The Strike in the American Novel. Metuchen,
N.J.: Scarecrow. Pp. 83-85.
Notes Dreiser's use of the strike to measure Hurst-
wood's disintegration.

J72-3 BRIDGEWATER, PATRICK. "Fictional Superman: Jack London and
Theodore Dreiser," Nietzsche in Anglosaxony. Leicester,
England: Leicester U. Press. Pp. 163-72.

J72-4 FURST, LILIAN R. "A Question of Choice in the Naturalistic
Novel: Zola's Thérèse Raquin and Dreiser's An American
Tragedy," Modern American Fiction: Insights and Foreign
Lights. Eds. Wolodymyr T. Zyla and Wendell M. Aycock.
Proceedings of the Comparative Literature Symposium.
Vol. 5. Lubbock: Interdepartmental Committee on Com-
parative Literature. Pp. 39-55.

J72-5 GERBER, PHILIP L. "Introduction," Trilogy of Desire.
New York: World. Pp. v-xv.

WORKS ON

J72-6   GRIFFIN, ROBERT J. "Carrie and Music: A Note on Dreiser's
         Technique," From Irving to Steinbeck: Studies of American
         Literature in Honor of Harry R. Warfel. Eds. Motley
         Deakin and Peter Lisca. Gainesville: U. Florida Press.
         Pp. 73-81.

J72-7   HOFFMAN, MICHAEL J. "From Realism to Naturalism: Sister
         Carrie and the Sentimentality of Nihilism," The Subversive
         Vision. Port Washington, N.Y.: Kennikat. Pp. 139-53.

J72-8   HUBBELL, JAY B. Who Are the Major American Writers? Durham:
         Duke U. Press. See Index.
             Considers Dreiser's reputation among critics, book
         reviewers, English professors, and anthologists.

J72-9   KATZ, JOSEPH. "Theodore Dreiser and Stephen Crane: Studies
         in a Literary Relationship," Stephen Crane in Transition:
         Centenary Essays. Ed. Joseph Katz. DeKalb: Northern
         Illinois U. Press. Pp. 174-204.

J72-10   LANG, HANS-JOACHIM. "Dreiser: Jennie Gerhardt," Der Ameri-
         kanische Roman: Von den Anfangen bis dur Gegenwart. Ed.
         Hans-Joachim Lang. Dusseldorf: August Bagel Verlag.
         Pp. 194-218, 400-05.

J72-11   MOOKERJEE, R. N. "The Emerging Social Critic: The Plays
         of Theodore Dreiser," Asian Response to American Litera-
         ture. Ed. C. D. Narasimhaiah. Delhi, India: Vikas.
         Pp. 151-57.

J72-12   POLI, BERNARD. "L'Irruption Peu Orthodoxe de 'Sister
         Carrie,'" La Roman Américain 1865-1917: Mythes de la
         Frontière et de la Ville. Paris: Libraire Armand Colin.
         Pp. 158-72.

J72-13   SUTTON, WILLIAM A. The Road to Winesburg: A Mosaic of the
         Imaginative Life of Sherwood Anderson. Metuchen, N.J.:
         Scarecrow. See Index.
             Frequent references to Dreiser, including a letter from
         Floyd Dell to Sutton denying Dreiser's involvement in the
         publication of Windy McPherson's Son.

J72-14   WESTLAKE, NEDA M. "Dummy: Twelve Men, by Theodore
         Dreiser," Proof: The Yearbook of American Bibliographical
         and Textual Studies. Ed. Joseph Katz. Vol. 2. Columbia:
         U. South Carolina Press. Pp. 153-74.

THEODORE DREISER: A BIBLIOGRAPHY

Parts of Books

1973

J73-1   HUSSMAN, LAWRENCE E., JR. "Foreword," The Bulwark. Portway
         Bath, England: Cedric Chivers Ltd. Pp. 5-15.

J73-2   LONGSTREET, STEPHEN. Chicago: 1860-1919. New York: McKay.
         See Index.
             Frequent references to and quotations from Dreiser,
         whom Longstreet knew and referred to as "the best his-
         torian an earlier Chicago ever had."

J73-3   PIZER, DONALD. "A Summer at Maumee: Theodore Dreiser Writes
         Four Stories," Essays Mostly on Periodical Publishing in
         America. Ed. James Woodress. Durham: Duke U. Press.
         Pp. 193-204.

J73-4   SALZMAN, JACK. "The Curious History of Dreiser's The Bul-
         wark," Proof: The Yearbook of American Bibliographical
         and Textual Studies. Ed. Joseph Katz. Vol. 3. Columbia:
         U. South Carolina Press. Pp. 21-61.

237

K

In an effort to demonstrate the force and diversity of Dreiser's impact on critics, fellow writers, and the public at large, we have ranged widely in this section, including not only the standard critical and biographical studies but also editorials, news stories, letters to the editor, and selected reviews of books about Dreiser. In regard to news stories, we have of necessity been quite selective, for events such as the suppression of The "Genius," Dreiser's activities in Harlan County, Kentucky, and his altercation with Sinclair Lewis received wide and often repetitious coverage. Thus, we have included only those items which were characterized by thoroughness, contained quotations from the principals involved, or dramatized the broad spectrum of public opinion. Syndicated articles have not been duplicated.

We have noted only the first republication and any republication in the books included in section I. There has been no attempt to describe the degree of revision involved in such republication, however. Generally, annotations have been limited in this section to the identification of editorials, parodies, caricatures, and letters to the editor.

An asterisk at the end of an entry based on a clipping (see K14-5) indicates that we were unable to locate the work in the place cited. In these instances, the asterisk signifies that the item does exist, but the bibliographical information may not be accurate.

1901

K01-1   ANON. "Literature," New York Commercial Advertiser, 18 Sept., p. 5. Repub: Kazin and Shapiro, p. 65; See I55-1. Salzman, p. 24; See I72-2.

K01-2   REEDY, WILLIAM MARION. St. Louis Mirror, 11 (26 Sept.), 4. Editorial.

Articles in Newspapers and Journals

K01-3 RAFTERY, JOHN. "By Bread Alone," St. Louis Mirror, 11 (5 Dec.), 5.

1907

K07-1 ANON. "Mr. Dreiser and His Critics," New York Sun, 18 June, p. 6. Repub: Kazin and Shapiro, pp. 66-67; See I55-1. Salzman, pp. 40-41; See I72-2. Editorial.

K07-2 MAYNADIER, EMILY W. "Praise for 'Sister Carrie'," New York Times Saturday Review of Books, 29 June, p. 420. Letter to editor.

K07-3 ANON. "Sister Carrie," Style and American Dressmaker, 6 (July), 4-5.

K07-4 LEWIS, SINCLAIR. "The Literary Zoo: Editors Who Write," Life, 50 (10 Oct.), 414-15.

K07-5 [Personality Sketch of Dreiser], Newspaperdom, 24 Oct. [PU].

K07-6 ANON. "Delineator's Editor," Editor and Publisher, 7 (28 Dec.), 2.

1910

K10-1 ANON. "The Great American Novel," Denver Republican, 5 Aug., p. 6. Editorial.

1911

K11-1 HARRIS, FRANK. "Twenty Favourite Books," Academy, 80 (27 May), 653-54.

K11-2 MACY, BALDWIN. "New York Letter," Chicago Evening Post, 4 Aug., p. 4.

K11-3 KENTON, EDNA. "Some Incomes in Fiction," Bookman, 34 (Oct.), 147-52.

K11-4 ANON. "Chronicle and Comment: The Story of a Book," Bookman, 34 (Nov.), 221-25.

K11-5 ANON. "Stories of Two Women," New York Herald, 2 Dec., p. 10.

WORKS ON

1912

K12-1   BENNETT, ARNOLD. "The Future of the American Novel," North
          American Review, 195 (Jan.), 76-83.

K12-2   KUTTNER, ALFRED B. "The Lyrical Mr. Dreiser," International,
          5 (Jan.), 21-22.

K12-3   DELL, FLOYD. "Theodore Dreiser's Chicago," Chicago Evening
          Post Friday Literary Review, 23 Feb., p. 1.

K12-4   CARROLL, LAWRENCE. "Sister Carrie," Reedy's Mirror, 21
          (25 Apr.), 6-7.

K12-5   MACY, BALDWIN. "New York Letter," Chicago Evening Post
          Friday Literary Review, 10 May, p. 6.

K12-6   SHERWOOD, MARGARET. "Characters in Recent Fiction,"
          Atlantic Monthly, 109 (May), 672-84.

K12-7   RICHARDS, EDMUND C. "As to Theodore Dreiser," Chicago
          Evening Post Friday Literary Review, 29 Nov., p. 4.
          Letter to editor with reply by editors.

K12-8   ANON. "Fiction Built on Fact," Minneapolis Sunday Journal,
          1 Dec., Part 2, p. 4. Editorial.

1913

K13-1   BULLOCK, SHAN F. "London Letter," Chicago Evening Post
          Friday Literary Review, 3 Jan., p. 4.

K13-2   JARMUTH, EDITH DE LONG. "'The Financier' Reviewed," New York
          Globe and Commercial Advertiser, 11 Apr., p. 10. Letter
          to editor, dated 8 Apr.

K13-3   HARRIS, FRANK. "American Novelists Today: Theodore
          Dreiser," Academy, 85 (2 Aug.), 133-34.

K13-4   DELL, FLOYD. "Chicago in Fiction (Part 1)," Bookman, 38
          (Nov.), 270-77.

K13-5   DELL, FLOYD. "Chicago in Fiction (Part 2)," Bookman, 38
          (Dec.), 375-79.

Theodore Dreiser: A Bibliography

Articles in Newspapers and Journals

1914

K14-1   DUFFY, RICHARD. "When They Were Twenty-One, II--A New York Group of Literary Bohemians," Bookman, 38 (Jan.), 521-31.

K14-2   UNTERMEYER, LOUIS. "In the Manner of: Thomas Hardy, James Oppenheim, Arnold Bennett, and Theodore Dreiser," Vanity Fair, 2 (Apr.), 33. Parody.

K14-3   ANON. "What Happened to 'The Titan,'" New York Evening Sun, 11 Apr., p. 9.

K14-4   ANON. "Bribes and Sordid Love Told in Book," Chicago Daily Journal, 18 May, pp. 1-2.

K14-5   "Yerkes' Life Basis of Bold Dreiser Novel," Chicago Evening Journal, 22 May* [PU].

K14-6   ANON. "Dreiser Does More Reporting," Minneapolis Sunday Journal, 31 May, Part 11, p. 2. Editorial.

K14-7   ANON. "Between the Lines," New York Evening Sun, 1 Aug., p. 7.

K14-8   [LYON, HARRIS MERTON]. "From an Old Farmhouse: The Author of The Titan," Reedy's Mirror, 23 (21 Aug.), 7-8. Repub: Theodore Dreiser: America's Foremost Novelist, pp. 5-12 (as "What Manner of Man He Is"; See I17-1).

K14-9   "Praises Writer, Hits Censor," Philadelphia Record, 21 Dec.* [PU].

1915

K15-1   BOURNE, RANDOLPH S. "Theodore Dreiser," New Republic, 2 (17 Apr.), Spring Literary Review, 7-8.

K15-2   MASTERS, EDGAR LEE. "Theodore Dreiser--A Portrait," New York Times Book Review, 31 Oct., p. 424. Repub: Edgar Lee Masters, The Great Valley. New York: Macmillan, 1916. Pp. 228-30 (as "Theodore Dreiser"). Theodore Dreiser: America's Foremost Novelist, pp. 3-4; See I17-1. A Book About Theodore Dreiser and His Work, pp. [4-5]; See I26-1. Kazin and Shapiro, pp. 15-16; See I55-1.

K15-3   FICKE, ARTHUR DAVISON. "Portrait of Theodore Dreiser," Little Review, 2 (Nov.), 6-7. Repub: Theodore Dreiser:

WORKS ON

America's Foremost Novelist, pp. 13-14 (as "To Theodore
Dreiser on Reading The 'Genius'"; See I17-1).

K15-4   KAUN, ALEXANDER S. "Choleric Comments," Little Review, 2
        (Nov.), 22-23.

K15-5   SCAVENGER, THE, pseud. "The Scavenger's Swan Song," Little
        Review, 2 (Nov.), 23-24.

K15-6   HERSEY, HAROLD. "Great Novelist Dreiser," New York Globe
        and Commercial Advertiser, 9 Nov., p. 10. Letter to
        editor dated 6 Nov.

K15-7   BRINSLEY, HENRY. "The Genius of Mr. Theodore Dreiser and
        Some Other Geniuses," Vanity Fair, 5 (Dec.), 41, 112.

K15-8   SHERMAN, STUART P. "The Naturalism of Mr. Dreiser," Nation,
        101 (2 Dec.), 648-50. Repub: Stuart P. Sherman, On Con-
        temporary Literature. New York: Holt, 1917. Pp. 85-101
        (as "The Barbaric Naturalism of Theodore Dreiser"). Kazin
        and Shapiro, pp. 71-80; See I55-1. Lydenberg, pp. 63-72;
        See I71-1.

K15-9   A., M. A. "Sex in Fiction," Nation, 101 (16 Dec.), 718.
        Letter to editor.

K15-10 ANON. "Our American Balzac," Minneapolis Sunday Journal,
        19 Dec., Editorial Section, p. 2. Repub: Salzman,
        pp. 250-51; See I72-2. Editorial.

K15-11 ANON. "Genius Misconceived," Minneapolis Sunday Journal,
        26 Dec., Editorial Section, p. 2. Editorial.

                              1916

K16-1   ANON. "Edgar Lee Masters' Tribute to Theodore Dreiser,"
        Current Opinion, 60 (Jan.), 48.

K16-2   "Realism and Naturalism," Philadelphia Press, 9 Jan., Maga-
        zine Section, p. 21 [PU].

K16-3   ANON. "The Conning Tower: The Meeting of Pericles and
        Aspasia. By Our Own Theodore Dreiser," New York Tribune,
        27 Jan., p. 9. Parody.

K16-4   HABBERSTAD, CLAUDE. "Is It?" New Republic, 6 (19 Feb.),
        76. Letter to editor.

                              242

THEODORE DREISER: A BIBLIOGRAPHY

Articles in Newspapers and Journals

K16-5   ANON. "Unrestrained Passion in the Novel," Chicago Herald,
14 Mar., p. 4.

K16-6   ANDERSON, SHERWOOD. "Dreiser," Little Review, 3 (Apr.), 5.
Repub: Sherwood Anderson, Horses and Men. New York:
Huebsch, 1923. Pp. xi-xii (as "Introduction"). A Book
About Theodore Dreiser and His Work, pp. [1-3]; See I26-1.

K16-7   MENCKEN, H. L. "Theodore Dreiser," Baltimore Evening Sun,
26 July, p. 6.

K16-8   MENCKEN, H. L. "More Dreiseriana," Baltimore Evening Sun,
1 Aug., p. 6.

K16-9   MENCKEN, H. L. "Two Dreiser Novels," Baltimore Evening Sun,
4 Aug., p. 8.

K16-10 ANON. "Editorial Notes," New Republic, 8 (26 Aug.), 79-80.

K16-11 ANON. "A Novelist's Wrong Angle on Life," Indianapolis
Sunday Star, 27 Aug., p. 16. Editorial.

K16-12 [YOUNG, GORDON RAY?]. "Comstockians Would Muzzle Another
American Novelist," Los Angeles Sunday Times, 27 Aug.,
Part 3, p. 18.

K16-13 E[DGETT], E[DWIN] F[RANCIS]. "Writers and Books," Boston
Evening Transcript, 2 Sept., Part 3, p. 9.

K16-14 FUESSLE, NEWTON A. "An Admirer of Dreiser," Reedy's Mirror,
25 (8 Sept.), 576. Letter to editor.

K16-15 "Curiosity and Censorship," New York Morning Telegraph,
9 Sept. [PU].

K16-16 M'NAB, TANSY. "Sweepings from Inkpot Alley: Mr. Dreiser
and the Censor," New York Tribune, 10 Sept., Part 5, p. 2.

K16-17 ANON. "'Genius' Put Under Ban," Cincinnati Enquirer,
14 Sept., p. 14.

K16-18 E[DGETT], E[DWIN] F[RANCIS]. "Writers and Books," Boston
Evening Transcript, 16 Sept., Part 3, p. 9.

K16-19 [HARVEY, ALEXANDER]. [The Suppression of The "Genius"],
Bang, 11 (25 Sept.), 1-8.

WORKS ON

K16-20 E[DGETT], E[DWIN] F[RANCIS]. "Writers and Books," Boston
        Evening Transcript, 30 Sept., Part 3, p. 7.

K16-21 ANON. "Writers Are Opposing Literary Censorship," New York
        Sun, 14 Oct., p. 6.

K16-22 ANON. "Theodore Dreiser and His Comstock Case," Interna-
        tional, 10 (Oct.), 293-94.

K16-23 POUND, EZRA. "Dreiser Protest," Egoist, 3 (Oct.), 159.

K16-24 ANON. "Confused Standards of Literary Censorship," Literary
        Digest, 53 (21 Oct.), 1033-34.

K16-25 ANON. "Our Most Suppressed Novelist," Current Opinion, 61
        (Nov.), 338-39.

K16-26 FRANK, WALDO. "Emerging Greatness," Seven Arts, 1 (Nov.),
        73-78. Repub: The Achievement of Sherwood Anderson. Ed.
        Ray Lewis White. Chapel Hill: U. North Carolina Press,
        1966. Pp. 20-24.

K16-27 LAIT, JACK. "Protests Against Damning Dreiser, Who Wrote
        The 'Genius': Attorney Says Censors Hunt 'Smut,'" Chicago
        Herald, 7 Nov., p. 18.

                              1917

K17-1   ANON. "Priests Attack 'Genius' Novel," Chicago Examiner,
        8 Jan., p. 6.

K17-2   ANON. "Art and Censorship and Theodore Dreiser," Out West,
        45 (Mar.), 55.

K17-3   "Girard's Topics of the Town," Philadelphia Public Ledger,
        12 Apr. [PU].

K17-4   HEDGES, M. H. "Mr. Dreiser," Dial, 62 (19 Apr.), 343.

K17-5   ANON. "Dreiser's Arraignment of Our Intellectual Aridity,"
        Current Opinion, 62 (May), 344-45.

K17-6   "Girard's Topics of the Town," Philadelphia Public Ledger,
        4 May, p. 10.

K17-7   BOURNE, RANDOLPH S. "The Art of Theodore Dreiser," Dial, 62
        (14 June), 507-09. Repub: Randolph S. Bourne, History

Articles in Newspapers and Journals

of a Literary Radical and Other Essays. New York:
Huebsch, 1920. Pp. 195-204. Kazin and Shapiro, pp. 92-95;
See I55-1. Lydenberg, pp. 81-85; See I71-1.

K17-8   WOODBRIDGE, HOMER E. "Mr. Dreiser and 'Celestina,'" Dial,
63 (28 June), 28. Letter to editor.

K17-9   MENCKEN, H. L. "The Dreiser Bugaboo," Seven Arts, 2 (Aug.),
507-17. Repub: Kazin and Shapiro, pp. 84-91; See I55-1.
Lydenberg, pp. 73-80; See I71-1.

K17-10 MENCKEN, H. L. "Sister Carrie's History," New York Evening
Mail, 4 Aug., p. 7.

K17-11 ANON. "Dreiser's Novels as a Revelation of the American
Soul," Current Opinion, 63 (Sept.), 191.

K17-12 GLAENZER, RICHARD B. "Snap-Shots of American Novelists:
Dreiser," Bookman, 46 (Sept.), 28. Repub: Richard B.
Glaenzer, Literary Snapshots. New York: Brentano's,
1920.

K17-13 MORDELL, ALBERT. "With a Persecuted Author," Philadelphia
Press, 9 Sept., Magazine Section, pp. 17, 19.

K17-14 ANDERSON, SHERWOOD. "An Apology for Crudity," Dial, 63
(8 Nov.), 437-38. Repub: Kazin and Shapiro, pp. 81-83;
See I55-1.

K17-15 ANON. "Casual Comment," Dial, 63 (22 Nov.), 533.

1918

K18-1   ANDERSON, MARGARET. "Mr. Mencken's Truisms," Little Review,
4 (Jan.), 13-14.

K18-2   ANON. "Dreiser en Passant," Bookman, 46 (Feb.), 655.

K18-3   YEWDALE, MERTON STARK. "Is Dreiser's The 'Genius' Immoral?"
New York Sun, 24 Feb., Section 6, p. 10.

K18-4   H[OLMES], R[ALPH] F. "Musings With the Muses," Detroit
Journal, 21 Mar., p. 4.

K18-5   ARENS, EGMONT. "The Right to Love," New York Call, 30 Mar.,
Call Magazine, pp. 6, 16.

WORKS ON

K18-6   ANON. "Call 'The Genius' Indecent," New York <u>Times</u>, 2 May, p. 19.

K18-7   ANON. "Dreiser Novel Is Proper Say Leading Novelists," New York <u>Sun</u>, 2 May, p. 16.

K18-8   ANON. "Dreiser Case Argued in Court," Chicago <u>Herald &</u> <u>Examiner</u>, 4 May, Fine Arts Supplement, p. 1.

K18-9   YEWDALE, MERTON STARK. "All Values Go Down Before Dreiser," Chicago <u>Herald & Examiner</u>, 4 May, Fine Arts Supplement, p. 1.

K18-10 ANON. "The Strength of Dreiser," <u>New Appeal</u> (Girard, Kans.), 18 May, p. 3.

K18-11 AUERBACH, JOSEPH S. "Authorship and Liberty," <u>North American</u> <u>Review</u>, 207 (June), 902-17. Repub: Joseph S. Auerbach, <u>Essays and Miscellanies</u>. New York: Harper, 1922. Vol. 3, 130-65 (as "Oral Argument Against the Suppression of The 'Genius'").

K18-12 ANON. "Five Judges Will Decide If 'The Genius' Is Genius, 'Tommyrot,' or Plain Filth," Brooklyn <u>Daily Eagle</u>, 9 June, Section 3, p. 2.

K18-13 HUNEKER, JAMES GIBBONS. "Old Philadelphia, Paris Forty Years Ago," Philadelphia <u>Press</u>, 2 Aug., p. 8.

K18-14 ANON. "Among the Publishers," <u>Publishers' Weekly</u>, 94 (31 Aug.), 634.

K18-15 MAURICE, ARTHUR B. "Makers of Modern American Fiction (Men): Dreiser and Dixon," <u>Mentor</u>, 6 (1 Sept.), 6-7.

K18-16 JAMESON, R. D. "Puritanic Taboos," <u>New Republic</u>, 16 (28 Sept.), 260. Letter to editor.

K18-17 HARRIS, FRANK. "Theodore Dreiser," <u>Pearson's Magazine</u>, 39 (Oct.), 346-51.

K18-18 KARSNER, DAVID. "America's Literary Sphinx," New York <u>Evening Post</u>, 19 Oct., Book Section, p. 8.

Theodore Dreiser: A Bibliography

Articles in Newspapers and Journals

1919

K19-1 ANON. "The Secret of Personality as Theodore Dreiser Reveals It," Current Opinion, 66 (Mar.), 175-76.

K19-2 S., H. B. [HENRY BLACKMAN SELL?]. "To Theodore Dreiser," Chicago Daily News, 30 Apr., p. 12. Letter to Dreiser.

K19-3 BYRNE, DONN. "Twelve Men," New York Times Review of Books, 11 May, p. 276. Letter to editor.

K19-4 WILLIAMS, BLANCHE C. "Twelve Men," New York Times Review of Books, 11 May, p. 276. Letter to editor.

K19-5 YOST, CHARLES E. "Theodore Dreiser," Fayette (Ohio) Review, 17 July [PU].

K19-6 ANON. "Does Any One Here Know Dreiser?--," Terre Haute [Ind.] Saturday Spectator, 2 Aug., p. 9.

K19-7 BOGART, GUY. "Theodore Dreiser," Colony Co-operator (Sept.), pp. 8-9, 15.

K19-8 McCARDELL, ROY L. "Theodore Dreiser: Master of the Matter-of-Fact," New York Morning Telegraph, 28 Dec., Magazine Section [PU].

1920

K20-1 ANON. "Brief Comment," Review, 2 (17 Apr.), 375.

K20-2 MEYER, ANNIE NATHAN. "Mr. Dreiser's 'Battle for Truth,'" Review, 2 (8 May), 486. Letter to editor.

K20-3 MEYER, ANNIE NATHAN. "Mr. Dreiser and the Broadway Magazine," Review, 2 (5 June), 597. Letter to editor.

K20-4 KARSNER, DAVID. "Theodore Dreiser: A Portrait," New York Call, 18 July, Call Magazine, pp. 6-7.

K20-5 SAYLER, OLIVER M. "Theodore Dreiser, Hoosier, Serves as Preceptor for the Younger Artists and Writers of Modern America," Topics (Indianapolis), 1 (18 Aug.), 5-6 [PU].

K20-6 RUNYON, DAMON. "Runyon Tells of Changing Broadway," New York American, 25 Oct., p. 14.

THEODORE DREISER: A BIBLIOGRAPHY

WORKS ON

K20-7   [DOUGLAS, GEORGE?]. "Theodore Dreiser," San Francisco
         Bulletin, 30 Oct., p. [20].

K20-8   [BROOKS, VAN WYCK?]. "A Reviewer's Note-Book," Freeman, 2
         (24 Nov.), 262-63.

K20-9   KARSNER, DAVID. "The Romance of Two Hoosier Brothers,"
         New York Call, 5 Dec., Magazine Section, pp. 6-7.

                              1921

K21-1   SHERMAN, STUART P. "The National Genius," Atlantic Monthly,
         127 (Jan.), 1-11. Repub: Stuart P. Sherman, The Genius
         of America: Studies in Behalf of the Younger Generation.
         New York: Scribners, 1923. Pp. 1-32 (as "The Genius of
         America").

K21-2   ANON. "Whose Flag Is It?" New Republic, 25 (9 Jan.), 304-
         06. Editorial.

K21-3   LANE, JOHN. "Theodore Dreiser," London Times Literary Sup-
         plement, 20 Jan., p. 44. Letter to editor.

K21-4   RASCOE, BURTON. "Reviewing the Reviewer," Freeman, 2
         (26 Jan.), 473-74. Letter to editor.

K21-5   L., F. S. A. "Theodore Dreiser," London Times Literary Sup-
         plement, 27 Jan., p. 60. Letter to editor.

K21-6   VAN DOREN, CARL. "Contemporary American Novelists: Theodore
         Dreiser," Nation, 112 (16 Mar.), 400-01. Repub: Carl
         Van Doren, Contemporary American Novelists, 1900-1920.
         New York: Macmillan, 1922. Pp. 74-83.

K21-7   [BROOKS, VAN WYCK?]. "A Reviewer's Notebook," Freeman, 3
         (8 June), 310-11.

K21-8   [ROBERTS], CARL ERIC BECHHOFER. "Impressions of Recent
         American Literature," London Times Literary Supplement,
         23 June, pp. 403-04.

K21-9   ANON. "Comment," Dial, 71 (Nov.), 622-24.

K21-10   MENCKEN, H. L. "The American Novel," Voices (London), 5
         (Nov.), 115-21. Repub: H. L. Mencken, Prejudices:
         Fourth Series. New York: Knopf, 1924. Pp. 278-93.

K21-11   BEACH, JOSEPH WARREN. "English Speech and American Writers,"
         New Republic, 29 (28 Dec.), 123-25.

Articles in Newspapers and Journals

1922

K22-1   FULLER, HENRY B. "Chicago Novelists," Literary Review, 3
        (18 Mar.), 501-02.

K22-2   WHITE, WILLIAM ALLEN. "Splitting Fiction Three Ways," New
        Republic, 30 (12 Apr.), Spring Literary Supplement,
        pp. 22, 24, 26. Repub: The Novel of Tomorrow and the
        Scope of Fiction. Indianapolis: Bobbs-Merrill, 1922.
        Pp. 123-33.

K22-3   WILLSON, ROBERT H. "Ye Poet Leaps in Lake to Nip Lily for
        Lady," San Francisco Examiner, 23 Aug., pp. 1-2.

K22-4   BERN, PAUL. "Take That, Mr. Dreiser," Los Angeles Times,
        22 Sept., Part 2, p. 4.

K22-5   RASCOE, BURTON. "A Bookman's Day Book," New York Tribune
        Magazine and Books, 31 Dec., p. 20. Repub: Burton
        Rascoe, A Bookman's Daybook. Ed. C. Hartley Grattan.
        New York: Liveright, 1929. Pp. 59-60 (as "Dreiser,
        Conservative Editor").

1923

K23-1   ANON. "The Gossip Shop," Bookman, 56 (Jan.), 661.

K23-2   TOWNE, CHARLES HANSON. "Some Magnificent Failures,"
        Literary Digest International Book Review, 1 (Feb.),
        12-13, 68.

K23-3   TARZAN. Brooklyn Daily Eagle, 3 Feb., p. 5. Letter to the
        editor.

K23-4   BOYNTON, PERCY. "American Authors of Today: Theodore
        Dreiser," English Journal, 12 (Mar.), 180-88. Repub:
        Percy Boynton, Some Contemporary Americans. Chicago:
        U. Chicago Press, 1924. Pp. 126-44.

K23-5   McFADDEN, JAMES G. "A Book About Myself," Literary Digest
        International Book Review, 1 (Mar.), 79. Letter to
        editor.

K23-6   MASTERS, EDGAR LEE. "Theodore Dreiser's 'A Book About
        Myself,'" Chicago Evening Post Literary Review, 16 Mar.,
        p. 4. Letter to editor dated 8 Mar.

WORKS ON

K23-7   VAN DOREN, CARL. "American Realism," New Republic, 34
        (21 Mar.), 107-09.

K23-8   DUFFUS, ROBERT L. "The Wherefore of Literary Anarchism,"
        New York Globe and Commercial Advertiser, 28 Apr., p. 10.

K23-9   RASCOE, BURTON. "A Bookman's Day Book," New York Tribune
        Book News and Reviews, 29 Apr., p. 30. Repub: Burton
        Rascoe, A Bookman's Daybook. Ed. C. Hartley Grattan.
        New York: Liveright, 1929. P. 97 (as "Dreiser's Proper
        Story").

K23-10 AUSTIN, MARY. "Sex in American Literature," Bookman, 57
        (June), 385-93.

K23-11 [JONES, LLEWELLYN?]. "Moral or Immoral?" Chicago Evening
        Post Literary Review, 31 Aug., p. 4. Editorial.

K23-12 ANON. "The Conquest of Canaan," New York Times, 11 Oct.,
        p. 20.

K23-13 RASCOE, BURTON. "A Bookman's Daybook," New York Tribune
        Magazine and Books, 25 Nov., p. 32. Repub: Burton
        Rascoe, A Bookman's Daybook. Ed. C. Hartley Grattan.
        New York: Liveright, 1929. Pp. 163-64 (as "Arthur
        Henry, Whitlock and Dreiser").

K23-14 KING, WYNCIE. "Theodore Dreiser," New York Times Book
        Review, 23 Dec., p. 6. Caricature.

                              1924

K24-1   ANON. "Present Tendencies in American Literature Assailed,"
        Current Opinion, 76 (Feb.), 165-67.

K24-2   RASCOE, BURTON. "Contemporary Reminiscences," Arts and
        Decoration, 20 (Apr.), 28, 57, 62.

                              1925

K25-1   MENCKEN, H. L. "The Case of Dreiser," Chicago Tribune,
        15 Mar., Part 8, pp. 1, 7. Repub: A Book About Theodore
        Dreiser and His Work, pp. [6-13]; See I26-1.

K25-2   CARTER, JOHN. "Dreiser Reduced Literature to Its Own Level,"
        New York Times Book Review, 9 Aug., p. 5.

Articles in Newspapers and Journals

K25-3 SEARCH-LIGHT, pseud. [Waldo Frank]. "Profiles: The
Colossus of Children," New Yorker, 1 (15 Aug.), 6-7. Re-
pub: Search-Light, pseud. [Waldo Frank], Time Exposures.
Boni & Liveright, 1926. Pp. 159-64 (as "Theodore Dreiser:
The Colossus of Children").

K25-4 GRATTAN, C. HARTLEY. "Mrs. Wharton and Mr. Dreiser," Nation,
121 (30 Sept.), 361.

K25-5 HALDEMAN-JULIUS, EMANUEL. "Dreiser Into His Own," Girard
[Kans.] Haldeman-Julius Weekly, 10 Oct., pp. 1-2.

K25-6 NORRIS, CHARLES G. "My Favorite Character in Fiction,"
Bookman, 62 (Dec.), 410-11.

1926

K26-1 DUFFUS, ROBERT L. "Dreiser," American Mercury, 7 (Jan.),
71-76. Repub: American Criticism: 1926. Ed. William A.
Drake. New York: Harcourt, 1926. Pp. 46-61.

K26-2 [SMALL, H. A.]. "Is T. Dreiser's Realism Only Reincarnation?"
San Francisco Chronicle, 17 Jan., Screen, Drama, Books,
Music and Art Section, p. 4D.

K26-3 E., G. D. "Merrily He Whirls Around," New York Morning Telegraph, 24 Jan., Section 4, p. 4.

K26-4 LEWIS, SINCLAIR. "The Remarks of Mr. Sinclair Lewis," Buzz
Saw (Kansas City, Mo.), 19 (28 Jan.), 1-4.

K26-5 [JONES, LLEWELLYN]. "Mr. Dreiser's English," Chicago Evening
Post Literary Review, 29 Jan., p. 4. Repub: Current Reviews. Ed. Lewis Worthington Smith. New York: Holt,
1926. Pp. 208-12.

K26-6 BODENHEIM, MAXWELL. "On Writing," Saturday Review of Literature, 2 (13 Feb.), 562. Repub: Salzman, pp. 449-50; See
I72-2. Letter to editor.

K26-7 ANON. "Theodore Dreiser Has Ceased To Be a Bogey Man to the
Critics," Kansas City [Mo.] Star, 20 Feb., p. 6.

K26-8 SMYTH, CLIFFORD. "Changing Realism," Literary Digest International Book Review, 4 (Mar.), 238.

WORKS ON

K26-9   MARTIN, QUINN. "The Magic Lantern: A Book That Would Make
        a Great Film," New York World, 7 Mar., Metropolitan
        Section, p. 4M.

K26-10 ANON. "When Mr. Dreiser Dropt into Church," Literary Digest,
        88 (27 Mar.), 52.

K26-11 WALKER, CHARLES R. "How Big Is Dreiser?", Bookman, 63 (Apr.),
        146-49.

K26-12 DIGBY, KENELM. "The Literary Lobby," New York Evening Post
        Literary Review, 3 Apr., p. 12.

K26-13 DIGBY, KENELM. "The Literary Lobby," New York Evening Post
        Literary Review, 10 Apr., p. 20.

K26-14 BENCHLEY, ROBERT. "Mr. Benchley Interviews Theodore Dreiser,"
        Life, 87 (15 Apr.), 10. Repub: Robert Benchley, The
        Early Worm. New York: Holt, 1927. Pp. 78-79 (as "An
        Interview with Theodore Dreiser"). Parody.

K26-15 FICKE, ARTHUR DAVISON. "Dreiser as Artist," Saturday Review
        of Literature, 2 (17 Apr.), 724. Letter to editor.

K26-16 DIGBY, KENELM. "The Literary Lobby," New York Evening Post
        Literary Review, 24 Apr., p. 12.

K26-17 MILLER, HENRY. "Dreiser's Style," New Republic, 46 (28 Apr.),
        306. Repub: Salzman, p. 486; See 172-2. Letter to
        editor.

K26-18 MENCKEN, H. L. "An American Literary Phenomenon--Theodore
        Dreiser," Vanity Fair, 26 (May), 50.

K26-19 DURGIN, CHESTER. "The Band Wagon: The Story Behind the
        Story," Long Island Daily Press, 22 May [PU].

K26-20 PRESTON, JOHN HYDE. "True Style," Saturday Review of Litera-
        ture, 2 (22 May), 814. Letter to editor.

K26-21 OAK, V. V. "The Awful Dreiser," Nation, 122 (2 June), 610.
        Letter to editor.

K26-22 KARSNER, DAVID. "Dreiser, the Daddy of American Realists,"
        New York Herald Tribune, 20 June, Section 7, pp. 3-4, 8-9.

K26-23 STRUNSKY, SIMEON. "About Books, More or Less: Prose Poems,"
        New York Times Book Review, 27 June, p. 4.

Articles in Newspapers and Journals

K26-24   STUART, HENRY LONGAN. "Fifty 'Outstanding Novels' of the
         Last Six Months: Dreiser's Monumental 'An American
         Tragedy' Leads the List," New York Times Book Review,
         27 June, pp. 3, 24-25.

K26-25   ANON. "The All-Star Literary Vaudeville," New Republic, 47
         (30 June), 158-63.

K26-26   TOWNE, CHARLES HANSON. "Behind the Scenes with Author and
         Editor," Literary Digest International Book Review, 4
         (July), 475-77.

K26-27   WALDMAN, MILTON. "Contemporary American Authors: VII--
         Theodore Dreiser," London Mercury, 14 (July), 283-91.
         Repub: Living Age, 331 (1 Oct. 1926), 43-50 (as "A
         German-American Insurgent").

K26-28   BEACH, JOSEPH WARREN. "The Naive Style," American Speech, 1
         (Aug.), 576-83. Repub: Joseph Warren Beach, The Outlook
         for American Prose. Chicago: U. Chicago Press, 1926.
         Pp. 177-96.

K26-29   HALDEMAN-JULIUS, EMANUEL. "What the Editor Is Thinking About:
         Theodore Dreiser," Girard [Kans.] Haldeman-Julius Weekly,
         7 Aug., p. 4. Repub: Emanuel Haldeman-Julius, The Fun I
         Get Out of Life. Girard, Kans.: Haldeman-Julius, n.d.
         Pp. 79-83.

K26-30   ANON. "Dreiser 'Crib' From Anderson Shocks Friends," New
         York Herald Tribune, 7 Sept., p. 9.

K26-31   BROUN, HEYWOOD. "It Seems to Me," New York World, 8 Sept.,
         p. 15.

K26-32   ANON. "George Ade Absolves Dreiser of Lifting His 'Swift
         Worker,'" New York Herald Tribune, 9 Sept., p. 2.

K26-33   ANON. "Freer Verse Than Usual," New York Times, 10 Sept.,
         p. 20.

K26-34   PATERSON, ISABEL. "Reading With Tears," Bookman, 64 (Oct.),
         192-97.

K26-35   ROBINSON, WILLIAM J. "An American Tragedy," Critic and Guide,
         25D (Oct.), 391-98.

K26-36   WALLACE, INEZ. "Ask Inez Wallace: Must We Have Another
         American Tragedy?" Cleveland Plain Dealer, 3 Oct.,
         Dramatic Section, p. 5.

WORKS ON

K26-37 ANON. "It's Nice to Dream About," Collier's, 78 (23 Oct.),
13.

K26-38 TAYLOR, G. R. STIRLING. "The United States as Seen by an
American Writer," Nineteenth Century, 100 (Dec.), 803-15.

K26-39 YBARRA, T. R. "Swinnerton Calls Our Authors Virile," New
York Times, 15 Dec., p. 5.

K26-40 TAYLOR, G. R. STIRLING. "Theodore Dreiser," Outlook
(London), 58 (18 Dec.), 607-08.

1927

K27-1 HORWILL, HERBERT W. "London Discusses Mr. Dreiser,"
New York Times Book Review, 9 Jan., p. 8.

K27-2 ADAMIC, LOUIS. "Theodore Dreiser: An Appreciation,"
Haldeman-Julius Monthly (Girard, Kans.), 1 (Jan.-Mar.),
93-97.

K27-3 "Remove the Cause," Miami News, 1 Feb. [PU].

K27-4 ANON. "Sex Stuff and Censorship," El Paso Times, 7 Feb.,
p. 4. Editorial.

K27-5 MORAND, PAUL. "Paris Letter," Dial, 82 (Mar.), 233-38.

K27-6 WELLS, H. G. "Wells Assays the Culture of America,"
New York Times, 15 May, Section 4, pp. 3, 20.

K27-7 STRUNSKY, SIMEON. "About Books, More or Less: Said Without
Flowers," New York Times Book Review, 29 May, p. 4.

K27-8 BURKE, THOMAS. "America's Villified Author," T. P.'s &
Cassell's Weekly (London), 8 (4 June), 178.

K27-9 H., J. "Theodore Dreiser Reported to Have Written a Musical
Comedy With Artless Title," New York World, 7 Oct., p. 15.

K27-10 ANON. "English Booktrade News: Thomas Burke on Dreiser,"
Publishers' Weekly, 112 (28 Oct.), 1637.

K27-11 WALKER, CHARLES R. "Business in the American Novel,"
Bookman, 66 (Dec.), 401-05.

Articles in Newspapers and Journals

1928

K28-1 BABBITT, IRVING. "The Critic and American Life," Forum, 79 (Feb.), 161-76.

K28-2 ANON. "Replies to Dreiser on Soviet Regime," New York Times, 28 Feb., p. 6.

K28-3 ELLISTON, H. B. "Mr. Dreiser and Russia," New York Times, 3 Mar., p. 16. Letter to editor.

K28-4 STRUNSKY, SIMEON. "About Books, More or Less: Paragraphs," New York Times Book Review, 4 Mar., p. 4.

K28-5 ANON. "Found Many Idle in Russia," New York Times, 5 Mar., p. 14.

K28-6 PATERSON, ISABEL. "Books and Other Things," New York Herald Tribune, 9 Mar., p. 15.

K28-7 FRANK, WALDO. "Our Arts: The Re-Discovery of America: XII," New Republic, 54 (9 May), 343-47.

K28-8 McDONALD, EDWARD D. "Dreiser Before Sister Carrie," Bookman, 67 (June), 369-74.

K28-9 CRUNCHER, JERRY. "Epitaphs for Living Lions," Forum, 80 (July), 78-81.

K28-10 WINNER, PERCY. "Dorothy Thompson Demands Dreiser Explain Parallel," New York Evening Post, 14 Nov., p. 6.

K28-11 GILKES, MARTIN. "Discovering Dreiser," New Adelphi, 2 (Dec.), 178-81.

1929

K29-1 CHESTERTON, G. K. "The Skeptic as a Critic," Forum, 81 (Feb.), 65-69.

K29-2 Y., SAM. "Book Worm," Muskogee [Okla.] Democrat, 5 Feb. [PU].

K29-3 STALNAKER, JOHN M., and FRED EGGAN. "American Novelists Ranked: A Psychological Study," English Journal, 18 (Apr.), 295-307.

WORKS ON

K29-4   BULLARD, F. LAURISTON. "Boston's Book Ban Likely To Live Long," New York Times, 28 Apr., Part 3, pp. 1, 7.

K29-5   ANON. "Enemies of Society," New Republic, 58 (8 May), 318-20.

K29-6   SCHRIFTGIESSER, KARL. "Boston Stays Pure," New Republic, 58 (8 May), 327-29.

K29-7   ANON. "Noted Writers Aid Textile Strikers," New York Times, 19 Aug., p. 39.

K29-8   JOHNSON, A. THEODORE. "Realism in Contemporary American Literature: Notes on Dreiser, Anderson, Lewis," Southwestern Bulletin (Memphis, Tenn.) (Sept.), pp. 3-16.

K29-9   HANSEN, HARRY. "The First Reader," Chicago Daily News, 20 Dec., p. 23.

1930

K30-1   BROE, AXEL. "Theodore Dreiser," Tilskueren (Copenhagen) (Jan.), 58-64.

K30-2   CONRAD, LAWRENCE HENRY. "Theodore Dreiser," Landmark, 12 (Jan.), 29-32.

K30-3   FITZGERALD, GEORGE L. "Dreiser's Credo," Forum, 83 (Jan.), p. xxxviii. Letter to editor.

K30-4   RIDDELL, JOHN, pseud. [Corey Ford]. "A Gallery of Dreiser," Vanity Fair, 33 (Feb.), 58-59, 82. Parody.

K30-5   LINCOLN, SELMA WALDEN. "An Answer to One of the 'Gallery of Women,'" Chicago Daily News, 26 Feb., p. 18. Letter dated 20 Feb.

K30-6   KELLY, CLAUDE. "American Victory or Tragedy: The Fallacy of Theodore Dreiser's Theories as Demonstrated by the Personal Victory of Ulysses S. Grant Over the Power of Circumstances (Part 1)," National Republic, 17 (Mar.), 16-17, 44.

K30-7   KELLY, CLAUDE. "American Victory or Tragedy (Part 2)," National Republic, 17 (Apr.), 28-29, 46.

K30-8   ANON. "Novelist Pays El Paso Visit," El Paso Herald, 25 Apr., p. 1.

Articles in Newspapers and Journals

K30-9   ANON. "Dreiser's Attack on Religion Elicits Scathing De-
         nunciation," El Paso Herald, 28 Apr., p. 2.

K30-10   ANON. "Getting the Goat," El Paso Herald, 29 Apr., p. 4.
         Editorial.

K30-11   NELLIGAN, GEORGE J. "Talking Things Over: Dreiser--Failure,"
         El Paso Herald, 30 Apr., pp. 4, 9. Letter to editor.

K30-12   BERCOVICI, KONRAD. "The Romantic Realist," Mentor, 18 (May),
         38-41, 73.

K30-13   HUTCHINS, T. A. "Talking Things Over: The Dreiser After-
         math," El Paso Herald, 8 May, p. 4. Letter to editor.

K30-14   ANON. "Mr. Dreiser Is Interviewed," New York Herald Tribune,
         9 July, p. 16. Editorial.

K30-15   ANON. "The Dark Blue Dreiser," Literary Digest, 106
         (26 July), 17.

K30-16   SIBLEY, W. G. "Along the Highway: Hardly a Masterpiece,"
         Chicago Journal of Commerce, 6 Aug., p. 14.

K30-17   ANON. "'Capturing' New York," New York Times, 15 Aug.,
         p. 16. Editorial.

K30-18   McCOLE, CAMILLE. "The Tragedy of Theodore Dreiser,"
         Catholic World, 132 (Oct.), 1-7.

K30-19   ANON. "Week by Week: Shall It Be Dreiser?" Commonweal, 12
         (22 Oct.), 626.

K30-20   LEWIS, SINCLAIR. "Text of Sinclair Lewis's Nobel Prize
         Address at Stockholm," New York Times, 13 Dec., p. 12.
         Repub: Kazin and Shapiro, pp. 111-12 (as "Our Formula
         for Fiction"; See I55-1).

                              1931

K31-1   DINAMOV, SERGEI. "Theodore Dreiser Is Coming Our Way,"
         Literature of the World Revolution (Moscow), No. 5 (1931),
         126-32.

K31-2   ANON. "Shaw Draws Fire From Hollywood," New York Times,
         3 Mar., p. 6.

K31-3   ANON. "An American Tragedy," New York Times, 21 Mar., p. 16.
         Editorial.

K31-4   ANON. "Lewis Is Slapped By Dreiser in Club," New York Times,
         21 Mar., p. 11.

K31-5   ANON. "After and Above the Melee," New York Times, 23 Mar.,
         p. 20.

K31-6   ANON. "Dreiser versus Lewis," Commonweal, 13 (1 Apr.), 594.
         Editorial.

K31-7   ANON. "Slap! Slap!" Literary Digest, 109 (11 Apr.), 15-16.

K31-8   ANON. "The Week," New Republic, 66 (22 Apr.), 258.

K31-9   ANON. "Theodore Dreiser Again," Commonweal, 13 (22 Apr.),
         677. Editorial.

K31-10   BARRETT, E. BOYD. "Modern Writers and Religion," Thinker, 3
         (May), 32-38.

K31-11   HANEY, LEWIS. "Dreiser Plan Has Many Faults," New York
         Evening Journal, 15 May, p. 38.

K31-12   PROSSER, F. D. "Mr. Dreiser's Remedy," New York Times,
         16 May, p. 16. Letter to editor.

K31-13   MAY, ARMAND. "Things to Consider," New York Times, 27 May,
         p. 26. Letter to editor.

K31-14   GREEN, WILLIAM. "Dreiser Says Union Assists Operators; Green
         Makes Denial: Green's Reply," Pittsburgh Press, 26 June,
         p. 2.

K31-15   GELLERT, HUGO. "The Titan," New Masses, 7 (Sept.), 6-7.

K31-16   GOLD, MICHAEL. "Six Open Letters: Dear Theodore Dreiser,"
         New Masses, 7 (Sept.), 5.

K31-17   INTERNATIONAL UNION OF REVOLUTIONARY WRITERS. "Greetings to
         Dreiser," New Masses, 7 (Sept.), 6.

K31-18   MUNSON, GORHAM B. "Our Post-War Novel," Bookman, 74 (Oct.),
         141-44.

K31-19   FISCHER, LOUIS. "Russia Adopts Dreiser," New York Herald
         Tribune Books, 4 Oct., p. 9.

Articles in Newspapers and Journals

K31-20 ANON. "Unkind Levity," New York <u>Times</u>, 7 Nov., p. 20. Editorial.

K31-21 SMITH, EDWARD B. "Judge Jones Exiles Some, Say Miners," Knoxville <u>News-Sentinel</u>, 7 Nov., pp. 1, 10.

K31-22 SMITH, EDWARD B. "Miners' Distress Seen By Writers," Knoxville <u>News-Sentinel</u>, 8 Nov., p. 6A.

K31-23 ANON. "Jury Indicts Dreiser at Pineville," Knoxville <u>News-Sentinel</u>, 10 Nov., pp. 1, 12.

K31-24 ANON. Dreiser Indicted By Kentucky Jury," New York <u>Times</u>, 11 Nov., p. 12.

K31-25 ANON. "Dreiser Indicted," Knoxville <u>News-Sentinel</u>, 12 Nov., p. 6. Editorial.

K31-26 WILLARD, DANIEL. "I Am Only a Railroad Man," <u>Liberty</u>, 8 (14 Nov.), 30-33.

K31-27 ANON. "Dreiser Indicted For Syndicalism," New York <u>Times</u>, 17 Nov., p. 14.

K31-28 ANON. "Free and Easy Indictments," New York <u>Times</u>, 18 Nov., p. 22. Editorial.

K31-29 ANON. "Investigating the Mines," <u>America</u>, 46 (21 Nov.), 151. Editorial.

K31-30 ANON. "Toothpicks," <u>New Republic</u>, 69 (25 Nov.), 32-33.

K31-31 ANON. "Dreiser's Feud With Kentucky," <u>Literary Digest</u>, 111 (28 Nov.), 9.

K31-32 DOS PASSOS, JOHN. "Harlan: Working Under the Gun," <u>New Republic</u>, 69 (2 Dec.), 62-67.

K31-33 ANON. "Anderson Decries Our 'Speakeasy' Era," New York <u>Times</u>, 7 Dec., p. 24.

1932

K32-1 DINAMOV, SERGEI. "Theodore Dreiser Continues the Struggle," <u>International Literature</u>, Nos. 2-3 (1932), 112-15.

THEODORE DREISER: A BIBLIOGRAPHY

WORKS ON

K32-2   RÜEGG, A. "Theodore Dreiser Abkehr vom Katholizismus,"
        Schweizerisches Rundschau, 31 (1932), 1084-95.

K32-3   ANON. "Dreiser Draws Up Communistic Plan," New York Times,
        18 Jan., p. 13.

K32-4   ANON. "Dreiser Places Himself," Kansas City [Mo.] Times,
        19 Jan., p. [18]. Editorial.

K32-5   ANON. "Theodore Dreiser," New Masses, 7 (Feb.), 28.

K32-6   SOSKIN, WILLIAM. "Reading and Writing," New York Evening
        Post, 26 Mar., p. 7.

K32-7   GRATTAN, C. HARTLEY. "Upton Sinclair on Current Literature,"
        Bookman, 75 (Apr.), 61-64.

K32-8   COCHRANE, R. H. "Correcting Mr. Dreiser," New York Times,
        15 Apr., p. 20. Letter to editor.

K32-9   DAVIS, ELMER. "The Red Peril," Saturday Review of Literature,
        8 (16 Apr.), 661-62. Repub: Salzman, pp. 643-46; See
        I72-2.

K32-10 ROCHESTER, ANNA. "Dreiser Was Right," New Republic, 70
        (20 Apr.), 275. Letter to editor.

K32-11 ANON. "Whither the American Writer?" Modern Quarterly, 6
        (Summer), 11-19.

K32-12 SEAVER, EDWIN. "American Writers and Kentucky," New Masses,
        7 (June), 9-10.

K32-13 GARDNER, PAUL. "Dreiser, Pirandothello, War and Waltzes,"
        Canadian Forum, 12 (Aug.), 437-38.

K32-14 BROOKS, OBED. "The Problem of the Social Novel," Modern
        Quarterly, 6 (Autumn), 77-82.

K32-15 HAZLITT, HENRY. "Our Greatest Authors: How Great Are They?"
        Forum, 88 (Oct.), 245-50.

K32-16 MARQUIS, DON. "205 Words," Saturday Review of Literature, 9
        (15 Oct.), 174.

K32-17 FADIMAN, CLIFTON. "Dreiser and the American Dream," Nation,
        135 (19 Oct.), 364-65.

THEODORE DREISER: A BIBLIOGRAPHY

Articles in Newspapers and Journals

K32-18 ANON. "Poor Dreiser," Bookman, 75 (Nov.), 682-84.

K32-19 ANON. "American Realism," New York Times, 4 Dec., Section 4, p. 1. Editorial.

K32-20 KINGSLEY, GRACE. "Hobnobbing in Hollywood," Los Angeles Times, 13 Dec., Part 2, p. 7.

1933

K33-1 GRATTAN, C. HARTLEY. "Dreiser a Hero," Saturday Review of Literature, 9 (14 Jan.), 377.

K33-2 LE VERRIER, CHARLES. "Un grand romancier américain: Theodore Dreiser," Revue Hebdomadaire, 42 (21 Jan.), 280-94.

K33-3 PAVESE, CESARE. "Dreiser e la sua battaglia sociale," La Cultura, 12 (Apr.-June), 431-37. Repub: Cesare Pavese, American Literature: Essays and Opinions. Trans. Edwin Fussell. Berkeley: U. California Press, 1970. Pp. 107-116 (as "Dreiser and His Social Battle").

K33-4 ANDERSON, SHERWOOD. "Sherwood Anderson to Theodore Dreiser," American Spectator, 1 (June), 1.

K33-5 ANON. "The Liberation of American Literature," London Times Literary Supplement, 15 June, pp. 401-02.

K33-6 HALEY, CARMEL O'NEILL. "The Dreisers," Commonweal, 18 (7 July), 265-67.

K33-7 ANON. "NRA and USSR," New York Times, 29 Aug., p. 16. Editorial.

K33-8 BIRSS, JOHN H. "Record of Theodore Dreiser: A Bibliographical Note," Notes and Queries, 165 (30 Sept.), 226.

K33-9 HANSEN, HARRY. "The First Reader," New York World-Telegram, 25 Nov., p. 17.

K33-10 McINTYRE, O. O. "Dinner With Dreiser," Cosmopolitan, 95 (Dec.), 56-57.

K33-11 WALDMAN, MILTON. "Tendencies of the Modern Novel," Fortnightly Review, 140 (Dec.), 717-25.

WORKS ON

1934

K34-1   M[ONROE], H[ARRIET]. "Comment: Dorothy Dudley's Frontiers,"
        Poetry, 43 (Jan.), 208-15.

K34-2   SCHNEIDER, ISIDOR. "Theodore Dreiser," Saturday Review of
        Literature, 10 (10 Mar.), 533-35.

K34-3   WEEKS, EDWARD. "A Modern Estimate of American Best Sellers,
        1875-1933," Publishers' Weekly, 125 (21 Apr.), 1507.

K34-4   GREGORY, HORACE. "Middle Western Gloom: Theodore Dreiser's
        Characters in Their Setting," Common Sense (May) [PU].

K34-5   CAMPBELL, LOUISE. "New Books: Speaking of Dreiser,"
        Philadelphia Evening Public Ledger, 18 July, p. 18.

1935

K35-1   GOLD, MICHAEL. "The Gun Is Loaded, Dreiser," New Masses, 15
        (7 May), 14-15.

K35-2   NEWMAN, LOUIS I. "Dreiser and Haman," Nation, 140 (15 May),
        572. Letter to editor dated 20 Apr.

K35-3   RODMAN, SELDEN. "Common Sense Protests," Nation, 140
        (15 May), 572. Letter to editor dated 25 Apr.

K35-4   ROTTENBERG, ABRAHAM. "Dreiser's Chauvinism," Nation, 140
        (15 May), 572. Letter to editor dated 18 Apr.

K35-5   SCHOENBERG, PHILIP. "Making the Jews Responsible," Nation,
        140 (15 May), 572-73. Letter to editor dated 20 Apr.

K35-6   SERWER, HARRY. "Racial Solidarity--a Myth," Nation, 140
        (15 May), 573. Letter to editor dated 13 Apr.

K35-7   TRACHTENBERG, JOSHUA. "Anti-Semites Both!" Nation, 140
        (15 May), 572. Letter to editor dated 23 Apr.

K35-8   WEIL, LEONARD D. "The Logical Solution," Nation, 140
        (15 May), 572. Letter to editor dated 15 Apr.

K35-9   ARVIN, NEWTON. "Fiction Mirrors America," Current History,
        42 (Sept.), 610-16.

Articles in Newspapers and Journals

1936

K36-1   SMITH, REBECCA W. "Portrait of an American: the National Character in Fiction," Southwest Review, 21 (Apr.), 245-60.

K36-2   COWLEY, MALCOLM. "Nobel Prize Oration," New Repbulic, 88 (19 Aug.), 36-38.

K36-3   CHAMBERLAIN, JOHN. "Theodore Dreiser," New Republic, 89 (23 Dec.), 236-38. Repub: After the Genteel Tradition. Ed. Malcolm Cowley. New York: Norton, 1937. Pp. 27-36. Kazin and Shapiro, pp. 127-32 (as "Theodore Dreiser Remembered"; See I55-1).

1937

K37-1   ANON. "Author Rejects Fame," New York Times, 5 Mar., p. 24. Editorial.

K37-2   FORD, FORD MADOX. "Theodore Dreiser," American Mercury, 40 (Apr.), 488-96. Repub: Ford Madox Ford, Portraits From Life. Boston: Houghton, 1937. Pp. 164-82. Kazin and Shapiro, pp. 21-35 (as "Portrait of Dreiser"; See I55-1).

K37-3   HUTH, JOHN F., JR. "Theodore Dreiser: 'The Prophet,'" American Literature, 9 (May), 208-17.

K37-4   ANON. "Dreiser Denies He Is Recognized," New York Times, 4 May, p. 21.

K37-5   ANON. "Footnotes on Headlines," New York Times, 9 May, Section 4, p. 2.

K37-6   ANON. "Dreiser Ordered to Repay Royalties," New York Times, 30 June, p. 21.

1938

K38-1   VIVAS, ELISEO. "Dreiser, An Inconsistent Mechanist," Ethics, 48 (July), 498-508. Repub: Eliseo Vivas, Creation and Discovery: Essays in Criticism and Aesthetics. New York: Noonday, 1955. Pp. 3-13. Kazin and Shapiro, pp. 237-45; See I55-1.

K38-2   HUTH, JOHN F., JR. "Dreiser and Success: An Additional Note," Colophon, 3 (Summer), 406-10.

WORKS ON

K38-3   NICHOLSON, GUY H. "Dreiser No Tennis Expert," New York Times,
         6 Aug., p. 9.

K38-4   AVARY, MYTRA. "Success--and Dreiser," Colophon, 3 (Autumn),
         598-604.

K38-5   LENGEL, WILLIAM C. "The 'Genius' Himself," Esquire, 10
         (Sept.), 55, 120, 124, 126.

K38-6   DICKSON, LOVAT. "The American Novel in England," Publishers'
         Weekly, 134 (29 Oct.), 1586-90.

K38-7   HUTH, JOHN F., JR. "Theodore Dreiser, Success Monger,"
         Colophon, 3 (Winter), 120-33.

                              1939

K39-1   CHURCHILL, DOUGLAS W. "Pointing at Hollywood," New York
         Times, 12 Mar., Section 11, p. 5.

K39-2   MASTERS, EDGAR LEE. "Dreiser at Spoon River," Esquire, 11
         (May), 66, 146, 151-52, 154, 156, 158.

                              1940

K40-1   VAN DOREN, CARL. "The Nation and the American Novel,"
         Nation, 150 (10 Feb.), 212.

K40-2   WALCUTT, CHARLES CHILD. "The Three States of Theodore
         Dreiser's Naturalism," PMLA, 55 (Mar.), 266-89. Repub:
         Charles Child Walcutt, American Literary Naturalism, A
         Divided Stream. Minneapolis: U. Minnesota Press, 1956.
         Pp. 180-221 (as "Theodore Dreiser: The Wonder and Terror
         of Life"). Kazin and Shapiro, pp. 246-69 (as "Theodore
         Dreiser and the Divided Stream"; See I55-1). Pizer,
         pp. 496-508 (as "Theodore Dreiser: The Wonder and Terror
         of Life"; See I70-1). Lydenberg, pp. 104-28 (as "Theodore
         Dreiser and the Divided Stream"; See I71-1).

K40-3   JOHNSON, OAKLEY. "Theodore Dreiser--Critic of Capitalist
         Society," People's Daily World, 31 Dec., p. 5.

Theodore Dreiser: A Bibliography

Articles in Newspapers and Journals

1941

K41-1   KAZIN, ALFRED. "The Lady and the Tiger: Edith Wharton and
          Theodore Dreiser," Virginia Quarterly Review, 17 (Winter),
          101-19. Repub: Alfred Kazin, On Native Grounds.
          New York: Harcourt, 1942. Pp. 73-90 (as "Two Educations:
          Edith Wharton and Theodore Dreiser"). Kazin and Shapiro,
          pp. 154-60 (as "Theodore Dreiser: His Education and
          Ours"; See I55-1).

K41-2   LORD, DAVID. "Dreiser Today," Prairie Schooner, 15 (Winter),
          230-39.

1942

K42-1   BOCKSTAHLER, OSCAR L. "Contributions to American Literature
          by Hoosiers of German Ancestry," Indiana Magazine of
          History, 38 (Sept.), 231-50.

K42-2   ANON. "Dreiser Flees As Abuse of Britain Stirs Storm of
          Protest," Toronto Evening Telegram, 22 Sept., p. 3.

K42-3   ANON. "Importation of Subversive Rot No Help to the War
          Effort," Toronto Evening Telegram, 22 Sept., p. 6.
          Editorial.

K42-4   MURRAY, GEORGE. "Poison Tongue of Mr. Dreiser," London
          Daily Mail, 22 Sept., p. 1 [PU].

K42-5   ANON. "Writers Assail Dreiser," New York Times, 25 Sept.,
          p. 6.

K42-6   ANON. "Writers' Board Censures Dreiser," New York PM,
          25 Sept., p. 12.

K42-7   MEYER, GEORGE W. "The Original Social Purpose of the
          Naturalistic Novel," Sewanee Review, 50 (Oct.-Dec.),
          563-70.

K42-8   ANON. "Dreiser," New Republic, 107 (5 Oct.), 397.

K42-9   PARRISH, ANNE, and JOSIAH TITZELL. "Writers Reply to Mr.
          Dreiser," New York Herald Tribune, 14 Oct., p. 22.

K42-10   ANON. "The Lion and the Paragraph," Portland Oregonian,
          21 Oct., p. 12.

WORKS ON

K42-11 RAHV, PHILLIP. "On the Decline of Naturalism," Partisan Re-
        view, 9 (Nov.-Dec.), 483-93. Repub: Phillip Rahv, Image
        and Idea. Norfolk, Conn.: New Directions, 1949. Pp. 128-
        38 (as "Notes on the Decline of Naturalism").

1943

K43-1   FARRELL, JAMES T. "James T. Farrell Revalues Dreiser's
        'Sister Carrie,'" New York Times Book Review, 4 July,
        p. 3. Repub: James T. Farrell, The League of Frightened
        Philistines. New York: Vanguard, 1945. Pp. 12-19 (as
        "Dreiser's Sister Carrie"). Kazin and Shapiro, pp. 182-87;
        See I55-1.

K43-2   ADAMS, J. DONALD. "Speaking of Books," New York Times Book
        Review, 18 July, p. 2.

1944

K44-1   ANON. "Academy's Award To Go to Dreiser," New York Times,
        28 Mar., p. 11.

K44-2   SMITH, WINIFRED. "The Worker as Hero," American Bookman, 1
        (Fall), 35-42.

1945

K45-1   FARRELL, JAMES T. "Some Aspects of Dreiser's Fiction,"
        New York Times Book Review, 29 Apr., pp. 7, 28.

K45-2   ARNAVON, CYRILLE. "Theodore Dreiser and Painting," American
        Literature, 17 (May), 113-26.

K45-3   FARRELL, JAMES T. "'An American Tragedy,'" New York Times
        Book Review, 6 May, pp. 6, 16.

K45-4   MELLETT, SUE. "Indiana In Literature," Indianapolis Star,
        3 June, Section 4, p. 18.

K45-5   SILLEN, SAMUEL. "'The Logic of My Life,'" Daily Worker,
        5 Aug., Magazine Section, pp. 1, 4.

K45-6   ANON. "Theodore Dreiser Dies at Age of 74," New York Times,
        29 Dec., pp. 1, 14.

Articles in Newspapers and Journals

K45-7   ANON. "Theodore Dreiser, Nation's Greatest Novelist, Dies at Age of 74," Sunday Worker, 30 Dec., p. 2.

K45-8   FAST, HOWARD. "He Knew the People," Sunday Worker, 30 Dec., p. 3.

K45-9   FOSTER, WILLIAM Z. "Communist Party's Tribute to Dreiser," Sunday Worker, 30 Dec., p. 2.

K45-10 SILLEN, SAMUEL. "His Art Led Him to Communism," Sunday Worker, 30 Dec., p. 3.

K45-11 ANON. "Los Angeles Communists to Honor Dreiser Memory," Daily Worker, 31 Dec., p. [6].

K45-12 ANON. "Realism's Trail Blazer," St. Louis Globe-Democrat, 31 Dec., p. 64.

K45-13 LERNER, MAX. "On Dreiser," New York PM, 31 Dec., p. 2. Repub: Max Lerner, Actions and Passions. New York: Simon, 1949. Pp. 43-46.

1946

K46-1   ANON. "Theodore Dreiser," New York Times, 1 Jan., p. 26. Editorial.

K46-2   ANON. "Topics of the Time," New York Times, 2 Jan., p. 18. Editorial.

K46-3   McCOY, ESTHER. "Theodore Dreiser Talks to a Friend," People's Daily World, 3 Jan., p. 1 [PU].

K46-4   ANON. "Russians Mourn Dreiser," New York Times, 5 Jan., p. 15.

K46-5   ANON. "Vale," Saturday Review of Literature, 29 (5 Jan.), 16.

K46-6   ANON. "Milestones," Time, 47 (7 Jan.), 77.

K46-7   ANON. "Transition," Newsweek, 27 (7 Jan.), 62.

K46-8   ANON. "Obituary Notes," Publishers' Weekly, 149 (12 Jan.), 178.

WORKS ON

K46-9   FARRELL, JAMES T. "Theodore Dreiser: In Memoriam," Saturday
         Review of Literature, 29 (12 Jan.), 15-17, 27-28. Repub:
         James T. Farrell, Literature and Morality. New York:
         Vanguard, 1947. Pp. 26-34.

K46-10   JONES, HOWARD MUMFORD. "Theodore Dreiser--A Pioneer Whose
         Fame Is Secure," New York Times Book Review, 13 Jan.,
         p. 6.

K46-11   MAYBERRY, GEORGE. "Dreiser: 1871-1945," New Republic, 114
         (14 Jan.), 56.

K46-12   BURGUM, EDWIN BERRY. "Theodore Dreiser, 1871-1945," New
         Masses, 58 (15 Jan.), 6.

K46-13   ARAGON, LOUIS. "When We Met Dreiser," New Masses, 58
         (29 Jan.), 6-7.

K46-14   BURGUM, EDWIN BERRY. "Dreiser and His America," New Masses,
         58 (29 Jan.), 7-9, 22. Repub: Edwin Berry Burgum, The
         Novel and the World's Dilemma. New York: Oxford Press,
         1947. Pp. 292-301 (as "Theodore Dreiser and the Ethics
         of American Life").

K46-15   DREIDEN, SIMON. "Theodore Dreiser in the Soviet Union,"
         New Masses, 58 (29 Jan.), 9.

K46-16   LAWSON, JOHN HOWARD. "Dreiser: 20th Century Titan," Sunday
         Worker, 3 Feb., Magazine Section, p. 9.

K46-17   BURGUM, EDWIN BERRY. "The America of Theodore Dreiser,"
         Book Find News, 2 (Mar.), 10-11, 21-22.

K46-18   DREISER, EDWARD. "My Brother, Theodore," Book Find News, 2
         (Mar.), 14-15.

K46-19   ELIAS, ROBERT H. "Theodore Dreiser: or, The World Well
         Lost," Book Find News, 2 (Mar.), 12-13, 22.

K46-20   JACKSON, CHARLES. "Theodore Dreiser and Style," Book Find
         News, 2 (Mar.), 16-17.

K46-21   LAWSON, JOHN HOWARD. "Tribute to Theodore Dreiser," Book
         Find News, 2 (Mar.), 19.

K46-22   SCHNEIDER, ISIDOR. "Dreiser . . . A Man of Integrity,"
         Book Find News, 2 (Mar.), 18, 22.

Articles in Newspapers and Journals

K46-23 SINCLAIR, UPTON, et al. "Theodore Dreiser: In Memoriam,"
        Book Find News, 2 (Mar.), 8-9.

K46-24 TJADER, MARGUERITE. "Dreiser's Last Year . . . The Bulwark
        in the Making," Book Find News, 2 (Mar.), 6-7, 20-21.

K46-25 ANON. "'The Bulwark' Has a History," Publishers' Weekly,
        149 (2 Mar.), 1390.

K46-26 HANSEN, HARRY. "Mencken Tells How He Tried to Reform
        Dreiser's Writing," Chicago Sunday Tribune, 24 Mar.,
        Part 4, p. 4.

K46-27 BRAZILLER, GEORGE. "How Will Dreiser Be Honored?" Book Find
        News, 2 (Apr.), 10.

K46-28 TJADER, MARGUERITE. "Theodore Dreiser: World Spirit,"
        Free World, 11 (Apr.), 56-57.

K46-29 JONES, HOWARD MUMFORD. "Dreiser Reconsidered," Atlantic
        Monthly, 177 (May), 162-70.

K46-30 RICHARDS, HODEE. "Dreiser's 'Bulwark': Summary of a Useful
        Life," People's Daily World, 8 May [PU]. Letter to editor.

K46-31 FARRELL, JAMES T. "Theodore Dreiser," Chicago Review, 1
        (Summer), 127-44. Repub: James T. Farrell, Selected
        Essays. Ed. Luna Wolf. New York: McGraw-Hill, 1964.
        Pp. 150-68.

K46-32 FARRELL, JAMES T. "Social Themes in American Realism,"
        English Journal, 35 (June), 309-15. Repub: James T.
        Farrell, Selected Essays. Ed. Luna Wolf. New York:
        McGraw-Hill, 1964. Pp. 3-13.

K46-33 ROLFE, EDWIN. "Theodore Dreiser," Poetry, 68 (June), 134-36.

K46-34 BROWN, CARROLL T. "Dreiser's Bulwark and Philadelphia
        Quakerism," Bulletin of the Friends Historical Association,
        35 (Autumn), 52-61.

K46-35 FLANAGAN, JOHN T. "Theodore Dreiser in Retrospect," South-
        west Review, 31 (Autumn), 408-11.

K46-36 TJADER, MARGUERITE. "Dreiser's Last Visit to New York,"
        Twice-a-Year, 15 (Fall-Winter), 217-28.

WORKS ON

K46-37   FAST, HOWARD. "Dreiser's Short Stories," New Masses, 60
         (3 Sept.), 11-12.

K46-38   LUDLOW, FRANCIS. "Plodding Crusader," College English, 8
         (Oct.), 1-7.

K46-39   ROSS, WOODBURN O. "Concerning Dreiser's Mind," American
         Literature, 18 (Nov.), 233-43.

                              1947

K47-1   RADIN, EDWARD. "The Original American Tragedy," New York
         Sunday Mirror, 26 Jan., Magazine Section, pp. 12-13.

K47-2   ANON. "Fulsome Praise: Dreiser and the Land of the Free,"
         Cresset, 11 (Feb.), 43-44.

K47-3   HELLESNES, NILS. "Theodore Dreiser," Syn Og Segn (Oslo), 53
         (Mar.), 116-20.

K47-4   COWLEY, MALCOLM. "Sister Carrie's Brother," New Republic,
         116 (26 May), 23-25. Repub: Kazin and Shapiro, pp. 171-
         74 (as Section 1 of "Sister Carrie: Her Fall and Rise";
         See I55-1). Lydenberg, pp. 52-56 (as Section 1 of "Sister
         Carrie's Brother"; See I71-1).

K47-5   COWLEY, MALCOLM. "The Slow Triumph of Sister Carrie," New
         Republic, 116 (23 June), 24-27. Repub: Kazin and
         Shapiro, pp. 174-81 (as Section 2 of "Sister Carrie: Her
         Fall and Rise"; See I55-1). Lydenberg, pp. 56-62 (as
         Section 2 of "Sister Carrie's Brother"; See I71-1).

K47-6   COWLEY, MALCOLM. "'Not Men': A Natural History of American
         Naturalism," Kenyon Review, 9 (Summer), 414-35. Repub:
         Evolutionary Thought in America. Ed. Stow Persons.
         New Haven: Yale U. Press, 1950. Pp. 300-33 (as "Natural-
         ism in American Literature").

K47-7   SILLEN, SAMUEL. "Final Volume of Dreiser Trilogy To Be Pub-
         lished This Fall," Daily Worker, 1 Aug., p. 11.

K47-8   HANSEN, HARRY. "'The Stoic', Third of Dreiser's Cowperwood
         Stories, Coming," Chicago Sunday Tribune, 31 Aug., Part 4,
         p. 5.

K47-9   ROCKWELL, KENNETH. "A Call on Dreiser," Dallas Daily Times
         Herald, 23 Nov., Part 6, p. 5.

THEODORE DREISER: A BIBLIOGRAPHY

Articles in Newspapers and Journals

1948

K48-1   MENCKEN, H. L. "That Was New York: The Life of an Artist,"
        New Yorker, 24 (17 Apr.), 64-71.

K48-2   REGAN, PATRICIA. "Realism--Or Is It?" Catholic World, 167
        (June), 235-42.

K48-3   FRANZ, ELEANOR W. "The Tragedy of the 'North Woods,'"
        New York Folklore Quarterly, 4 (Summer), 85-97.

1949

K49-1   PEARSON, NORMAN H. "Idealist in Conflict with Society,"
        Saturday Review of Literature, 32 (29 Jan.), 14-15.

K49-2   HOWE, IRVING. "Dreiser Undone," Nation, 168 (5 Feb.), 159-60.

K49-3   KAZIN, ALFRED. "Dreiser," New Yorker, 25 (26 Feb.), 91-93.
        Repub: Alfred Kazin, The Inmost Leaf. New York: Har-
        court, 1955. Pp. 236-41.

K49-4   BIZZARI, E. "Dreiser postumo," Fiera Letteraria, 6
        (16 May), 6.

K49-5   MORRIS, LLOYD. "Heritage of a Generation of Novelists,"
        New York Herald Tribune Books, 26 (25 Sept.), 12-13, 74.

1950

K50-1   ANON. "Edgar Lee Masters," Saturday Review of Literature, 33
        (25 Mar.), 21.

K50-2   BROOKS, VAN WYCK. "Theodore Dreiser," University of Kansas
        City Review, 16 (Spring), 187-97.

K50-3   BOWRON, BERNARD. "The Making of an American Scholar,"
        Monthly Review, 2 (Oct.), 212-22.

K50-4   MARX, LEO. "The Teacher," Monthly Review, 2 (Oct.), 205-10.

K50-5   MATTHIESSEN, F. O. "Of Crime and Punishment," Monthly Re-
        view, 2 (Oct.), 189-204. Repub: Matthiessen, pp. 187-
        211; See I51-2.

WORKS ON

1951

K51-1   MATTHIESSEN, F. O. "Dreiser's Politics," Tomorrow, 10
(Jan.), 10-17. Repub: Matthiessen, pp. 213-33; See
I51-2.

K51-2   VAN VECHTEN, CARL. "Theodore Dreiser as I Knew Him," Yale
University Library Gazette, 25 (Jan.), 87-92. Repub:
Carl Van Vechten, Fragments of an Unwritten Autobiography.
New Haven: Yale U. Press. Vol. 2, 3-15.

K51-3   BERRYMAN, JOHN. "Through Dreiser's Imagination the Tides of
Real Life Billowed," New York Times Book Review, 4 Mar.,
pp. 7, 29. Repub: Highlights of Modern Literature. Ed.
Francis Brown. New York: NAL, 1954. Pp. 118-23. Kazin
and Shapiro, pp. 149-53 (as "Dreiser's Imagination"; See
I55-1).

K51-4   KUSELL, SALLY. "Dreiser's Style," New York Times Book Review, 8 Apr., p. 26. Letter to editor.

K51-5   HOFSTADTER, RICHARD. "Native Sons of Literature," Nation,
172 (28 Apr.), 398.

K51-6   BELLOW, SAUL. "Dreiser and the Triumph of Art," Commentary,
11 (May), 502-03. Repub: Kazin and Shapiro, pp. 146-48;
See I55-1.

K51-7   KWIAT, JOSEPH J. "Dreiser and the Graphic Artist," American
Quarterly, 3 (Summer), 127-41.

K51-8   KRIM, SEYMOUR. "Theodore Dreiser," Hudson Review, 4
(Autumn), 474-77.

K51-9   TRILLING, LIONEL. "Dreiser, Anderson, Lewis, and the Riddle
of Society," Reporter, 5 (13 Nov.), 37-40.

K51-10 LEAVER, FLORENCE. "Theodore Dreiser, Beyond Naturalism,"
Mark Twain Quarterly, 9 (Winter), 5-9.

K51-11 ANON. "A Re-examination of Dreiser," London Times Literary
Supplement, 21 Dec., pp. 813-14.

1952

K52-1   STEINBRECHER, GEORGE, JR. "Inaccurate Accounts of Sister
Carrie," American Literature, 23 (Jan.), 490-93.

Articles in Newspapers and Journals

K52-2   SILLEN, SAMUEL. "Dreiser Predicted Wall Street's Attack on America's Essential Freedoms," People's Daily World, 3 Jan. [PU].

K52-3   KWIAT, JOSEPH J. "Dreiser's The 'Genius' and Everett Shinn, the 'Ash Can' Painter," PMLA, 67 (Mar.), 15-31.

K52-4   SHAPIRO, CHARLES. "The Role of Attitudes in the Novel," Folio, 18 (Nov.), 15-20.

K52-5   KERN, ALEXANDER. "Dreiser's Difficult Beauty," Western Review, 16 (Winter), 129-36. Repub: Kazin and Shapiro, pp. 161-68; See I55-1.

1953

K53-1   WIRZBERGER, KARL-HEINZ. "Die neueste amerikanische Dreiser forschung," Zeitschrift für Anglistik und Amerikanistik, 1 (Heft 2, 1953), 186-95.

K53-2   GEISMAR, MAXWELL. "Dreiser and the Dark Textures of Life," American Scholar, 22 (Spring), 215-21.

K53-3   KWIAT, JOSEPH J. "The Newspaper Experience: Crane, Norris, and Dreiser," Nineteenth-Century Fiction, 8 (Sept.), 99-117.

K53-4   AHNEBRINK, LARS. "Dreiser's Sister Carrie and Balzac," Symposium, 7 (Nov.), 306-22.

1954

K54-1   WIRZBERGER, KARL-HEINZ. "Das leben und schaffen Theodore Dreisers," Zeitschrift für Anglistik und Amerikanistik, 2 (Heft 1, 1954), 5-42.

K54-2   CRAWFORD, BRUCE. "Theodore Dreiser: Letter-Writing Citizen," South Atlantic Quarterly, 53 (Apr.), 231-37.

K54-3   WESTLAKE, NEDA M. "Theodore Dreiser's Notes on Life," Library Chronicle, 20 (Summer), 69-75.

K54-4   ANON. "The Girl in Big Moose Lake," The Monthly Letter of the Limited Editions Club, No. 253 (Aug.), 1-4.

Theodore Dreiser: A Bibliography

WORKS ON

K54-5   COHEN, LESTER. "Theodore Dreiser: A Personal Memoir,"
          Discovery, No. 4 (Sept.), 99-126.

K54-6   LEISY, ERNEST E. "Dreiser's Mennonite Origin," Mennonite
          Life, 9 (Oct.), 179-80.

                              1955

K55-1   ROSENBERG, BERNARD. "Mr. Trilling, Theodore Dreiser (and
          Life in the U. S.)," Dissent, 2 (Spring), 171-78.

K55-2   LYDENBERG, JOHN. "Theodore Dreiser: Ishmael in the Jungle,"
          Monthly Review, 7 (Aug.), 124-36. Repub: American Radi-
          cals. Ed. Harvey Goldberg. New York: Monthly Review
          Press, 1957. Pp. 37-52. Lydenberg, pp. 22-35; See I71-1.

K55-3   FILLER, LOUIS. "Dreamers, and the American Dream," Southwest
          Review, 40 (Autumn), 359-63.

K55-4   BECKER, GEORGE J. "Theodore Dreiser: The Realist as Social
          Critic," Twentieth Century Literature, 1 (Oct.), 117-27.

K55-5   GEISMAR, MAXWELL. "A Novelist True to Himself in a Shifting
          World," New York Times Book Review, 20 Nov., p. 4.

K55-6   ÅHNEBRINK, LARS. "Garland and Dreiser: An Abortive Friend-
          ship," Midwest Journal, 7 (Winter), 285-92.

K55-7   FRIEDRICH, GERHARD. "Theodore Dreiser's Debt to Woolman's
          Journal," American Quarterly, 7 (Winter), 385-92.

K55-8   SILLEN, SAMUEL. "Notes on Dreiser," Masses and Mainstream,
          8 (Dec.), 12-19.

                              1956

K56-1   FARRELL, JAMES T. "Dreiser," New York Times Book Review,
          8 Jan., p. 22. Letter to editor.

K56-2   GRANA, GIANNI. "La Rinàscita del naturalismo in Americana:
          Anderson e Dreiser," Fiera Letteraria, No. 3 (15 Jan.), 4.

K56-3   EDWARDS, OLIVER. "Moby Theo," London Times, 19 Jan., p. 11.

K56-4   RAPIN, RENE. "Dreiser's Jennie Gerhardt, Chapter LXII,"
          Explicator, 14 (May), 54.

Articles in Newspapers and Journals

K56-5   KRIM, SEYMOUR. "Dreiser and His Critics," Commonweal, 64
         (1 June), 229-31.

K56-6   KRUTCH, JOSEPH WOOD. "In These Days Our Literature in All
         Its Might Came of Age," New York Times Book Review,
         7 Oct., pp. 6-7, 40.

                              1957

K57-1   GLICKSBERG, CHARLES I. "Fiction and Philosophy," Arizona
         Quarterly, 13 (Spring), 5-17.

K57-2   WILLEN, GERALD. "Dreiser's Moral Seriousness," University of
         Kansas City Review, 23 (Spring), 181-87. Repub: Lyden-
         berg, pp. 96-103; See 171-1.

K57-3   THOMAS, J. D. "The Natural Supernaturalism of Dreiser's
         Novels," Rice Institute Pamphlets, 44 (Apr.), 112-25.

K57-4   FLINT, R. W. "Dreiser: The Press of Life," Nation, 184
         (Apr.), 371-73.

K57-5   FREIDRICH, GERHARD. "A Major Influence on Theodore Dreiser's
         The Bulwark," American Literature, 29 (May), 180-93.

K57-6   NOBLE, DAVID W. "Dreiser and Veblen: The Literature of
         Cultural Change," Social Research, 24 (Autumn), 311-29.
         Repub: Studies in American Culture: Dominant Ideas and
         Images. Eds. Joseph J. Kwiat and Mary C. Turpie. Min-
         neapolis: U. Minnesota Press, 1960. Pp. 139-52.

                              1958

K58-1   DURHAM, FRANK. "Mencken as Missionary," American Literature,
         29 (Jan.), 478-83.

K58-2   ADAMS, J. DONALD. "Speaking of Books," New York Times Book
         Review, 16 Feb., p. 2.

K58-3   SOLOMON, ERIC. "A Source for Fitzgerald's The Great Gatsby,"
         Modern Language Notes, 73 (Mar.), 186-88.

K58-4   ADAMS, J. DONALD. "Speaking of Books," New York Times Book
         Review, 6 Apr., p. 2.

WORKS ON

K58-5   NATHAN, GEORGE JEAN. "Memories of Fitzgerald, Lewis, and
        Dreiser," Esquire, 50 (Oct.), 148-54.

K58-6   ANISIMOV, IVAN I. "Put', prolozhennyi Draizerom," Inostran-
        naĩa literatura, No. 11 (Nov.), 219-32.

K58-7   STEWART, RANDALL. "Dreiser and the Naturalistic Heresy,"
        Virginia Quarterly, 34 (Winter), 100-16.

                                1959

K59-1   THOMAS, J. D. "The Supernatural Naturalism of Dreiser's
        Novels," Rice Institute Pamphlets, 46 (Apr.), 53-69.

K59-2   TAKAHASHI, ATSUKO. "A Study of Theodore Dreiser's Thought,"
        Essays and Studies in British and American Literature
        (Tokyo Women's Christian College), 7 (Summer), 71-102.

K59-3   HALSEY, VAN R. "Fiction and the Businessman: Society
        Through All Its Literature," American Quarterly, 11 (Fall),
        391-402.

K59-4   HANDY, WILLIAM J. "A Re-examination of Dreiser's Sister
        Carrie," Texas Studies in Language and Literature, 1
        (Autumn), 380-93. Repub: William J. Handy, Modern Fic-
        tion: A Formalist Approach. Carbondale: Southern
        Illinois U. Press, 1971 (as "Dreiser's Sister Carrie").

K59-5   SIMPSON, CLAUDE M., JR. "Sister Carrie Reconsidered," South-
        west Review, 44 (Winter), 44-53. Repub: Sister Carrie.
        Boston: Houghton, 1959. Pp. v-xix (as "Introduction").

K59-6   STEWART, RANDALL. "Moral Crisis as Structural Principle in
        Fiction: A Few American Examples," Christian Scholar, 42
        (Dec.), 284-89. Repub: Randall Stewart, Regionalism and
        Beyond: Essays of Randall Stewart. Ed. George Core.
        Nashville: Vanderbilt U. Press, 1968. Pp. 185-93.

                                1960

K60-1   HOFFMAN, FREDERICK J. "The Scene of Violence: Dostoevsky
        and Dreiser," Modern Fiction Studies, 6 (Summer), 91-105.
        Repub: Frederick J. Hoffman, The Mortal No: Death and
        the Modern Imagination. Princeton: Princeton U. Press.
        Pp. 179-201. Salzman, Merrill Studies, pp. 26-31; See
        I71-3.

Theodore Dreiser: A Bibliography

Articles in Newspapers and Journals

K60-2   BERNARD, KENNETH. "The Flight of Theodore Dreiser," University of Kansas City Review, 26 (June), 251-59.

K60-3   CHANG, WANG-ROK. "The Bulwark: Dreiser's Last Stand," English Language and Literature, 8 (June), 36-42.

K60-4   THOMAS, J. D. "Three American Tragedies: Notes on the Responsibilities of Fiction," South Central Bulletin, 20 (Winter), 11-15.

K60-5   COHEN, LESTER. ". . . And the Sinner--Horace Liveright," Esquire, 54 (Dec.), 107-08.

K60-6   FINKELSTEIN, SIDNEY. "Six Ways of Looking at Reality," Mainstream, 13 (Dec.), 31-42.

1961

K61-1   MILLGATE, MICHAEL. "Theodore Dreiser and the American Financier," Studi Americani, 7 (1961), 133-45. Repub: Michael Millgate, American Social Fiction: James to Cozzens. New York: Barnes, 1964. Pp. 67-86 (as "Theodore Dreiser").

K61-2   MARKELS, JULIAN. "Dreiser and the Plotting of Inarticulate Experience," Massachusetts Review, 2 (Spring), 431-48. Repub: Pizer, pp. 527-41, See I70-1. Salzman, Merrill Studies, pp. 45-55; See I71-3.

K61-3   GINGRICH, ARNOLD. "How To Become the Second-Best Authority on Almost Anything," Esquire, 55 (Apr.), 6.

K61-4   COURSEN, HERBERT R., JR. "Clyde Griffiths and the American Dream," New Republic, 145 (4 Sept.), 21-22.

K61-5   FARRELL, JAMES T. "James T. Farrell Recalls H. L. Mencken," Toledo Blade, 26 Nov., Section 2, p. 7. Letter to editor.

K61-6   BLOOM, ROBERT. "Past Indefinite: The Sherman-Mencken Debate on an American Tradition," Western Humanities Review, 15 (Winter), 73-81.

K61-7   HEUSTON, DUSTIN. "Theodore Dreiser: Naturalist or Theist," Brigham Young University Studies, 3 (Winter), 41-49.

THEODORE DREISER: A BIBLIOGRAPHY

1962

K62-1   PUTZEL, MAX. "Dreiser, Reedy, and 'De Maupassant, Junior,'" _American Literature_, 33 (Jan.), 466-84.

K62-2   MUNSON, GORHAM. "The Magic of the Short Story," _Connotation_, 1 (Spring), 2-9.

K62-3   ASKEW, MELVIN W. "The Pseudonymic American Hero," _Bucknell Review_, 10 (Mar.), 224-31.

K62-4   RICHMAN, SIDNEY. "Theodore Dreiser's The Bulwark: A Final Resolution," _American Literature_, 34 (May), 229-45.

K62-5   BLACKSTOCK, WALTER. "Dreiser's Dramatizations of Art, the Artist, and the Beautiful in American Life," _Southern Quarterly_, 1 (Oct.), 63-86.

K62-6   WARREN, ROBERT PENN. "An American Tragedy," _Yale Review_, 52 (Oct.), 1-15. Repub: Lydenberg, pp. 129-40; See I71-1. Salzman, _Merrill Studies_, pp. 99-111; See I71-3.

K62-7   FREEDMAN, WILLIAM A. "A Look at Dreiser as Artist: The Motif of Circularity in _Sister Carrie_," _Modern Fiction Studies_, 8 (Winter), 384-92.

1963

K63-1   NAGAHARA, MAKOTO. "Dreiser at the Turn of the Century-- _Sister Carrie_," _Ritsumeikan Bungaku_, No. 212 (Feb.), 17-36. In Japanese.

K63-2   GREBSTEIN, SHELDON N. "Dreiser's Victorian Vamp," _Midcontinent American Studies Journal_, 4 (Spring), 3-12. Repub: Pizer, pp. 541-51; See I70-1.

K63-3   WILSON, WILLIAM E. "The Titan and the Gentleman," _Antioch Review_, 23 (Spring), 25-34.

K63-4   SATŌ, SHŌHEI. "The World of Theodore Dreiser," _Gakuen_, No. 280 (Apr.), 18-40. In Japanese.

K63-5   CONROY, JACK. "Theodore Dreiser," _Inland: The Magazine of the Middle West_, No. 40 (Autumn), 9, 13-15. Repub: _American Book Collector_, 15 (Feb. 1965), 11-16.

Articles in Newspapers and Journals

K63-6   MOERS, ELLEN. "The Finesse of Dreiser," American Scholar, 33 (Winter), 109-14. Repub: Pizer, pp. 558-67; See I70-1. Lydenberg, pp. 153-62; See I71-1.

K63-7   LEHAN, RICHARD. "Dreiser's An American Tragedy: A Critical Study," College English, 25 (Dec.), 187-93. Repub: The Modern American Novel. Ed. Max Westbrook. New York: Random, 1966. Pp. 21-33.

K63-8   PHILLIPS, WILLIAM L. "The Imagery of Dreiser's Novels," PMLA, 78 (Dec.), 572-85. Repub: Pizer, pp. 551-58; See I70-1. Salzman, Merrill Studies, pp. 85-92; See I71-3.

1964

K64-1   LONG, ROBERT E. "Sister Carrie and the Rhythm of Failure in Fitzgerald," Fitzgerald Newsletter, No. 25 (Spring), 146-47.

K64-2   HAKUTANI, YOSHINOBU. "Dreiser and French Realism," Texas Studies in Language and Literature, 6 (Summer), 200-12.

K64-3   HAKUTANI, YOSHINOBU. "Sinclair Lewis and Dreiser: A Study in Continuity and Development," Discourse, 7 (Summer), 254-76.

K64-4   SAMUELS, CHARLES THOMAS. "Mr. Trilling, Mr. Warren, and An American Tragedy," Yale Review, 53 (Summer), 629-40. Repub: Lydenberg, pp. 163-73; See I71-1.

K64-5   HOWE, IRVING. "The Stature of Theodore Dreiser," New Republic, 151 (25 July), 19-21. Repub: An American Tragedy. New York: NAL, 1964. Pp. 815-20 (as first half of "Afterword"). Lydenberg, pp. 141-45 (as first half of "Dreiser and Tragedy: The Stature of Theodore Dreiser"; See I71-1). Salzman, Merrill Studies, pp. 32-37 (as first half of "An American Tragedy"; See I71-3).

K64-6   HOWE, IRVING. "Dreiser and the Tragedy," New Republic, 151 (22 Aug.), 25-28. Repub: An American Tragedy. New York: NAL, 1964. Pp. 820-28 (as second half of "Afterword"). Lydenberg, pp. 145-52 (as second half of "Dreiser and Tragedy: The Stature of Theodore Dreiser"; See I71-1). Salzman, Merrill Studies, pp. 37-44 (as second half of "An American Tragedy"; See I71-3).

WORKS ON

K64-7   WILLIAMS, PHILIP. "The Chapter Titles of Sister Carrie,"
        American Literature, 36 (Nov.), 359-65.

K64-8   DUDDING, GRIFFITH. "A Note Concerning Theodore Dreiser's
        Philosophy," Library Chronicle, 30 (Winter), 36-37.

K64-9   HANDY, WILLIAM J. "Saul Bellow and the Naturalistic Hero,"
        Texas Studies in Literature and Language, 5 (Winter),
        538-45.

                              1965

K65-1   BINNI, FRANCESCO. "Dreiser olfre il Naturalismo," Studi
        Americani, 11 (1965), 251-69.

K65-2   SWANBERG, W. A. "Dreiser Among the Slicks," Horizon, 7
        (Spring), 54-61.

K65-3   WAGNER, VERN. "The Maligned Style of Theodore Dreiser,"
        Western Humanities Review, 19 (Spring), 175-84.

K65-4   HICKS, GRANVILLE. "A Liar in Search of the Truth," Saturday
        Review, 48 (24 Apr.), 31-32.

K65-5   MOORE, HARRY T. "Dreiser: The Greatest? Tedious Bore?
        Sex Fiend? Trail Blazer? Hard Rock? Hypocrite?"
        Chicago Tribune Books Today, 25 Apr., p. 1. Repub: Harry
        T. Moore, Age of the Modern and Other Literary Essays.
        Carbondale: Southern Illinois U. Press, 1971. Pp. 73-76
        (as "Dreiser and the Inappropriate Biographer").

K65-6   SPILLER, ROBERT E. "A Giant Still Asking To Be Accounted
        For," New York Times Book Review, 16 May, pp. 4-5.

K65-7   EDWARDS, OLIVER. "A Compelling Novel," London Times, 5 Aug.,
        p. 13.

K65-8   FLANAGAN, JOHN T. "Dreiser's Style in An American Tragedy,"
        Texas Studies in Language and Literature, 7 (Autumn),
        285-94.

K65-9   MACAULEY, ROBIE. "Let Me Tell You About the Rich," Kenyon
        Review, 27 (Autumn), 645-71.

K65-10 SWANBERG, W. A. "Mencken and Dreiser," Menckaniana, No. 15
        (Fall), 6-8.

THEODORE DREISER: A BIBLIOGRAPHY

Articles in Newspapers and Journals

K65-11   OLSEN, HUMPHREY A. "Vincennes an Interlude in Famous Novel-
         ist's life," Vincennes [Ind.] Sun-Commercial, 29 Dec.,
         p. 11.

K65-12   PIZER, DONALD. "Nineteenth-Century American Naturalism: An
         Essay in Definition," Bucknell Review, 13 (Dec.), 1-18.
         Repub: Donald Pizer, Realism and Naturalism in Nineteenth-
         Century American Literature. Carbondale: Southern
         Illinois U. Press, 1966. Pp. 11-32 (as "Late Nineteenth-
         Century American Naturalism"). Pizer, pp. 567-73; See
         I71-1.

                              1966

K66-1   ANZILOTTI, ROLANDO. "Il viaggio di Dreiser in Italia,"
         Studi Americani, 12 (1966), 323-98.

K66-2   BUTLER, GERALD J. "The Quality of Emotional Greatness,"
         Paunch, No. 25 (Feb.), 5-17.

K66-3   EARNEST, ERNEST. "The American Ariel," South Atlantic
         Quarterly, 65 (Spring), 192-200.

K66-4   FILLER, LOUIS. "Sense, Sentimentality, and Theodore Dreiser,"
         Salamagundi, 1 (Spring), 90-97.

K66-5   STODDARD, DONALD R. "Mencken and Dreiser: An Exchange of
         Roles," Library Chronicle, 32 (Spring), 117-36.

K66-6   DEBOUZY, MARIANNE. "Theodore Dreiser," Les Langues Modernes,
         60 (Mar.-Apr.), 37-42.

K66-7   FLANAGAN, JOHN T. "Theodore Dreiser's Chicago," Revue des
         Langues Vivantes, 32 (Mar.-Apr.), 131-44.

K66-8   KATZ, JOSEPH. "Theodore Dreiser at Indiana University,"
         Notes and Queries, 13 (Mar.), 100-01.

K66-9   MAILER, NORMAN. "Modes and Mutations," Commentary, 41 (Mar.),
         37-40.

K66-10   TIPPETTS, SALLY L. "The Theatre in Dreiser's Sister Carrie,"
         Notes and Queries, 13 (Mar.), 99-100.

K66-11   VON SZELISKI, JOHN J. "Dreiser's Experiment with Tragic
         Drama," Twentieth Century Literature, 12 (Apr.), 31-40.

WORKS ON

K66-12 MOERS, ELLEN. "New Light on Dreiser in the 1890's," Columbia Library Columns, 15 (May), 10-24.

K66-13 LANE, LAURIAT, JR. "The Double in An American Tragedy," Modern Fiction Studies, 12 (Summer), 213-20.

K66-14 LEONARD, NEIL. "Theodore Dreiser and the Film," Film Heritage, 2 (Fall), 7-16.

K66-15 NUGENT, WALTER T. K. "Carter H. Harrison and Dreiser's 'Walden Lucas,'" Newberry Library Bulletin, 6 (Sept.), 222-30.

K66-16 MAYFIELD, SARA. "Another Fitzgerald Myth Exploded by Mencken," Fitzgerald Newsletter, No. 32 (Winter), 1.

1967

K67-1 KHAINDRAVA, L. "Problema zhenshchiny v romanakh Draizera," Literaturnaia Gruziia (Tbilisi), 3 (1967), 90-95.

K67-2 KHAINDRAVA, L. "Teodor Draizer o sud'be zhenshchiny v kapitalisticheskom mire," Trudy Tbiliskogo pedagogicheskogo instituta, 19 (1967), 233-47.

K67-3 MAZETS'KII, G. "Okrilenii zhovtnem. Do pitannia pro evolyutsiyu svitoglyadu i tvorchosti Teodora Draizera," Radyans'ske literaturoznavstvo (Kiev), 10 (1967), 19-25.

K67-4 YAMAMOTO, SHUJI. "Religion of Theodore Dreiser: Its Four Aspects," Kyushu American Literature, 10 (1967), 70-74.

K67-5 TJADER, MARGUERITE. "Rabota Draizera nad romanom 'Oplot,'" Voprosy Literatury, 11 (Jan.), 139-52.

K67-6 SALZMAN, JACK. "The Publication of Sister Carrie: Fact and Fiction," Library Chronicle, 33 (Spring), 119-33.

K67-7 HAKUTANI, YOSHINOBU. "Sister Carrie and the Problem of Literary Naturalism," Twentieth Century Literature, 13 (Apr.), 3-17.

K67-8 PURDY, STROTHER B. "An American Tragedy and L'Étranger," Comparative Literature, 19 (Summer), 252-68.

K67-9 BLACKSTOCK, WALTER. "The Fall and Rise of Eugene Witla: Dramatic Vision of Artistic Integrity in The 'Genius,'" Language Quarterly, 5 (Fall-Winter), 15-18.

THEODORE DREISER: A BIBLIOGRAPHY

Articles in Newspapers and Journals

K67-10   LONG, ROBERT E. "Dreiser and Frederic: The Upstate New York Exile of Dick Diver," Fitzgerald Newsletter, No. 37 (Winter), 1-2.

1968

K68-1   FURMANCZYK, WIESLAW. "The Conception of External Forces in Theodore Dreiser's Philosophical Notes," Acta Philologica, 1 (1968), 23-42.

K68-2   WALCUTT, CHARLES CHILD. "Sister Carrie: Naturalism or Novel of Manners," Genre, 1 (Jan.), 76-85.

K68-3   ADLER, BETTY. "Unmasked," Menckeniana, No. 25 (Spring), 16.

K68-4   SCOTT, KENNETH W. "Did Dreiser Cut Up Jack Harkaway?" Markham Review, No. 2 (May), 1-4.

K68-5   SODERBERGH, PETER A. "Theodore Dreiser in Pittsburgh, 1894," Western Pennsylvania Historical Magazine, 51 (July), 229-42.

K68-6   KATZ, JOSEPH. "Theodore Dreiser: Enter Chicago, Hope, and Walt Whitman," Walt Whitman Review, 14 (Dec.), 169-71.

1969

K69-1   POSTNOV, YU. S. "Masterstvo T. Draizera v romane 'Sestra Kerri,'" Voprosy yazyka i literatury (Novosibirskii universitet), 3 (1969), 75-85.

K69-2   SALZMAN, JACK. "Dreiser and Ade: A Note on the Text of Sister Carrie," American Literature, 40 (Jan.), 544-48.

K69-3   DOWELL, RICHARD W. "Sister Carrie: An Attack on the Gospel of Wealth," Indiana English Journal, 3 (Spring), 3-10.

K69-4   STESSIN, LAWRENCE. "The Businessman in Fiction," Literary Review, 12 (Spring), 281-89.

K69-5   KATOPE, CHRISTOPHER G. "Sister Carrie and Spencer's First Principles," American Literature, 41 (Mar.), 64-75.

K69-6   MULQUEEN, JAMES E. "Sister Carrie: A Modern Pilgrim's Progress," CEA Critic, 31 (Mar.), 8-20.

THEODORE DREISER: A BIBLIOGRAPHY

WORKS ON

K69-7   CAMPBELL, CHARLES L. "An American Tragedy: or, Death in the Woods," Modern Fiction Studies, 15 (Summer), 251-59.

K69-8   WYCHERLEY, H. ALAN. "Mechanism and Vitalism in Dreiser's Non-fiction," Texas Studies in Literature and Language, 11 (Summer), 1039-49.

K69-9   INGE, M. THOMAS. "Theodore Dreiser's Sister Carrie: Essay Topics," Exercise Exchange, 16 (Summer/Fall), 2-3.

K69-10 SALZMAN, JACK. "The Critical Recognition of Sister Carrie: 1900-1907," Journal of American Studies, 3 (July), 123-33.

K69-11 SAMUELS, CHARLES THOMAS. "The Irrepressible Dreiserian," New Republic, 161 (19 July), 25-26, 30-31.

K69-12 THOMAS, J. D. "Epimetheus Bound: Theodore Dreiser and the Novel of Thought," Southern Humanities Review, 3 (Fall), 346-57.

K69-13 PIZER, DONALD. "Theodore Dreiser's 'Nigger Jeff': The Development of an Aesthetic," American Literature, 41 (Nov.), 331-41.

K69-14 GRIFFIN, ERNEST G. "Sympathetic Materialism: A Rereading of Theodore Dreiser," Humanities Association Bulletin, 20 (Winter), 59-68.

1970

K70-1   CHUNTONOVA, NINA. "Ta, kotoraia ne boyalas' zhit'," Molodoi kommunist, No. 4 (1970), 120-25.

K70-2   HOVEY, RICHARD B., and RUTH S. RALPH. "Dreiser's The 'Genius': Motivation and Structure," Hartford Studies in Literature, No. 2 (1970), 169-83.

K70-3   PIZER, DONALD. "Dreiser Studies: Work To Be Done," Dreiser Newsletter, 1 (Spring), 10-13.

K70-4   PIZER, DONALD. "The Problem of Philosophy in the Novel," Bucknell Review, 18 (Spring), 53-62. Repub: Pizer, pp. 583-87; See I70-1.

K70-5   SWANBERG, W. A. "Airmail Interview," Dreiser Newsletter, 1 (Spring), 2-6.

284

THEODORE DREISER: A BIBLIOGRAPHY

Articles in Newspapers and Journals

K70-6   DOWELL, RICHARD W. "'On the Banks of the Wabash': A Musical Whodunit," Indiana Magazine of History, 66 (June), 95-109.

K70-7   MOOKERJEE, R. N. "Victims of a 'Degrading Doctrine': Dreiser's An American Tragedy," Indian Journal of American Studies, 1 (July), 23-32.

K70-8   ADAMS, RICHARD P. "Permutations of American Romanticism," Studies in Romanticism, 9 (Fall), 249-68.

K70-9   LEHAN, RICHARD. "Assessing Dreiser," Dreiser Newsletter, 1 (Fall), 1-3.

K70-10 MOERS, ELLEN. "Airmail Interview," Dreiser Newsletter, 1 (Fall), 4-10.

K70-11 SEARS, DONALD A., and MARGARET BOURLAND. "Journalism Makes the Style," Journalism Quarterly, 47 (Autumn), 504-09.

K70-12 FLEISSNER, R. F. "The Macomber Case: A Sherlockian Analysis," Baker Street Journal, 20 (Sept.), 154-56, 69.

K70-13 SWANBERG, W. A. "The Double Life of Theodore Dreiser," Critic, 29 (Nov.-Dec.), 20-27.

K70-14 KANE, PATRICIA. "Reading Matter as a Clue to Dreiser's Character," South Dakota Review, 8 (Winter), 104-06.

K70-15 DANCE, DARYL C. "Sentimentalism in Dreiser's Heroines, Carrie and Jennie," CLA Journal, 14 (Dec.), 127-42.

1971

K71-1   GILENSON, BORIS. "Sotsial'naia sila, preobrazuyuschaia mir," Inostrannaia literatura, No. 8 (1971), 191-96.

K71-2   GONCHAROV, L. N. "Teodor Draizer--borets za peredovuiu kulturu prosveshchenie S Sh A," Sovetskaia pedagogika, No. 11 (1971), 129-33.

K71-3   MOOKERJEE, R. N. "Dreiser's Ambivalent Naturalism: A Note on Sister Carrie," Rajasthan University Studies in English, 5 (1971), 36-48.

K71-4   NARTOV, K. "Issledovatel' tragicheskoi Ameriki," Literatura v shkole, 4 (1971), 92-94.

WORKS ON

K71-5   PASKALEVA, DONKA. "Pred 100-godishninata ot rozhdenieto na
         Teodor Draizer," Bibliotekar (Sofia), 18 (1971), 39-40.

K71-6   PIRINSKA, PAVLINA. "Teodor Draizer i Amerika," Literaturna
         misel (Sofia), 15 (1971), 133-45.

K71-7   PRESS, VIKTOR. "Velikii Amerikanets," Oktiabr', No. 8
         (1971), 209-12.

K71-8   SEQUEIRA, ISAAC. "A Note on the Influence of Dreiser's
         Tropistic Theory of Life on His Naturalistic Fiction,"
         Osmania Journal of English Studies, 8 (1971), 29-35.

K71-9   SHIRIAEVA, A. A. "T. Draizer," Srednee spetsial'noe obra-
         zovanie, 7 (1971), 48-50.

K71-10   ANON. "Reappraising Theodore Dreiser," London Times Literary
         Supplement, 1 Jan., p. 13.

K71-11   CHATTERJEE, RAJ. "Genius Bright and Base," Times of India,
         19 Jan., p. 8.

K71-12   DAHLBERG, EDWARD. "Dahlberg on Dreiser, Anderson, and Dahl-
         berg," New York Times Book Review, 31 Jan., pp. 2, 30-31.

K71-13   LABRIE, RODRIGUE E. "American Naturalism: An Appraisal,"
         Markham Review, 2 (Feb.), 88-90.

K71-14   GERBER, PHILIP L. "A Tragedy Ballad," Dreiser Newsletter, 2
         (Spring), 5-6.

K71-15   LEHAN, RICHARD. "Airmail Interview," Dreiser Newsletter, 2
         (Spring), 11-17.

K71-16   LOVING, JEROME M. "The Rocking Chair Structure of Sister
         Carrie," Dreiser Newsletter, 2 (Spring), 7-10.

K71-17   MOULTON, PHILLIPS P. "The Influence of the Writings of John
         Woolman," Quaker History, 60 (Spring), 3-13.

K71-18   WADLINGTON, WARWICK. "Pathos and Dreiser," Southern Review,
         7 (Spring), 411-29.

K71-19   WARREN, ROBERT PENN. "Homage to Theodore Dreiser on the
         Centenary of His Birth," Southern Review, 7 (Spring),
         345-410. Repub: Warren; See I71-4.

Articles in Newspapers and Journals

K71-20 GERBER, PHILIP L. "Dreiser's Financier: A Genesis," _Journal of Modern Literature_, 1 (Mar.), 354-74.

K71-21 MOURI, ITARU. "Reconsideration of _Sister Carrie_--The Significance of the Latent World," _Studies in English Literature_ (English Literary Society of Japan), 47 (Mar.), 199-215. In Japanese; English synopsis in the English number of Vol. 47, pp. 172-74.

K71-22 SALZMAN, JACK. "Dreiser Then and Now," _Journal of Modern Literature_, 1 (Mar.), 421-30.

K71-23 WITEMEYER, HUGH. "Gaslight and Magic Lamp in _Sister Carrie_," _PMLA_, 86 (Mar.), 236-40.

K71-24 GERBER, PHILIP L. "The Alabaster Protégé: Dreiser and Berenice Fleming," _American Literature_, 43 (May), 217-30.

K71-25 MOOKERJEE, R. N. "Dreiser's Use of Hindu Thought in _The Stoic_," _American Literature_, 43 (May), 273-78.

K71-26 MOERS, ELLEN. "When New York Made It," New York _Times Book Review_, 16 May, pp. 31-32.

K71-27 JURNAK, SHEILA HOPE. "Popular Art Forms in _Sister Carrie_," _Texas Studies in Literature and Language_, 13 (Summer), 313-20.

K71-28 MOOKERJEE, R. N. "The Literary Naturalist as Humanist: The Last Phase of Theodore Dreiser," _Midwest Quarterly_, 12 (Summer), 369-81.

K71-29 MENCKEN, H. L. "Minority Report: Third Series," _Menckeniana_, No. 38 (Summer), 1-2. Repub: _Dreiser Newsletter_, 5 (Spring 1974), 5 (as "Mencken on Dreiser").

K71-30 KELLER, DEAN H. "Dreiser's _Concerning Dives and Lazarus_," _Serif_, 8 (June), 31-32.

K71-31 DOUGLAS, GEORGE H. "Dreiser's Enduring Genius," _Nation_, 212 (28 June), 826-28.

K71-32 ANON. "Apostle of Naturalism," _MD_, 15 (July), 111-17.

K71-33 GILENSON, BORIS. "Dreiser in the Soviet Union," _Soviet Life_, No. 8 (Aug.), 55-57.

WORKS ON

K71-34 ZASURSKIĬ, YASEN N. "Khudozhnik besposhchadnoi pravdy," Literaturnaia gazete, 25 Aug., p. 15.

K71-35 DOWELL, RICHARD W. "Dreiser's Contribution to 'On the Banks of the Wabash': A Fiction Writer's Fiction!" Indiana English Journal, 6 (Fall), 7-13.

K71-36 PALMER, ERWIN. "Theodore Dreiser, Poet," South and West, 10 (Fall), 26-44.

K71-37 SCHMIDT-VON BARDELEBEN, RENATE. "Dreiser on the European Continent. Part One: Theodore Dreiser, the German Dreisers, and Germany," Dreiser Newsletter, 2 (Fall), 4-10.

K71-38 TJADER, MARGUERITE. "Airmail Interview," Dreiser Newsletter, 2 (Fall), 11-17.

K71-39 ZASURSKIĬ, YASEN N. "Spory o Draizere," Literaturnaia gazete, 22 Sept., p. 15.

K71-40 GENT, GEORGE. "Two Subjects for Centennial: Dreiser and Johnson," New York Times, 12 Oct., p. 48.

K71-41 McILVAINE, ROBERT M. "A Literary Source for the Caesarean Section in A Farewell to Arms," American Literature, 43 (Nov.), 444-47.

K71-42 HAKUTANI, YOSHINOBU. "Theodore Dreiser's Editorial and Free-Lance Writing," Library Chronicle, 37 (Winter), 70-85.

1972

K72-1 GILENSON, BORIS. "Our Friend Dreiser (On the centenary of his birth)," trans. Monica Whyte, Soviet Literature, No. 4 (1972), 172-75.

K72-2 HAJEK, FRIEDERIKE. "American Tragedy--Zwei Aspekte: Dargestellt in Richard Wrights Native Son und in Theodore Dreisers An American Tragedy," Zeitschrift für Anglistik und Amerikanistik, 20 (1972), 262-79.

K72-3 KERN, ALEXANDER C. "Dreiser and Fitzgerald as Social Critics," Papers of the Midwest Modern Language Association, No. 2 (1972), 80-87.

Articles in Newspapers and Journals

K72-4   RECCHIA, EDWARD. "Naturalism's Artistic Compromises in
         Sister Carrie and The Octopus," Literatur in Wissenschaft
         und Unterricht, 5 (1972), 277-85.

K72-5   FURMANCZYK, WIESLAW. "Theodore Dreiser's Philosophy in
         Notes on Life," Dreiser Newsletter, 3 (Spring), 9-12.

K72-6   SALZMAN, JACK. Introduction to "I Find the Real American
         Tragedy by Theodore Dreiser," Resources for American
         Literature Study, 2 (Spring), 3-4.

K72-7   SCHMIDT-VON BARDELEBEN, RENATE. "Dreiser on the European
         Continent. Part Two: The Reception of Dreiser in Western
         Europe," Dreiser Newsletter, 3 (Spring), 1-8.

K72-8   VANCE, WILLIAM L. "Dreiserian Tragedy," Studies in the Novel,
         4 (Spring), 39-51.

K72-9   DESAI, RUPIN W. "Delusion and Reality in Sister Carrie,"
         PMLA, 87 (Mar.), 309-10. Letter to editor.

K72-10   McILVAINE, ROBERT. "A Literary Source for Hurstwood's Last
         Scene," Research Studies, 40 (Mar.), 44-46.

K72-11   GERBER, PHILIP. "Dreiser Meets Balzac at the 'Allegheny
         Carnegie,'" Carnegie Magazine, 46 (Apr.), 137-39.

K72-12   WEIR, SYBIL B. "The Image of Women in Dreiser's Fiction.
         1900-1925," Pacific Coast Philology, 7 (Apr.), 65-71.

K72-13   BYERS, JOHN R., JR. "Dreiser's Hurstwood and Jefferson's
         Rip Van Winkle," PMLA, 87 (May), 514-16. Letter to
         editor.

K72-14   WITEMEYER, HUGH. "Sister Carrie: Plus ca change . . . ,"
         PMLA, 87 (May), 514. Letter to editor.

K72-15   LUNDÉN, ROLF. "The Antithetic Pattern of Theodore Dreiser's
         Art," American Studies in Scandinavia, No. 7 (Summer),
         39-56.

K72-16   ØVERLAND, ORM. "The Inadequate Vehicle: Dreiser's Finan-
         cier 1912-1945," American Studies in Scandinavia, No. 7
         (Summer), 18-38.

K72-17   ROSE, ALAN HENRY. "Sin and the City: The Users of Disorder
         in the Urban Novel," Centennial Review, 16 (Summer),
         203-20.

WORKS ON

K72-18 DEW, MARJORIE. "Realistic Innocence: Cady's Footnote to a Definition of American Literary Realism," American Literary Realism 1870-1910, 5 (Fall), 487-89.

K72-19 WESTLAKE, NEDA. "Airmail Interview," Dreiser Newsletter, 3 (Fall), 6-12.

K72-20 WILSON, GIL. "A Proposal for a Dreiser Mural," Dreiser Newsletter, 3 (Fall), 1-5.

K72-21 DOWELL, RICHARD W. "Medical Diary Reveals First Dreiser Visit to the University of Pennsylvania," Library Chronicle, 38 (Winter), 92-96.

K72-22 ELIAS, ROBERT H. "Bibliography and the Biographer," Library Chronicle, 38 (Winter), 25-44.

K72-23 GERBER, PHILIP. "Dreiser's Debt to Jay Cooke," Library Chronicle, 38 (Winter), 67-77.

K72-24 KATZ, JOSEPH. "Theodore Dreiser's Ev'ry Month," Library Chronicle, 38 (Winter), 46-66.

K72-25 McALEER, JOHN J. "An American Tragedy and In Cold Blood," Thought, 47 (Winter), 569-86.

K72-26 McALEER, JOHN J. "Dreiser's 'Notes on Life': Response to an Impenetrable Universe," Library Chronicle, 38 (Winter), 78-91.

K72-27 PIZER, DONALD. "Dreiser's Novels: The Editorial Problem," Library Chronicle, 38 (Winter), 7-24.

1973

K73-1 GERBER, PHILIP. "The Financier Himself: Dreiser and C. T. Yerkes," PMLA, 88 (Jan.), 112-21.

K73-2 BROGUNIER, JOSEPH. "Dreiser in Paperback: Riches and Rags," Dreiser Newsletter, 4 (Spring), 1-4.

K73-3 FORREY, ROBERT. "Theodore Dreiser," Dreiser Newsletter, 4 (Spring), 23-24.

K73-4 GROSS, DALTON H. "George Sterling's Letters to Theodore Dreiser: 1920-1926," Dreiser Newsletter, 4 (Spring), 14-20.

Theodore Dreiser: A Bibliography

Articles in Newspapers and Journals

K73-5   HUSSMAN, LAWRENCE E., JR. "Dreiser's Emotional Power,"
         Dreiser Newsletter, 4 (Spring), 12-13.

K73-6   STONE, WILLIAM B. "Dreiser and C. T. Yerkes," PMLA, 88
         (Oct.), 1188-89. Letter to editor.

K73-7   BURGAN, MARY A. "'Sister Carrie' and the Pathos of Natural-
         ism," Criticism, 15 (Fall), 336-49.

K73-8   DOUGLAS, GEORGE H. "Ludwig Lewisohn on Theodore Dreiser,"
         Dreiser Newsletter, 4 (Fall), 1-6.

K73-9   DOWELL, RICHARD W. "Dreiser's Address to the Future,"
         Dreiser Newsletter, 4 (Fall), 10-11.

K73-10   ENGLAND, D. GENE. "A Further Note on the 'Dreiser' Annota-
         tions," Dreiser Newsletter, 4 (Fall), 9-10.

K73-11   MOERS, ELLEN. "A 'New' First Novel by Arthur Henry,"
         Dreiser Newsletter, 4 (Fall), 7-9.

L

REVIEWS

With the exception of the 1926, 1928 and 1935 editions of Moods, the revised edition of The Financier, and the Constable edition of Plays, reviews of all editions of a particular work are listed in chronological order under the title of the work. Because of this classified arrangement, the first two digits in the entry number signify the year of publication of the first edition of the work, not the year of publication of the review. The year of publication of the review is given in the entry itself.

As a general rule, we have omitted reviews of less than 150 words unless we found they were significant because of the reviewers, the contents, or the sources in which they appeared. Only one appearance of a syndicated review is presented.

We have noted the first book republication of a review plus any additional republication in books included in section I. Textual changes and deletions in connection with republication are not indicated.

An asterisk at the end of an entry based on a clipping or republication (see L11-12 and L14-45) indicates that we were unable to locate the review in the place cited. In these instances, the asterisk signifies that the review does exist, but the bibliographical information may not be accurate.

SISTER CARRIE (1900)

L00-1   M., I. F. "A Round of the Latest Fiction," Louisville Times,
         20 Nov. 1900, p. 7. Repub: Kazin and Shapiro, pp. 53-54;
         See I55-1. Salzman, p. 1; See I72-2.

L00-2   ANON. "Mere Mention: 'Sister Carrie,'" Detroit Free Press,
         24 Nov. 1900, p. 11. Repub: Salzman, p. 2; See I72-2.

L00-3   [KENTON, EDNA]. "Glances at New Books," Chicago Daily News,
         30 Nov. 1900, p. 14. Repub: Salzman, pp. 2-3; See I72-2.

L00-4   ANON. "Book Reviews," Hartford [Conn.] Courant, 6 Dec. 1900,
         p. 10. Repub: Salzman, p. 3; See I72-2.

L00-5   Toledo Blade, 8 Dec. 1900 [PU]. Repub: Salzman, p. 3; See
         I72-2.

L00-6   ANON. "Literature: Sister Carrie," New York Commercial Ad-
         vertiser, 19 Dec. 1900, p. [6]. Repub: Kazin and Shapiro,
         pp. 55-58; See I55-1. Salzman, pp. 4-5; See I72-2.

L00-7   ANON. "New Books and Announcements," Albany Journal, 22 Dec.
         1900, p. 9. Repub: Salzman, p. 5; See I72-2.

L00-8   SEIBEL, GEORGE. "A Novel of City Life," Pittsburgh Commer-
         cial Gazette, 28 Dec. 1900, p. 7. Repub: Salzman,
         pp. 5-6; See I72-2.

L00-9   ANON. "Two Good Novels and Another," Churchman, 82 (29 Dec.
         1900), 814. Repub: Salzman, p. 6; See I72-2.

L00-10   ANON. "A Feminine Type," San Francisco Chronicle, 30 Dec.
         1900, p. 28. Repub: Salzman, p. 6; See I72-2.

L00-11   ANON. "A Novel of To-day," Recreation, 14 (Jan. 1901), 66.
         Repub: Salzman, p. 6; See I72-2.

L00-12   LITTE, pseud. [William Marion Reedy]. "Sister Carrie: A
         Strangely Strong Novel in a Queer Milieu," St. Louis
         Mirror, 10 (3 Jan. 1901), 6-7. Repub: Salzman, pp. 6-8;
         See I72-2.

L00-13   New Haven Journal Courier, 12 Jan. 1901 [PU]. Repub:
         Salzman, pp. 8-9; See I72-2.

L00-14   ANON. "Must Not Defy Social Law," Chicago Chronicle, 14 Jan.
         1901, p. 10. Repub: Salzman, p. 9; See I72-2.

WORKS ON

L00-15 ANON. "Recent Publications: Sister Carrie," Indianapolis Journal, 14 Jan. 1901, p. 4. Repub: Salzman, p. 9; See I72-2.

L00-16 HORTON, GEORGE. "Strong Local Novel," Chicago Times-Herald, 16 Jan. 1901, p. 9. Repub: Salzman, p. 10; See I72-2.

L00-17 ANON. "In the World of Books," Seattle Post-Intelligencer, 20 Jan. 1901, p. 29. Repub: Salzman, p. 11; See I72-2.

L00-18 ANON. "New Books: A Study in 'Realism,'" Denver Republican, 20 Ján. 1901, p. 29. Repub: Salzman, pp. 10-11; See I72-2.

L00-19 RICE, WALLACE. Chicago American, 26 Jan. 1901 [PU]. Repub: Salzman, p. 12; See I72-2.

L00-20 Syracuse Post-Standard, ? Feb. 1901 [PU]. Repub: Kazin and Shapiro, p. 61; See I55-1. Salzman, pp. 12-13; See I72-2.

L00-21 The Interior, 21 Feb. 1901 [PU]. Repub: Salzman, p. 13; See I72-2.

L00-22 ANON. "New Fiction," Louisville Courier-Journal, 23 Feb. 1901, p. 5. Repub: Salzman, p. 14; See I72-2.

L00-23 ANON. "Among the New Books," Chicago Daily Tribune, 25 Feb. 1901, p. 6. Repub: Salzman, pp. 14-15; See I72-2.

L00-24 VAN WESTRUM, A. SCHADE. "The Decadence of Realism," Book Buyer, 22 (Mar. 1901), 136-37.

L00-25 KERFOOT, J. B. "The Latest Books," Life, 37 (7 Mar. 1901), 187.

L00-26 ANON. "New Books of the Week: Sister Carrie," Indianapolis News, 9 Mar. 1901, p. 23. Repub: Salzman, pp. 17-18; See I72-2.

L00-27 ANON. "Books Worth Reading: Dollar Library, No. 6," London Daily Express, 12 Aug. 1901, p. 2.

L00-28 ANON. "Fiction: Sister Carrie," Edinburgh Scotsman, 12 Aug. 1901, p. 2. Repub: Salzman, p. 18; See I72-2.

L00-29 London Daily Mail, 13 Aug. (?) 1901 [PU]. Repub: Salzman, p. 18; See I72-2.

Reviews: SISTER CARRIE

L00-30 ANON. "New Novels," Manchester Guardian, 14 Aug. 1901,
        p. 9. Repub: Salzman, pp. 18-19; See I72-2.

L00-31 ANON. "Fiction: Sister Carrie," Academy, 61 (24 Aug. 1901),
        153. Repub: Salzman, pp. 20-21; See I72-2.

L00-32 ANON. "Novels of the Week," Spectator (London), 87 (24 Aug.
        1901), 257. Repub: Salzman, pp. 19-20; See I72-2.

L00-33 "American Fiction," London Daily Chronicle, 26 Aug. 1901 [PU].
        Repub: Salzman, pp. 21-22; See I72-2. Salzman repub-
        lishes part of the Daily Chronicle review as appearing in
        the London Express.

L00-34 ANON. "Sister Carrie," Newark Sunday News, 1 Sept. 1901,
        Magazine Section, p. 2. Repub: Kazin and Shapiro,
        pp. 62-64; See I55-1. Salzman, pp. 15-17; See I72-2.

L00-35 Eversham Journal, 7 Sept. 1901 [PU]. Repub: Salzman,
        pp. 22-23; See I72-2.

L00-36 [WATTS-DUNTON, THEODORE]. "New Novels: Sister Carrie,"
        Athenaeum, 7 Sept. 1901, pp. 312-13. Repub: Salzman,
        pp. 23-24; See I72-2.

L00-37 GILDER, JEANNETTE L. "Among the New Books: Withdrawn
        Novel Is to Be Given a Second Publication," Chicago Daily
        Tribune, 27 Apr. 1907, p. 8. Repub: Salzman, p. 25;
        See I72-2.

L00-38 COOPER, FREDERIC TABER. "The Fetich of Form and Some Recent
        Novels," Bookman, 25 (May 1907), 287. Repub: Salzman,
        p. 26; See I72-2.

L00-39 RHODES, HARRISON. "Mr. Dreiser's 'Sister Carrie,'" Bookman,
        25 (May 1907), 298-99. Repub: Salzman, pp. 27-29; See
        I72-2.

L00-40 ANON. "New Books: Romances for May," New York Sun, 11 May
        1907, p. 7.

L00-41 ANON. "Sister Carrie," New York Times Saturday Review of
        Books, 25 May 1907, p. 332. Repub: Salzman, p. 29;
        See I72-2.

L00-42 ANON. "Late Works of Fiction," New York World, 1 June 1907,
        p. 10.

THEODORE DREISER: A BIBLIOGRAPHY

WORKS ON

L00-43 ANON. "'Sister Carrie,'" New York Evening Sun, 1 June 1907,
       p. 4. Repub: Salzman, pp. 30-31; See I72-2.

L00-44 [REPPLIER, AGNES?]. "Among the Books: Sister Carrie,"
       Philadelphia Public Ledger, 1 June 1907, p. 10. Repub:
       Salzman, pp. 29-30; See I72-2.

L00-45 ANON. "Books of the Day: Sister Carrie," Boston Evening
       Transcript, 5 June 1907, p. 20. Repub: Salzman, pp. 32-
       33; See I72-2.

L00-46 ANON. "The Career of 'Sister Carrie,'" Boston Daily Ad-
       vertiser, 5 June 1907, p. 7. Repub: Salzman, pp. 31-32;
       See I72-2.

L00-47 Buffalo Times, 6 June 1907 [PU].

L00-48 St. Louis Mirror, 6 June 1907 [PU].

L00-49 ANON. "A Plain Tale from the Life," Kansas City [Mo.] Star,
       8 June 1907, p. 5. Repub: Salzman, pp. 33-34; See
       I72-2.

L00-50 ANON. "With the Novelists," Newark Evening News, 8 June
       1907, Second Section, p. 12. Repub: Salzman, pp. 34-35;
       See I72-2.

L00-51 Buffalo Courier, 8 June 1907 [PU]. Repub: Salzman, p. 34;
       See I72-2.

L00-52 LYON, HARRIS MERTON. "Theodore Dreiser's 'Sister Carrie':
       A Review of a Re-published Book," Houston Post, 9 June
       1907, p. 26. Repub: Salzman, pp. 35-38; See I72-2.

L00-53 ANON. "American Realism," Los Angeles Sunday Times, 16 June
       1907, Part 6, p. 14. Repub: Salzman, pp. 38-40; See
       I72-2.

L00-54 ROBERTSON, CARL T. "A Week's Selection of Fiction: 'Sister
       Carrie,'" Cleveland Plain Dealer, 16 June 1907, p. 7.
       Repub: Salzman, p. 40; See I72-2.

L00-55 Baltimore American, 17 June 1907 [PU].

L00-56 St. Louis Republic, 22 June 1907 [PU].

L00-57 ANON. "Triumphant Vindication of a Suppressed Novel," Balti-
       more Sun, 26 June 1907, p. 12. Repub: Salzman, pp. 41-
       42; See I72-2.

L00-58 Advance (Chicago), 27 June 1907 [PU]. Repub: Salzman, pp. 42-43; See I72-2.

L00-59 NON, A., pseud. "Major and Minor," Musical Leader and Concert Goer, 13 (27 June 1907), 13. Repub: Salzman, p. 42; See I72-2.

L00-60 ANON. "Books: 'Sister Carrie,'" Denver Republican, 30 June 1907, p. 19.

L00-61 ANON. "Recent Fiction and the Critics: Sister Carrie," Current Literature, 43 (July 1907), 109-110.

L00-62 COOPER, FREDERIC TABER. "The Fallacy of Tendencies in Fiction: Sister Carrie," Forum, 39 (July 1907), 117-18. Repub: Salzman, pp. 43-44; See I72-2.

L00-63 ANON. "Recent Publications: Sister Carrie," New Orleans Daily Picayune, 1 July 1907, p. 14. Repub: Salzman, pp. 44-45; See I72-2.

L00-64 ANON. "New Books: Sister Carrie," Boston Journal, 4 July 1907, p. 11. Repub: Salzman, p. 46; See I72-2.

L00-65 ANON. "The Matinee Girl," New York Dramatic Mirror, 6 July 1907, p. 2.

L00-66 BRASTOW, VIRGINIA. "In the Book World: 'Sister Carrie,'" San Francisco Bulletin, 6 July 1907, p. 15.

L00-67 ANON. "New Books Reviewed," Hartford [Conn.] Courant, 8 July 1907, p. 10. Repub: Salzman, pp. 46-47; See I72-2.

L00-68 HINSDALE, LAURA F. "Biography of a Country-Bred Girl in a Metropolis," Denver Rocky Mountain News, 15 July 1907, p. 7.

L00-69 ANON. "Sister Carrie," Washington Evening Star, 20 July 1907, Part 3, p. 6. Repub: Salzman, pp. 47-48; See I72-2.

L00-70 ANON. "The New Fiction," Chicago Evening Post, 27 July 1907, p. 8.

L00-71 ANON. "'Sister Carrie,'" Louisville Courier-Journal, 27 July 1907, p. 9. Repub: Salzman, pp. 48-49; See I72-2.

THEODORE DREISER: A BIBLIOGRAPHY

WORKS ON

L00-72 ANON. "Some Summer Novels," Indianapolis Star, 27 July 1907,
p. 11. Repub: Salzman, p. 49; See I72-2.

L00-73 ANON. "Books and Bookmen: A 'Purpose' Novel," New York
Press, 31 July 1907, p. 5. Repub: Kazin and Shapiro,
p. 68, under incorrect date; See I55-1. Salzman, pp. 45-
46, under incorrect date; See I72-2.

L00-74 Harrisburg [Pa.] Star-Independent, 31 July 1907 [PU].

L00-75 CORYN, SIDNEY G. P. "Books and Authors: Sister Carrie,"
Argonaut, 61 (3 Aug. 1907), 73. Repub: Salzman, p. 50;
See I72-2.

L00-76 ANON. "Literary Matters: 'Sister Carrie,'" Detroit Journal,
10 Aug. 1907, p. 12.

L00-77 ANON. "New Publications: Some Summer Fiction," New Orleans
Times-Democrat, 25 Aug. 1907, Part Third, p. 2.

L00-78 Paris Modes, Sept. 1907 [PU]. Repub: Salzman, pp. 50-51;
See I72-2.

L00-79 ANON. "Sister Carrie's Romance," Boston Herald, 14 Sept.
1907, p. 5.

L00-80 MOYER, REED. "Our Literary Letter," Mobile [Ala.] Register,
15 Sept. 1907, p. 13.

L00-81 COATES, JOSEPH HORNER. "'Sister Carrie,'" North American
Review, 186 (Oct. 1907), 288-91. Repub: Salzman,
pp. 51-53; See I72-2.

L00-82 HUBNER, CHARLES W. "Literary Gossip: 'Sister Carrie,'"
Atlanta Journal, 16 Nov. 1907, p. 7.

L00-83 ANON. "New Books," Milwaukee Evening Wisconsin, 22 Nov.
1907, p. 15.

L00-84 NON, A., pseud. "Major and Minor," Musical Leader and Concert Goer, 14 (28 Nov. 1907), 13. Repub: Salzman,
p. 53; See I72-2.

L00-85 ANON. "Book Review: 'Sister Carrie,'" Akron Beacon
Journal, 30 Nov. 1907, p. 4. Repub: Salzman, pp. 53-54;
See I72-2.

L00-86 ANON. "A Fascinating Story," Salt Lake City Tribune,
25 Feb. 1912, p. 20.

298

L00-87 ANON. "With Authors and Books," Chicago Record-Herald,
29 Feb. 1912, p. 6.

L00-88 Hartford [Conn.] Times, 1 Mar. 1912 [PU].

L00-89 ANON. "American Vanity Fair," Boston Daily Globe, 2 Mar.
1912, p. 11.

L00-90 ANON. "Sister Carrie," Washington Evening Star, 2 Mar. 1912,
Part 2, p. 9.

L00-91 "On the Library Table: New Books," Utica Press, 3 Mar. 1912
[PU].

L00-92 ANON. "The Latest in Books: 'Sister Carrie,' by Theodore
Dreiser," Grand Rapids Evening Press, 7 Mar. 1912, p. 11.

L00-93 "Mr. Dreiser's First Novel," Brooklyn Standard Union, 8 Mar.
1912 [PU].

L00-94 ANON. "Sister Carrie," Portland [Oreg.] Evening Telegram,
9 Mar. 1912, p. 19.

L00-95 [BASHFORD, HERBERT?]. "Sister Carrie," San Francisco
Bulletin, 9 Mar. 1912, p. [14].

L00-96 Cleveland Plain Dealer, 9 Mar. 1912 [PU].

L00-97 Detroit Free Press, 9 Mar. 1912 [PU].

L00-98 ANON. "A Tale of Boston: Mr. Russell Sullivan's New Novel
and Other Examples of Current Tendencies in Fiction,"
Providence Sunday Journal, 10 Mar. 1912, Third Section,
p. 9.

L00-99 STANARD, MARY NEWTON. "On the Reviewer's Table: 'Sister
Carrie,'" Richmond Times-Dispatch, 10 Mar. 1912, Society
Section, p. 12.

L00-100 ROBINSON, HELEN RING. "Views and Reviews," Denver Rocky
Mountain News, 11 Mar. 1912, p. 10.

L00-101 ANON. "The New Fiction," New Orleans Daily Picayune, 17 Mar.
1912, Part Three, p. 10.

L00-102 ANON. "Sister Carrie," New Orleans Times-Democrat, 17 Mar.
1912, Part Four, p. 7.

WORKS ON

L00-103 "'Sister Carrie,'" Waterbury Democrat, 23 Mar. 1912 [PU].

L00-104 "A Realistic Story," Newark Call, 24 Mar. 1912 [PU].

L00-105 ANON. "'Sister Carrie,'" Springfield Sunday Republican, 24 Mar. 1912, p. 31.

L00-106 ANON. "Sister Carrie Reprinted," Philadelphia Inquirer, 30 Mar. 1912, p. 6.

L00-107 ANON. "Springtime Literature: Sister Carrie," Boston Herald, 30 Mar. 1912, p. 4.

L00-108 Trenton Advertiser, 31 Mar. 1912 [PU].

L00-109 CABELL, ISA CARRINGTON. "Recent Fiction," Bellman, 12 (6 Apr. 1912), 436.

L00-110 "Sister Carrie," Brooklyn Times, 6 Apr. 1912 [PU].

L00-111 "Sister Carrie," New Haven Journal Courier, 6 Apr. 1912 [PU].

L00-112 ANON. "Many New Volumes for Spring Readers: 'Sister Carrie,'" Dallas Morning News, 8 Apr. 1912, p. 4.

L00-113 ANON. "'Sister Carrie' Once More," Brooklyn Daily Eagle, 20 Apr. 1912, p. 5.

L00-114 ANON. "Second Edition of 'Sister Carrie,'" Baltimore Sun, 5 May 1912, Part 4, p. 7.

L00-115 "Sister Carrie," Boston Zion's Herald, 8 May 1912 [PU].

L00-116 "Current Fiction: 'Sister Carrie,'" Des Moines Register Leader, 11 May 1912 [PU].

L00-117 COOK, PAUL. "The Book Shelf: 'Sister Carrie,'" Birmingham [Ala.] Age-Herald, 12 May 1912, p. 33.

L00-118 MASON, WALT. "Among the Booksmiths," Kansas City [Mo.] Star, 19 May 1912, Editorial Section, p. 3D.

L00-119 "Miss in Her Teens," London Daily Chronicle, 16 July 1912 [PU].

L00-120 ANON. "Current Fiction: Sister Carrie," Nation, 95 (25 July 1912), 80.

Reviews: JENNIE GERHARDT

L00-121 H[ACKETT], F[RANCIS]. "Sister Carrie," New Republic, 14
    (23 Feb. 1918), 116-17.

L00-122 "'Sister Carrie,'" Toronto Saturday Night, 19 Oct. 1918 [PU].

L00-123 ANON. "New Novels: Sister Carrie," London Times Literary
    Supplement, 12 May 1927, p. 334.

L00-124 TAYLOR, RACHEL ANNAND. "The Beginning of Dreiser,"
    Spectator (London), 138 (14 May 1927), Literary Supple-
    ment, 859, 861.

L00-125 ANON. "Books Worth Reading," John O'London's Weekly, 17
    (11 June 1927), 299.

L00-126   "New Novels: Sister Carrie," London Daily Telegraph,
    1 July 1927 [PU].

L00-127 GEISMAR, MAXWELL. "Jezebel on the Loop," Saturday Review,
    36 (4 July 1953), 12.

JENNIE GERHARDT (1911)

L11-1   ANON. "Jennie Gerhardt's Love," New York World, 21 Oct. 1911,
    p. 10.

L11-2   ANON. "Realism," New York Tribune, 21 Oct. 1911, p. 8. Re-
    pub: Salzman, p. 57; See I72-2.

L11-3   ANON. "Dreiser's New Novel Reaches Friends Here," Kansas
    City [Mo.] Journal, 22 Oct. 1911, Second Section, p. 1B.
    Repub: Salzman, pp. 57-58; See I72-2.

L11-4   ANON. "Love Stories of Many Years Told in Mr. Nevill's
    'Romantic Past,'" New York Herald, 28 Oct. 1911, p. 8.
    Repub: Salzman, pp. 59-60; See I72-2.

L11-5   ANON. "Some New Books of the Week," New York Globe and
    Commercial Advertiser, 28 Oct. 1911, p. 8. Repub:
    Salzman, pp. 60-61; See I72-2.

L11-6   P., P. M. "Of Many Sorts: Another 'Real Story,'" Syracuse
    Post-Standard, 28 Oct. 1911, p. 4.

L11-7   MENCKEN, H. L. "A Novel of the First Rank," Smart Set, 35
    (Nov. 1911), 153-55. Repub: H. L. Mencken's Smart Set
    Criticism. Ed. William H. Nolte. Ithaca, N.Y.: Cornell

WORKS ON

U. Press, 1968. Pp. 244-48 (as "A Modern Tragedy").
Salzman, pp. 61-64; See 172-2.

L11-8   DELL, FLOYD. "A Great Novel," Chicago Evening Post Friday
Literary Review, 3 Nov. 1911, p. 1. Repub: Salzman,
pp. 64-68; See 172-2.

L11-9   ANON. "New Fiction: 'Jennie Gerhardt,'" Detroit Free Press,
4 Nov. 1911, p. 11. Repub: Salzman, p. 70; See 172-2.

L11-10 SHUMAN, EDWIN L. "Significant New Fiction," Chicago Record-
Herald, 4 Nov. 1911, p. 5. Repub: Salzman, pp. 68-69;
See 172-2.

L11-11 WARREN, FREDERIC BLOUNT. "Reviews of Some of the Season's
New Books," New York Morning Telegraph, 5 Nov. 1911 [PU].
Repub: Salzman, p. 70; See 172-2.

L11-12 "'Jennie Gerhardt' a Great Book," Kansas City [Mo.] Post,
9 Nov. 1911* [PU]. Repub: Salzman, p. 72; See 172-2.

L11-13 ANON. "More Craving for Love," Chicago Daily Journal,
11 Nov. 1911, p. 13.

L11-14 ANON. "Study of Femininity," Boston Daily Globe, 11 Nov.
1911, p. 9 (Morning ed.); p. 7 (Evening ed.).

L11-15 PEATTIE, ELIA W. "A New Novel by Robert Herrick: Some
Other New Fiction," Chicago Daily Tribune, 11 Nov. 1911,
p. 11. Repub: Salzman, p. 71; See 172-2.

L11-16 ANON. "Recent Publications: Jennie Gerhardt," New Orleans
Daily Picayune, 12 Nov. 1911, Third Part, p. 10.

L11-17 BIBLIOPHILE, THE, pseud. "The Book Shelf: 'Jennie Gerhardt,'" Birmingham [Ala.] Age-Herald, 12 Nov. 1911, p. 44.

L11-18 "Jennie Gerhardt," Philadelphia Telegraph, 15 Nov. 1911 [PU].

L11-19 ANON. "A Consideration of Current Fiction: Jennie Gerhardt,"
Continent, 42 (16 Nov. 1911), 1650.

L11-20 ANON. "In the Realm of Imagination," Boston Herald, 18 Nov.
1911, p. 8.

L11-21 ANON. "New Books in Brief: 'Jennie Gerhardt,'" Chicago
Inter Ocean, 18 Nov. 1911, p. 5.

L11-22 ANON. "Notices of New Books: 'Jennie Gerhardt,'" Burlington [Ia.] Saturday Evening Post, 18 Nov. 1911, p. 4 [i.e. 6].

L11-23 ANON. "Passing Reference to a Few of the New Books Seen in the Stalls: Real Life on the Printed Page," Pittsburg Press, 18 Nov. 1911, p. [4].

L11-24 [BASHFORD, HERBERT?]. "Jennie Gerhardt. One of the Most Distinctive Novels of the Year," San Francisco Bulletin, 18 Nov. 1911, p. [17]. Repub: Salzman, p. 72; See I72-2.

L11-25 ANON. "Jennie Gerhardt on a Big Canvas," New York Times Review of Books, 19 Nov. 1911, p. 728. Repub: Salzman, pp. 73-74; See I72-2.

L11-26 ANON. "Literary Notes: Jennie Gerhardt," Peoria [Ill.] Herald-Transcript, 19 Nov. 1911, p. 24. Repub: Salzman, p. 74; See I72-2.

L11-27 ANON. "Story Books and Others: Story of a Woman," Buffalo Express, 19 Nov. 1911, Part 2, p. 17.

L11-28 "Theodore Dreiser's Second Novel," New Orleans Times-Democrat, 19 Nov. 1911* [PU]. Repub: Salzman, p. 73; See I72-2.

L11-29 ANON. "Mirthful Knights in Modern Days: Jennie Gerhardt," Dallas Morning News, 20 Nov. 1911, p. 4. Repub: Salzman, p. 74; See I72-2.

L11-30 ANON. "Book Reviews: Jennie Gerhardt. A Novel," Washington Evening Star, 25 Nov. 1911, Part 2, p. 9. Repub: Salzman, pp. 75-76; See I72-2.

L11-31 "A Bold, Pitiful Story," Brooklyn Standard Union, 25 Nov. 1911 [PU].

L11-32 [MARKHAM, EDWIN]. "Theodore Dreiser's Second Novel," New York American, 25 Nov. 1911, p. 8. Repub: Salzman, pp. 58-59, under incorrect date; See I72-2.

L11-33 New Haven Journal and Courier, 25 Nov. 1911 [PU]. Repub: Salzman, p. 75; See I72-2.

L11-34 Waterbury [Conn.] Democrat, 25 Nov. 1911 [PU]. Repub: Salzman, p. 75; See I72-2.

WORKS ON

L11-35 ANON. "Some of the New Books This Week," St. Paul [Minn.] Pioneer Press, 26 Nov. 1911, Section 3, p. 4.

L11-36 MENCKEN, H. L. "The Free Lance," Baltimore Evening Sun, 27 Nov. 1911 [PU].

L11-37 ANON. "Among the Books," Cleveland News, 29 Nov. 1911, Magazine Section, p. 10.

L11-38 REEDY, WILLIAM MARION. "Jennie Gerhardt," St. Louis Mirror, 20 (30 Nov. 1911), 4.

L11-39 WINTER, CALVIN. "Theodore Dreiser's 'Jennie Gerhardt,'" Bookman, 34 (Dec. 1911), 432-34. Repub: Salzman, pp. 76-78; See I72-2.

L11-40 ANON. "'Jennie Gerhardt' Is Sordid Realism," Philadelphia Press, 2 Dec. 1911, p. 7. Repub: Salzman, pp. 78-79; See I72-2.

L11-41 ANON. "A Luckless Woman," Boston Daily Advertiser, 2 Dec. 1911, p. 8.

L11-42 ANON. "New Books: Realistic and Sad," New York Sun, 2 Dec. 1911, p. 8.

L11-43 ANON. "'Jennie Gerhardt,'" San Francisco Chronicle, 3 Dec. 1911, Magazine Section, p. [6]. Repub: Salzman, pp. 79-80; See I72-2.

L11-44 SINCLAIR, UPTON. "Some Comment on Books," New York Call, 3 Dec. 1911, Magazine Section, p. 13.

L11-45 Baltimore Evening News, 5 Dec. 1911 [PU]. Repub: Salzman, p. 80; See I72-2.

L11-46 ANON. "Literature: Jennie Gerhardt," Independent, 71 (7 Dec. 1911), 1267-68. Repub: Salzman, pp. 80-81; See I72-2.

L11-47 ANON. "Jennie Gerhardt," Philadelphia Inquirer, 9 Dec. 1911, p. 10.

L11-48 LESTER, WILLIAM R. "Realistic Novel of Present Time," Philadelphia North American, 9 Dec. 1911, p. 15.

L11-49 New York Evening Mail, 9 Dec. 1911* [PU]. Repub: Salzman, p. 81; See I72-2.

Reviews: JENNIE GERHARDT

L11-50 ANON. "Book Talk: A Woman's Life Story," Columbus Ohio State Journal, 10 Dec. 1911, Society Section, p. 6.

L11-51 ANON. "In the Literary World: Jennie Gerhardt," Nashville Tennessean and American, 10 Dec. 1911, Section Two, p. 11.

L11-52 "Jennie Gerhardt," Brooklyn Citizen, 10 Dec. 1911 [PU].

L11-53 MENCKEN, H. L. "'Jennie Gerhardt,'" Los Angeles Sunday Times Magazine, 10 Dec. 1911, Holiday Book Section, p. 4.

L11-54 GUITERMAN, ARTHUR. "Rhymed Reviews: Jennie Gerhardt," Life, 58 (14 Dec. 1911), 1104.

L11-55 ANON. "On the Library Table," Utica [N.Y.] Press, 15 Dec. 1911 [PU]. Repub: Salzman, p. 82; See I72-2.

L11-56 ANON. "Strong But Not Pleasant," Hartford [Conn.] Times, 15 Dec. 1911, p. 21.

L11-57 KINSLEY, P. A. "Variety of Plots Nicely Trimmed: A Girl and Her Lovers," Philadelphia Record, 16 Dec. 1911, p. 11.

L11-58 SMITH, EMILY FRANCES. "Books Worth While: 'Jennie Gerhardt,'" Independent (Kansas City, Mo.), 26 (16 Dec. 1911), 6.

L11-59 ANON. "Books and Bookmen: 'Jennie Gerhardt,'" New York Press, 23 Dec. 1911, p. 5. Repub: Salzman, p. 82; See I72-2.

L11-60 B[LOCK], A[NITA] C. "One of the New Books: Jennie Gerhardt," New York Call, 24 Dec. 1911, Magazine Section, p. 15. Repub: Salzman, pp. 82-84; See I72-2.

L11-61 ANON. "An American Novelist," Nation (London), 10 (30 Dec. 1911), 564.

L11-62 ANON. "'Jennie Gerhardt,'" Oshkosh [Wis.] Daily Northwestern, 30 Dec. 1911, p. 6.

L11-63 ANON. "The Latest Books: Jennie Gerhardt," Argonaut, 69 (30 Dec. 1911), 449.

L11-64 "Jennie Gerhardt," Pittsburgh Index, 30 Dec. 1911 [PU].

L11-65 New York Satire, 30 Dec. 1911 [PU].

WORKS ON

L11-66   Advance (Chicago), Jan. 1912 [PU]. Repub: Salzman, pp. 84-85; See I72-2.

L11-67   ANON. "Book Reviews: Jennie Gerhardt: Theodore Dreiser's Second Novel of American Life," Craftsman, 21 (Jan. 1912), 458-59. Repub: Salzman, pp. 85-86; See I72-2.

L11-68   ANON. "Recent Fiction and the Critics: Jennie Gerhardt," Current Literature, 52 (Jan. 1912), 114.

L11-69   ANON. "The Season's Best Fiction: Some Novels of Distinction," American Review of Reviews, 45 (Jan. 1912), 123.

L11-70   KERFOOT, J. B. "A Row of Books," Everybody's Magazine, 26 (Jan. 1912), 284.

L11-71   RICHMOND, JOHN. "The Realism of Theodore Dreiser," Metropolitan Magazine, 35 (Jan. 1912), 50. Repub: Salzman, pp. 86-87; See I72-2.

L11-72   FIELD, ROSWELL. "Dreiser's Novel Nearly Great," Chicago Examiner, 4(?) Jan. 1912 [PU]. Repub: Salzman, p. 88; See I72-2.

L11-73   KERFOOT, J. B. "The Antics of Maiden Aunts," Life, 59 (4 Jan. 1912), 65. Repub: Salzman, pp. 87-88; See I72-2.

L11-74   CABELL, ISA CARRINGTON. "Recent Books," Bellman, 12 (6 Jan. 1912), 20. Repub: Salzman, pp. 88-89; See I72-2.

L11-75   ANON. "Current Fiction: Jennie Gerhardt," Nation, 94 (11 Jan. 1912), 34-35. Repub: Salzman, pp. 89-90; See I72-2.

L11-76   LESLIE, JAMES EDWARD. "Book News," Pittsburg Dispatch, 14 Jan. 1912* [PU].

L11-77   ANON. "Current Fiction: Jennie Gerhardt," New York Evening Post, 27 Jan. 1912, Saturday Supplement, p. 7.

L11-78   LUBLIN, CURTIS. "The Case of 'Jennie Gerhardt,'" Town and Country, 66 (3 Feb. 1912), 22.

L11-79   ANON. "Jennie Gerhardt: A Type," Toronto Sunday World, 4 Feb. 1912 [PU].

L11-80   ANON. "James Burrill Angell: Jennie Gerhardt," Portland [Oreg.] Evening Telegram, 10 Feb. 1912, p. 19.

Reviews: JENNIE GERHARDT

L11-81 "Jennie Gerhardt," Brooklyn Times, 10 Feb. 1912 [PU].

L11-82 NON, A., pseud. "Major and Minor," Musical Leader and Concert Goer, 23 (15 Feb. 1912), 19.

L11-83 ANON. "Recent Fiction," Dial, 52 (16 Feb. 1912), 131-32. Repub: Salzman, p. 90; See I72-2.

L11-84 ANON. "A Grim Tale, Out of the Common and Well Told," Indianapolis Star, 10 Mar. 1912, p. 17.

L11-85 London Times, 12 Mar. 1912* [PU].

L11-86 ANON. [Jennie Gerhardt], Cleveland Town Topics, 16 Mar. 1912, p. 22.

L11-87 ANON. "A New Novel by Theodore Dreiser," Newark Evening News, 16 Mar. 1912, p. 28. Repub: Salzman, p. 91; See I72-2.

L11-88 DAINGERFIELD, ELIZABETH. "Jennie Gerhardt," Lexington Herald, 24 Mar. 1912, Fourth Section, p. 2. Repub: Salzman, pp. 91-92; See I72-2.

L11-89 NON, A., pseud. "Major and Minor," Musical Leader and Concert Goer, 23 (2 May 1912), 19. Repub: Salzman, p. 92; See I72-2.

L11-90 LANDON, ROWANA HEWITT. Columbus [Ohio] Dispatch, 11 May 1912 [PU]. Repub: Salzman, pp. 92-93; See I72-2.

L11-91 H., M. O. "'Jennie Gerhardt,'" Toronto Globe, 13 July 1912, p. 18.

L11-92 K[ERFOOT], J. B. "Hints for Highbrows," Life, 59 (13 June 1912), 1210.

L11-93 ANON. "The Test of Time: 'Jennie Gerhardt,'" Indianapolis News, 14 Feb. 1914, p. 7.

L11-94 SACKVILLE-WEST, V. "Reviews: New Novels," The Nation & Athenaeum, 44 (2 Feb. 1929), 620, 622.

L11-95 TAYLOR, RACHEL ANNAND. "Fiction: Sad Fields and Sick Cities," Spectator (London), 142 (2 Feb. 1929), 169-70.

L11-96 ANON. "A Life of Sacrifice," Glasgow Herald, 7 Feb. 1929 [PU].

WORKS ON

L11-97   W., J. D.   "A Woman in May Fair," Cambria Daily Leader,
         9 Feb. 1929 [PU].

L11-98   ANON.   "Jennie Gerhardt," London Times Literary Supplement,
         14 Feb. 1929, p. 116.

L11-99   SEYMOUR-SMITH, MARTIN.   "Stupefying Power," Spectator, 223
         (16 Aug. 1969), 210.   Reviewed with The Financier and
         The Titan.

THE FINANCIER (1912)

L12-1   [MENCKEN, H. L.].   "Today's Book," Baltimore Evening Sun,
         29 Oct. 1912, p. 4.

L12-2   ANON.   "Books of the Week: By Theodore Dreiser," New York
         Globe and Commercial Advertiser, 2 Nov. 1912, p. 7.

L12-3   ANON.   "Fiction: 'Traction' Interests," New York Tribune,
         2 Nov. 1912, p. 11.   Repub: Salzman, pp. 97-98; See
         I72-2.

L12-4   ANON.   "The Financier," New York American, 2 Nov. 1912, p. 6.

L12-5   ANON.   "Good Native Stories," Brooklyn Daily Eagle, 2 Nov.
         1912, Picture and Sporting Section, p. 7.   Repub: Salzman,
         pp. 98-99; See I72-2.

L12-6   ANON.   "A Hero of High Finance," New York World, 2 Nov. 1912,
         p. 6.   Repub: Salzman, p. 98; See I72-2.

L12-7   FORD, JAMES L.   "'The Financier' Is a 'Loaf of Human Life,'"
         New York Herald, 2 Nov. 1912, p. 14.

L12-8   ANON.   "A Story of Money and Love," Salt Lake City Tribune,
         3 Nov. 1912, Magazine Section, p. [9].

L12-9   E[DGETT], E[DWIN] F[RANCIS].   "Theodore Dreiser," Boston
         Evening Transcript, 6 Nov. 1912, p. 24.   Repub: Salzman,
         pp. 99-100; See I72-2.

L12-10   ANON.   "An Unsuccessful Financier," New York Evening Mail,
         9 Nov. 1912, p. 8.   Repub: Salzman, p. 101; See I72-2.

L12-11   ANON.   "Of an Early Financier," Buffalo Express, 10 Nov. 1912,
         Part 2, p. 19.

L12-12 MENCKEN, H. L. "Dreiser's Novel: The Story of a Financier Who Loved Beauty," New York Times Review of Books, 10 Nov. 1912, p. 654. Repub: Salzman, pp. 101-04; See I72-2.

L12-13 ANON. "Theodore Dreiser's New Novel," New York Evening Sun, 11 Nov. 1912, p. [8]. Repub: Salzman, pp. 104-05; See I72-2.

L12-14 ANON. "Year's Strongest Novels," Continent, 43 (14 Nov. 1912), 1616-17.

L12-15 Waco [Tex.] Times Herald, 14 Nov. 1912 [PU].

L12-16 MENCKEN, H. L. "The Free Lance," Baltimore Evening Sun, 15 Nov. 1912, p. 6.

L12-17 ANON. "Fiction: 'The Financier,'" Detroit Free Press, 16 Nov. 1912, p. 6.

L12-18 ANON. "The Financier," Philadelphia Press, 16 Nov. 1912, p. 8. Repub: Salzman, p. 105; See I72-2.

L12-19 ANON. "The Financier," Portland [Oreg.] Evening Telegram, 16 Nov. 1912, p. 19.

L12-20 ANON. "The Financier," St. Louis Post-Dispatch, 16 Nov. 1912, p. 4. Repub: Salzman, pp. 107-08; See I72-2.

L12-21 ANON. "A Philadelphia Novel," Philadelphia Inquirer, 16 Nov. 1912, p. 16.

L12-22 ANON. "Stirring, Poignant, Dramatic," Salt Lake City Herald-Republican, 16 Nov. 1912, p. [14].

L12-23 [BASHFORD, HERBERT?]. "The Financier. Theodore Dreiser Writes Another Big Novel," San Francisco Bulletin, 16 Nov. 1912, p. [18]. Repub: Salzman, p. 106; See I72-2.

L12-24 LESTER, W. R. "Dreiser's 'The Financier,'" Philadelphia North American, 16 Nov. 1912, p. 13.

L12-25 ROBERTSON, CARL T. "On the Book Shelves: Fiction Received," Cleveland Plain Dealer, 16 Nov. 1912, p. 8. Repub: Salzman, pp. 105-06; See I72-2.

L12-26 ANON. "'The Financier,'" San Francisco Chronicle, 17 Nov. 1912, Magazine Section, p. [6]. Repub: Salzman, pp. 108-09; See I72-2.

WORKS ON

L12-27   ANON. "Some Recent Novels," Providence Sunday Journal,
         17 Nov. 1912, Third Section, p. 9. Repub: Salzman,
         p. 108; See I72-2.

L12-28   ANON. "Books and Bookmen: 'The Financier,'" New York Press,
         18 Nov. 1912, p. 11.

L12-29   JEWETT, C. T. "News of Authors and Their Books," Terre Haute
         [Ind.] Star, 18 Nov. 1912, p. 4.

L12-30   SAGE, WILLIAM E. "Mary Johnston's Great Novel of the War:
         'The Financier,'" Cleveland Leader, 18 Nov. 1912, p. 6.
         Repub: Salzman, p. 109; See I72-2.

L12-31   "Our Book Table," San Francisco   Zion's Herald, 20 Nov.
         1912 [PU].

L12-32   ANON. "The Latest in Books," Grand Rapids Evening Press,
         21 Nov. 1912, p. 16.

L12-33   CARY, LUCIAN. "A Big Novel," Chicago Evening Post Friday
         Literary Review, 22 Nov. 1912, p. 1. Repub: Salzman,
         pp. 109-12; See I72-2.

L12-34   ANON. "Book Reviews: The Financier," Washington Evening
         Star, 23 Nov. 1912, Part 2, p. 9.

L12-35   ANON. "In 'The Financier,'" Boston Daily Globe, 23 Nov.
         1912, p. 9 (Morning ed.); p. [13] (Evening ed.).

L12-36   ANON. "The News of the New Books: 'The Financier' Did Not
         Get His Training in Sunday School," Kansas City [Mo.]
         Star, 23 Nov. 1912, p. 7.

L12-37   "'The Financier,'" Kansas City [Mo.] Post, 23 Nov. 1912* [PU].

L12-38   ANON. "'Simkin's on Equity' by Texas Writer: 'The
         Financier,'" Dallas Morning News, 25 Nov. 1912, p. 3.

L12-39   ANON. "Cowperwood the Primitive," Boston Daily Advertiser,
         28 Nov. 1912, p. 8.

L12-40   ANON. "The Financier," Hartford [Conn.] Courant, 28 Nov.
         1912, p. 21. Repub: Salzman, pp. 112-13; See I72-2.

L12-41   ANON. "New Books: The Career of a Money Maker," New York
         Sun, 30 Nov. 1912, Second Section, p. 2.

THEODORE DREISER: A BIBLIOGRAPHY

L12-42 K., D. S. "The Financier," Boston Times, 30 Nov. 1912 [PU].
        Repub: Salzman, pp. 113-14; See I72-2.

L12-43 LENGEL, W. C. "Criticism," Wichita Beacon, 30 Nov. 1912 [PU].

L12-44 New York Morning Telegraph, 30 Nov. 1912 [PU].

L21-45 ANON. "Literature and Art," Current Literature, 53 (Dec.
        1912), 696-97.

L21-46 COOPER, FREDERIC TABER. "Theory of Endings and Some Recent
        Novels: The Financier," Bookman, 36 (Dec. 1912), 435-36.
        Repub: Salzman, pp. 115-17; See I72-2.

L21-47 ANON. "A Strong Novel of Finance by Theodore Dreiser,"
        Baltimore Sun, 1 Dec. 1912, Part 3, p. 7. Repub: Salzman,
        pp. 117-18; See I72-2.

L21-48 C., R. "New Novels: An American Novel," Manchester Guardian,
        4 Dec. 1912, p. 4.

L21-49 ANON. "Good Books for Christmas," Chicago Banker, 7 Dec.
        1912, p. 19.

L12-50 "A Very Long Novel by Theodore Dreiser," Toronto Mail Empire,
        7 Dec. 1912 [PU].

L12-51 ANON. "The Financier," Newark Sunday Call, 8 Dec. 1912,
        Part 3, p. 9.

L12-52 ANON. "Recent Publications: The Financier," New Orleans
        Daily Picayune, 8 Dec. 1912, Third Part, p. 14.

L12-53 MENCKEN, H. L. "'The Financier.' Powerful Novel of Modern
        Commerce by Theodore Dreiser," Los Angeles Times Magazine,
        8 Dec. 1912, Holiday Book Section, p. 6.

L12-54 PECKHAM, H. H. "Theodore Dreiser Scores a Success," Raleigh
        [N.C.] News and Observer, 8 Dec. 1912* [PU]. Repub:
        Salzman, pp. 118-19; See I72-2.

L12-55 Good Health Clinic (Syracuse, N.Y.), 12 Dec. 1912 [PU].

L12-56 Des Moines Register Leader, 14 Dec. 1912 [PU]. Repub:
        Salzman, p. 119; See I72-2.

L12-57 LESTER, W. R. "Strong Novel of American Life," Philadelphia
        North American, 14 Dec. 1912, p. 15.

WORKS ON

L12-58 ANON. "Book Notices: The Financier," Bookseller, Newsdealer, and Stationer, 37 (15 Dec. 1912), 671.

L12-59 ANON. "Literary Notes: 'The Financier,'" Augusta [Ga.]
Chronicle, 15 Dec. 1912, Section B, p. 3. Repub: Salzman,
pp. 114-15, as appearing in Harper's Monthly Magazine,
Dec. 1912; See I72-2. We could not locate the review in
Harper's.

L12-60 ANON. "No Hero Stalks Through His Pages," Kansas City [Mo.]
Journal, 15 Dec. 1912, p. 7A. Repub: Salzman, pp. 120-21,
under incorrect date; See I72-2.

L12-61 Trenton [N.J.] Advertiser, 15 Dec. 1912 [PU].

L12-62 "Fiction's Mirror: Millionaire Natural History," London
Daily Chronicle, 17 Dec. 1912 [PU].

L12-63 ANON. "Current Fiction: The Financier," Nation, 95 (19 Dec.
1912), 589-90. Repub: Salzman, pp. 121-22; See I72-2.

L12-64 RINGMASTER, THE, pseud. [H. L. Mencken]. "The Literary Show:
A Great American Novel," Town Topics, 68 (19 Dec. 1912),
19-20. Repub: Salzman, pp. 122-24; See I72-2.

L12-65 ANON. "Current Fiction," New York Evening Post, 21 Dec.
1912, Saturday Supplement, p. 9.

L12-66 "Books and Their Writers: America's Greatest Novelist,"
Yorkshire Observer, 21 Dec. 1912 [PU].

L12-67 ANON. "Notices of New Books: 'The Financier,'" Burlington
[Ia.] Saturday Evening Post, 28 Dec. 1912, p. 4.

L12-68 MENCKEN, H. L. "Again the Busy Fictioneers," Smart Set, 39
(Jan. 1913), 153, 155-57.

L12-69 REEDY, WILLIAM MARION. "Reflections: Dreiser's Great Book,"
St. Louis Mirror, 21 (2 Jan. 1913), 2. Repub: Salzman,
pp. 124-26; See I72-2.

L12-70 "Novels of the Week," London Evening(?) Standard, 3 Jan.
1913 [PU].

L12-71 ANON. "Two American Novelists," Nation (London), 12 (4 Jan.
1913), 613.

Reviews: THE FINANCIER

L12-72 ANON. "The Financier," Charlotte [N.C.] Observer, 12 Jan.
         1913, p. 20. Repub: Salzman, p. 126; See I72-2.

L12-73 ANON. "The Financier: A Novel," New Orleans Times-Democrat,
         12 Jan. 1913, Magazine Section, p. 7.

L12-74 ANON. "Recent Oferings [sic.] of Story Writers," Newark
         Evening News, 18 Jan. 1913, p. 24.

L12-75 Brooklyn Times, 18 Jan. 1913 [PU].

L12-76 M., I. E. "Vanity of Vanities," Chicago Tribune, 19 Jan.
         1913* [PU]. Repub: Salzman, pp. 126-27; See I72-2.

L12-77 ANON. "The Latest Books: The Financier," Argonaut, 72
         (25 Jan. 1913), 58. Repub: Salzman, p. 127; See I72-2.

L12-78 ANON. "News of Books," Denver Times, 25 Jan. 1913, p. 7.

L12-79 CABELL, ISA CARRINGTON. "The Bellman's Bookshelf," Bellman,
         14 (25 Jan. 1913), 117.

L12-80 MASON, WALT. "Among the Booksmiths," St. Joseph [Mo.] News-
         Press, 31 Jan. 1913, p. 11. Repub: Salzman, p. 128;
         See I72-2.

L12-81 ANON. "A Few Thought-Compelling Novels," American Review of
         Reviews, 47 (Feb. 1913), 242.

L12-82 ANON. "The Financier," Book News Monthly, 31 (Feb. 1913),
         448. Repub: Salzman, pp. 128-29; See I72-2.

L12-83 ALSPAUGH, AUDRIE. "Dreiser's 'Financier,' a Big Theme,"
         Chicago Daily Tribune, 1 Feb. 1913, p. 8. Repub: Salz-
         man, p. 131; See I72-2.

L12-84 PAYNE, WILLIAM MORTON. "Recent Fiction," Dial, 54 (1 Feb.
         1913), 99-100. Repub: Salzman, pp. 130-31; See I72-2.

L12-85 SHUMAN, EDWIN L. "Novels by Two Realists," Chicago Record-
         Herald, 1 Feb. 1913, p. 7. Repub: Salzman, pp. 129-30;
         See I72-2.

L12-86 GUITERMAN, ARTHUR. "Rhymed Review: The Financier," Life,
         61 (13 Feb. 1913), 313.

L12-87 ANON. "Passing Reference to a Few of the New Books Seen in
         The Stalls: Finance in Days of Panics," Pittsburg Press,
         15 Feb. 1913, p. [4].

WORKS ON

L12-88   Los Angeles Graphic, 15 Feb. 1913 [PU]. Repub: Salzman,
          pp. 131-32; See I72-2.

L12-89   New Haven Journal and Courier, 17 Feb. 1913 [PU].

L12-90   ANON. "The New Books: Mr. Dreiser's Financier," Independent,
          74 (27 Feb. 1913), 470-71. Repub: Salzman, pp. 132-34;
          See I72-2.

L12-91   ANON. "Yerkes in Fiction," Public (Chicago), 16 (28 Feb.
          1913), 211.

L12-92   HAMILTON, JAMES SHELLEY. "What Are You Reading?" Delineator,
          81 (Mar. 1913), 206.

L12-93   WOOD, GARDNER W. "Books of the Day: The Financier,"
          McClure's Magazine, 40 (Mar. 1913), 231, 235. Repub:
          Salzman, pp. 134-35; See I72-2.

L12-94   ANON. "For Book Lovers," Ainslee's, 31 (Apr. 1913), 156.
          Repub: Salzman, p. 135; See I72-2.

L12-95   DAWSON, CONINGSBLY. "A Row of Books," Everybody's Magazine,
          28 (Apr. 1913), 570-71.

L12-96   ANON. "Considering the Fictionists," Vogue, 41 (1 Apr. 1913),
          94, 96.

L12-97   ANON. "Books and Literature: The Financier," Cotton &
          Finance (New York), 2 (5 Apr. 1913), 173.

L12-98   ANON. "Recent Reflections of a Novel Reader," Atlantic
          Monthly, 111 (May 1913), 689-91. Repub: Salzman,
          pp. 135-37; See I72-2.

L12-99   ANON. "A Novel of Serious Strength," Springfield Sunday Re-
          publican, 4 May 1913, p. 35.

L12-100   San Francisco Evening Post, 13 Sept. 1913 [PU].

L12-101   ANON. "The Bookshelf of a Workingman," New York Weekly
          People, 28 Oct. 1922, p. 4.

A TRAVELER AT FORTY (1913)

L13-1   DELL, FLOYD. "Discovering a New Novelist," Chicago Evening
          Post, 12 Sept. 1913, p. 9.

Reviews: A TRAVELER AT FORTY

L13-2   ANON. "Writers and Books," New York Evening Post, 19 Nov.
         1913, p. 6.

L13-3   ANON. "Dreiser as a Traveler," St. Louis Globe-Democrat,
         29 Nov. 1913, p. 8.

L13-4   Boston Traveler and Evening Herald, 29 Nov. 1913 [PU].

L13-5   Buffalo Commercial, 29 Nov. 1913 [PU].

L13-6   E[DGETT], E[DWIN] F[RANCIS]. "A Traveler at Forty," Boston
         Evening Transcript, 3 Dec. 1913, p. 24. Repub: Salzman,
         pp. 141-42; See I72-2.

L13-7   GILDER, JEANNETTE L. "Mr. Dreiser on His Travels," Chicago
         Daily Tribune, 3 Dec. 1913, p. 15.

L13-8   COLSON, ETHEL M. "Gossip Out of Bookland," Chicago Record-
         Herald, 5 Dec. 1913, p. 6.

L13-9   SOLON, ISRAEL. "A Novelist in Europe," Chicago Evening Post,
         5 Dec. 1913, p. [13]. Repub: Salzman, pp. 142-43;
         See I72-2.

L13-10   [MORDELL, ALBERT]. "Novel Book of Travels," Philadelphia
         Record, 6 Dec. 1913, p. 11. Repub: Salzman, pp. 144-45;
         See I72-2.

L13-11   ANON. "A Traveler at Forty," Portland [Oreg.] Evening Tele-
         gram, 6 Dec. 1913, Section 2 (Annual Booklover's Edition),
         p. 5.

L13-12   BASHFORD, HERBERT. "A Traveler at Forty," San Francisco
         Bulletin, 6 Dec. 1913, p. [14]. Repub: Salzman, p. 145;
         See I72-2.

L13-13   D[AWSON], N. P. "Mr. Dreiser Travels," New York Globe and
         Commercial Advertiser, 6 Dec. 1913, p. 6. Repub: Salzman,
         p. 144; See I72-2.

L13-14   ANON. "Dreiser as a Traveler," Buffalo Express, 7 Dec. 1913,
         Part 2, p. 22.

L13-15   FITCH, GEORGE HAMLIN. "Impressions of Europe," San Francisco
         Chronicle, 7 Dec. 1913, p. 22. Repub: Salzman, pp. 145-
         46; See I72-2.

L13-16   ANON. "Travel and Nature Studies," Continent, 44 (11 Dec.
         1913), 1751.

WORKS ON

L13-17　HASSELGRAVE, CHARLES E.　"A Holiday Trip into the Land of Books," Independent, 76 (11 Dec. 1913), 507-08.　Repub: Salzman, pp. 146-47; See I72-2.

L13-18　ANON.　"Mr. Dreiser Abroad," New York Tribune, 13 Dec. 1913, p. 9.

L13-19　ANON.　"Mr. Dreiser in Europe," Providence Daily Journal, 13 Dec. 1913, p. 6.　Repub:　Salzman, pp. 149-50, under incorrect date; See I72-2.

L13-20　ANON.　"Unusual Travel Rook [sic.]," Boston Daily Globe, 13 Dec. 1913, p. 4.　Repub:　Salzman, pp. 147-48; See I72-2.

L13-21　LESTER, WILLIAM R.　"Views of People in Strange Lands," Philadelphia North American, 13 Dec. 1913, p. 12.　Repub: Salzman, p. 147; See I72-2.

L13-22　ANON.　"Some Recent Publications Received by the Post:　A Traveler at Forty," Houston Post, 14 Dec. 1913, p. 39.

L13-23　ANON.　"Literature:　A Traveler at Forty," Nation, 97 (18 Dec. 1913), 591-92.　Repub:　Salzman, pp. 148-49; See I72-2.

L13-24　ANON.　"Traveler at Forty Worthily Sketched," New York Morning Telegraph, 20 Dec. 1913 [PU].

L13-25　ANON.　"Book Reviews:　A Traveler at Forty," Washington Evening Star, 20 Dec. 1913, Part 2, p. 7.　Repub:　Salzman, p. 150; See I72-2.

L13-26　ANON.　"A Dispassionate Observer," New York Evening Post, 20 Dec. 1913, Saturday Supplement, p. 4.

L13-27　ANON.　"Two Novelists Abroad," Brooklyn Daily Eagle, 20 Dec. 1913, p. 8.

L13-28　COLSON, ETHEL M.　"Sincere and Sparkling," Chicago Record-Herald, 20 Dec. 1913, p. 8.　Repub:　Salzman, pp. 150-51; See I72-2.

L13-29　[MARKHAM, EDWIN?].　"A Traveler at Forty," New York American, 20 Dec. 1913, p. 7; p. 9 (Greater New York ed.).　Repub: Salzman, pp. 151-52; See I72-2.

Reviews: A TRAVELER AT FORTY

L13-30   ANON.   "'A Traveler at Forty,'" Hartford [Conn.] Post, 21
Dec. 1913 [PU].

L13-31   C., W. J.   "New Books: A Traveler at Forty," Detroit
Tribune, 21 Dec. 1913, Financial and Realty Section,
p. [6]. Repub: Salzman, p. 152; See I72-2.

L13-32   ANON.   "Mr. Dreiser," New York Times Review of Books, 28 Dec.
1913, p. 763. Repub: Salzman, pp. 152-54; See I72-2.

L13-33   ANON.   "Books of Travel and Description," American Review of
Reviews, 49 (Jan. 1914), 119.

L13-34   ANON.   "The New Books: A Traveler at Forty," Outlook, 106
(3 Jan. 1914), 48.

L13-35   ANON.   "A Traveler at Forty," Argonaut, 74 (3 Jan. 1914), 7.

L13-36   M[ENCKEN], H. L.   "Dreiser in Foreign Parts," Baltimore
Evening Sun, 3 Jan. 1914, p. 3.

L13-37   ANON.   "A Traveler at Forty," Louisville Courier-Journal,
5 Jan. 1914, p. 6.

L13-38   ANON.   "A Self-Centered Traveler," New York Evening Mail,
10 Jan. 1914, p. 8.

L13-39   ANON.   "Best Things on Shelves for Followers of Books:
Philandering Abroad," New York Press, 11 Jan. 1914, Part
4, p. 7. Repub: Salzman, pp. 154-55; See I72-2.

L13-40   ANON.   "Books of the Day," Chicago Daily News, 15 Jan. 1914,
p. 15.

L13-41   Christian Intelligencer, 21 Jan. 1914 [PU]. Repub: Salzman,
pp. 155-56; See I72-2.

L13-42   KERFOOT, J. B.   "The Latest Books," Life, 63 (22 Jan. 1914),
152. Repub: Salzman, p. 156; See I72-2.

L13-43   ANON.   "A Traveler's Impressions," Philadelphia Public
Ledger, 24 Jan. 1914, p. 18.

L13-44   K., D. S.   "A Delightful Book of Travel," Boston Times,
24 Jan. 1914 [PU]. Repub: Salzman, pp. 156-57; See
I72-2.

L13-45   Christian Advocate, 29 Jan. 1914 [PU].

WORKS ON

L13-46 ANON. "Theodore Dreiser, Hoosier, Sees Europe at Forty,"
Indianapolis News, 31 Jan. 1914, p. 11. Repub: Salzman,
pp. 158-59; See I72-2.

L13-47 ANON. "A Traveler at Forty," Hartford [Conn.] Courant,
31 Jan. 1914, p. [19]. Repub: Salzman, pp. 157-58; See
I72-2.

L13-48 ANON. "'A Traveler at Forty,'" New York World, 31 Jan. 1914,
p. 7.

L13-49 A., E. F. "A Traveller at Forty," Travel, 22 (Feb. 1914),
58.

L13-50 DELL, FLOYD. "Mr. Dreiser and the Dodo," Masses, 5 (Feb.
1914), 17. Repub: Salzman, pp. 162-64; See I72-2.

L13-51 HENRY, STUART. "Theodore Dreiser's 'A Traveler at Forty,'"
Bookman, 38 (Feb. 1914), 673-74. Repub: Salzman,
pp. 160-62; See I72-2.

L13-52 LEE, J. M. "A Traveler at Forty," Book News Monthly, 32
(Feb. 1914), 297. Repub: Salzman, p. 164; See I72-2.

L13-53 MENCKEN, H. L. "Anything But Novels," Smart Set, 42 (Feb.
1914), 153-54. Repub: Salzman, pp. 159-60; See I72-2.

L13-54 ANON. "A Traveler at Forty," Vogue, 43 (1 Feb. 1914), 88.

L13-55 LUBLIN, CURTIS. "Some Recent Books," Town & Country, 68
(7 Feb. 1914), 19, 25. Repub: Salzman, pp. 164-65; See
I72-2.

L13-56 ANON. "Books: A Traveler at Forty," Milwaukee Evening
Wisconsin, 13 Feb. 1914, p. 13.

L13-57 ANON. "A Finer World Within the World," Spur (New York),
13 (15 Feb. 1914), 44.

L13-58 LEWIS, SINCLAIR. "Intimate Travel Talks by World-Famed
Writers," St. Louis Republic, 21 Feb. 1914, p. 4. Repub:
Salzman, pp. 165-66; See I72-2.

L13-59 TOWNE, CHARLES HANSON. "A Traveller--And Sporty. By
Theodore Dry, Sir," New York Tribune, 26 Feb. 1914, p. 6.

L13-60 BURTON, RICHARD. "The Bellman's Book Plate," Bellman, 16
(21 Mar. 1914), 361.

L13-61   DAWSON, N. P. "Adventures All: A Row of Books," Everybody's
Magazine, 30 (Apr. 1914), 514.

L13-62   ANON. "Reviews of New Books: Dreiser, Theodore," Literary
Digest, 48 (9 May 1914), 1124.

L13-63   ANON. "At Last a Real Travel Book," Kansas City [Mo.] Star,
16 May 1914, p. 12. Repub: Salzman, p. 166; See I72-2.

L13-64   ANON. "A Traveler at Forty: By Theodore Dreiser," Craftsman,
26 (June 1914), 355-56.

L13-65   "As an American Sees Us," Yorkshire Post, 29 June 1914 [PU].

L13-66   "An American's View of England," Eastern Morning News,
29 June 1914 [PU].

L13-67   ANON. "Some Travel Books," Athenaeum, 18 July 1914, Holiday
Supplement, p. 94.

L13-68   Boston Congregationalist, 20 Aug. 1914 [PU].

L13-69   ANON. "A Strenuous Tour," London Pall Mall Gazette, 5 Jan.
1915* [PU].

L13-70   DILLON, MICHAEL FRANCIS. "With the Writers of Books: A
Book of Travel," Indianapolis Indiana Catholic and Record,
17 Mar. 1916, p. 4. Repub: Salzman, pp. 166-67, under
incorrect name of newspaper and date; See I72-2.

L13-71   DOUGLAS, GEORGE. "Dreiser," San Francisco Bulletin, 4 Sept.
1920, p. 12.

THE TITAN (1914)

L14-1   ANON. "Glimpses of New Books: The Titan," Little Rock
Arkansas Democrat, 20 May 1914, p. 10.

L14-2   JONES, LLEWELLYN. "The Book of the Week: Realism of the
Chair," Chicago Evening Post, 22 May 1914, p. 15.

L14-3   ANON. "Views and Reviews of Current Fiction: The Eighteen-
Eighties," New York Tribune, 23 May 1914, p. 11. Repub:
Salzman, pp. 171-72; See I72-2.

L14-4   ANON. "Financier Becomes Titan," New York World, 23 May
1914, p. 8. Repub: Salzman, pp. 175-76; See I72-2.

WORKS ON

L14-5 D[AWSON], N. P. "Mr. Dreiser Continued," New York Globe and Commercial Advertiser, 23 May 1914, p. 8.

L14-6 E[DGETT], E[DWIN] F[RANCIS]. "Dreiser and His Titan," Boston Evening Transcript, 23 May 1914, Part 3, p. 8. Repub: Salzman, pp. 173-75; See I72-2.

L14-7 LESTER, WILLIAM R. "Magnate's Career in Dreiser Novel," Philadelphia North American, 23 May 1914, p. 15.

L14-8 S., H. S. "Theodore Dreiser's 'Titan,'" Baltimore Evening Sun, 23 May 1914, p. 4. Repub: Salzman, pp. 172-73; See I72-2.

L14-9 HAWTHORNE, HILDEGARDE. "Mr. Dreiser's Trilogy," New York Times Review of Books, 24 May 1914, pp. 241-42. Repub: Salzman, pp. 176-78; See I72-2.

L14-10 ANON. "Books and Literary Notes," Terre Haute [Ind.] Star, 25 May 1914, p. 6.

L14-11 ANON. "The Latest Books: 'The Titan,'" Akron Beacon Journal, 27 May 1914, p. 2. Central Press Association review.

L14-12 REEDY, WILLIAM MARION. "Reflections: Dreiser's 'Titan,'" Reedy's Mirror, 23 (29 May 1914), 3. Repub: Salzman, pp. 178-79; See I72-2.

L14-13 ANON. "A Nasty Novel," St. Louis Post-Dispatch, 30 May 1914, p. 4.

L14-14 ANON. "Rabid Realism," Philadelphia Press, 30 May 1914, p. 8.

L14-15 ANON. "The Titan: A Business Novel," Philadelphia Public Ledger, 30 May 1914, p. 12.

L14-16 BASHFORD, HERBERT. "The Titan," San Francisco Bulletin, 30 May 1914, p. 8.

L14-17 MACY, JOHN. "The Titan: Mr. Dreiser's New Novel," Boston Herald, 30 May 1914, p. 4.

L14-18 GRAVES, REV. CHARLES. "Among the Books," Albany Knickerbocker Press, 31 May 1914, p. 6.

L14-19 COOPER, FREDERIC TABER. "Summer-Time Fiction: The Titan," Bookman, 39 (June 1914), 447. Repub: Salzman, pp. 180-81; See I72-2.

L14-20 ANON. "The Titan," Louisville Courier-Journal, 1 June 1914,
p. 6. Repub: Salzman, p. 181; See I72-2.

L14-21 Bookseller, 1 June 1914 [PU].

L14-22 BARBER, S. E. "Book Review: The Titan," Memphis News
Scimitar, 2 June 1914, p. [4].

L14-23 UPDEGRAFF, ALLAN. "Theodore Dreiser's American Superman,"
Baltimore News, 3 June 1914 [PU]. Repub: Salzman,
pp. 181-82; See I72-2.

L14-24 ANON. "Books Talked About: Theodore Dreiser's American
Superman," Cincinnati Enquirer, 6 June 1914, p. 10.

L14-25 ANON. "Is This Yerkes in Fiction?" Brooklyn Daily Eagle,
6 June 1914, Picture and Sporting Section, p. 5. Repub:
Salzman, pp. 182-83; See I72-2.

L14-26 ANON. "Some of the New Books and People Who Write Them:
The Titan," Chicago Daily Journal, 6 June 1914, p. 13.
Repub: Salzman, pp. 183-85; See I72-2.

L14-27 ANON. "With the New Novels," New York Evening Post, 6 June
1914, Supplement Section, p. 5. Repub: Salzman,
pp. 185-86; See I72-2.

L14-28 "The Titan," Boston Times, 6 June 1914 [PU]. Repub: Salzman,
p. 183; See I72-2.

L14-29 BOWERS, EDWIN F. "Reviews of New Books: 'The Titan,'"
New York Call, 7 June 1914, p. 14.

L14-30 Rochester Post Express, 8 June 1914 [PU]. Repub: Salzman,
p. 185; See I72-2.

L14-31 ANON. "Books of the Day," Chicago Daily News, 9 June 1914,
p. 11.

L14-32 ANON. "Current Fiction: The Titan," Nation, 98 (11 June
1914), 697-98.

L14-33 "Books and Authors: The Titan," Scoop (Chicago), 13 June
1914 [PU].

L14-34 COLSON, ETHEL M. "Realism and Romance," Chicago Record-
Herald, 13 June 1914, p. 9. Repub: Salzman, pp. 186-87;
See I72-2.

WORKS ON

L14-35 ANON. "A Master of Immortality," Providence Sunday Journal,
14 June 1914, Third Section, p. [8]. Repub: Salzman,
pp. 187-88; See I72-2.

L14-36 CARY, LUCIAN. "Recent Fiction," Dial, 56 (16 June 1914),
504. Repub: Salzman, p. 189; See I72-2.

L14-37 WILLIAMS, S. C. "A Mirabeau of Finance," Boston Daily Advertiser, 17 June 1914, p. 4.

L14-38 GUITERMAN, ARTHUR. "Rhymed Reviews: The Titan," Life, 63
(18 June 1914), 1132.

L14-39 RINGMASTER, THE, pseud. [H. L. Mencken]. "The Literary Show:
Dreiser and His Titan," Town Topics, 71 (18 June 1914),
17-18.

L14-40 ANON. "'The Titan' Not for Infants," Kansas City [Mo.] Star,
20 June 1914, p. 12.

L14-41 J., F. "Trilogy of Desire Lurid But Tiresome," Toronto Mail
Empire, 20 June 1914 [PU].

L14-42 ANON. "On the Reviewer's Table: 'The Titan,'" Richmond
[Va.] Times-Dispatch, 21 June 1914, Section 4, p. 10.

L14-43 ANON. "'The Titan,'" San Francisco Chronicle, 21 June 1914,
p. 31.

L14-44 "The Titan," Toronto World, 21 June 1914 [PU].

L14-45 New York Evening Sun, 22 June 1914.* Repub: Salzman,
pp. 189-90; See I72-2.

L14-46 ANON. "Books of the Day," Toronto Globe, 24 June 1914, p. 6.

L14-47 ANDERSON, MARGARET STEELE. "Dreiser's Story of Chicago.
The Titan," Louisville Evening Post, 27 June 1914, p. 5.
Repub: Salzman, pp. 190-91; See I72-2.

L14-48 HUNEKER, JAMES. "The Seven Arts: 'The Titan,'" Puck, 75
(27 June 1914), 21.

L14-49 ANON. "Fiction: Amorous Money-Maker," Los Angeles Sunday
Times, 28 June 1914, Part 3, p. 23. Repub: Salzman,
p. 191; See I72-2.

THEODORE DREISER: A BIBLIOGRAPHY

L14-50 ANON. "New Publications: The Titan," New Orleans Times-
Picayune, 28 June 1914, Magazine Section, p. 6.

L14-51 ANON. "Book Reviews," Magazine of Wall Street, 14 (July
1914), 287.

L14-52 ANON. "Literature and Art: The Financier Gets Out of Jail,"
Current Opinion, 57 (July 1914), 47-48.

L14-53 WING, DeWITT C. "An Unreeling Realist," Little Review, 1
(July 1914), 49-51. Repub: Salzman, pp. 191-92; See
I72-2.

L14-54 ANON. "The Loves and Labors of a Business Titan," New York
Sun, 4 July 1914, p. 5.

L14-55 "Another Dreiser Book," Bond Buyer, 4 July 1914 [PU].

L14-56 ANON. "The Titan," Pittsburgh Post, 11 July 1914, p. 5.
Repub: Salzman, pp. 192-93, as appearing in the Pittsburgh Sun on 10 July; See I72-2. We could not locate the
review in the Sun.

L14-57 "The Bookshelf," Toronto Saturday Night, 11 July 1914 [PU].

L14-58 ANON. "New Books and Magazines," Rochester [N.Y.] Democrat
and Chronicle, 17 July 1914, p. 5.

L14-59 ANON. "Mr. Dreiser's New Novel," Newark Evening News,
18 July 1914, p. 12. Repub: Salzman, pp. 193-94; See
I72-2.

L14-60 Argonaut, 25 July 1914 [PU].

L14-61 BIBLIOPHILE, THE, pseud. "The Book Shelf: 'The Titan,'"
Birmingham [Ala.] Age-Herald, 26 July 1914, p. 24.

L14-62 LONG, LILY A. "The American Business Baron," St. Paul
Pioneer Press, 26 July 1914, Third Section, p. 6.

L14-63 ANON. "Book Reviews: The Titan," Craftsman, 26 (Aug. 1914),
564.

L14-64 BRINSLEY, HENRY. "Manhood vs. the Artistic Temperment,"
Vanity Fair, 2 (Aug. 1914), 49.

L14-65 MAN, A., pseud. "A Note on Theodore Dreiser," International:
A Review of Two Worlds, 8 (Aug. 1914), 249. Repub:
Salzman, pp. 200-01; See I72-2.

WORKS ON

L14-66 MENCKEN, H. L. "Adventures Among the New Novels," Smart Set,
        43 (Aug. 1914), 153-57. Repub: Salzman, pp. 194-98;
        See I72-2.

L14-67 SKIDELSKY, BERENICE C. "The Titan," Book News Monthly, 32
        (Aug. 1914), 591. Repub: Salzman, pp. 198-99; See I72-2.

L14-68 ANON. "Imbecile Books and Others," Rochester [N.Y.] Herald,
        1 Aug. 1914 [PU].

L14-69 ANON. "Life Interpreted Through Fiction," Vogue, 44 (1 Aug.
        1914), 57, 80.

L14-70 ANON. "The Titan," Portland [Oreg.] Evening Telegram, 1 Aug.
        1914, p. 11.

L14-71 J., C. K. "'The Titan,'" Los Angeles Graphic, 8 Aug. 1914
        [PU].

L14-72 KERFOOT, J. B. "The Latest Books," Life, 64 (13 Aug. 1914),
        268. Repub: Salzman, pp. 201-02; See I72-2.

L14-73 [MORDELL, ALBERT]. "New Dreiser Novel Has Business Theme,"
        Philadelphia Record, 15 Aug. 1914, p. 7.

L14-74 ALSPAUGH, AUDRIE. "'The Titan' a Record, Not Literature,"
        Chicago Daily Tribune, 22 Aug. 1914, p. 10. Repub:
        Salzman, p. 202; See I72-2.

L14-75 ANON. "The Titan," New York American, 29 Aug. 1914, p. 7.

L14-76 GILDER, JEANNETTE L. "Books of the Day: The Titan,"
        McClure's Magazine, 43 (Sept. 1914), 223-24.

L14-77 "A Story of Chicago," St. Louis Globe Democrat, 6 Sept. 1914*
        [PU].

L14-78 ANON. "Books of the Day: 'The Titan,'" New York Evening
        Mail, 19 Sept. 1914, p. 6.

L14-79 ANON. "Books: The Titan," Milwaukee Evening Wisconsin,
        22 Sept. 1914, p. 9. Repub: Salzman, pp. 202-03; See
        I72-2.

L14-80 ANON. "Recent Reflections of a Novel-Reader," Atlantic
        Monthly, 114 (Oct. 1914), 523. Repub: Salzman, pp. 203-
        04; See I72-2.

L14-81 ANON. "The New Books: The Failure of Success," Independent,
80 (12 Oct. 1914), 63.

L14-82 ANON. "News and Reviews of Recent Books," Seattle Post-
Intelligencer, 17 Oct. 1914, p. 6. Repub: Salzman,
pp. 204-05; See I72-2.

L14-83 ANON. "Book Reviews," Rochester [N.Y.] Union and Advertiser,
20 Nov. 1914, p. 17.

L14-84 ANON. "'The Titan' Is Second in Trilogy," Chicago Examiner,
13 Dec. 1914, Society and Club News Section, p. [7].

L14-85 Columbus [Ohio] Dispatch, 9 Jan. 1915 [PU].

L14-86 GARNETT, EDWARD. "A Gossip on Criticism," Atlantic Monthly,
117 (Feb. 1916), 182-84.

L14-87 ANON. "In the Book-Mart," Spartanburg [S.C.] Herald,
7 Feb. 1915, p. 4.

L14-88 HUEFFER, FORD MADOX. "A Literary Portrait: Chicago,"
Outlook (London), 6 Mar. 1915 [PU].

L14-89 LOCKE, W. J. "A Colossus of Finance," London Pall Mall
Gazette, 6 Mar. 1915, p. 5.

L41-90 ANON. "New Novels: 'The Titan,'" London Times Literary
Supplement, 11 Mar. 1915, p. 86.

L14-91 ANON. "Fiction: 'The Titan,'" Athenaeum, 13 Mar. 1915,
p. 235.

L14-92 GARNETT, EDWARD. "A Book of the Day: A Novel of Size,"
London Daily News and Leader, 18 Mar. 1915 [PU].

L14-93 C., G. "New Novels: Man or Monster?" Manchester Guardian,
25 Mar. 1915, p. 5.

L14-94 ANON. "Notice of Books: The Titan," Bookseller, 63 (26 Mar.
1915), 320.

L14-95 ANON. "The Apotheosis of the Blackguard," Saturday Review
(London), 119 (3 Apr. 1915), 359.

L14-96 "New Novels: 'The Titan,'" Westminster Gazette, 3 Apr.
1915 [PU].

THEODORE DREISER: A BIBLIOGRAPHY

L14-97   ANON. "New Novels: The Titan," London <u>Times Literary</u>
         <u>Supplement</u>, 5 July 1928, p. 502.

L41-98   ANON. "New Novels," London <u>Times</u>, 6 July 1928, p. 22.

L41-99   ANON. "Books and Writers: A Hero from Chicago," Birmingham
         <u>Post</u>, 21 Aug. 1928 [PU].

THE "GENIUS" (1915)

L15-1   SCAVENGER, THE, <u>pseud</u>. "The Dionysian Dreiser," <u>Little</u>
         <u>Review</u>, 2 (Oct. 1915), 10-13. Repub: Salzman, pp. 209-
         12; <u>See</u> I72-2.

L15-2   ANON. "Fiction: The 'Genius,'" <u>Bookseller, Newsdealer and</u>
         <u>Stationer</u>, 43 (1 Oct. 1915), 394. Repub: Salzman,
         p. 212; <u>See</u> I72-2.

L15-3   ANON. "Mr. Dreiser's 'Genius,'" New York <u>World</u>, 2 Oct. 1915,
         p. 8. Repub: Salzman, pp. 213-14; <u>See</u> I72-2.

L15-4   ANON. "Theodore Dreiser Writes Story of Genius Whose Life
         Was a Failure," St. Louis <u>Globe-Democrat</u>, 2 Oct. 1915,
         p. 6.

L15-5   ANON. "Views and Reviews of Current Fiction: The 'Genius,'"
         New York <u>Tribune</u>, 2 Oct. 1915, p. 8. Repub: Salzman,
         pp. 212-13; <u>See</u> I72-2.

L15-6   BAIRD, LEONARD. "A Verdict in Verse," New York <u>Morning</u>
         <u>Telegraph</u>, 2 Oct. 1915 [PU].

L15-7   COLSON, ETHEL M. "New Books Covering Wide Range: Dreiser's
         Latest Epic," Chicago <u>Herald</u>, 2 Oct. 1915, p. 7. Repub:
         Salzman, p. 214; <u>See</u> I72-2.

L15-8   Cincinnati <u>Commercial Tribune</u>, 3 Oct. 1915 [PU].

L15-9   ANON. "Books of the Day," Chicago <u>Daily News</u>, 6 Oct. 1915,
         p. 13.

L15-10   REEDY, WILLIAM MARION. "The Genius of Theodore Dreiser,"
         <u>Reedy's Mirror</u>, 24 (8 Oct. 1915), 239. Repub: Salzman,
         pp. 214-15; <u>See</u> I72-2.

L15-11   ANON. "A Genius and Also a Cur," Brooklyn <u>Daily Eagle</u>,
         9 Oct. 1915, p. 8. Repub: Salzman, pp. 215-16; <u>See</u> I72-2.

L15-12 ANON. "Latest Fiction: 'The Genius,'" Detroit Free Press, 9 Oct. 1915, p. 6.

L15-13 DODGE, LOUIS. "'The "Genius"' Once Again Proves Theodore Dreiser Great Novelist," St. Louis Republic, 9 Oct. 1915, p. 10. Repub: Salzman, pp. 217-18, as appearing in the St. Louis Republican; See I72-2.

L15-14 E[DGETT], E[DWIN] F[RANCIS]. "The Genius," Boston Evening Transcript, 9 Oct. 1915, Part 3, p. 9. Repub: Salzman, pp. 216-17; See I72-2.

L15-15 LESTER, WILLIAM R. "New-Century Life Study in Dreiser's 'The Genius,'" Philadelphia North American, 9 Oct. 1915, p. 8.

L15-16 ANON. "Around the Library Table: 'The Genius,'" Salt Lake City Herald-Republican, 10 Oct. 1915, Magazine Section, p. 8.

L15-17 ANON. "Three New Novels of American Life: The Genius," New York Times Review of Books, 10 Oct. 1915, p. 362. Repub: Salzman, p. 218; See I72-2.

L15-18 ANON. "Mr. Dreiser's Latest Novel," Providence Sunday Journal, 10 Oct. 1915, Fifth Section, p. 8. Repub: Salzman, pp. 218-19; See I72-2.

L15-19 BOYNTON, H. W. "Varieties of Realism," Nation, 101 (14 Oct. 1915), 461-62. Repub: Salzman, pp. 220-21, under incorrect title; See I72-2.

L15-20 WILLIAMS, SIDNEY. "An Amorous Specimen of Genius," Boston Herald, 16 Oct. 1915, p. 4.

L15-21 ANON. "Book Reviews: The 'Genius,'" Washington Sunday Star, 17 Oct. 1915, Part 7, p. [10]. Repub: Salzman, pp. 219-20, under incorrect date; See I72-2.

L15-22 MASTERS, EDGAR LEE. "An American 'Genius,'" Chicago Evening Post, 22 Oct. 1915, p. 11. Repub: Salzman, pp. 221-24; See I72-2.

L15-23 ANON. "A Riot of Eroticism," St. Louis Post-Dispatch, 23 Oct. 1915, p. 5. Repub: Salzman, p. 224; See I72-2.

L15-24 W., C. [CLEMENT WOOD?]. "Genius and Today," New York Call, 24 Oct. 1915, Magazine Section, p. 14. Repub: Salzman, pp. 224-25; See I72-2.

WORKS ON

L15-25 ANON. "The 'Genius,'" Louisville Courier-Journal, 25 Oct.
1915, p. 6. Repub: Salzman, p. 225; See I72-2.

L15-26 D[AWSON], N. P. "Books of the Week: Theodore Dreiser,"
New York Globe and Commercial Advertiser, 30 Oct. 1915,
p. 8. Repub: Salzman, pp. 225-26; See I72-2.

L15-27 ANON. "Book of the Week," Denver Rocky Mountain News,
31 Oct. 1915, Section 2, p. 6.

L15-28 ANON. "Some of the New Fiction: Mr. Dreiser's 'The
"Genius,"'" Springfield Sunday Republican, 31 Oct. 1915,
Second Section, p. 15.

L15-29 COOPER, FREDERIC TABER. "Some Novels of the Month: The
Genius," Bookman, 42 (Nov. 1915), 322-23. Repub: Salzman, pp. 230-31; See I72-2.

L15-30 POWYS, JOHN COWPER. "Theodore Dreiser," Little Review, 2
(Nov. 1915), 7-13. Repub: The Little Review Anthology.
Ed. Margaret Anderson. New York: Hermitage House, 1953.
Pp. 46-51. Salzman, pp. 226-29; See I72-2.

L15-31 BASHFORD, HERBERT. "Theodore Dreiser Creates Wonderful
Character In Book," San Francisco Bulletin, 6 Nov. 1915,
p. [12].

L15-32 LEWIS, ADDISON. "Dreiser's 'Genius,'" Bellman, 19 (6 Nov.
1915), 524. Repub: Salzman, p. 231; See I72-2.

L15-33 Los Angeles Graphic, 6 Nov. 1915 [PU]. Repub: Salzman,
pp. 231-32; See I72-2.

L15-34 ROBERTSON, CARL T. "On the Book Shop Shelves," Cleveland
Plain Dealer, 6 Nov. 1915, p. 6.

L15-35 ANON. "'The "Genius,"'" San Francisco Chronicle, 7 Nov.
1915, Special Feature Section, p. 23.

L15-36 ANON. "Some of the Latest Books: The Genius," Buffalo
Express, 7 Nov. 1915, p. 35.

L15-37 ANON. "The New Books: Too Much Genius," Independent, 84
(8 Nov. 1915), 237. Repub: Salzman, p. 232; See I72-2.

L15-38 HALE, EDWARD E. "Recent Fiction," Dial, 59 (11 Nov. 1915),
422.

L15-39   KERFOOT, J. B. "The Latest Books," Life, 66 (11 Nov. 1915),
         914. Repub: Salzman, p. 232; See I72-2.

L15-40   MORDELL, ALBERT. "Dreiser's 'The Genius,'" Philadelphia
         Record, 13 Nov. 1915, p. 11. Repub: Salzman, pp. 232-33;
         See I72-2.

L15-41   "Recent Fiction: 'The "Genius,"'" Argonaut, 13 Nov. 1915
         [PU].

L15-42   ANON. "The Genius," Bookseller, Newsdealer, and Stationer,
         43 (15 Nov. 1915), 693.

L15-43   ANON. "New Novels: The 'Genius,'" London Times Literary
         Supplement, 18 Nov. 1915, p. 416.

L15-44   ANON. "A Good and Realistic Tale of Vast Extent," New York
         Sun, 20 Nov. 1915, p. 9.

L15-45   ANON. "Very 'Artistic' Temperament," New York Evening Post,
         20 Nov. 1915, Feature Supplement, p. 6. Repub: Salzman,
         pp. 236-37; See I72-2.

L15-46   BOURNE, RANDOLPH. "Dreiser as Hero," New Republic, 5
         (20 Nov. 1915), Fall Literary Review, pp. 5-6. Repub:
         Salzman, pp. 233-36; See I72-2.

L15-47   FORD, JAMES L. "The Sex Question Dominating Theme In 'The
         Genius,'" New York Herald, 20 Nov. 1915, p. 7. Repub:
         Salzman, p. 236; See I72-2.

L15-48   ANON. "Book Reviews in Tabloid: The Genius," Atlanta
         Constitution, 28 Nov. 1915, Magazine Section, p. [6].

L15-49   PURVIS, WILLIAM. "The Artist as Blackguard," London Daily
         Chronicle, 28 Nov. 1915 [PU].

L15-50   LENGEL, WILLIAM C. "The Genius?" The International: A
         Review of Two Worlds, 9 (Dec. 1915), 382-84.

L15-51   MENCKEN, H. L. "A Literary Behemoth," Smart Set, 47 (Dec.
         1915), 150-54. Repub: Salzman, pp. 237-42; See I72-2.

L15-52   M., A. "New Novels: One of the Americas," Manchester
         Guardian, 2 Dec. 1915, p. 4.

L15-53   "Mr. Dreiser's New Novel," London Evening Standard and St.
         James Gazette, 3 Dec. 1915 [PU].

THEODORE DREISER: A BIBLIOGRAPHY

WORKS ON

L15-54 "The Genius," London Globe, 4 Dec. 1915 [PU].

L15-55 PEATTIE, ELIA W. "Mr. Dreiser Chooses a Tom-Cat for a Hero," Chicago Daily Tribune, 4 Dec. 1915, p. 15. Repub: Salzman, pp. 242-44; See I72-2.

L15-56 Cincinnati Times Star, 6 Dec. 1915 [PU].

L15-57 LUBLIN, CURTIS. "Some Recent Books," Town & Country, 70 (10 Dec. 1915), 28, 48.

L15-58 M[ONTGELAS], A[LBRECHT]. "Dreiser's 'Genius,'" Chicago Examiner, 11 Dec. 1915, p. 16. Repub: Salzman, pp. 244-46; See I72-2.

L15-59 DELL, FLOYD. "The 'Genius' and Mr. Dreiser," New Review, 3 (15 Dec. 1915), 362-63. Repub: Salzman, pp. 246-49; See I72-2.

L15-60 ANON. "Book News: Theodore Dreiser's Latest Is Longest, but Falls Short of His Other Work," Kansas City [Mo.] Star, 18 Dec. 1915, p. 5. Repub: Salzman, pp. 249-50; See I72-2.

L15-61 ANON. "'The "Genius,"'" Newark Evening News, 18 Dec. 1915, p. 26.

L15-62 WEST, REBECCA. "A Book of the Day: The Artist," London Daily News, 23 Dec. 1915 [PU].

L15-63 ANON. "The Appeal Book Shelf: The 'Genius,'" Girard [Kans.] Appeal to Reason, 25 Dec. 1915, p. 5.

L15-64 ANON. "Literature and Art: The New Massive Novel of Theodore Dreiser," Current Opinion, 60 (Jan. 1916), 47-48.

L15-65 SKIDELSKY, BERENICE C. "The Genius," Book News Monthly, 34 (Jan. 1916), 218. Repub: Salzman, p. 251; See I72-2.

L15-66 ANON. "Books: A Genius and A 'Genius,'" Harper's Weekly, 62 (1 Jan. 1916), 20. Repub: Salzman, p. 252; See I72-2.

L15-67 "Fiction Here: A Novel of Passion," London Daily Chronicle, 3 Jan. 1916 [PU].

L15-68 ANON. "An Alp of Words," Minneapolis Journal, 4 Jan. 1916, p. 17.

L15-69 S., R. "Books of the Week: An American Novel," Bystander (London), 5 Jan. 1916 [PU].

L15-70 "How Dreiser Writes: Sex and Struggle," Sidney (New South Wales) Sun, 6 Jan. 1916 [PU].

L15-71 ANON. "A Methodical Novel," Nation (London), 18 (8 Jan. 1916), 550, 552.

L15-72 "Why Should Novelists Fill So Many Pages," Philadelphia Telegraph, 14 Jan. 1916 [PU].

L15-73 KAUN, ALEXANDER. "Homo Americanus," Daily Maroon, 19 Jan. 1916 [PU].

L15-74 ANON. "New Books and Magazines," Rochester [N.Y.] Democrat-Chronicle, 21 Jan. 1916, p. 9.

L15-75 Ithaca [N.Y.] Daily News, 22 Jan. 1916 [PU].

L15-76 GILMAN, LAWRENCE. "The Book of the Month: The Biography of an Amorist," North American Review, 203 (Feb. 1916), 290-93.

L15-77 ANON. "What They Read: The 'Genius,'" Vogue, 47 (1 Feb. 1916), 80, 82. Repub: Salzman, p. 252; See I72-2.

L15-78 "The Genius," Outlook (London), 12 Feb. 1916 [PU].

L15-79 HUNEKER, JAMES. "The Seven Arts," Puck, 79 (12 Feb. 1916), 10.

L15-80 "Amatory Adventures," Philadelphia Press, 27 Feb. 1916, Seventh Section [PU].

L15-81 ANON. "Novels That Arouse Debate," Continent, 47 (16 Mar. 1916), 37.

L15-82 MASSINGHAM, HAROLD. "The American Novel," Bookman (London), 50 (Apr. 1916), 21-22.

L15-83 DELL, FLOYD. "Talks With Live Authors: Theodore Dreiser," Masses, 8 (Aug. 1916), 36.

L15-84 E[DGETT], E[DWIN] F[RANCIS]. "Writers and Books," Boston Evening Transcript, 1 Sept. 1923, Book Section, p. 6.

WORKS ON

L15-85 "'The Genius,' Republished," Fort Wayne Journal Gazette,
1 Sept. 1923 [PU].

L15-86 M., I. G. "New Books at Random: The 'Genius,'" Washington
Evening Star, 4 Sept. 1923, p. 6.

L15-87 LEARY, DANIEL BELL. "Truth About Some Suppressed Books,"
Buffalo Evening News, 8 Sept. 1923, Saturday Literary and
Magazine Supplement, p. 10.

L15-88 WINN, JANE FRANCES. "Book Review: 'The Genius,'" St. Louis
Globe-Democrat, 8 Sept. 1923, p. 14.

L15-89 HARRIGAN, HARVEY. "The 'Genius' Again Ventures Forth,"
New York Call, 9 Sept. 1923, Call Magazine, p. 10.

L15-90 FORD, THOMAS F. "Mr. Dreiser Tries Again," Los Angeles
Times, 16 Sept. 1923, Part 3, p. 32.

L15-91 [HALLER, RICHARD V.?]. "Theodore Dreiser's Novel 'The
Genius' Republished," Portland Sunday Oregonian, 23 Sept.
1923, Section Five, p. 5.

L15-92 ANON. "Dreiser's 'Genius' Returns From a Five Years Exile,"
Kansas City [Mo.] Star, 29 Sept. 1923, p. 16.

L15-93 JACKSON, C. M. "Dreiser's 'Genius' Once More At Large; Ban
Now Removed," San Francisco Bulletin, 29 Sept. 1923, p. 20.

L15-94 ANON. "Book Reviews: The 'Genius,'" Nashville Tennessean,
30 Sept. 1923, Magazine Section, p. 3.

L15-95 DEXTER, BYRON. "The 'Genius,'" Atlanta Journal, 30 Sept.
1923, Atlanta Journal Magazine, p. 28.

L15-96 DOORLY, MARGARET H. "The 'Genius,'" Omaha Sunday World-
Herald, 7 Oct. 1923, Magazine Section, p. 12.

L15-97 ANON. "They Suppressed It in 1915," Milwaukee Journal,
12 Oct. 1923, p. 12.

L15-98 BIDDLE, FRANCIS P. "Dreiser's 'The Genius,' Reissued After
Eight Years' Suppression, Unusual Book of Rugged Power,"
Philadelphia Public Ledger, 13 Oct. 1923, p. 14.

L15-99 SANDERS, CHAUNCEY ELWOOD. "Books and Writers: Comment By
the Way," Austin [Tex.] Statesman, 28 Oct. 1923, p. 6.

Reviews: PLAYS OF THE NATURAL AND THE SUPERNATURAL

L15-100 "The 'Genius,'" New London [Conn.] Day, 8(?) Dec. 1923 [PU].

L15-101 "'The Elephant Now Goes Round,'" Greensboro [N.C.] News, 16 Dec. 1923 [PU].

L15-102 "The Genius," New York Jewish Tribune, 4 Jan. 1924 [PU].

L15-103 "'The Genius,'" Iowa City Daily Iowan, 27 Jan. 1924 [PU].

L15-104 "The Bookshelf of a Workingman," New York Weekly People, ? Mar. 1924 [PU].

L15-105 GARLAND, ROBERT. Baltimore Post, 21 Mar. 1924 [PU].

PLAYS OF THE NATURAL AND THE SUPERNATURAL (1916)

L16-1   ANON. "The Plays of Strindberg and Dreiser," Boston Herald, 26 Feb. 1916, p. 4.

L16-2   ANON. "Word Pictures of Life of Working Class Thrill," St. Louis Globe-Democrat, 26 Feb. 1916, p. 7. Repub: Salzman, p. 257; See I72-2.

L16-3   COLSON, ETHEL M. "The Dreiser Plays and Mrs. Atherton's Latest," Chicago Herald, 26 Feb. 1916, p. 5. Repub: Salzman, pp. 255-56; See I72-2.

L16-4   D[AWSON], N. P. "Plays by Mr. Dreiser," New York Globe and Commercial Advertiser, 26 Feb. 1916, p. 8. Repub: Salzman, pp. 256-57; See I72-2.

L16-5   LESLIE, JAMES EDWARD. Pittsburg Dispatch, 26 Feb. 1916, p. 11. Repub: Salzman, pp. 257-58; See I72-2.

L16-6   [PRICE, ARTHUR L.?]. "Book Reviews: Plays of the Natural and the Supernatural," San Francisco Call and Post, 4 Mar. 1916, p. [14]. Repub: Salzman, p. 258; See I72-2.

L16-7   ANON. "Miscellaneous: 'Plays of the Natural and the Super-natural,'" Detroit Free Press, 5 Mar. 1916, Part 4, p. 13.

L16-8   ANON. "Very Original Plays," New York Evening Sun, 11 Mar. 1916, p. 7.

L16-9   ANON. "Mr. Dreiser's Plays," New York Sun, 12 Mar. 1916, Sixth Section, p. 10. Repub: Salzman, pp. 258-59; See I72-2.

THEODORE DREISER: A BIBLIOGRAPHY

WORKS ON

L16-10 ANON. "A Flock of Poets and Dramatists. A Mad Swede, a
Sane Irishman. A Parodist Among Song Birds," Brooklyn
Daily Eagle, 18 Mar. 1916, Section 2, p. 4. Repub:
Salzman, p. 260; See I72-2.

L16-11 M., D. L. [DOROTHEA LAURENCE MANN?]. "With the Supernatural,"
Boston Evening Transcript, 18 Mar. 1916, Part 3, p. 9.
Repub: Salzman, pp. 259-60; See I72-2.

L16-12 PEATTIE, ELIA W. "Dreiser's Plays Natural and Supernatural,"
Chicago Daily Tribune, 18 Mar. 1916, p. 7.

L16-13 ANON. "Among Some Worthy Books: 'Plays of the Natural and
the Supernatural,'" Los Angeles Sunday Times, 19 Mar.
1916, Part 3, p. 24. Repub: Salzman, pp. 260-61; See
I72-2.

L16-14 JONES, LLEWELLYN. "The Book of the Week: Men and Ghosts,"
Chicago Evening Post, 24 Mar. 1916, p. 10. Repub:
Salzman, pp. 263-64; See I72-2.

L16-15 ANON. "Plays of the Natural and the Supernatural," Burlington [Ia.] Saturday Evening Post, 25 Mar. 1916, p. 4.

L16-16 ANON. "Here Are Some Plays: Dreiser's Plays," Buffalo
Express, 26 Mar. 1916, p. 35. Repub: Salzman, p. 264;
See I72-2.

L16-17 ANON. "Reviews and Criticisms of Books and Magazines: Plays
of the Natural and the Supernatural," New Orleans Times-
Picayune, 26 Mar. 1916, Magazine Section, p. 2.

L16-18 ANON. "Book News: Theodore Dreiser Has Written Some Very
Novel, but Rather Disappointing Plays," Kansas City [Mo.]
Star, 1 Apr. 1916, p. 5.

L16-19 ANON. "Drama and Poetry," Bookseller, 1 Apr. 1916 [PU].

L16-20 ANON. "Book of the Week," Denver Rocky Mountain News,
2 Apr. 1916, Section 2, p. 6.

L16-21 BARROWS, JACK. Denver Times, 5 Apr. 1916 [PU]. Repub:
Salzman, pp. 264-65; See I72-2.

L16-22 ANON. "The Appeal Book Shelf: Seven One-Act Plays,"
Girard [Kans.] Appeal to Reason, 15 Apr. 1916, p. 5.
Repub: Salzman, p. 265; See I72-2.

Reviews: PLAYS OF THE NATURAL AND THE SUPERNATURAL

L16-23 D[OUGLAS], G[EORGE]. "Fourth Dimensional Dramas," San Francisco Chronicle, 23 Apr. 1916, Special Feature Section,
p. 23. Repub: Salzman, pp. 261-62, under incorrect date;
See I72-2.

L16-24 ANON. "Plays and Pageants," American Review of Reviews, 53
(May 1916), 634. Repub: Salzman, p. 265; See I72-2.

L16-25 MOSES, MONTROSE J. "Plays by Theodore Dreiser," Book News
Monthly, 34 (May 1916), 414-15. Repub: Salzman, pp. 265-
67; See I72-2.

L16-26 [HOPPER, ANNA L.?]. "Plays by Theodore Dreiser," Louisville
Courier-Journal, 8 May 1916, p. 6.

L16-27 ANON. "Plays by Dreiser," Indianapolis News, 20 May 1916,
p. 20. Repub: Salzman, p. 267; See I72-2.

L16-28 ANON. "Theodore Dreiser's Plays," Springfield [Mass.] Union,
28 May 1916 [PU]. Repub: Salzman, p. 267, as appearing
in the Springfield Republican; See I72-2. We could not
locate the review in the Republican.

L16-29 MENCKEN, H. L. "A Soul's Adventures," Smart Set, 49 (June
1916), 154. Repub: Salzman, p. 268; See I72-2.

L16-30 "Seven Plays By Dreiser," Philadelphia Press, 18 June 1916,
Seventh Section [PU]. Repub: Salzman, p. 269; See I72-2.

L16-31 ANON. "Music and Drama," Independent, 86 (26 June 1916), 554.

L16-32 R[EEDY], W[ILLIAM] M[ARION]. "What I've Been Reading,"
Reedy's Mirror, 25 (14 July 1916), 463. Repub: Salzman,
p. 269; See I72-2.

L16-33 ANON. "Plays of the Natural and the Supernatural," Philadelphia Public Ledger, 15 July 1916, p. 7. Repub:
Salzman, p. 270; See I72-2.

L16-34 ANON. "Book Chat: Theodore Dreiser's Plays," Detroit
Saturday Night, 22 July 1916, p. 20.

L16-35 ANON. "Some Recent Books of Unusual Interest: Plays of the
Natural and the Supernatural," New England Magazine,
NS 55 (Aug. 1916), 117-18.

L16-36 BLIVEN, BRUCE. "Some Spooky Drama," Outlook, Aug. 1916.
Repub: Salzman, p. 270; See I72-2.

WORKS ON

L16-37 [SHERMAN, STUART P.]. "The Understanding of Mr. Dreiser,"
        Nation, 103 (12 Oct. 1916), 355. Repub: Salzman,
        pp. 271-72; See I72-2.

L16-38 ANON. "What They Read: Plays of the Natural and Super-
        natural," Vogue, 48 (15 Oct. 1916), 118, 120.

L16-39 ANON. "Book of the Week: Freak Plays," Everyman (London),
        9 (3 Nov. 1916), 70.

L16-40 "Some Plays," Outlook (London), 25 Nov. 1916 [PU].

L16-41 ANON. "Books: A New Dramatic Form," Spectator (London),
        118 (3 Feb. 1917), 139-40.

L16-42 HITCHCOCK, ELIZABETH S. "Book Reviews: 'Plays of the
        Natural and Supernatural,'" Detroit Times, 19 Feb. 1917,
        p. 5. Repub: Salzman, p. 272; See I72-2.

L16-43 WOODBRIDGE, HOMER E. "Some Experiments in American Drama,"
        Dial, 62 (17 May 1917), 440.

L16-44 Theatre, July 1917 [PU].

A HOOSIER HOLIDAY (1916)

L16-45 MENCKEN, H. L. "The Creed of a Novelist," Smart Set, 50
        (Oct. 1916), 138-43. Repub: H. L. Mencken, The Creed of
        a Novelist. New York: John Lane, [1916]. 16 pp. [an
        advertising pamphlet for A Hoosier Holiday]. H. L.
        Mencken's Smart Set Criticism. Ed. William H. Nolte.
        Ithaca, N.Y.: Cornell U. Press, 1968. Pp. 248-56.
        Salzman, pp. 275-81; See I72-2.

L16-46 Bookseller, 15 Nov. 1916 [PU].

L16-47 E[DGETT], E[DWIN] F[RANCIS]. "Theodore Dreiser on a Hoosier
        Holiday," Boston Evening Transcript, 15 Nov. 1916, Part 2,
        p. 8. Repub: Salzman, p. 281; See I72-2.

L16-48 ANON. "New Books and Magazines," Rochester [N.Y.] Democrat
        and Chronicle, 19 Nov. 1916, p. 27.

L16-49 ANON. "Theo. Dreiser on Wheels," New York World, 19 Nov.
        1916, Editorial Section, p. 4.

Reviews: A HOOSIER HOLIDAY

L16-50   SELL, HENRY BLACKMAN. "'A Hoosier Holiday' by Theodore
         Dreiser," Chicago Daily News, 22 Nov. 1916, p. 11. Re-
         pub: Salzman, pp. 281-83; See 172-2.

L16-51   ROSE, W. R. "All in the Day's Work," Cleveland Plain Dealer,
         23 Nov. 1916, p. 8.

L16-52   D[AWSON], N. P. "Mr. Dreiser on Holiday," New York Globe and
         Commercial Advertiser, 25 Nov. 1916, p. 6. Repub:
         Salzman, p. 283; See 172-2.

L16-53   ANON. "A Hoosier Holiday with Theodore Dreiser," New York
         Sun, 26 Nov. 1916, Section 6, p. 2. Repub: Salzman,
         p. 284; See 172-2.

L16-54   ANON. "Travel in America," Dial, 61 (30 Nov. 1916), 474.
         Repub: Salzman, p. 284; See 172-2.

L16-55   ANON. "Books for Christmas Giving," Book News Monthly, 35
         (Dec. 1916), 148.

L16-56   ANON. "Motoring in the West," Brooklyn Daily Eagle, 2 Dec.
         1916, Christmas Book Supplement, p. 2. Repub: Salzman,
         p. 285; See 172-2.

L16-57   ANON. "Mr. Dreiser Goes Traveling," Chicago Daily Tribune,
         2 Dec. 1916, p. 8. Repub: Salzman, p. 285; See 172-2.

L16-58   ANON. "Mr. Dreiser Undertakes a Motor Tour," Boston Herald,
         2 Dec. 1916* [PU].

L16-59   ANON. "Theodore Dreiser's New Book Affords a Near View of
         American Scenes," New York Herald, 2 Dec. 1916, p. 7.
         Repub: Salzman, p. 286; See 172-2.

L16-60   "An Indiana Novelist Revisits Boyhood Haunts," Philadelphia
         Press, 3 Dec. 1916, Seventh Section, pp. 1, 6 [PU]. Re-
         pub: Salzman, pp. 286-87; See 172-2.

L16-61   ANON. "Travel Books: A Hoosier Holiday," American Hebrew,
         100 (8 Dec. 1916), 191.

L16-62   ANON. "A Hoosier Holiday," New York Evening Sun, 9 Dec.
         1916, p. 7. Repub: Salzman, p. 287; See 172-2.

L16-63   ANON. "Good Books for Adults," Seattle Post-Intelligencer,
         10 Dec. 1916, Part 5, p. 9.

337

WORKS ON

L16-64 YOUNG, GORDON RAY. "Theodore Dreiser," Los Angeles Sunday Times, 10 Dec. 1916, Part 3, p. 26. Repub: Salzman, p. 287; See I72-2.

L16-65 ANON. "Theodore Dreiser Revisits Indiana," Indianapolis Star, 11 Dec. 1916, p. 5. Repub: Salzman, pp. 287-88; See I72-2.

L16-66 W., T. "The Sex Questioner," Louisville Courier-Journal, 11 Dec. 1916, p. 6.

L16-67 R[EEDY], W[ILLIAM] M[ARION]. "What I've Been Reading," Reedy's Mirror, 25 (15 Dec. 1916), 839-40. Repub: Salzman, pp. 289-91, under incorrect date; See I72-2.

L16-68 COLSON, ETHEL M. "Holiday Jaunt With Theodore Dreiser," Chicago Herald, 16 Dec. 1916, p. 9. Repub: Salzman, p. 291; See I72-2.

L16-69 New York Evening Post, 16 Dec. 1916* [PU]. Repub: Salzman, pp. 291-92; See I72-2.

L16-70 BASHFORD, HERBERT. "Most Outstanding American Novelist Reveals New Vein," San Francisco Bulletin, 30 Dec. 1916, p. 14. Repub: Salzman, p. 292; See I72-2.

L16-71 ANON. "'A Hoosier Holiday,'" Springfield [Mass.] Sunday Republican, 31 Dec. 1916, Second Section, p. 15.

L16-72 M[ONTGELAS], A[LBRECHT]. "'A Hoosier Holiday,'" Chicago Examiner, 6 Jan. 1917, p. 10.

L16-73 ANON. "Around the Library Table: 'A Hoosier Holiday,'" Salt Lake City Herald-Republican, 7 Jan. 1917, p. 1

L16-74 ANON. "Reviews of New Books: A Hoosier Holiday," Washington Sunday Star, 14 Jan. 1917, Part 4, p. 2. Repub: Salzman, pp. 292-93; See I72-2.

L16-75 D[OUGLAS], G[EORGE]. "'A Hoosier Holiday,'" San Francisco Chronicle, 14 Jan. 1917, Editorial, Music, Drama and Special Feature Section, p. 22. Repub: Salzman, pp. 294-95; See I72-2.

L16-76 WOOD, CLEMENT. "The Stuff We Are Made Of," New York Call, 14 Jan. 1917, Magazine and Editorial Section, p. 14. Repub: Salzman, pp. 293-94; See I72-2.

Reviews: A HOOSIER HOLIDAY

L16-77 [YOST, CHARLES?]. Fayette [Ohio] Review, Feb. 1917 [PU].

L16-78 ANON. "Book Notes," Milwaukee Evening Wisconsin, 13 Feb.
1917, p. 11.

L16-79 ANON. "The Books: Priggish and Ponderous," Minneapolis
Journal, 13 Feb. 1917, p. 19.

L16-80 KERFOOT, J. B. "The Latest Books," Life, 69 (15 Feb. 1917),
272.

L16-81 J[ONES], L[LEWELLYN]. "Mr. Dreiser's Soul," Chicago Evening
Post, 2 Mar. 1917, p. 7. Repub: Salzman, pp. 295-96;
See I72-2.

L16-82 ANON. "Mr. Dreiser's Favorite Hero," Nation, 104 (8 Mar.
1917), 268-69. Repub: Salzman, pp. 296-97; See I72-2.

L16-83 BALL, SUSAN W. "Womans World," Terre Haute [Ind.] Saturday
Spectator, 24 Mar. 1917, pp. 10-11. Repub: Salzman,
pp. 297-99; See I72-2.

L16-84 F., W. O. "A Hoosier Holiday," Terre Haute [Ind.] Saturday
Spectator, 31 Mar. 1917, pp. 23-24.

L16-85 TUCKER, MARION. "Out-of-Door Books," Churchman, 115 (12 May
1917), 551. Repub: Salzman, p. 300; See I72-2.

L16-86 ANON. "A Hoosier Holiday," Indianapolis News, 26 May 1917,
p. 3. Repub: Salzman, pp. 299-300; See I72-2.

L16-87 JENKINS, WILLIAM E. "A Hoosier Holiday," Indiana University
Alumni Quarterly, 4 (July 1917), 415-17.

L16-88 ANON. "Other Books Worth While," Literary Digest, 56
(26 Jan. 1918), 36.

L16-89 ANON. "Mr. Dreiser on a Journey," London Times, 12 Apr.
1932, p. 20.

L16-90 ANON. "A Hoosier Holiday," London Times Literary Supplement,
14 Apr. 1932, p. 268.

L16-91 PRITCHETT, V. S. "Mr. Dreiser Goes Home," Spectator (London),
148 (11 June 1932), 835-36.

THEODORE DREISER: A BIBLIOGRAPHY

WORKS ON

FREE AND OTHER STORIES (1918)

L18-1   Boston Post, 24 Aug. 1918 [PU]. Repub: Salzman, p. 303;
        See I72-2.

L18-2   E[DGETT], E[DWIN] F[RANCIS]. "Theodore Dreiser and the
        Short Story," Boston Evening Transcript, 28 Aug. 1918,
        Part 2, p. 6. Repub: Salzman, pp. 303-04; See I72-2.

L18-3   ANON. "Book of the Day," Philadelphia Inquirer, 29 Aug.
        1918, p. 10. Repub: Salzman, p. 304; See I72-2.

L18-4   [HOPPER, ANNA L.?]. "Stories by Dreiser," Louisville
        Courier Journal, 2 Sept. 1918, p. 5. Repub: Salzman,
        pp. 304-05; See I72-2.

L18-5   ANON. "Books and Reading," New York Evening Post, 3 Sept.
        1918, p. 6.

L18-6   CLINE, LEONARD L. "Dreiser Tries Short Stories," Detroit
        Sunday News, 8 Sept. 1918, Society Section, p. 10. Re-
        pub: Salzman, p. 305; See I72-2.

L18-7   ANON. "Dross and Gold," Philadelphia Press, 14 Sept. 1918,
        p. 8. Repub: Salzman, pp. 306-07; See I72-2.

L18-8   ANON. "Garnered Short Stories," New York Evening Sun,
        14 Sept. 1918, p. 7.

L18-9   ANON. "Short Stories," New York Evening Post, 14 Sept. 1918,
        Book Section, p. 2. Repub: Salzman, pp. 305-06; See
        I72-2.

L18-10 D[AWSON], N. P. "Mr. Dreiser's Short Stories," New York
        Globe and Commercial Advertiser, 14 Sept. 1918, p. 8.

L18-11 ANON. "'Free and Other Stories,'" Springfield [Mass.]
        Sunday Republican, 22 Sept. 1918, Sports, Auto and Maga-
        zine Section, p. 13A. Repub: Salzman, pp. 309-10; See
        I72-2.

L18-12 ANON. "Latest Works of Fiction: Free," New York Times
        Review of Books, 22 Sept. 1918, p. 398. Repub: Salzman,
        pp. 307-08; See I72-2.

L18-13 ANON. "New Books to Claim the Attention of the Readers:
        Free and Other Stories," Buffalo Express, 22 Sept. 1918,
        p. 54.

Reviews: FREE AND OTHER STORIES

L18-14 FORREST, BELFORD. "Among the Books: 'Free and Other
        Stories,'" Albany Knickerbocker Press, 22 Sept. 1918,
        Fourth Section, p. 4. Repub: Salzman, pp. 308-09;
        See I72-2.

L18-15 SCARBOROUGH, DOROTHY. "Dreiser's Vignettes of States of
        Mind," New York Sun, 22 Sept. 1918, Section 5, p. 8.
        Repub: Salzman, p. 308; See I72-2.

L18-16 ANON. "'Free and Other Stories,'" Richmond [Va.] Journal,
        23(?) Sept. 1918 [PU]. Repub: Salzman, p. 310; See I72-2.

L18-17 ANON. "'It Is Easier to Be Critical than to Be Correct,'"
        Baltimore Evening Sun, 28 Sept. 1918, p. 4.

L18-18 YOUNG, GORDON RAY. "Drama, Essays and Fiction: 'Free and
        Other Stories,'" Los Angeles Sunday Times, 29 Sept. 1918,
        Part 3, p. 22. Repub: Salzman, p. 310; See I72-2.

L18-19 ANON. "Novels and Short Stories," American Review of
        Reviews, 58 (Oct. 1918), 445.

L18-20 H[ARRIS], F[RANK]. "Books Worth Reading," Pearson's Magazine,
        39 (Oct. 1918), 359. Repub: Salzman, pp. 310-11; See
        I72-2.

L18-21 "'Free and Other Stories,'" Rochester [N.Y.] Post Express,
        15 Oct. 1918 [PU]. Repub: Salzman, pp. 311-12; See
        I72-2.

L18-22 KARSNER, DAVID. "Theodore Dreiser's Short Stories," New York
        Call, 27 Oct. 1918, Call Magazine, p. 11. Repub:
        Salzman, pp. 312-13; See I72-2.

L18-23 MENCKEN, H. L. "Dithyrambs Against Learning," Smart Set, 57
        (Nov. 1918), 143-44. Repub: Salzman, pp. 313-14; See
        I72-2.

L18-24 "Deiser's [sic.] Short Stories," Indianapolis Star, 6 Nov.
        1918* [PU].

L18-25 ANON. "Dreiser's Short Stories," Nashville Tennesseean,
        8 Dec. 1918, Woman's Section, p. 12. Repub: Salzman,
        p. 314; See I72-2.

L18-26 REEDY, WILLIAM MARION. "A Round of Random Reading:
        Dreiser's Short Stories," Reedy's Mirror, 27 (13 Dec.
        1918), 641. Repub: Salzman, pp. 314-15; See I72-2.

WORKS ON

L18-27   ANON. "The Books: Dreiser Again," Minneapolis Journal,
         20 Dec. 1918, p. 11. Repub: Salzman, p. 315; See I72-2.

L18-28   ANON. "Notes on New Books: Free and Other Stories," Dial,
         65 (28 Dec. 1918), 630, 632. Repub: Salzman, pp. 316-17;
         See I72-2.

L18-29   BEFFEL, JOHN NICHOLAS. "Dreiser's Story Book Is Sad As-
         semblage," Chicago Herald & Examiner, 3 Apr. 1919, p. 14.
         Repub: Salzman, p. 317; See I72-2.

L18-30   STEPHENSON, HENRY THEW. "Free and Other Stories," Indiana
         University Alumni Quarterly, 6 (July 1919), 434.

L18-31   ANON. "A Real American," London Times Literary Supplement,
         21 Aug. 1919, p. 446. Reviewed with Twelve Men.

L18-32   MAN OF KENT, A, pseud. "Rambling Remarks: Mr. Dreiser as
         a Writer of Short Stories," British Weekly, 66 (4 Sept.
         1919), 493. Reviewed with Twelve Men.

L18-33   ANON. "A Quintet," Nation (London), 25 (27 Sept. 1919), 776.

TWELVE MEN (1919)

L19-1   WEBB, DORIS. "A Different Dreiser," Publishers' Weekly, 95
         (15 Mar. 1919), 822.

L19-2   ANON. "The New Books: Groups of Short Stories," The Inde-
         pendent, 97 (22 Mar. 1919), 414.

L19-3   MENCKEN, H. L. "H. L. Mencken Tells of Dreiser's New Book,"
         New York Sun, 13 Apr. 1919, Section 7, p. 4. Repub:
         Salzman, pp. 319-21; See I72-2.

L19-4   ANON. "In Bookland: Dreiser's 'Twelve Men' Real," Newark
         Evening News, 26 Apr. 1919, p. 8. Repub: Salzman,
         p. 322; See I72-2.

L19-5   ANON. "Twelve Men," Philadelphia Public Ledger, 26 Apr.
         1919, p. 15.

L19-6   BROUN, HEYWOOD. "'Twelve Men' by Dreiser," New York Tribune,
         26 Apr. 1919, p. 10. Repub: Salzman, pp. 321-22; See
         I72-2.

L19-7   D[AWSON], N. P. "Twelve Men," New York Globe and Commercial Advertiser, 26 Apr. 1919, p. 12. Repub: Salzman, pp. 322-24; See I72-2.

L19-8   ANON. "Dreiser's 'Twelve Men,'" New York World, 27 Apr. 1919, Editorial Section, p. 6E.

L19-9   ANON. "Twelve Men," New York Times Review of Books, 27 Apr. 1919, p. 234. Repub: Salzman, pp. 324-25; See I72-2.

L19-10 KARSNER, DAVID. "Theodore Dreiser's 'Twelve Men,'" New York Call, 27 Apr. 1919, Call Magazine, p. 10* [PU]. Repub: Salzman, pp. 325-26; See I72-2.

L19-11 E[DGETT], E[DWIN] F[RANCIS]. "Theodore Dreiser Dissects Humanity," Boston Evening Transcript, 30 Apr. 1919, Part 2, p. 6. Repub: Salzman, pp. 326-27; See I72-2.

L19-12 G., J. W. Wisconsin Literary Magazine, May 1919 [PU].

L19-13 A., M. "Theodore Dreiser," New Republic, 19 (3 May 1919), 30-31. Repub: Salzman, pp. 327-29; See I72-2.

L19-14 B., C. "Dreiser's Rare Genius Is Shown In 'Twelve Men,'" Baltimore Evening Sun, 3 May 1919, p. 8. Repub: Salzman, pp. 332-33; See I72-2.

L19-15 New York Morning Telegraph, 3 May 1919 [PU]. Repub: Salzman, pp. 331-32; See I72-2.

L19-16 RASCOE, BURTON. "Dreiser Gives Us His Best Effort in 'Twelve Men,'" Chicago Daily Tribune, 3 May 1919, p. 12. Repub: Salzman, pp. 329-31; See I72-2.

L19-17 ANON. "Mr. Dreiser Picks a Jury," Syracuse Post-Standard, 4 May 1919, p. 4.

L19-18 ANON. "Panoramic Portraits Sketched By Dreiser," Nashville Tennessean and American, 4 May 1919, Amusement and Automobile Section, p. 5.

L19-19 "Clean-Cut American Types," Trenton Times, 4 May 1919 [PU].

L19-20 [FORD, JAMES L.?]. "About a Dozen," New York Herald, 4 May 1919, Third Section, p. 8.

L19-21 SMITS, LEE J. "Dreiser Draws Full-Length Character," Detroit Sunday News, 4 May 1919, p. 14.

WORKS ON

L19-22 ANON. "Books and Authors: 'Twelve Men,'" Grand Rapids
        [Mich.] News, 10 May 1919, p. 4.

L19-23 ANON. "A Dozen Personalities," New York Review, 10 May 1919,
        p. 6.

L19-24 ANON. "Dreiser and Just a Dozen," Boston Herald, 10 May 1919,
        p. 7.

L19-25 ANON. "Dreiser's New Book," Philadelphia Evening Public
        Ledger, 10 May 1919, p. 9.

L19-26 ANON. "The Phenomenal Dreiser," New York Evening Sun,
        10 May 1919, p. 13. Repub: Salzman, pp. 333-34; See
        I72-2.

L19-27 ANON. "Books in Review: 'Twelve Men,'" Seattle Post-
        Intelligencer, 11 May 1919, Part 3, p. 9.

L19-28 ANON. "Books of the Week," Providence Sunday Journal,
        11 May 1919, Sixth Section, p. 7. Repub: Salzman,
        pp. 334-35; See I72-2.

L19-29 ANON. "'Twelve Men,'" San Francisco Chronicle, 11 May 1919,
        Editorial, Music, Theatrical News and Features Section,
        p. 2E. Repub: Salzman, p. 335, under incorrect date;
        See I72-2.

L19-30 FORREST, BELFORD. "Among the Books: 'Twelve Men,'" Albany
        Knickerbocker Press, 11 May 1919, Fourth Section, p. 4.

L19-31 ANON. "Portraits as Fiction," Brooklyn Daily Eagle, 17 May
        1919, p. 6.

L19-32 ANON. "Twelve Portraits by Theodore Dreiser," Philadelphia
        Press, 17 May 1919, p. 11. Repub: Salzman, pp. 335-36;
        See I72-2.

L19-33 ANON. "Dreiser's New Book Has a Dozen American Character
        Sketches," New York American, 18 May 1919, Editorial and
        City Life Section, p. CE-3.

L19-34 ANON. "Reviews of New Books: Twelve Men," Washington
        Sunday Star, 18 May 1919, Part 2, p. 9.

L19-35 Baltimore News, 18 May 1919 [PU]. Repub: Salzman, p. 336;
        See I72-2.

L19-36   YOUNG, GORDON RAY.   "'Twelve Men,'" Los Angeles Sunday Times,
         18 May 1919, Part 3, p. 33.

L19-37   ANON.   "American Types," Nation, 108 (24 May 1919), 838.
         Repub: Salzman, pp. 336-38; See I72-2.

L19-38   ANON.   "Theodore Dreiser's 'Twelve Men,'" St. Louis Post-
         Dispatch, 24 May 1919, p. 6.

L19-39   ANON.   "Dreiser's Portraits," Springfield [Mass.] Sunday
         Republican, 25 May 1919, Sports, Auto and Magazine Section,
         p. 17A. Repub: Salzman, pp. 338-39; See I72-2.

L19-40   ANON.   "A Baker's Dozen of Dreiserian Portraits," Current
         Opinion, 66 (June 1919), 389-90.

L19-41   ANON.   "Novels, Foreign and American," American Review of
         Reviews, 59 (June 1919), 671.

L19-42   Albany Telegram, 1 June 1919 [PU].

L19-43   H[OLMES], R[ALPH] F.   "Musings with the Muses," Detroit
         Journal, 4 June 1919, p. 4.

L19-44   ANON.   "Book Reviews: Twelve Men," American Hebrew, 109
         (6 June 1919), 109.

L19-45   J[ONES], L[LEWELLYN].   "Twelve Men as Seen by Dreiser,"
         Chicago Evening Post, 13 June 1919, p. [9]. Repub:
         Salzman, pp. 339-40; See I72-2.

L19-46   "Dreiser's New Book," Fresno Republican, 15 June 1919 [PU].

L19-47   HARRIS, FRANK.   "'Twelve Men,' by Theodore Dreiser,"
         Pearson's Magazine, 41 (July 1919), 422. Repub: Salzman,
         pp. 340-42; See I72-2.

L19-48   BOYNTON, H. W.   "Straight Goods," The Review, 1 (5 July 1919),
         169-70.

L19-49   "Twelve Men," Montreal Gazette, 12 July 1919 [PU].

L19-50   ANON.   "A Reader's Notes," Indianapolis Star, 14 July 1919,
         p. 6. Repub: Salzman, p. 342; See I72-2.

L19-51   MENCKEN, H. L.   "Novels Chiefly Bad," Smart Set, 59 (Aug.
         1919), 140-41.

WORKS ON

L19-52 POWYS, JOHN COWPER. "Real American Book by Genius Is Star in Literary Heavens," San Francisco Bulletin, 23 Aug. 1919, p. 19. Repub: Salzman, pp. 342-43; See I72-2.

L19-53 D[ELL], F[LOYD]. "American Fiction," Liberator, 2 (Sept. 1919), 46-47.

L19-54 ANON. "New Books Reviewed: Twelve Men," North American Review, 210 (Oct. 1919), 567-68.

L19-55 ANON. "Review of New Books," Literary Digest, 63 (11 Oct. 1919), 73.

L19-56 ANON. "The Book Shelf: 'Twelve Men,'" Birmingham [Ala.] Age-Herald, 26 Oct. 1919, Section C, p. 7.

L19-57 Bookseller, 15 Nov. 1919 [PU].

L19-58 DRUCKER, REBECCA. "Dreiser and O'Higgins," New York Tribune, 29 Nov. 1919, p. 10. Repub: Salzman, pp. 343-44; See I72-2.

L19-59 JENKINS, WILLIAM E. "Twelve Men," Indiana University Alumni Quarterly, 7 (Jan. 1920), 74-75.

L19-60 FINGER, CHARLES J. "Out of the Grip," Reedy's Mirror, 29 (6 May 1920), 373-74.

L19-61 HAWORTH, JAMES R. "Twelve Men By Dreiser in New Form," Huntington [W. Va.] Herald Advertiser, 29 July 1928 [PU].

L19-62 FITZGERALD, GERRY. St. Louis Times, 5 Aug. 1928 [PU].

L19-63 "Here Are Twelve Men," Wheeling [W. Va.] Register, 12 Aug. 1928 [PU].

L19-64 "In New Dress," Manchester [N.H.] Leader, 1 Sept. 1928 [PU].

L19-65 "New Additions to the Modern Library," Chester [Pa.] Times, 10 Sept. 1928 [PU].

L19-66 ANON. "Twelve Men," London Times Literary Supplement, 2 Oct. 1930, p. 780.

THE HAND OF THE POTTER (1919)

L19-67 [LEWISOHN, LUDWIG]. "Tragedy and Trifles," Nation, 109 (6 Sept. 1919), 340. Repub: Salzman, pp. 347-48; See I72-2.

L19-68 D., R. [REBECCA DRUCKER?]. "Grim Play by Dreiser," New York Tribune, 6 Sept. 1919, p. 9. Repub: Salzman, pp. 348-49; See I72-2.

L19-69 ANON. "Books: 'The Hand of the Potter,'" St. Louis Republic, 8 Sept. 1919, p. 9.

L19-70 ANON. "Mr. Dreiser's Play," New York Review, 13 Sept. 1919 [PU].

L19-71 ANON. "Notes and Views on Plays and Players," Indianapolis News, 13 Sept. 1919, p. 16. Repub: Salzman, p. 349, under incorrect date; See I72-2.

L19-72 ANON. "'Hand of Potter' Is Sex Play," New York American, 14 Sept. 1919 [PU].

L19-73 ANON. "A Dreiserian Play," Boston Evening Transcript, 17 Sept. 1919, Part 3, p. 4.

L19-74 ANON. "Books of the Fortnight: The Hand of the Potter," Dial, 67 (20 Sept. 1919), 276. Repub: Salzman, p. 350; See I72-2.

L19-75 ANON. "Super-Dreiser," New York Evening Sun, 20 Sept. 1919, p. [11]. Repub: Salzman, p. 349; See I72-2.

L19-76 D[AWSON], N. P. "The Hand of the Potter," New York Globe and Commercial Advertiser, 20 Sept. 1919, p. 8.

L19-77 ANON. "Reviews of the Books: The Hand of the Potter," Washington Sunday Star, 21 Sept. 1919, Part 3, p. 4. Repub: Salzman, pp. 350-51; See I72-2.

L19-78 FORREST, BELFORD. "Among the Books: 'The Hand of the Potter,'" Albany Knickerbocker Press, 21 Sept. 1919, Fourth Section, p. 6. Repub: Salzman, p. 350; See I72-2.

L19-79 ANON. "New Books and Gossip," Pittsburg Dispatch, 25 Sept. 1919, p. 6.

WORKS ON

L19-80 ANON. "Mr. Dreiser's Latest Play," Chicago Evening Post,
        26 Sept. 1919, p. [13].

L19-81 ANON. "Books of the Day: 'The Hand of the Potter,'" Phila-
        delphia Inquirer, 27 Sept. 1919, p. 12.

L19-82 "'The Hand of the Potter,'" Los Angeles Times, 28(?) Sept.
        1919 [PU].

L19-83 NATHAN, GEORGE JEAN. "Dreiser's Play--and Some Others,"
        Smart Set, 60 (Oct. 1919), 131-33. Repub: George Jean
        Nathan, The Theatre, the Drama, the Girls. New York:
        Knopf, 1921. Pp. 85-90. Salzman, pp. 351-53; See I72-2.

L19-84 ANON. "The New Books: Hand of the Potter," Outlook, 123
        (1 Oct. 1919), 191. Repub: Salzman, p. 353; See I72-2.

L19-85 BUTCHER, FANNY. "Tabloid Book Review," Chicago Sunday
        Tribune, 5 Oct. 1919, Part 7, p. 5.

L19-86 BENNETT, JESSE LEE. "The Incomplete Sceptic," New Republic,
        20 (8 Oct. 1919), 297-98. Repub: Salzman, pp. 353-55;
        See I72-2.

L19-87 ANON. "Dreiser's Published Play," Brooklyn Daily Eagle,
        11 Oct. 1919, p. 9.

L19-88 [BLACK, CONSTANCE]. "'It Is Easier to Be Critical than to
        Be Correct,'" Baltimore Evening Sun, 11 Oct. 1919, p. 6.
        Repub: Salzman, pp. 357-58, as appearing in the Baltimore
        Sun; See I72-2. We could not locate the review in the
        Sun.

L19-89 RASCOE, BURTON. "Dreiser Shakes the Potter's Hand," Chicago
        Daily Tribune, 11 Oct. 1919, p. 13. Repub: Salzman,
        pp. 355-57; See I72-2.

L19-90 ANON. "The Drama," Denver Rocky Mountain News, 12 Oct. 1919,
        Section 2, p. 4. Repub: Salzman, p. 360; See I72-2.

L19-91 STONE, JOHN T. "Choice of Material Spoils Dreiser Play,"
        Detroit Sunday News, 12 Oct. 1919, Magazine Section,
        p. 15. Repub: Salzman, pp. 358-59; See I72-2.

L19-92 ANON. "A Little Too Much Realism," Trenton [N.J.] Sunday
        Times-Advertiser, 19 Oct. 1919, Part Two, p. 3. Repub:
        Salzman, p. 360; See I72-2.

Reviews: THE HAND OF THE POTTER

L19-93 ANON. "A Play By Theodore Dreiser," Indianapolis Sunday
Star, 19 Oct. 1919, Part 7, p. 9. Repub: Salzman,
p. 360; See 172-2.

L19-94 BECKER, M. L. "A Dreiser Play," New York Evening Post,
25 Oct. 1919, p. 11 [PU]. Repub: Salzman, pp. 360-61;
See 172-2.

L19-95 ANON. "A Play By Dreiser," Springfield [Mass.] Sunday Republican, 26 Oct. 1919, Magazine and Auto Section, p. 16A.

L19-96 ANON. "Published Drama," Providence Sunday Journal, 26 Oct.
1919, Sixth Section, p. 7. Repub: Salzman, p. 362;
See 172-2.

L19-97 HOLMES, RALPH F. Springfield [Mass.] Morning Union, 26 Oct.
1919. Repub: Salzman, pp. 361-62; See 172-2.

L19-98 WOOLLCOTT, ALEXANDER. "Hand of the Potter," New York Times
Review of Books, 26 Oct. 1919, p. 598. Repub: Salzman,
p. 361; See 172-2.

L19-99 ANON. "Reviews: The Hand of the Potter," The New Age, 26
(6 Nov. 1919), 15.

L19-100 ANON. "'The Hand of the Potter,'" San Francisco Chronicle,
16 Nov. 1919, Editorial, Music, Theatrical News and
Features Section, p. [2E]. Repub: Salzman, pp. 362-63,
under incorrect date; See 172-2.

L19-101 ANON. "Vogue of Printed Plays Steadily Gaining Favor,"
Philadelphia Press, 22 Nov. 1919, p. 11. Repub: Salzman,
p. 363; See 172-2.

L19-102 ANON. "'The Hand of the Potter' by Dreiser," Baltimore News,
29 Nov. 1919 [PU]. Repub: Salzman, pp. 363-64; See
172-2.

L19-103 KARSNER, DAVID. "A Tragedy," New York Call, 6 Dec. 1919,
p. [10]. Repub: Salzman, pp. 364-65; See 172-2.

L19-104 ANON. "A Pathological Play," New York Medical Review,
6 Mar. 1920, pp. 431-32 [PU]. Repub: Salzman, pp. 365-
66; See 172-2.

L19-105 ANON. "Dreiser's Play," Philadelphia Evening Public Ledger,
5 June 1920, p. 10.

WORKS ON

L19-106 G., K. M. "The Hand of the Potter," Journal of Social
Hygiene, 6 (July 1920), 424-25.

HEY RUB-A-DUB-DUB (1920)

L20-1 ANON. "Theodore Dreiser Writes a Modern Prose Rubaiyat,"
Philadelphia North American, 13 Mar. 1920, p. 8. Repub:
Salzman, p. 369; See I72-2.

L20-2 D[AWSON], N. P. "'Hey Rub-a-Dub-Dub,'" New York Globe and
Commercial Advertiser, 13 Mar. 1920 p. 6.

L20-3 BUTCHER, FANNY. "Fiction," Chicago Sunday Tribune, 14 Mar.
1920, p. 9. Repub: Salzman, p. 370; See I72-2.

L20-4 H[OLMES], R[ALPH] F. "Musing with the Muses," Detroit
Journal, 17 Mar. 1920, p. 4. Repub: Salzman, pp. 370-71;
See I72-2.

L20-5 ANON. "Battling Dreiser--and Less Striking Writers," New
York Evening Post, 20 Mar. 1920, Book Section, p. 2.
Repub: Salzman, pp. 371-72; See I72-2.

L20-6 ANON. "Dreiser's Beliefs in New Book," New York American,
21 Mar. 1920, Editorial Section, p. CE-2.

L20-7 ANON. "Miscellaneous Books," New York Sun and Herald,
21 Mar. 1920, Section 4, p. 10.

L20-8 G., B. F. "Dreiser in Particular," Philadelphia Press,
21 Mar. 1920, Section 2, p. 7. Repub: Salzman, pp. 372-
73; See I72-2.

L20-9 ANON. "Books of the Day," Philadelphia Inquirer, 23 Mar.
1920, p. 12. Repub: Salzman, p. 373; See I72-2.

L20-10 ANON. "Dreiser and His Drum," Providence Sunday Journal,
28.Mar. 1920, Sixth Section, p. 7.

L20-11 H[OLMES], R[ALPH] F. "Musing with the Muses," Detroit
Journal, 31 Mar. 1920, p. 4.

L20-12 ANON. "New Books in Brief: Hey Rub-A-Dub-Dub," Current
Opinion, 68 (Apr. 1920), 570.

L20-13 B., J. "Dreiser's New Element," Brooklyn Daily Eagle,
3 Apr. 1920, p. 8. Repub: Salzman, p. 374; See I72-2.

L20-14 H[OLMES], R[ALPH] F. "Musing with the Muses," Detroit
Journal, 3 Apr. 1920, p. 4.

L20-15 ANON. "Reviews of New Books: Hey Rub-A-Dub-Dub," Washington
Sunday Star, 4 Apr. 1920, p. 28.

L20-16 HAAG, JACKSON D. "Frank Exposition of Dreiser's Philosophy,"
Detroit News, 4 Apr. 1920, Magazine Section, p. 10. Repub: Salzman, pp. 375-76; See I72-2.

L20-17 H[OLMES], R[ALPH] F. "Musing with the Muses," Detroit
Journal, 7 Apr. 1920, p. 4.

L20-18 RASCOE, BURTON. "The Books of the Week," Chicago Daily
Tribune, 10 Apr. 1920, p. 7. Repub: Salzman, p. 376;
See I72-2.

L20-19 DE CASSERES, BENJAMIN. "Mr. Dreiser Talks of Many Things,"
New York Times Review of Books, 11 Apr. 1920, p. 167.
Repub: Salzman, pp. 376-78; See I72-2.

L20-20 HANSEN, HARRY. "Of New and Ancient Things," Chicago Daily
News, 14 Apr. 1920, p. 12. Repub: Salzman, p. 378; See
I72-2.

L20-21 M[ORE], P[AUL] E[LMER]. "Theodore Dreiser, Philosopher,"
The Review, 2 (17 Apr. 1920), 380-81. Repub: Salzman,
pp. 379-82; See I72-2.

L20-22 MACOMBER, BEN. "Dreiser Likes the Noise His Thwacking
Cudgels Produce," San Francisco Chronicle, 18 Apr. 1920,
Editorial, Music, Theatrical News and Features Section,
p. 2E.

L20-23 ANON. "Brave Mr. Dreiser," New York Review, 24 Apr. 1920.
Repub: Salzman, pp. 373-74; See I72-2.

L20-24 ANON. "New Books: Hey Rub-A-Dub-Dub," Catholic World, 111
(May 1920), 260-61.

L20-25 H[ARRIS], F[RANK]. "A Word to Dreiser," Pearson's Magazine,
45 (May 1920), 902-04. Repub: Salzman, pp. 384-86;
See I72-2.

L20-26 MENCKEN, H. L. "More Notes From a Diary," Smart Set, 62
(May 1920), 138-40. Repub: H. L. Mencken's Smart Set
Criticism. Ed. William H. Nolte. Ithaca, N.Y.: Cornell
U. Press, 1968. Pp. 256-59 (as "De Profundis"). Salzman,
pp. 382-84; See I72-2.

THEODORE DREISER: A BIBLIOGRAPHY

L20-27 BROOKS, VAN WYCK. "According to Dreiser," Nation, 110 (1 May 1920), 595-96. Repub: Salzman, pp. 386-87; See I72-2.

L20-28 ANON. "Mr. Dreiser's Views," Springfield [Mass.] Sunday Republican, 2 May 1920, Magazine and Auto Section, p. 13a.

L20-29 H[ACKETT], F[RANCIS]. "Mystery, Terror and Confusion," New Republic, 22 (26 May 1920), 423-24. Repub: Salzman, pp. 388-90; See I72-2.

L20-30 ANON. "Books and Authors: 'Hey Rub-a-Dub-Dub,'" Grand Rapids [Mich.] News, 26 June 1920, p. 6 [i.e. 4].

L20-31 ANON. "America Gives the World Nothing Spiritual, Says Dreiser," New York Tribune, 4 July 1920, Magazine and Book Section, p. 11. Repub: Salzman, pp. 390-92; See I72-2.

L20-32 B., W. W. [WARREN WILMER BROWN?]. "Who Ever Saw Dreiser in a Sportive Mood?" Baltimore News, 31 July 1920. Repub: Salzman, pp. 392-93; See I72-2.

L20-33 ANON. "Briefer Mention: Hey Rub-A-Dub-Dub," Dial, 69 (Sept. 1920), 320. Repub: Salzman, p. 393; See I72-2.

L20-34 ANON. "Dreiser's Latest 'Shocking' Book," Cincinnati Star, 4 Sept. 1920. Repub: Salzman, pp. 393-94; See I72-2.

L20-35 ANON. "A Reader's Notes," Indianapolis Star, 18 Apr. 1921, p. 6.

L20-36 HALE, WILL T. "Hey, Rub-a-Dub-Dub," Indiana University Alumni Quarterly, 8 (Oct. 1921), 485-86.

L20-37 ANON. "Mr. Dreiser Moralizes," London Times Literary Supplement, 9 Apr. 1931, p. 282.

A BOOK ABOUT MYSELF (1922)

L22-1 LEIGHTON, EDITH. "Literary Confessions," Bookman, 56 (Dec. 1922), 498. Repub: Salzman, p. 397; See I72-2.

L22-2 D[AWSON], N. P. "'A Book About Myself,'" New York Globe and Commercial Advertiser, 21 Dec. 1922, p. 12.

L22-3 A[DAMS], F[RANKLIN] P. "The Conning Tower," St. Louis Post-Dispatch, 22 Dec. 1922, p. 21.

THEODORE DREISER: A BIBLIOGRAPHY

Reviews: A BOOK ABOUT MYSELF

L22-4   LEWIS, TRACY HAMMOND. "News and Views: The Frank Mr.
        Dreiser," New York Morning Telegraph, 22 Dec. 1922 [PU].

L22-5   ANON. "Theodore Dreiser Looking Backward," New York Times
        Book Review, 24 Dec. 1922, p. 14. Repub: Salzman,
        pp. 397-98; See I72-2.

L22-6   MINOT, JOHN CLAIR. "Theodore Dreiser," Boston Herald,
        27 Dec. 1922, p. 17.

L22-7   PAVA, MALCOLM. "Theodore Dreiser," Buffalo Saturday Night,
        27(?) Dec. 1922 [PU].

L22-8   ANON. "Books and Reading," New York Evening Post, 28 Dec.
        1922, p. 6.

L22-9   EDGETT, EDWIN FRANCIS. "The Apologia of Theodore Dreiser,"
        Boston Evening Transcript, 30 Dec. 1922, Book Section,
        p. 4.

L22-10 COOPER, FREDERIC TABER. "Dreiser on Himself," New York
        Herald, 31 Dec. 1922, Section Eight, p. 20.

L22-11 MANKIEWICZ, HERMAN J. "Dreiser, About Dreiser," New York
        World, 31 Dec. 1922 [PU].

L22-12 RASCOE, BURTON. "The Interesting Dullness of Dreiser's
        Life," New York Tribune, 31 Dec. 1922, Magazine and Book
        Section, p. 17. Repub: Salzman, pp. 399-402; See I72-2.

L22-13 POTTER, E. G. Chicago Tribune [Paris ed.], 1 Jan. 1923.
        Repub: Salzman, p. 402; See I72-2.

L22-14 Cleveland News, 6 Jan. 1923 [PU].

L22-15 "Dreiser Tells Us All About Career As Writing Man," San
        Francisco Bulletin, 6 Jan. 1923* [PU].

L22-16 PEARSON, EDMUND LESTER. "New Books and Old," Independent,
        110 (6 Jan. 1923), 25.

L22-17 WILLIAMS, SIDNEY. "Harry Kemp Examines Himself, and Theodore
        Dreiser, Ditto," Philadelphia North American, 6 Jan. 1923,
        p. 12.

L22-18 ANON. "Theodore Dreiser Tells the Story of His Reportorial
        Youth With Emotional Divagations," Providence Sunday
        Journal, 7 Jan. 1923, Fifth Section, p. 13.

THEODORE DREISER: A BIBLIOGRAPHY

L22-19 CURRIE, GEORGE. "Dreiser Exposes Himself," Brooklyn Daily
        Eagle, 13 Jan. 1923, p. 5.

L22-20 HYDE, HENRY M. "Dreiser at His Worst," Baltimore Evening
        Sun, 13 Jan. 1923, p. 6.

L22-21 St. Louis Star, 13 Jan. 1923 [PU].

L22-22 "Theodore Dreiser in Penning His Life Emphasizes Unhappy
        Features of His Existence," Philadelphia Public Ledger,
        13 Jan. 1923 [PU].

L22-23 "'A Book About Myself,'" Fort Wayne Journal Gazette, 14 Jan.
        1923 [PU].

L22-24 C., E. "'A Book About Myself,'" Atlanta Journal, 14 Jan.
        1923, Atlanta Journal Magazine, p. 14.

L22-25 H., J. G. "Dreiser's Own Book Entertaining Work," Richmond
        [Va.] Times-Dispatch, 14 Jan. 1923, Part Two, p. 5.

L22-26 M., I. G. "New Books at Random," Washington Evening Star,
        16 Jan. 1923, p. 6. Repub: Salzman, pp. 402-04; See
        I72-2.

L22-27 HANSEN, HARRY. "Robert Herrick on Marriage," Chicago Daily
        News, 17 Jan. 1923, p. 14.

L22-28 ANON. "Theodore Dreiser," Terre Haute [Ind.] Tribune,
        19 Jan. 1923, p. 4. Repub: Salzman, pp. 404-05; See
        I72-2.

L22-29 KRUTCH, JOSEPH WOOD. "Dreiser's Wanderjahre," New York
        Evening Post Literary Review, 20 Jan. 1923, p. 396.

L22-30 ALLEN, FRANK WALLER. "Books and Bookmen: A Book About My-
        self," Springfield Illinois State Journal, 21 Jan. 1923,
        p. 20.

L22-31 HALLER, RICHARD V. "A Book About Myself," Portland Sunday
        Oregonian, 21 Jan. 1923, Section Five, p. 3.

L22-32 HUNT, FRANK A. "Life of Dreiser As Told by Himself," Salt
        Lake City Telegram, 21 Jan. 1923, Magazine Section, p. 1.

L22-33 "The 'Memoirs' Vogue," Pittsburg Dispatch, 21 Jan. 1923 [PU].

Reviews: A BOOK ABOUT MYSELF

L22-34   PINOCHET, TANCREDO. "La Autobiografia de un Periodista,"
         Diario De La Marina, 23 Jan. 1923 [PU].

L22-35   ANON. "The Latest Books," Life, 81 (25 Jan. 1923), 22.

L22-36   G., M. D. T. "Today's Book Review: His Newspaper Days,"
         Syracuse Post-Standard, 25 Jan. 1923, p. 4.

L22-37   ANON. "Unhappy Theodore Dreiser in 'A Book About Myself,'"
         Kansas City [Mo.] Star, 27 Jan. 1923, p. 6.

L22-38   BUTCHER, FANNY. "Books," Chicago Sunday Tribune, 28 Jan.
         1923, Part 8, p. 19.

L22-39   "Dreiser's Story," Philadelphia Evening Public Ledger,
         30 Jan. 1923 [PU].

L22-40   Cornell Era, 60 (Feb. 1923), 23 [PU].

L22-41   LA GALLIENNE, RICHARD. "Certain Literary Sins of Theodore
         Dreiser," Literary Digest International Book Review, 1
         (Feb. 1923), 10-11, 70-71. Repub: Salzman, pp. 405-08;
         See I72-2.

L22-42   J[ONES], L[LEWELLYN]. "Theodore Dreiser's Reminiscences,"
         Chicago Evening Post Literary Review, 2 Feb. 1923, p. 7.

L22-43   Minneapolis Minnesota Daily Star, 2 Feb. 1923 [PU].

L22-44   BOYNTON, H. W. "Book Reviews: Der Arme Theodor," Inde-
         pendent, 110 (3 Feb. 1923), 99-100. Repub: Salzman,
         pp. 408-11; See I72-2.

L22-45   MACOMBER, BEN. "As His Own Dante Theodore Dreiser Conducts
         Excursion Through Inferno of Youthful Soul," San Francisco
         Chronicle, 4 Feb. 1923, Screen, Drama, Music, Books and
         Art Section, p. D5. Repub: Salzman, p. 412; See I72-2.

L22-46   ANON. "Literary Outlook: A Book About Myself," Chicago
         Journal of Commerce, 5 Feb. 1923, p. 4.

L22-47   KARSNER, DAVID. "Here and There and Everywhere," New York
         Call, 9 Feb. 1923, p. [8]. Repub: Salzman, pp. 413-14,
         under incorrect date; See I72-2.

L22-48   BROWN, WARREN WILMER. "Dreiser's Book About Himself Is
         Weighty," Baltimore News, 11 Feb. 1923 [PU].

WORKS ON

L22-49 FORD, THOMAS F. "Mr. Dreiser Tells the World," Los Angeles
Times, 18 Feb. 1923, Part 3, p. 38.

L22-50 KENDRICK, AMES. "Even the Poets Join Attack on Dreiser,"
Washington Herald Times, 18 Feb. 1923 [PU].

L22-51 EATON, WALTER PRICHARD. "Boy, Page Diogenes," Judge, 84
(24 Feb. 1923), 22.

L22-52 ANON. "Dreiser Begs Alms from His Readers," Kansas City
[Mo.] Journal-Post, 25 Feb. 1923, Magazine Section, p. 4.

L22-53 BAYM, MAX I. "On Dreiser," Detroit Free Press, 25 Feb. 1923,
Magazine Section, pp. 3-4. Repub: Salzman, pp. 415-16;
See I72-2.

L22-54 DOORLY, MARGARET H. "A Book About Myself," Omaha Sunday
World-Herald, 25 Feb. 1923, Magazine Section, p. 13.

L22-55 Catholic Review, Mar. 1923 [PU].

L22-56 MENCKEN, H. L. "Adventures Among Books--III," Smart Set, 70
(Mar. 1923), 143-44. Repub: Salzman, pp. 414-15; See
I72-2.

L22-57 TEETER, LOUIS. "A Book About Myself," Illinois Magazine,
4 Mar. 1923 [PU].

L22-58 "A Book About Myself," York [Pa.] Gazette Daily, 10 Mar.
1923 [PU].

L22-59 EATON, G. D. "The Contribution Box: 'A Book About Myself,'"
St. Louis Post-Dispatch, 10 Mar. 1923, p. 7.

L22-60 ROUTH, MARGARET. "Dreiser's Intimate Biography," St. Paul
Pioneer Press, 18 Mar. 1923, Fourth Section, p. 4.

L22-61 G., E. "Shorter Notices: A Book About Myself," Freeman, 7
(21 Mar. 1923), 46. Repub: Salzman, pp. 416-17; See
I72-2.

L22-62 ANON. "A Book About Myself," Modern Review, 1 (Apr. 1923),
129.

L22-63 MADOWSKY, THEODORE. "A Book About Myself," Forum, 69 (Apr.
1923), 1472-74. Repub: Salzman, pp. 417-18; See I72-2.

L22-64 "Book Reviews," Olympia [Wash.] Recorder, 2 Apr. 1923 [PU].

Reviews: THE COLOR OF A GREAT CITY

L22-65 L[EWISOHN], L[UDWIG]. "Books: Portrait of an Artist,"
        Nation, 116 (4 Apr. 1923), 394.

L22-66 Long Island Daily Press, 7 Apr. 1923 [PU].

L22-67 BARRY, JOHN D. "Living This Life: 'A Book About Myself,'"
        Minneapolis Morning Tribune, 14 Apr. 1923, p. 24. Repub:
        Salzman, pp. 418-19; See I72-2.

L22-68 ANON. "Dreiser's Notable Autobiography," San Francisco Call
        and Post, 5 May 1923, p. 23. Repub: Salzman, pp. 419-20;
        See I72-2.

L22-69 SEAVER, EDWIN. "Theodore Dreiser Himself," Advance, 15 June
        1923, p. 6 [PU]. Repub: Salzman, pp. 420-21; See I72-2.

L22-70 P., Z. F. "Book Reviews: A Book About Myself," American
        Hebrew, 113 (3 Aug. 1923), 255.

L22-71 HALE, WILL T. "A Book About Myself," Indiana University
        Alumni Quarterly, 12 (Jan. 1925), 90-91.

L22-72 ANON. "A Novelist's Youth," London Times Literary Supplement,
        26 Sept. 1929, p. 741.

L22-73 "A Novelist's Autobiography," The Age (Melbourne, Australia),
        9 Nov. 1929 [PU].

L22-74 T., C. P. "An American Odyssey," Time and Tide (London),
        29 Nov. 1929 [PU].

L22-75 WILLIAMS, ORLO. "A Book About Myself," Criterion, 9 (Jan.
        1930), 327-30.

L22-76 CAMERON, MAY. "Author! Author!: After 'Dawn,'" New York
        Evening Post, 6 Aug. 1931, p. 11.

L22-77 HANSEN, HARRY. "The First Reader," New York World-Telegram,
        12 Aug. 1931, p. 23.

THE COLOR OF A GREAT CITY (1923)

L23-1 Cleveland News, 15 Dec. 1923 [PU].

L23-2 STALLINGS, LAURENCE. "The First Reader: An Anglophile's
       Confession," New York World, 21 Dec. 1923, p. 9.

WORKS ON

L23-3 ANON. "Dreiser Pens Great Story," San Francisco <u>Bulletin</u>, 22 Dec. 1923, p. 19.

L23-4 ANON. "As the Uncommercial Traveler," New York <u>Times Book Review</u>, 23 Dec. 1923, p. 7. Repub: Salzman, pp. 425-26; <u>See</u> I72-2.

L23-5 ANON. "Dreiser Tells of Old Sam'l Clampitt's Junk-Yard, Etc.," <u>Time</u>, 2 (24 Dec. 1923), 14.

L23-6 HANSEN, HARRY. "Where Novels Begin," Chicago <u>Daily News</u>, 26 Dec. 1923, p. 14.

L23-7 JOHNSON, NUNNALLY. "Dreiser," Brooklyn <u>Daily Eagle</u>, 29 Dec. 1923, p. 3.

L23-8 WINN, JANE FRANCES. "Book Review: 'The Color of a Great City,'" St. Louis <u>Globe-Democrat</u>, 29 Dec. 1923, p. 15.

L23-9 BABB, STANLEY E. "Book News and Book Reviews: 'The Color of a Great City,'" Galveston <u>Daily News</u>, 30 Dec. 1923, p. 24.

L23-10 COOPER, FREDERIC TABER. "Dreiser Surveys Chameleonlike New York," New York <u>Herald</u>, 30 Dec. 1923, Section Nine, p. 17.

L23-11 COWDIN, MARGARET BARLOW. "Books and Bookmen: The Color of a Great City," Springfield <u>Illinois State Journal</u>, 30 Dec. 1923, Part Four, p. 6.

L23-12 R[OGERS], J. W., JR. "Sordid, Gray Writings of Dreiser Reveals Sympathy for Suffering Humanity; Has Sense of Beauty," Dallas <u>Daily Times Herald</u>, 30 Dec. 1923, Third Section, p. [2].

L23-13 "Shady Side of New York Life," Trenton <u>Times</u>, 30 Dec. 1923 [PU].

L23-14 BROWN, WARREN WILMER. "Dreiser Wordy in Latest Product," Baltimore <u>News</u>, 1 Jan. 1924 [PU].

L23-15 F., M. M. "The Office Window," Elkhart [Ind.] <u>Daily Truth</u>, 5 Jan. 1924 [PU].

L23-16 LEOF, MADELIN. "Theodore Dreiser Tries New York and Describes His Impressions in 'The Color of a Great City,'" Philadelphia <u>Public Ledger</u>, 5 Jan. 1924, p. 13.

THEODORE DREISER: A BIBLIOGRAPHY

Reviews: THE COLOR OF A GREAT CITY

L23-17 MOLONEY, S. J. "Dreiser Rises to Heights of the Great City," Salt Lake City Telegram, 6 Jan. 1924, Magazine Section, p. 1.

L23-18 ANON. "The New Books: Color of a Great City (the)," Outlook, 136 (9 Jan. 1924), 70. Repub: Salzman, pp. 426-27; See I72-2.

L23-19 C., S. L. [SHERWIN LAWRENCE COOK?]. "The Color of a Great City," Boston Evening Transcript, 9 Jan. 1924, Part 3, p. 4.

L23-20 Fort Wayne News-Sentinal, 12 Jan. 1924 [PU].

L23-21 MENCKEN, H. L. "Mencken Becomes Reminiscent Over Dreiser's New York," Baltimore Evening Sun, 12 Jan. 1924, p. 6. Repub: Salzman, pp. 427-28; See I72-2.

L23-22 McCORD, DAVID F. "Dreiser's Notebook," Springfield Illinois State Register, 13 Jan. 1924, p. 4.

L23-23 WEEKS, HOWARD. "Dreiser Out of His Field," Detroit News, 13 Jan. 1924, Metropolitan Section, p. 16.

L23-24 MacDONALD, W. A. "Mostly Books," Attleboro Sun, 17 Jan. 1924 [PU].

L23-25 "Dreiser Paints Prose Pictures of 38 Phases of New York Life," Columbia Missourian, 20 Jan. 1924 [PU].

L23-26 Salem [Oreg.] Statesman, 20 Jan. 1924 [PU].

L23-27 WARWICK, DIANA. "Life and Letters," Life, 83 (24 Jan. 1924), 22.

L23-28 BULLIET, C. J. "Books and Writers," Louisville Herald, 27 Jan. 1924 [PU].

L23-29 KARSNER, DAVID. "Dreiser's Tableaux," New York Tribune, 27 Jan. 1924, Magazine and Book Section, p. 19. Repub: Salzman, pp. 428-30; See I72-2.

L23-30 Q. "Today's Book Review: Sketches of New York," Syracuse Post-Standard, 28 Jan. 1924, p. 4.

L23-31 FULLER, HENRY B. "The Color of a Great City," New Republic, 37 (30 Jan. 1924), 263-64.

WORKS ON

L23-32 KESLER, CARL. "The Raw Material of Which Dreiser Made
        Great Novels," Quincy Herald, 1 Feb. 1924 [PU].

L23-33 TAYLOR, ALLAN. "'The Color of a Great City,'" Atlanta
        Journal, 3 Feb. 1924, Atlanta Journal Magazine, p. 22.

L23-34 "Dreiser's Impressions," Argonaut, 9 Feb. 1924 [PU].

L23-35 McCARDELL, LEE. "Books and Letters," Norfolk Virginian
        Pilot, 12 Feb. 1924 [PU].

L23-36 G., M. N. "Dreiser's Manhattan," Rockford Republic, 13 Feb.
        1924, p. 13.

L23-37 KRUTCH, J[OSEPH] W[OOD]. "Books: Plain and Colored,"
        Nation, 118 (13 Feb. 1924), 176.

L23-38 COWLEY, MALCOLM. "Black and White," New York Evening Post
        Literary Review, 16 Feb. 1924, p. 520.

L23-39 BOCERE, pseud. "About Books and Things: Color--And Much
        Else," Warren Chronicle, 25 Feb. 1924 [PU].

L23-40 Winston-Salem Sentinel, 1 Mar. 1924 [PU].

L23-41 ANON. "The Bookshelf of a Workingman," New York Weekly
        People, 8 Mar. 1924, p. 4.

L23-42 BUTCHER, FANNY. "Theodore Dreiser's Latest Book True to His
        Character," Chicago Daily Tribune, 8 Mar. 1924, p. 9.

L23-43 BRENT, CHESTER H. Roanoke [Va.] World-News, 10 Mar. 1924
        [PU].

L23-44 EATON, G. D. "Dreiser's Book As Whole Fails to Live up to
        Expectations--Good in Spots," Detroit Free Press, 16 Mar.
        1924, Magazine Section, pp. 9-10.

L23-45 V., J. L. "Dreiser Inarticulate," Circle, 19 Mar. 1924 [PU].

L23-46 ANON. "'The Color of a Great City,'" St. Louis Post-Dispatch,
        22 Mar. 1924, p. 6.

L23-47 HAINES, HELEN E. "Mr. Dreiser in a Great City," Pasadena
        Star-News, 22(?) Mar. 1924 [PU].

L23-48 JACKSON, JOSEPH H. "Dreiser Paints New York in Series of
        Powerful Sketches," San Francisco Chronicle, 23 Mar. 1924,
        Screen, Drama, Books, Music and Art Section, p. D5.

Reviews: THE COLOR OF A GREAT CITY

L23-49 MAURICE, ARTHUR BARTLETT. "The Splendid Quest for Bohemia," Literary Digest International Book Review, 2 (Apr. 1924), 378, 380.

L23-50 MINOT, JOHN CLAIR. "Dreiser's New York," Boston Herald, 5 Apr. 1924, p. 14.

L23-51 P., Z. F. "In the World of Books: The Color of a Great City," American Hebrew, 114 (18 Apr. 1924), 724.

L23-52 ANON. "Reviews of New Books: The Color of a Great City," Washington Sunday Star, 27 Apr. 1924, Part 2, p. 12.

L23-53 ANON. "Recent Books in Brief Review," Bookman, 59 (May 1924), 353. Repub: Salzman, pp. 430-31; See I72-2.

L23-54 B., R. "Mr. Theodore Dreiser at Home," Christian Science Monitor, 24 May 1924, p. 8. Repub: Salzman, p. 431; See I72-2.

L23-55 STURGES-JONES, MARION. "'The Color of a Great City,'" Camden Courier, 27 May 1924 [PU].

L23-56 FORD, THOMAS F. "Old New York's Seamy Side," Los Angeles Sunday Times, 15 June 1924, Part 3, p. 36. Repub: Salzman, pp. 432-33; See I72-2.

L23-57 SANDERS, CHAUNCEY ELWOOD. "Books and Writers: The Color of a Great City," Austin [Tex.] Statesman, 29 June 1924, p. 6. Repub: Salzman, p. 433, under incorrect date; See I72-2.

L23-58 RESIKA, ABRAHAM. "Once Over: The Color of a Great City," Liberator, 7 (July 1924), 31. Repub: Salzman, p. 434; See I72-2.

L23-59 ADLER, BETTY. "Book Reviews," Davenport [Ia.] Times, 26 July 1924. Repub: Salzman, pp. 434-36; See I72-2.

L23-60 BABB, W. O. "New York's Color," Dallas Morning News, 27 July 1924, Part 3, p. 10. Repub: Salzman, p. 434, under incorrect date; See I72-2.

L23-61 "The Color of a Great City," Atlantic City [N.J.] Union, 11 Apr. 1925 [PU].

L23-62 ANON. "New York Sketches," London Times Literary Supplement, 14 Aug. 1930, p. 652.

WORKS ON

AN AMERICAN TRAGEDY (1925)

L25-1   BUTCHER, FANNY. "Dreiser Rewards Waiters with Two Realistic Volumes," Chicago Daily Tribune, 2 Jan. 1926, p. 13.

L25-2   RENNELS, MARY. "Be Normal," Cleveland Town Topics, 2 Jan. 1926, p. 20. Repub: Salzman, pp. 439-40; See I72-2.

L25-3   ANON. "Books and Authors: Dreiser Again in Limelight," Trenton [N.J.] Sunday Times-Advertiser, 3 Jan. 1926, p. 8.

L25-4   BABB, STANLEY E. "Theodore Dreiser's New Novel, 'An American Tragedy,'" Galveston Daily News, 3 Jan. 1926, p. 6.

L25-5   HARRIS, JULIA COLLIER. "Dreiser's Long Expected Novel Depicts the Turmoil and the Tragedy of Youth," Columbus [Ohio] Enquirer Sun, 3 Jan. 1926 [PU]. Repub: Salzman, pp. 445-47; See I72-2.

L25-6   SHERMAN, STUART. "Mr. Dreiser in Tragic Realism," New York Herald Tribune Books, 3 Jan. 1926, pp. 1-3. Repub: Stuart P. Sherman, The Main Stream. New York: Scribner, 1927. Pp. 134-44. Salzman, Merrill Studies, pp. 17-24; See I71-3. Salzman, Theodore Dreiser, pp. 440-45; See I72-2.

L25-7   ANON. "Literary Outlook," Chicago Journal of Commerce, 4 Jan. 1926, p. 16.

L25-8   ANDERSON, SHERWOOD. "Dreiser," Saturday Review of Literature, 2 (9 Jan. 1926), 475. Repub: Wayne Gard, Book Reviewing. New York: Knopf, 1928. Pp. 88-92. Salzman, Merrill Studies, pp. 2-4; See I71-3. Salzman, Theodore Dreiser, pp. 447-49; See I72-2.

L25-9   CURRIE, GEORGE. "Passed in Review," Brooklyn Daily Eagle, 9 Jan. 1926, p. 5.

L25-10 DOUGLAS, GEORGE. "Dreiser's Novel," San Francisco Bulletin, 9 Jan. 1926, Feature Section, p. 3.

L25-11 EDGETT, EDWIN FRANCIS. "Theodore Dreiser Writes Another Novel," Boston Evening Transcript, 9 Jan. 1926, Book Section, p. 3.

L25-12 LOVE, ROBERTUS. "A Tremendous Tract," St. Louis Post-Dispatch, 9 Jan. 1926, p. 5.

THEODORE DREISER: A BIBLIOGRAPHY

Reviews: AN AMERICAN TRAGEDY

L25-13   RASCOE, BURTON. "An American Tragedy," New York Sun, 9 Jan.
1926, p. 10. Repub: Salzman, pp. 450-51; See I72-2.

L25-14   TOUCHSTONE, pseud. [Harry Esty Dounce]. "Books," New Yorker,
1 (9 Jan. 1926), 23.

L25-15   WILLIAMS, SIDNEY. "Mr. Dreiser's 'An American Tragedy' and
Stephen McKenna's 'The Oldest God,'" Philadelphia Inquirer, 9 Jan. 1926, p. 20.

L25-16   ANON. "The Tribune Library: An American Tragedy," Tulsa
Tribune, 10 Jan. 1926, Editorial and Magazine Section,
p. [7].

L25-17   CRAWFORD, JOHN W. "Theodore Dreiser Invests 'An American
Tragedy' with Mastery in Tracing Human Behavior," New York
World, 10 Jan. 1926, Third Section, p. 6M. Repub:
Salzman, pp. 454-56; See I72-2.

L25-18   DUFFUS, ROBERT L. "Dreiser's Undisciplined Power," New York
Times Book Review, 10 Jan. 1926, pp. 1, 6. Repub:
Salzman, pp. 451-54; See I72-2.

L25-19   E., G. D. "Dreiser's Novel at Last," New York Morning Telegraph, 10 Jan. 1926, Section 4, p. 7.

L25-20   SMALL, H. A. "Dreiser Once Again Invites Critical Dead Cats
and Lilies," San Francisco Chronicle, 10 Jan. 1926,
Screen, Drama, Books, Music and Art Section, p. 4D.

L25-21   "An American Tragedy," Fairmont West Virginian, 12 Jan. 1926
[PU].

L25-22   CURRIE, GEORGE. "Passed in Review," Brooklyn Daily Eagle,
16 Jan. 1926, p. 5.

L25-23   DARROW, CLARENCE. "Touching a Terrible Tragedy," New York
Evening Post Literary Review, 16 Jan. 1926, pp. 1-2.
Repub: Salzman, Merrill Studies, pp. 5-9; See I71-3.
Salzman, Theodore Dreiser, p. 456; See I72-2.

L25-24   LAWSON, W. ELSWORTH. "Book-Land Glimpses," Foxboro [Mass.]
Reporter, 16 Jan. 1926, p. 4 [PU]. Repub: Salzman,
pp. 457-58; See I72-2.

L25-25   New York Graphic, 16 Jan. 1926 [PU].

363

L25-26 LLOYD-SMITH, PARKER. "In 'An American Tragedy,' Dreiser Paves Broad Road of Realism," Albany Knickerbocker Press, 17 Jan. 1926, Sunday Magazine, p. 6.

L25-27 SAYLER, OLIVER M. Footlight and Lamplight, 2 (21 Jan. 1926), 1 [PU].

L25-28 JONES, LLEWELLYN. "Voluminous Tragedy," Chicago Evening Post Literary Review, 22 Jan. 1926, p. 1. Repub: Current Reviews. Ed. Lewis Worthington Smith. New York: Holt, 1926. Pp. 203-08.

L25-29 GOLDBERG, ISAAC. "In the World of Books: Theodore Dreiser's 'An American Tragedy' and Some American Comedies," Haldeman-Julius Weekly, 23 Jan. 1926, p. 3.

L25-30 CAHAN, ABRAHAM. "Dreiser's New Novel and What the Critics Say About It," Jewish Daily Forward, 24 Jan. 1926, p. 3. Repub: Salzman, pp. 461-64; See I72-2.

L25-31 CHITTICK, V. L. O. "The Work of Ten Years," Portland Sunday Oregonian, 24 Jan. 1926, Section Five, p. 3. Repub: Salzman, pp. 459-61; See I72-2.

L25-32 FORD, LILLIAN C. "Dreiser's American Tragedy," Los Angeles Sunday Times, 24 Jan. 1926, Part 3, p. 25.

L25-33 GOULD, JOHN. "Dreiser Tells Real Story With Rare Skill and Ruthlessness in 'An American Tragedy,'" Wichita Daily News, 24 Jan. 1926 [PU].

L25-34 DAVIDSON, DONALD. "The Spyglass: Theodore Dreiser," Nashville Tennessean, 31 Jan. 1926, Firing Line Section, p. 6. Repub: Donald Davidson, The Spyglass: Views and Reviews, 1924-1930. Ed. John Tyree Fain. Nashville: Vanderbilt U. Press, 1963. Pp. 67-70. Salzman, pp. 465-66; See I72-2.

L25-35 ELLINGSON, H. K. "Literary Notes: Dreiser's New Novel," Colorado Springs Sunday Gazette and Telegraph, 31 Jan. 1926, Section 3, p. 4.

L25-36 MAXWELL, JOHN. "An American Tragedy--By Dreiser," Indiana-polis Sunday Star, 31 Jan. 1926, Part 5, p. 14. Repub: Salzman, pp. 464-65; See I72-2.

L25-37 GORMAN, HERBERT S. "A Canvas of Living Figures," Book Review, Feb. 1926, p. 19. Repub: Salzman, pp. 467-68; See I72-2.

THEODORE DREISER: A BIBLIOGRAPHY

L25-38 HANNA, PHIL TOWNSEND. "An American Tragedy," California Sports, Feb. 1926, pp. 28, 38, 42 [PU].

L25-39 PATERSON, ISABEL. "Murders--Ancient and Modern," McNaught's Monthly, 5 (Feb. 1926), 59-60.

L25-40 TULLY, JIM. "Mr. Dreiser Writes An American Tragedy," Literary Digest International Book Review, 4 (Feb. 1926), 167, 169.

L25-41 KINSLEY, P. A. "Of Youth's Greatest Folly is 'An American Tragedy,'" Philadelphia Record, 6 Feb. 1926, p. 12.

L25-42 WALKER, CHARLES R. "Dreiser Moves Upward," Independent, 116 (6 Feb. 1926), 166. Repub: Salzman, pp. 468-69; See I72-2.

L25-43 BELLAMANN, HENRY. "The Literary Highway," Sunday Record, 7 Feb. 1926 [PU].

L25-44 KRUTCH, JOSEPH WOOD. "Crime and Punishment," Nation, 122 (10 Feb. 1926), 152. Repub: Salzman, Merrill Studies, pp. 10-12; See I71-3. Salzman, Theodore Dreiser, pp. 469-71; See I72-2.

L25-45 PEARSON, EDMUND. "The Book Table," Outlook, 142 (10 Feb. 1926), 222-23.

L25-46 AIKMAN, DUNCAN. "Book News: 'An American Tragedy,'" El Paso Times, 14 Feb. 1926, p. 18.

L25-47 M. [JOHN H. McGINNIS?]. "After Long Silence Dreiser Writes Two-Volume 'American Tragedy,'" Dallas Morning News, 14 Feb. 1926, Section 3, p. 3. Repub: Salzman, pp. 471-72; See I72-2.

L25-48 ANON. "An American Tragedy," Saturday Review of Literature, 2 (20 Feb. 1926), 569-70.

L25-49 BROUN, HEYWOOD. "It Seems to Me," New York World, 20 Feb. 1926, p. 11. Repub: Salzman, p. 473; See I72-2.

L25-50 MOUNT, GRETCHEN. "Theodore Dreiser Surpasses Even Himself," Detroit Free Press, 21 Feb. 1926, Magazine Section, p. 3. Repub: Salzman, pp. 473-75; See I72-2.

L25-51 SHULTZ, VICTOR. "Dreiser's Powerful New Book," Des Moines Sunday Register, 21 Feb. 1926 [Society and Editorial Section], p. E-7.

WORKS ON

L25-52 SMITH, DELOS. "A Masterpiece," New Orleans Tribune, 28 Feb.
        1926 [PU]. Repub: Salzman, pp. 475-76, as appearing in
        the New York World; See 172-2. We could not locate the
        review in the World.

L25-53 LINSCOTT, R. N. "An American Tragedy, by Theodore Dreiser,"
        The Atlantic's Bookshelf, Mar. 1926, p. [8]. Repub:
        Salzman, pp. 479-80; See 172-2.

L25-54 MENCKEN, H. L. "The Library: Dreiser in 840 Pages,"
        American Mercury, 7 (Mar. 1926), 379-81. Repub: H. L.
        Mencken, A Mencken Chrestomathy. New York: Knopf, 1949.
        Pp. 501-05. Salzman, Merrill Studies, pp. 12-17; See
        171-3. Salzman, Theodore Dreiser, pp. 476-79; See 172-2.

L25-55 McCRACKEN, W. LYNN. "Book Reviews Column," Great Falls
        [N.Y.] Times, 4 Mar. 1927 [PU].

L25-56 ANON. "Books and Authors: An American Tragedy," America,
        34 (6 Mar. 1926), 505.

L25-57 ANON. "Dreiser's 'The American Tragedy,'" Argonaut, 93
        (6 Mar. 1926), 5. Repub: Salzman, pp. 480-81; See 172-2.

L25-58 MORRISON, C. M. "Dreiser's Powerful New Novel, 'An American
        Tragedy,' Unfolds Harrowing Life Story of Youth," Newark
        Public Ledger, 6(?) Mar. 1926 [PU].

L25-59 SKIDELSKY, BERENICE. "What They Read," Vogue, 67 (15 Mar.
        1926), 186.

L25-60 WHIPPLE, T. K. "Theodore Dreiser," New Republic, 46 (17 Mar.
        1926), 113-15. Repub: Salzman, pp. 481-85; See 172-2.

L25-61 ANON. "Theodore Dreiser's 'American Tragedy,'" Springfield
        [Mass.] Sunday Union and Republican, 21 Mar. 1926, Maga-
        zine Section, p. 5A.

L25-62 ANON. "The Bookshelf of a Workingman," New York Weekly
        People, 27 Mar. 1926, p. 4.

L25-63 ANON. "Fiction," Cleveland Open Shelf, 4 (Apr. 1926), p. 53.

L25-64 PHELPS, WILLIAM LYON. "As I Like It," Scribner's Magazine,
        79 (Apr. 1926), 433-34. Repub: Salzman, pp. 486-87;
        See 172-2.

Reviews: AN AMERICAN TRAGEDY

L25-65   POWYS, JOHN COWPER. "An American Tragedy," Dial, 80 (Apr.
          1926), 331-38. Repub: Salzman, pp. 487-93; See I72-2.

L25-66   SILVERSON, HARRY. "A Study of Environment," Industrial
          Pioneer, Apr. 1926 [PU].

L25-67   TONER, WILLIAMS M. "An American Tragedy," Indiana University
          Alumni Quarterly, 13 (Apr. 1926), 164-65.

L25-68   VAN DOREN, CARL. "The Roving Critic: Beyond Good and Evil,"
          Century Magazine, 111 (Apr. 1926), 763-65. Repub:
          Salzman, pp. 493-95; See I72-2.

L25-69   BRENNECKE, ERNEST, JR. "Books: An American Tragedy,"
          Commonweal, 3 (28 Apr. 1926), 696-97. Repub: Salzman,
          pp. 495-97; See I72-2.

L25-70   W[EBSTER], P[AUL] F[RANCIS]. "Book Reviews," New York Uni-
          versity Daily News, 28 Apr. 1926, p. 5 [PU].

L25-71   SEAVER, EDWIN. "Theodore Dreiser and the American Novel,"
          New Masses, 1 (May 1926), 24.

L25-72   R., A. "Books: The American Tragedy," New Haven Union,
          23 May 1926 [PU].

L25-73   CESTRE, C. "Theodore Dreiser: An American Tragedy," Revue
          Anglo-Americaine, 3 (Aug. 1926), 567-71.

L25-74   ANON. "The Book Shelf," Bellingham [Wash.] Sunday Reveille,
          26 Sept. 1926, p. 7.

L25-75   K[AYDEN], E. M. "An American Tragedy," Sewanee Review, 34
          (Oct.-Dec. 1926), 495-97. Repub: Salzman, pp. 497-99;
          See I72-2.

L25-76   BLAIR, EMILY NEWELL. "Some Books Worth While," Good House-
          keeping, 83 (Oct. 1926), 51, 156, 159-60.

L25-77   ROBINSON, WILLIAM J. "Editorials: An American Tragedy,"
          Critic and Guide, 25D (Oct. 1926), 391-98.

L25-78   ANON. "New Novels: An American Tragedy," London Times
          Literary Supplement, 7 Oct. 1926, p. 672. Repub: American
          Writing Today: Its Independence and Vigor. Ed. Allan
          Angoff. New York: New York U. Press, 1957. Pp. 362-64.

L25-79   ANON. "Fiction: An American Tragedy," Spectator (London),
          137 (9 Oct. 1926), 602.

Theodore Dreiser: A Bibliography

WORKS ON

L25-80 HARWOOD, H. C. "New Books," Outlook (London), 58 (9 Oct. 1926), 351.

L25-81 MUIR, EDWIN. "Fiction," Nation and Athenaeum, 40 (16 Oct. 1926), 88-89.

L25-82 LYND, ROBERT. "The Young Murderer," Observer (London), 24 Oct. 1926, p. 7.

L25-83 ROBERTS, R. ELLIS. "A Murder Trial," London Daily News, 26 Oct. 1926 [PU].

L25-84 "An American Tragedy," London Daily Telegraph, 29 Oct. 1926 [PU].

L25-85 HARTLEY, L. P. Saturday Review (London), 142 (30 Oct. 1926) 522.

L25-86 P., T. "The Real American: A Great Novel," T. P.'s & Cassell's Weekly, 30 Oct. 1926, pp. 12-13 [PU].

L25-87 "Realism in U. S.," Birmingham Gazette, 4 Nov. 1926 [PU].

L25-88 M., A. N. "New Novels: Mr. Theodore Dreiser," Manchester Guardian, 5 Nov. 1926, p. 7.

L25-89 "'An American Tragedy,'" London Sunday Times, 7 Nov. 1926 [PU].

L25-90 DIXON, G. C. "An American Genius," London Daily Mail, 20 Nov. 1926 [PU].

L25-91 ROBERTS, R. ELLIS. "Theodore Dreiser," Bookman (London), 71 (Dec. 1926), 158-59.

L25-92 P., R. S. [ROGER PIPPETT?]. "Tragedy of Dollar Dictation," London Daily Herald, 29 Dec. 1926, p. 9.

L25-93 BENNETT, ARNOLD. "Books and Persons," London Evening Standard, 30 Dec. 1926 [PU].

L25-94 SCOTT, GEORGE RYLEY. "Dreiser at His Best and Worst," New Age, 40 (30 Dec. 1926), 106-07.

L25-95 D., I. F. "A Tremendous Book," Evanston [Ill.] News Index, 6 Jan. 1927* [PU].

368

Reviews: THE FINANCIER Revised edition

L25-96   S., P. "New Novels," New Statesman, 28 (15 Jan. 1927),
         420-21.

L25-97   NEVINSON, HENRY W. "From Life: An Average Criminal," New
         Leader, 21 Jan. 1927 [PU].

L25-98   THOROGOOD, HORACE. "A Great Novel," The Star (London),
         7 Feb. 1927 [PU].

L25-99   J., H. "Legal Literature," Butterworth's Fortnightly Notes
         (Wellington, New Zealand), 21 June 1927 [PU].

L25-100 FREEMAN, JOHN. "An American Tragedy," London Mercury, 16
         (Oct. 1927), 607-14.

MOODS: CADENCED AND DECLAIMED (1926)

L26-1   SHULTZ, VICTOR. "Poems by Two Pessimistic Novelists,"
         Des Moines Sunday Register, 5 Sept. 1926 [Society and
         Editorial Section], p. E-7.

THE FINANCIER. Revised edition (1927)

L27-1   HANSEN, HARRY. "The First Reader: Theodore Dreiser Revises,"
         New York World, 18 Apr. 1927, p. 11.

L27-2   ANON. "A Talk About Books: Dreiser at His Strongest in Re-
         vised 'The Financier,'" Battle Creek [Mich.] Enquirer and
         Evening News, 24 Apr. 1927, p. 4.

L27-3   ANON. "Dreiser Rewritten," New York Times Book Review,
         1 May 1927, p. 9.

L27-4   "Dreiser Revises 'the Financier,'" Trenton Times-Advertiser,
         5 June 1927 [PU].

L27-5   M., I. G. "New Books at Random," Washington Evening Star,
         14 June 1927, p. 8.

L27-6   GOLDBERG, ISAAC. "In the World of Books: Dreiser Revised,"
         Haldeman-Julius Weekly, 30 July 1927, p. 4.

L27-7   DARGAN, WOODS. "Dreiser at His Best," Asheville [N.C.]
         Times, 7 Aug. 1927 [PU].

Theodore Dreiser: A Bibliography

L27-8   ANON. "New Novels: The Financier," London Times Literary Supplement, 3 Nov. 1927, p. 786.

L27-9   GIBBS, DONALD. "Dreiser the Dull," Forum, 78 (Dec. 1927), 955-56. Reviewed with Chains.

L27-10 TOWER, ROY A. "The Financier (Rev. ed.)," Indiana University Alumni Quarterly, 16 (Jan. 1929), 108-09.

CHAINS (1927)

L27-11 BOYNTON, H. W. "Dreiser Broods Again," New York Sun, 14 May 1927, p. 9. Repub: Salzman, pp. 503-04; See I72-2.

L27-12 ANON. "A Dreiser Group," Springfield Illinois State Journal, 15 May 1927, Part 3, p. 6. Repub: Salzman, p. 504; See I72-2.

L27-13 STUART, HENRY LONGAN. "As Usual, Mr. Dreiser Spares Us Nothing," New York Times Book Review, 15 May 1927, p. 2. Repub: Salzman, pp. 504-06; See I72-2.

L27-14 ELLINGSON, H. K. "Literary Notes: Dreiser's New Book," Colorado Springs Sunday Gazette and Telegraph, 22 May 1927, Section 3, pp. 4-5. Repub: Salzman, p. 509; See I72-2.

L27-15 HANSEN, HARRY. "The First Reader," New York World, 22 May 1927, Book Section, p. 8M. Repub: Salzman, p. 510; See I72-2.

L27-16 VAN DOREN, CARL. "Lesser Novels," New York Herald Tribune Books, 22 May 1927, pp. 3-4. Repub: Salzman, pp. 508-09; See I72-2.

L27-17 AUBURN, WALTER J. "Lesser American Tragedies," Chicago Daily News, 25 May 1927, p. 14. Repub: Salzman, pp. 511-12; See I72-2.

L27-18 PINCKARD, H. R. "Short Stories by Dreiser Are Above Average," Huntington [W. Va.] Advertiser, 25 May 1927 [PU]. Repub: Salzman, pp. 510-11; See I72-2.

L27-19 T., J. E. Washington [Del.] News, 26 May 1927 [PU]. Repub: Salzman, p. 512; See I72-2.

L27-20 ALCESTE, pseud. [Ernest Boyd]. "Recent Books," New Yorker, 3 (28 May 1927), 88.

L27-21 LANGFELD, WILLIAM R. "Theodore Dreiser in Abridgment," Philadelphia Record, 28 May 1927, p. 4. Repub: Salzman, pp. 512-13; See I72-2.

L27-22 LECHLITNER, RUTH. "A Pachyderm Needs Room to Turn In," New York Evening Post Literary Review, 28 May 1927, p. 3. Repub: Salzman, pp. 506-07, under incorrect date; See I72-2.

L27-23 B[ECK], C[LYDE] B. "Life's Ironies," Detroit News, 29 May 1927, Part 3, p. 12. Repub: Salzman, pp. 507-08, under incorrect date; See I72-2.

L27-24 SCHRIFTGIESSER, KARL. "Theodore Dreiser in His Minor Mood," Boston Evening Transcript, 11 June 1927, Book Section, p. 2. Repub: Salzman, pp. 513-16; See I72-2.

L27-25 McFEE, WILLIAM. "Americana," New Republic, 51 (15 June 1927), 104-05. Repub: Salzman, pp. 516-17; See I72-2.

L27-26 MUNSON, GORHAM B. "Odds and Ends," Saturday Review of Literature, 3 (25 June 1927), 928. Repub: Salzman, pp. 517-18; See I72-2.

L27-27 Y[UST], W[ALTER]. "Theodore Dreiser's Short Stories and His Revised Novel," Philadelphia Public Ledger, 25 June 1927, p. 8. Includes brief mention of The Financier, revised ed. Repub: Salzman, pp. 518-19; See I72-2.

L27-28 HOLDER, V. E. "Chains by Theodore Dreiser," Larus, 1 (July 1927), 29.

L27-29 ANON. "Books and Authors: Chains, Lesser Novels and Stories," America, 37 (16 July 1927), 335.

L27-30 GERBER, MARIAN. "Gold in the Ore," Asheville [N.C.] Times, 24 July 1927 [PU]. Repub: Salzman, p. 519; See I72-2.

L27-31 "What They Read," Vogue, 1 Aug. 1927 [PU]. Repub: Salzman, pp. 519-20; See I72-2.

L27-32 ANON. "The Bookshelf of a Workingman," New York Weekly People, 6 Aug. 1927, p. 4. Repub: Salzman, pp. 520-21; See I72-2.

WORKS ON

L27-33 VERNON, GRENVILLE. "Books: Chains," Commonweal, 6 (28 Sept. 1927), 506-07.

L27-34 ANON. "New Novels: Chains," London Times Literary Supplement, 8 Mar. 1928, p. 168.

L27-35 HARWOOD, H. C. "New Books," Outlook (London), 61 (10 Mar. 1928), 310.

L27-36 SEMBOWER, ALTA BRUNT. "Chains," Indiana University Alumni Quarterly, 15 (Apr. 1928), 221-22.

MOODS: CADENCED AND DECLAIMED (1928)

L28-1 HANSEN, HARRY. "The First Reader," New York World, 9 Aug. 1928, p. 11. Repub: Salzman, pp. 523-24; See I72-2.

L28-2 YUST, WALTER. "Of Making Many Books--," Philadelphia Public Ledger, 10 Aug. 1928, p. 9. Repub: Salzman, pp. 524-25; See I72-2.

L28-3 CURRIE, GEORGE. "Passed in Review," Brooklyn Daily Eagle, 15 Aug. 1928, Section 1, p. 10A. Repub: Salzman, pp. 525-26; See I72-2.

L28-4 ANON. "Dreiser's Credo Index to His Character," San Francisco Bulletin, 18 Aug. 1928, p. 12. Repub: Salzman, pp. 526-27; See I72-2.

L28-5 BOYNTON, H. W. "Cadences of an Exile," New York Sun, 18 Aug. 1928, p. [21]. Repub: Salzman, pp. 528-29; See I72-2.

L28-6 "Dreiser Finds His Voice," Cincinnati Times Star, 18 Aug. 1928 [PU]. Repub: Salzman, pp. 529-30; See I72-2.

L28-7 GORMAN, ARTHUR J. "Dreiser's Moods Are Published," Pittsburgh Press, 18 Aug. 1928, p. 3. Repub: Salzman, p. 526; See I72-2.

L28-8 ANON. "Dreiser's Moods Take Verse Form in Neat Volume," San Francisco Chronicle, 19 Aug. 1928, Screen, Drama, Music, Books and Art Section, p. 10D. Repub: Salzman, p. 531; See I72-2.

L28-9 ANON. "Film Capital Satirizes Itself," Miami Daily News, 19 Aug. 1928, Second Section, p. 3. A N. E. A. review of Moods and Carl Van Vechten's Spider Boy that appeared,

Reviews: MOODS: CADENCED AND DECLAIMED

in whole or in part, in at least 16 newspapers. Repub:
Salzman, p. 525; See I72-2.

L28-10 HOWARD, DON. "Looking at Literature," Salt Lake City Telegram, 19 Aug. 1928, Magazine Section, p. 1. Repub:
Salzman, pp. 530-31; See I72-2.

L28-11 ROBERT, ROY. "Theodore Dreiser Again in His Strange Attitudes
With 'Moods,'" Atlanta Sunday American, 19 Aug. 1928 [PU].
Repub: Salzman, p. 531; See I72-2.

L28-12 [LOVE, ROBERTUS]. "By the Book Editor: 'Moods, Cadenced and
Declaimed,'" St. Louis Globe-Democrat, 25 Aug. 1928, p. 14.
Repub: Salzman, p. 532; See I72-2.

L28-13 Cincinnati Commercial Tribune, 26 Aug. 1928 [PU]. Repub:
Salzman, pp. 532-33; See I72-2.

L28-14 GROBMAN, MARGARET. "Dreiser Tries His Hand at Brevity,"
Chicago Evening Post Literary Review, 31 Aug. 1928,
p. [1]. Repub: Salzman, p. 534; See I72-2.

L28-15 Y., SAM. "Book Worm," Muskogee [Okla.] Democrat, 31 Aug.
1928 [PU]. Repub: Salzman, pp. 533-34; See I72-2.

L28-16 VAN VUREN, FLOYD. "In Printing House Square," Milwaukee
Journal, 1 Sept. 1928, p. 4.

L28-17 P., M. L. "'Moods' of Dreiser," Syracuse Post-Standard,
2 Sept. 1928, p. 4. Repub: Salzman, p. 534; See I72-2.

L28-18 Pueblo [Colo.] Star Journal, 2 Sept. 1928 [PU]. A rewritten
version of the N. E. A. review; See L28-9. Repub:
Salzman, p. 535; See I72-2.

L28-19 MacMILLAN, ELEANOR T. "New Books: Moods Cadenced and Declaimed," Portland Oregon Sunday Journal, 2 Sept. 1928,
Magazine Section, p. 3.

L28-20 NEIHARDT, JOHN G. "What Happens?" St. Louis Post-Dispatch,
3 Sept. 1928, p. 17. Repub: Salzman, pp. 535-36; See
I72-2.

L28-21 BALLOU, ROBERT O. "Traditions of Biography Are Broken by
Oscar Graf," Chicago Daily News, 5 Sept. 1928, p. 16.

L28-22 GOLDBERG, ISAAC. "In the World of Books: Theodore Dreiser
as Poet," Haldeman-Julius Weekly, 8 Sept. 1928, p. 1.
Repub: Salzman, pp. 536-37; See I72-2.

THEODORE DREISER: A BIBLIOGRAPHY

WORKS ON

L28-23 ANON. "The Thoughts and Moods of Theodore Dreiser," Kansas
City [Mo.] Journal-Post, 9 Sept. 1928, Journal-Post Magazine, p. 12. Repub: Salzman, pp. 537-38; See I72-2.

L28-24 "Moods Cadenced and Declaimed," Asbury Park [N.J.] Press,
9 Sept. 1928 [PU].

L28-25 ANON. "Dreiser Among the Poets--Half a Dozen Other New
Volumes," Kansas City [Mo.] Star, 15 Sept. 1928, p. 6.

L28-26 "Moods, Cadenced and Declaimed," Concord [N.H.] Independent,
22 Sept. 1928 [PU]. Repub: Salzman, p. 538; See I72-2.

L28-27 LAMAR, LUCIUS M. C. "Experimental Poetry of Theodore
Dreiser Now Issued for Trade," Dallas Morning News,
23 Sept. 1928, Editorial, Amusement and Radio Section,
p. 3. Repub: Salzman, pp. 538-39; See I72-2.

L28-28 ANON. "Theodore Dreiser Declaiming Some Candenced [sic.]
Moods," Philadelphia Inquirer, 29 Sept. 1928, p. 17.

L28-29 Holyoke [Mass.] Telegram, 29 Sept. 1928 [PU].

L28-30 "Theodore Dreiser's Long Awaited Poems," East St. Louis
[Ill.] Journal, 30 Sept. 1928 [PU].

L28-31 TASKER, J. DANA. "Dreiser as Poet," Outlook, 150 (24 Oct.
1928), 1036. Repub: Salzman, p. 539; See I72-2.

L28-32 ROSE, DONALD F. "Take It or Leave It: Stylists and Pessi-
mists," Forum, 80 (Nov. 1928), xiv.

L28-33 ANON. "Moods of Dreiser," Newark Evening News, 10 Nov. 1928,
Magazine Section, p. 4-x.

L28-34 R., G. R. B. [GERTRUDE R. B. RICHARDS?]. "Moods: Theodore
Dreiser's Excursions into Poetry," Boston Evening Transcript, 10 Nov. 1928, Book Section, p. 2. Repub: Salzman,
pp. 539-40; See I72-2.

L28-35 GINSBERG, LOUIS. "Dreiser's Poetry," Voices, No. 46 (Jan.
1929), 32-33.

L28-36 TOWER, ROY A. "Moods, Cadenced and Declaimed," Indiana
University Alumni Quarterly, 16 (Jan. 1929), 109.

Reviews: DREISER LOOKS AT RUSSIA

DREISER LOOKS AT RUSSIA (1928)

L28-37 HANSEN, HARRY. "The First Reader: Dreiser in Russia,"
        New York World, 10 Nov. 1928, p. 11. Repub: Salzman,
        pp. 543-44; See I72-2.

L28-38 PATERSON, ISABEL. "Books and Other Things," New York Herald
        Tribune, 13 Nov. 1928, p. 23. Repub: Salzman, pp. 544-
        45; See I72-2.

L28-39 LISSEY, JEANNETTE. "The Fly Leaf," Jamaica [N.Y.] Press,
        17 Nov. 1928 [PU]. Repub: Salzman, pp. 545-46; See
        I72-2.

L28-40 "Russia Viewed by Theodore Dreiser," Davenport Times, 17 Nov.
        1928 [PU].

L28-41 BECK, CLYDE. "Tragedy of Empire and the New Russia,"
        Detroit News, 18 Nov. 1928, Part 12, p. 8. Repub:
        Salzman, p. 546; See I72-2.

L28-42 ANON. "Mr. Dreiser Sees Things Good and Bad in the New
        Russia," Kansas City [Mo.] Star, 24 Nov. 1928, p. 6.

L28-43 ANON. "Theodore Dreiser Too Individualistic to Stomach
        Sovietism," Philadelphia Record, 24 Nov. 1928, p. 11.
        Repub: Salzman, pp. 546-47; See I72-2.

L28-44 W., E. H. "Dreiser Looks at Russia," La Porte [Ind.]
        Herald-Argus, 27 Nov. 1928 [PU].

L28-45 G[IBBS], W[ALCOTT]. "Recent Books," New Yorker, 4 (1 Dec.
        1928), 115.

L28-46 R., G. R. B. [GERTRUDE R. B. RICHARDS?]. "Dreiser on
        Russia," Boston Evening Transcript, 1 Dec. 1928, Book
        Section, p. 7. Repub: Salzman, pp. 547-48; See I72-2.

L28-47 NAZAROFF, ALEXANDER I. "Soviet Russia at the Beginning of
        Its Second Decade," New York Times Book Review, 2 Dec.
        1928, pp. 7, 28. Repub: Salzman, p. 548; See I72-2.

L28-48 ROSS, HOWARD S. "Books: Dreiser Looks at Russia," Ottawa
        Evening Citizen, 3 Dec. 1928 [PU].

L28-49 ANON. "One of the 57 Varieties," New York Weekly People,
        8 Dec. 1928, p. 3. Repub: Salzman, pp. 549-50; See
        I72-2.

WORKS ON

L28-50   EDGETT, EDWIN FRANCIS. "About Books and Authors," Boston
         Evening Transcript, 8 Dec. 1928, Book Section, p. 10.

L28-51   GORMAN, ARTHUR. "Rasputin Is Subject of Biography," Pitts-
         burgh Press, 8 Dec. 1928, p. 10. Repub: Salzman, p. 548;
         See I72-2.

L28-52   H., E. E. "Dreiser Says His Say on Russia," Albany Knicker-
         bocker Press, 16 Dec. 1928, Fourth Section, p. 6. Repub:
         Salzman, pp. 550-51; See I72-2.

L28-53   GANNETT, LEWIS. "Dreiser Gropes in Russia," New York
         Herald Tribune Books, 23 Dec. 1928, p. 3. Repub: Salzman,
         pp. 551-53; See I72-2.

L28-54   C[URTIS], J[OHN] G[OULD]. "The Russian Scene--Two Views,"
         Erie Daily Times, 29 Dec. 1928, Saturday Theatre, Radio
         and Magazine Supplement, p. 11. Repub: Salzman, p. 553;
         See I72-2.

L28-55   LOHMAN, HELEN. "Three Books About Russia After Ten Years of
         the Soviet," Philadelphia Inquirer, 5 Jan. 1929, p. 14.
         Repub: Salzman, pp. 553-54; See I72-2.

L28-56   [HORAN, KENNETH?]. "Dreiser Writes a Russian Tragedy,"
         Chicago Journal of Commerce, 19 Jan. 1929, p. 4. Repub:
         Salzman, pp. 554-55; See I72-2.

L28-57   DANA, HARRY. "Russia Looks at Dreiser--And Miss Thompson,"
         New Masses, 4 (Feb. 1929), 22.

L28-58   Forum, Feb. 1929 [PU]. Repub: Salzman, pp. 555-56; See
         I72-2.

L28-59   CORT, DAVID. "What They Read: Plagiarist," Vogue, 73
         (16 Feb. 1929), 126, 128. Repub: Salzman, pp. 556-57;
         See I72-2.

L28-60   VERNADSKY, G. "Russia Today," Yale Review, 18 (Spring 1929),
         600-03. Repub: Salzman, pp. 558-59; See I72-2.

L28-61   ANON. "Briefer Mention: Dreiser Looks at Russia," Dial, 86
         (Mar. 1929), 265. Repub: Salzman, p. 557; See I72-2.

L28-62   LLOYD, JESSIE. "Two Americans Look at Russia," Nation, 128
         (13 Mar. 1929), 317. Repub: Salzman, pp. 557-58; See
         I72-2.

Reviews: A GALLERY OF WOMEN

L28-63 SHANKS, EDWARD. "The Russian Enigma," Saturday Review
        (London), 147 (11 May 1929), 644.

L28-64 ANON. "Dreiser Looks at Russia," New Statesman, 33 (15 June
        1929), 316.

L28-65 PLOMER, WILLIAM. "Contemporary Russia," Nation and Athenaeum,
        45 (15 June 1929), 372.

L28-66 ANON. "The Picture of Russia," London Times Literary Supple-
        ment, 27 June 1929, pp. 501-02.

L28-67 ANON. "More Books on Russia," Spectator (London), 143
        (24 Aug. 1929), 255.

L28-68 O'NEILL, H. C. "Mr. Dreiser In Soviet Russia," London(?)
        Daily News, 5 Sept. 1929 [PU].

L28-69 TOWER, ROY A. "Dreiser Looks at Russia," Indiana University
        Alumni Quarterly, 16 (Oct. 1929), 548-49.

A GALLERY OF WOMEN (1929)

L29-1   KNIGHT, GRANT C. "Fiction: A Gallery of Women," Bookman,
        70 (Nov. 1929), 320-21. Repub: Salzman, pp. 563-64;
        See I72-2.

L29-2   PATERSON, ISABEL. "Books and Other Things," New York Herald
        Tribune, 29 Nov. 1929, p. 15. Repub: Salzman, pp. 564-
        65; See I72-2.

L29-3   SOSKIN, WILLIAM. "Books on Our Table: There Are More Ex-
        citing Women than Those on Display in Dreiser's 'A Gallery
        of Women,'" New York Evening Post, 29 Nov. 1929, p. 15.
        Repub: Salzman, pp. 565-67; See I72-2.

L29-4   DIVINE, CHARLES. "Dreiser, with Modern Brush, Paints 'A
        Gallery of Women,'" New York Telegram, 30 Nov. 1929,
        pp. 11, 16. Repub: Salzman, pp. 568-70; See I72-2.

L29-5   HANSEN, HARRY. "The First Reader: Dreiserian Women,"
        New York World, 30 Nov. 1929, p. 13. Repub: Salzman,
        pp. 567-68; See I72-2.

L29-6   ANON. "Theodore Dreiser in the Maze of Feminine Psychology,"
        New York Times Book Review, 1 Dec. 1929, p. 2. Repub:
        Salzman, pp. 570-71; See I72-2.

WORKS ON

L29-7   HOBSON, THAYER. "--And Nothing But the Truth," New York
        Herald Tribune Books, 1 Dec. 1929, pp. 5-6.* Repub:
        Salzman, pp. 571-72; See I72-2.

L29-8   YUST, WALTER. "Of Making Many Books," Philadelphia Public
        Ledger, 2 Dec. 1929, p. 11. Repub: Salzman, pp. 573-74;
        See I72-2.

L29-9   [KENNELL, RUTH E.]. "Hell Hath No Fury Like a Woman Scorned,"
        Chicago Daily News, 11 Dec. 1929, p. 22.

L29-10 B[UTCHER], F[ANNY]. "Dreiser's New Books Reflect Word
        Spending," Chicago Daily Tribune, 14 Dec. 1929, pp. 13, 17.

L29-11 S[MITH], A[GNES] W. "Recent Books," New Yorker, 5 (14 Dec.
        1929), 134.

L29-12 PORTERFIELD, ALLEN W. "An American Achievement," Outlook and
        Independent, 153 (18 Dec. 1929), 628-29. Repub: Salzman,
        pp. 575-77; See I72-2.

L29-13 McFEE, WILLIAM. "The Mountain in Labor," New York Sun,
        21 Dec. 1929, p. [22]. Repub: Salzman, pp. 574-75; See
        I72-2.

L29-14 MAURY, JEAN WEST. "A Gallery of Varied Dreiserian Women,"
        Boston Evening Transcript, 28 Dec. 1929, Book Section,
        p. 2. Repub: Salzman, p. 577; See I72-2.

L29-15 HEALY, ELISABETH S. "Books and Authors: A Gallery of Women
        by Theodore Dreiser," Havana [Cuba] Post, 13 Jan. 1929,
        p. 12.

L29-16 C., A. P. "Failures Caused by Sex," Syracuse Post-Standard,
        19 Jan. 1930, p. 4. Repub: Salzman, pp. 578-79; See
        I72-2.

L29-17 WELL, MAJOR ALEX. "Dreiser Pens Realistic Women," Albany
        Knickerbocker Press, 19 Jan. 1930, Society and Magazine
        Section, p. 16. Repub: Salzman, pp. 577-78; See I72-2.

L29-18 ANON. "The Book Revue," Theatre Guild, 7 (Feb. 1930), 4.

L29-19 MENCKEN, H. L. "The Library: Ladies, Mainly Sad," American
        Mercury, 19 (Feb. 1930), 254-55. Repub: Salzman,
        pp. 579-80; See I72-2.

L29-20 RIDDELL, JOHN, pseud. [Corey Ford]. "A Gallery of Dreiser,"
        Vanity Fair, 33 (Feb. 1930), 58-59.

L29-21 BROWN, ROLLO WALTER. "Fifteen Women," Saturday Review of Literature, 6 (8 Feb. 1930), 707-08. Repub: Salzman, pp. 581-83; See I72-2.

L29-22 ANON. "Fiction: Social and Character Studies," Cleveland Open Shelf, 4 (Apr. 1930), 61.

L29-23 RASCOE, BURTON. "Dreiser's Portraits," Plain Talk, 6 (Apr. 1930), 498-500. Repub: Salzman, pp. 583-85; See I72-2.

L29-24 ROSS, MARY. "Women in Fiction," Atlantic Bookshelf, Apr. 1930, p. 14.

L29-25 G., G. "Theodore Dreiser Is a Man Who Understands Women," New York Herald Tribune, 10 Apr. 1930* [PU].

L29-26 LINTOTT, H. J. B. "Novels," Nation and Athenaeum, 47 (12 Apr. 1930), 58.

L29-27 PARSONS, I. M. "Fiction: Americana," Spectator (London), 144 (12 Apr. 1930), 634.

L29-28 ANON. "Fair Women," Saturday Review (London), 149 (19 Apr. 1930), 492.

L29-29 PROTEUS, pseud. "Current Literature," New Statesman, 35 (26 Apr. 1930), 84.

L29-30 STOKES, W. N. "In These Stories Theodore Dreiser Analyzes Women," Dallas Morning News, 27 Apr. 1930, Feature Section, p. 8.

L29-31 "Fiction," Portland [Maine] Evening Express, 6 May 1930* [PU].

PLAYS, NATURAL AND SUPERNATURAL. Constable edition (1930)

L30-1 ANON. "'The Green Pastures' and Other Plays," London Times Literary Supplement, 15 May 1930, p. 410.

DAWN (1931)

L31-1 READER, THE, pseud. "Off the Press," New York American, 4 May 1931* [PU].

L31-2 WILDES, HARRY EMERSON. "Of Making Many Books--," Philadelphia Public Ledger, 7 May 1931, p. 13. Repub: Salzman, p. 587; See I72-2.

WORKS ON

L31-3   HANSEN, HARRY. "The First Reader," New York World-Telegram, 8 May 1931, p. 27. Repub: Salzman, pp. 592-93, under incorrect date; See I72-2.

L31-4   PATERSON, ISABEL. "Books and Other Things," New York Herald Tribune, 8 May 1931, p. 21. Repub: Salzman, pp. 588-90; See I72-2.

L31-5   SOSKIN, WILLIAM. "Books on Our Table: 'Dawn,' the Story of Theodore Dreiser's Youth, Impressively and Well Written," New York Evening Post, 8 May 1931, p. 11. Repub: Salzman, pp. 590-92; See I72-2.

L31-6   BUTCHER, FANNY. "Dreiser Tells Life Story in Frank Fashion," Chicago Daily Tribune, 9 May 1931, p. 12.

L31-7   MORDELL, ALBERT. "Theodore Dreiser Dares to Give Complete Picture of His Youth," Philadelphia Record, 9 May 1931, p. 10D. Repub: Salzman, pp. 595-96; See I72-2.

L31-8   RASCOE, BURTON. "Dreiser's Early Youth," New York Sun, 9 May 1931, p. 9. Repub: Salzman, pp. 593-95; See I72-2.

L31-9   BRITTEN, FLORENCE HAXTON. "When He Was Very Young," New York Herald Tribune Books, 10 May 1931, pp. 1-2. Repub: Salzman, pp. 596-97; See I72-2.

L31-10 JACK, PETER MONRO. "Dreiser's Confession of His Early Years," New York Times Book Review, 10 May 1931, p. 5. Repub: Salzman, pp. 597-600; See I72-2.

L31-11 MASSOCK, RICHARD. Albert Lea [Minn.] Tribune, 12 May 1931 [PU].

L31-12 HARRINGTON, JANETTE T. "Scanning the Shelves," Ohio State Lantern, 14 May 1931 [PU].

L31-13 McDERMOTT, WILLIAM F. "A Point of View: Theodore Dreiser Spills It All," Cleveland Plain Dealer, 16 May 1931, p. 7.

L31-14 PATERSON, ISABEL. "Books and Other Things," New York Herald Tribune, 18 May 1931, p. 11.

L31-15 W., J. T. "Theodore Dreiser Begins Autobiography," Springfield Weekly Republican, 21 May 1931, p. 8.

L31-16 HARRIS, WILLIAM E. "The Days of Theodore Dreiser's Youth," Boston Evening Transcript, 23 May 1931, Book Section, p. 8.

THEODORE DREISER: A BIBLIOGRAPHY

L31-17 W[HARTON], D[ON]. "The New Books: Dawn," Outlook & Inde-
        pendent, 158 (27 May 1931), 120. Repub: Salzman,
        p. 600; See 172-2.

L31-18 CONSTANT READER, pseud. [Dorothy Parker]. "Reading and
        Writing: Words, Words, Words," New Yorker, 7 (30 May
        1931), 64-66. Repub: Dorothy Parker, Constant Reader.
        New York: Viking, 1970. Pp. 138-43. Salzman, pp. 600-03;
        See 172-2.

L31-19 ANON. "An Appreciation of Dreiser's Dawn," Constable's
        Quarterly, No. 2 (Summer 1931), 35-39.

L31-20 K[LEIN], H[ERBERT]. "Book Notes: Dawn," Left, 1 (Summer &
        Autumn 1931), 89.

L31-21 CLARK, EDWIN. "Self-Revelations," Yale Review, 20 (June
        1931), 857-58. Repub: Salzman, pp. 603-04; See 172-2.

L31-22 HORRWITZ, E. "Witness of Theodore Dreiser," Dawn, 1 (June
        1931), 342 [PU].

L31-23 HAZLITT, HENRY. "Another Book About Himself," Nation, 132
        (3 June 1931), 613-14. Repub: Salzman, pp. 604-07; See
        172-2.

L31-24 HERRICK, ROBERT. "Dreiseriana," Saturday Review of Litera-
        ture, 7 (6 June 1931), 875. Repub: Salzman, pp. 607-10;
        See 172-2.

L31-25 ELLINGSON, H. K. "Literary Notes: Theodore Dreiser,"
        Colorado Springs Sunday Gazette and Telegraph, 14 June
        1931, Section 3, p. 4. Repub: Salzman, p. 610; See
        172-2.

L31-26 McG[INNIS, JOHN H.]. "Years of Theodore Dreiser's Youth Are
        Completely and Sincerely Recreated," Dallas Morning News,
        14 June 1931, Feature Section, p. 8. Repub: Salzman,
        pp. 610-12; See 172-2.

L31-27 CHAMBERLAIN, JOHN. "An American Record," Forum, 86 (July
        1931), vi.

L31-28 MENCKEN, H. L. "The Library: Footprints on the Sands of
        Time," American Mercury, 23 (July 1931), 383. Repub:
        Salzman, p. 612; See 172-2.

THEODORE DREISER: A BIBLIOGRAPHY

WORKS ON

L31-29 THOMPSON, ALAN REYNOLDS. "Biography: Dawn," Bookman, 73 (July 1931), 533-34. Repub: Salzman, pp. 613-14; See I72-2.

L31-30 ANON. "Mr. Dreiser's Youth," London Times Literary Supplement, 23 July 1931, p. 575.

L31-31 CHURCH, RICHARD. "The American Balzac," Spectator (London), 147 (25 July 1931), 133-34.

L31-32 F., H. I'A. "Books of the Day: Mr. Dreiser's Autobiography," Manchester Guardian, 3 Aug. 1931, p. 3.

L31-33 ARVIN, NEWTON. "An American Case History," New Republic, 67 (5 Aug. 1931), 319-20. Repub: Salzman, pp. 614-17; See I72-2.

L31-34 ANON. "A Middle-West Childhood," London Times, 7 Aug. 1931, p. 15.

L31-35 BURDETT, OSBERT. "Mr. Dreiser's Boyhood," Saturday Review (London), 152 (8 Aug. 1931), 186.

L31-36 PIPPETT, ROGER. "A Novelist Tells the Truth About Himself," London Daily Herald, 13 Aug. 1931 [PU].

L31-37 HERMANN, JOHN. "Honest Autobiography," New Masses, 7 (Sept. 1931), 19. Repub: Salzman, pp. 617-18; See I72-2.

L31-38 AGAR, HERBERT. "Dawn," English Review, 53 (Oct. 1931), 641-42.

L31-39 ANON. "Two American Autobiographies," New Statesman and Nation, 2 (3 Oct. 1931), 408.

TRAGIC AMERICA (1932)

L32-1 ANON. "Dreiser Scores Capitalistic System in New Book on 'Tragic America,'" Indianapolis Star, 18 Jan. 1932, pp. 1-2.

L32-2 GANNETT, LEWIS. "Books and Things," New York Herald Tribune, 18 Jan. 1932, p. 11. Repub: Salzman, p. 622; See I72-2.

L32-3 HANSEN, HARRY. "The First Reader," New York World-Telegram, 18 Jan. 1932, p. 21. Repub: Salzman, pp. 625-26; See I72-2.

Reviews: TRAGIC AMERICA

L32-4   SOSKIN, WILLIAM. "Reading and Writing," New York Evening
        Post, 18 Jan. 1932, p. 9. Repub: Salzman, pp. 623-25;
        See I72-2.

L32-5   TOWNE, CHARLES HANSON. "A Number of Things," New York
        American, 18 Jan. 1932, p. [11]. Repub: Salzman,
        pp. 621-22, under incorrect date; See I72-2.

L32-6   ANON. "Predicted Dreiser Book Appears," Springfield Illinois
        State Journal, 19 Jan. 1932, p. 6. Repub: Salzman,
        p. 626; See I72-2.

L32-7   BLUMENBERG, BEN. "Dreiser Indicts Capitalism," New Leader,
        13 (23 Jan. 1932), 10. Repub: Salzman, pp. 626-27; See
        I72-2.

L32-8   BOYD, J. IRWIN. "Dreiser Indicts Leaders but Spies Better
        Future," Philadelphia Public Ledger, 23 Jan. 1932, p. 16.
        Repub: Salzman, p. 628; See I72-2.

L32-9   CHASE, STUART. "Mr. Dreiser in a China Shop," New York
        Herald Tribune Books, 24 Jan. 1932, pp. 1-2. Repub:
        Salzman, pp. 631-33; See I72-2.

L32-10 STRUNSKY, SIMEON. "Mr. Dreiser Prescribes for Us," New York
        Times Book Review, 24 Jan. 1932, p. 10. Repub: Salzman,
        pp. 628-30; See I72-2.

L32-11 RASCOE, BURTON. "Dreiser Sees Red," New York Sun, 29 Jan.
        1932, p. 27. Repub: Salzman, pp. 633-35; See I72-2.

L32-12 C[OATES], R[OBERT] M. "Books, Books, Books," New Yorker, 7
        (30 Jan. 1932), 53-54.

L32-13 DAVIDSON, GUSTAV. Sunday Mirror, 31 Jan. 1932 [PU].

L32-14 GILLIS, REV. JAMES M. "What's Right with the World--Not So
        Tragic America," Catholic News, 6 Feb. 1932, p. 5. Repub:
        Salzman, pp. 635-36; See I72-2.

L32-15 N., S. E. "An American Indicts America," Sydney Mail,
        17 Feb. 1932, pp. 14, 25 [PU].

L32-16 JONES, ELIOT. "Dreiser vs. the U. S.," Saturday Review of
        Literature, 8 (27 Feb. 1932), 555. Repub: Salzman,
        pp. 636-37; See I72-2.

THEODORE DREISER: A BIBLIOGRAPHY

L32-17 ANON. "Current Literature: Tragic America," Sydney Morning Herald, 12 Mar. 1932, p. 8.

L32-18 LILJEHOLM, H. ERIC. "Dreiser Attacks Labor's Lethargy," Albany Knickerbocker Press, 20 Mar. 1932, Fourth Section, p. 4. Repub: Salzman, pp. 637-38; See I72-2.

L32-19 C., S. C. "Mr. Dreiser Astray," Christian Science Monitor, 26 Mar. 1932, p. 5 (Central ed.). Repub: Salzman, pp. 638-39; See I72-2.

L32-20 WILSON, EDMUND. "Equity for Americans," New Republic, 70 (30 Mar. 1932), 185-86. Repub: Salzman, pp. 639-42; See I72-2.

L32-21 THOMAS, NORMAN. "Books and Drama: Dreiser as Economist," Nation, 134 (6 Apr. 1932), 402-03. Repub: Salzman, pp. 642-43; See I72-2.

L32-22 STEVENS, BENNETT. "The Gnats and Dreiser," New Masses, 7 (May 1932), 24. Repub: Salzman, pp. 646-48; See I72-2.

L32-23 LASKI, H. J. "Books of the Day: An American Critic," Manchester Guardian, 21 July 1932, p. 5.

L32-24 RATCLIFFE, S. K. "Two American Extremes," Spectator (London), 149 (30 July 1932), 160.

L32-25 ANON. "Mr. Dreiser as Sociologist," London Times Literary Supplement, 4 Aug. 1932, p. 550.

L32-26 AGAR, HERBERT. "Decline and Fall," New Statesman and Nation, 4 (6 Aug. 1932), 160.

MOODS: PHILOSOPHIC AND EMOTIONAL (CADENCED AND DECLAIMED) (1935)

L35-1 ROBINSON, TED. "Caveat Lector! Week's Book Fare Offers a Brutal Tale, Fantasy, Dreiser's Poetry," Cleveland Plain Dealer, 23 June 1935, Women's Magazine and Amusement Section, p. 13.

L35-2 WALTON, EDA LOU. "Very Free Verse by Dreiser," New York Herald Tribune Books, 23 June 1935, p. 4.

L35-3 A., R. "Gifts From Parnassus: Moods," Cincinnati Enquirer, 29 June 1935, p. 7.

Reviews: AMERICA IS WORTH SAVING

L35-4   BENÉT, WILLIAM ROSE. "The Phoenix Nest: Contemporary
        Poetry," Saturday Review of Literature, 12 (29 June 1935),
        18.

L35-5   SALOMON, LOUIS B. "A Few Minutes with Authors: 'Moods,
        Philosophical and Emotional,' Cadenced and Declaimed,"
        Louisville Times, 29 June 1935, p. 4.

L35-6   SHERMAN, JOHN K. "Great Novelist Becomes a Poor Poet in
        'Moods,'" Minneapolis Star, 29 June 1935 [PU].

L35-7   CHAMBLISS, JAC. "In a Collection of 250 Prose Poems Which
        Make Up His First New Book Since 1931, Theodore Dreiser
        Formulates His Emotional Attitudes," Chattanooga Times,
        30 June 1935 [PU].

L35-8   HUTCHISON, PERCY. "Theodore Dreiser's Poetry in Prose,"
        New York Times Book Review, 7 July 1935, p. 10.

L35-9   W., J. T. "Dreiser's Poems," Springfield Weekly Republican,
        3 Oct. 1935, p. 8.

AMERICA IS WORTH SAVING (1941)

L41-1   SILLEN, SAMUEL. "Dreiser's J'Accuse," New Masses, 38
        (28 Jan. 1941), 24-26.

L41-2   HOWE, QUINCY. "Cooperative Monopolies," New York Herald
        Tribune Books, 2 Feb. 1941, p. 12. Repub: Salzman,
        pp. 651-52; See I72-2.

L41-3   ANON. "Counsel from Hollywood," Time, 37 (3 Feb. 1941),
        74-76. Repub: Salzman, p. 652; See I72-2.

L41-4   ANON. "Briefly Noted: America Is Worth Saving," New Yorker,
        16 (8 Feb. 1941), 58. Repub: Salzman, p. 654; See I72-2.

L41-5   DUFFUS, R[OBERT] L. "Theodore Dreiser Mounts the Soapbox,"
        New York Times Book Review, 9 Feb. 1941, p. 22. Repub:
        Salzman, pp. 652-54; See I72-2.

L41-6   HICKS, GRANVILLE. "Dreiser to the Rescue," Saturday Review
        of Literature, 23 (22 Feb. 1941), 13. Repub: Salzman,
        pp. 655-56; See I72-2.

L41-7   ANON. "Books in Brief: America Is Worth Saving," Christian
        Century, 58 (26 Feb. 1941), 290-91. Repub: Salzman,
        p. 659, under incorrect date; See I72-2.

WORKS ON

L41-8   RILEY, LESTER LEAKE. "Along the Bookshelves: America Is
         Worth Saving," Churchman, 155 (1 Apr. 1941), 18. Repub:
         Salzman, p. 656; See I72-2.

L41-9   GISSEN, MAX. "What Must America Do?" New Republic, 104
         (26 May 1941), 736-37. Repub: Salzman, pp. 656-58; See
         I72-2.

L41-10   PERRY, RALPH BARTON. "The Anatomy of Democracy," Virginia
         Quarterly Review, 17 (Summer 1941), 444-46.

THE BULWARK (1946)

L46-1   ANON. "The Bulwark," Kirkus Book Service, 14 (15 Jan. 1946),
         21-22.

L46-2   SEAVER, EDWIN. "'The Bulwark,' by Theodore Dreiser," Book
         Find News, 2 (Mar. 1946), 3-5. Repub: Salzman, pp. 661-
         63; See I72-2.

L46-3   ANON. "Theodore Dreiser's Last Novel," Newark Evening News,
         21 Mar. 1946, p. 12.

L46-4   GANNETT, LEWIS. "Books and Things," New York Herald Tribune,
         21 Mar. 1946, p. 23. Repub: Salzman, p. 664; See I72-2.

L46-5   McFEE, WILLIAM. "The Reviews," New York Sun, 21 Mar. 1946,
         p. 23.

L46-6   NORTH, STERLING. "Dreiser's Last Testament," New York Post,
         21 Mar. 1946, p. 25. Repub: Salzman, pp. 664-65; See
         I72-2.

L46-7   POORE, CHARLES. "Books of the Times," New York Times,
         21 Mar. 1946, p. 23. Repub: Salzman, p. 663; See I72-2.

L46-8   CALDERWOOD, NATALIE H. "The Old and New Dreiser," Kansas
         City [Mo.] Star, 23 Mar. 1946, p. 5. Repub: Salzman,
         pp. 668-69; See I72-2.

L46-9   PARSONS, MARGARET. "Book Chat: New Dreiser," Worcester
         [Mass.] Evening Gazette, 23 Mar. 1946, p. 8.

L46-10   SPILLER, ROBERT E. "Dreiser as Master Craftsman," Saturday
         Review of Literature, 29 (23 Mar. 1946), 23. Repub:
         Salzman, pp. 666-68; See I72-2.

L46-11 WILSON, EDMUND. "Books: Theodore Dreiser's Quaker and
        Graham Greene's Priest," New Yorker, 22 (23 Mar. 1946),
        88, 91, 92, 94. Repub: Salzman, p. 668; See I72-2.

L46-12 M., T. J. "'The Bulwark' Accentuates Dreiser's Loss to
        Letters," Atlanta Constitution, 24 Mar. 1946, Section C,
        p. 15. Repub: Salzman, pp. 670-71; See I72-2.

L46-13 PRESTON, JOHN HYDE. "Hero of Dreiser's Last Novel Resembles
        His Creator," New York PM, 24 Mar. 1946, Sunday Magazine
        Section, pp. m7-m8.

L46-14 ROBERTS, MARY-CARTER. "Reviewing the New Books: Theodore
        Dreiser's Posthumous Novel Not His Best," Washington
        Sunday Star, 24 Mar. 1946, Section C, p. 4. Repub:
        Salzman, pp. 669-70; See I72-2.

L46-15 ROGERS, W. G. "Does Dreiser's Last Novel Do His Best Work
        Credit?" New Haven Register, 24 Mar. 1946 [PU]. Repub:
        Salzman, pp. 681-82; See I72-2.

L46-16 BURKE, HARRY R. "Dreiser's Final Novel Is Recantation of
        Old Doubts," St. Louis Globe-Democrat, 24 Mar. 1946,
        Section E, p. [5]. Repub: Salzman, pp. 674-75; See
        I72-2.

L46-17 FLANAGAN, JOHN T. "Dreiser's Powerful, Posthumous Novel,"
        Chicago Sun Book Week, 24 Mar. 1946, p. 1. Repub:
        Salzman, p. 669; See I72-2.

L46-18 GREGORY, HORACE. "In the Large Stream of American Tradition,"
        New York Herald Tribune Weekly Book Review, 24 Mar. 1946,
        pp. 1-2. Repub: Salzman, pp. 671-74; See I72-2.

L46-19 HYDE, FREDERIC G. "Pithy Story of Quaker Life Rounds Out
        Dreiser's Work," Philadelphia Inquirer, 24 Mar. 1946,
        Society Section, p. 14.

L46-20 J[ORDAN]-S[MITH], P[AUL]. "Decline in National Ideal of
        Honesty Told by Dreiser," Los Angeles Times, 24 Mar. 1946,
        Part 3, p. 4.

L46-21 McVICKER, DAPHNE ALLOWAY. "Dreiser's Last Book Is Disap-
        pointing," Columbus [Ohio] Citizen, 24 Mar. 1946 [PU].

L46-22 MATTHIESSEN, F. O. "God, Mammon and Mr. Dreiser," New York
        Times Book Review, 24 Mar. 1946, pp. 1, 42, 44. Repub:
        Salzman, pp. 675-78; See I72-2.

WORKS ON

L46-23   PECKHAM, DOROTHY T.   "Fails in His Family Life," Worcester
         [Mass.] Sunday Telegram, 24 Mar. 1946, Section 3, p. 4.

L46-24   PHILLIPS, EUGENE.   "A Vigorous Human Novel, Theodore
         Dreiser's Last," Milwaukee Journal, 24 Mar. 1946, Edi-
         torial Section, p. 3.

L46-25   R., R. T.   "Dreiser's Posthumous Novel: Work Written in
         Desperation," Dallas Morning News, 24 Mar. 1946, Section
         Four, p. 4.   Repub: Salzman, pp. 680-81; See I72-2.

L46-26   RASCOE, BURTON.   "Does Dreiser's Final Novel Reveal Spiritual
         Creed?"   Chicago Sunday Tribune, 24 Mar. 1946, Part 4,
         pp. 3, 8.   Repub: Salzman, pp. 679-80; See I72-2.

L46-27   ROBINSON, MAUDE.   "A Quaker Tragedy: Dreiser's Last Novel
         Will Stir No Storm," Salt Lake City Tribune, 24 Mar. 1946,
         Section D, p. 2.

L46-28   S., W. T.   "Dreiser's Posthumous Novel," Providence Sunday
         Journal, 24 Mar. 1946, Section 6, p. 8.

L46-29   STEDMAN, ALEX.   "First of Two Dreiser Novels Invites Reading
         of Second, Too," Fort Worth Star-Telegram, 24 Mar. 1946,
         Section 2, p. 5.

L46-30   ANON.   "Dreiser the Great," Newsweek, 27 (25 Mar. 1946),
         102-03.   Repub: Salzman, pp. 684-85; See I72-2.

L46-31   ANON.   "Valedictory," Time, 47 (25 Mar. 1946), 102-06.   Re-
         pub: Salzman, pp. 682-83; See I72-2.

L46-32   PRICE, EMERSON.   "Book Reviews," Cleveland Press, 26 Mar.
         1946, p. 9.   Repub: Salzman, pp. 683-84; See I72-2.

L46-33   L[AYCOCK], E[DWARD] A.   "A Bulwark Overwhelmed," Boston
         Evening Globe, 27 Mar. 1946, p. 18.

L46-34   ANON.   "Books on Parade," San Francisco Call-Bulletin,
         29 Mar. 1946, p. [12].

L46-35   CARBERRY, EDWARD.   Cincinnati Post, 30 Mar. 1946 [PU].   Re-
         pub: Salzman, p. 685; See I72-2.

L46-36   ANON.   "Book Notes of a Miami Author: Dreiser's Last Book
         Unfolds Quaker's Life," Miami Herald, 31 Mar. 1946,
         Section B, p. 4.

L46-37 BROWN, CHARLES. "Despite the Critics, Dreiser Is Secure on His Literary Hill," Oklahoma City Daily Oklahoman, 31 Mar. 1946, p. 23C. Repub: Salzman, p. 687; See I72-2.

L46-38 "Dreiser's Last Novel," Columbus [Ohio] Dispatch, 31 Mar. 1946 [PU].

L46-39 FARRALL, HELEN K. "Strength and Compassion Set Dreiser's Posthumous Novel Apart," Des Moines Sunday Register, 31 Mar. 1946, Section 7, p. 11-x. Repub: Salzman, pp. 687-88; See I72-2.

L46-40 H., R. F. "Theodore Dreiser on the Spiritual Values," Springfield [Mass.] Republican, 31 Mar. 1946 [PU]. Repub: Salzman, p. 686; See I72-2.

L46-41 HANSEN, HARRY. "Dreiser on Faith," New York World-Telegram, 31 Mar. 1946 [PU]. Repub: Salzman, pp. 665-66; See I72-2.

L46-42 JACKSON, MARGOT. "Novels All: 'The Bulwark,'" Akron Beacon Journal, 31 Mar. 1946, Section B, p. 4.

L46-43 MAYBERRY, GEORGE. "Dreiser: The Last Chapter," New Republic, 114 (1 Apr. 1946), 449-50. Repub: Salzman, pp. 688-89; See I72-2.

L46-44 SROOG, ARNOLD. "'The Bulwark' True Dreiser: Unerring American Portrait," Daily Worker, 1 Apr. 1946, p. 11. Repub: Salzman, pp. 689-90; See I72-2.

L46-45 JACKSON, JOSEPH HENRY. "Bookman's Notebook," San Francisco Chronicle, 3 Apr. 1946, p. 16. Repub: Salzman, p. 690; See I72-2.

L46-46 ANON. "Library Notes," Greenfield [Mo.] Dade County Advocate, 4 Apr. 1946, p. 6.

L46-47 SONNICHSEN, C. L. "The Book Shelf: The Bulwark," El Paso Herald-Post, 5 Apr. 1946, p. 4.

L46-48 GARDINER, HAROLD C. "Faith and Worldliness," America, 75 (6 Apr. 1946), 14.

L46-49 NEVIN, ROBERT S. "Novel by Theodore Dreiser Magnificently Written," Dayton Journal Herald, 6 Apr. 1946* [PU].

WORKS ON

L46-50   BECK, CLYDE. "Theodore Dreiser's Posthumous Novel," Detroit
         News, 7 Apr. 1946, Home and Society Section, p. 19.

L46-51   F[OOTE], R[OBERT] O. "Posthumous Dreiser," Pasadena Star-
         News, 7 Apr. 1946, p. 21.

L46-52   FULLER, JOHN G. "'The Bulwark,'" Boston Sunday Post, 7 Apr.
         1946, p. A-2.

L46-53   HOYT, ELIZABETH NORTH. "A Quaker Background," Cedar Rapids
         [Ia.] Gazette, 7 Apr. 1946, Section Three, p. 2.

L46-54   WILSON, KEITH. "Dreiser's Last Novel," Omaha Sunday World-
         Herald, 7 Apr. 1946, Section C, p. 18. Repub: Salzman,
         p. 691; See I72-2.

L46-55   BEATTY, RICHMOND C. "Family Disintegration," Nashville
         Banner, 10 Apr. 1946, Midweek Society and Feature Section,
         p. 16.

L46-56   SMITH, THEODORE. "Reviews and News of Books," San Francisco
         News, 13 Apr. 1946 [PU].

L46-57   FIREBAUGH, JOSEPH J. "Major Theme Is Religious in Two Post-
         humous Novels," St. Louis Post-Dispatch, 14 Apr. 1946,
         Editorial Section, p. 2D.

L46-58   Q., S. A. "Dreiser's Last Book," Richmond [Va.] Times-Dis-
         patch, 14 Apr. 1946, Section 4, p. 12.

L46-59   ANON. "Dreiser, Theodore. The Bulwark," Best Sellers, 6
         (15 Apr. 1946), 19-20.

L46-60   MacDONALD, NORMAN. "Godly Quaker Dreiser Theme," Boston
         Herald, 17 Apr. 1946, p. 19.

L46-61   MURRAY, MARIAN. "The Bulwark," Hartford [Conn.] Times,
         18 Apr. 1946, p. 24.

L46-62   TRILLING, LIONEL. "Dreiser and the Liberal Mind," Nation,
         162 (20 Apr. 1946), 466, 468-70, 472. Repub: Salzman,
         pp. 692-98; See I72-2.

L46-63   WARE, RUNA ERWIN. "Book Notes: The Bulwark," Augusta [Ga.]
         Chronicle, 21 Apr. 1946, p. 1-D.

L46-64   "Books," Beverly Hills Script, 27 Apr. 1946 [PU].

Reviews: THE BULWARK

L46-65   B[ROADDUS], M[ARIAN] H[OWE]. "The Bulwark," El Paso Times,
          28 Apr. 1946, p. 6.

L46-66   MILLER, MARGARET. "Novel of Quaker Life Issued Posthumously,"
          San Diego Union, 28 Apr. 1946, Section C, p. 7.

L46-67   WEBSTER, HARVEY CURTIS. "Dreiser Puts Down His Last Great
          Words," Louisville Courier-Journal, 28 Apr. 1946, Section
          3, p. 12.

L46-68   ANON. "What's New," Senior Scholastic, 48 (29 Apr. 1946),
          26.

L46-69   RUBINSTEIN, ANNETTE. "A Pillar of Society," New Masses, 59
          (30 Apr. 1946), 23-24. Repub: Salzman, pp. 698-700;
          See I72-2.

L46-70   KENNEDY, JOHN S. "Fiction in Focus: The Bulwark," Sign, 25
          (May 1946), 60.

L46-71   JONES, HOWARD MUMFORD. "Dreiser Reconsidered," Atlantic
          Monthly, 177 (1 May 1946), 162, 164, 166, 168, 170.
          Repub: Salzman, pp. 700-04; See I72-2.

L46-72   L., T. T. "In Faith We Stand," Columbia [Mo.] Missourian,
          2 May 1946 [PU].

L46-73   WILLIS, MARIANNA. "Book Review," Glendora Press-Gleaner,
          3 May 1946 [PU].

L46-74   WALSH, LEE. "Of Books and Writings: 'The Bulwark,'"
          Washington Daily News, 4 May 1946, p. 12.

L46-75   RAGAN, MARJORIE. "Theodore Dreiser's Last Novel," Raleigh
          [N.C.] News and Observer, 5 May 1946, Section 4, p. 5.

L46-76   SULLIVAN, RICHARD F. "Spencerism to Asceticism," Hartford
          [Conn.] Courant, 5 May 1946, Magazine Section, p. 14.

L46-77   "You'll Want to Read This," Burbank Daily Review, 14 May
          1946 [PU].

L46-78   "The Bulwark," Portland [Maine] Press-Herald, 16 May 1946
          [PU].

L46-79   HOOVER, GLADYS. "Dreiser's Latest," San Jose Mercury Herald
          and News, 19 May 1946, p. 16.

TheodoRE DREISER: A Bibliography

ORKS ON

L46-80 LARSEN, MARGARET P. "Library Notes," Coleraine [Minn.]
        Itasca Iron News, 23 May 1946, p. 6.

L46-81 C., R. "Dreiser's Posthumous Book Recalls an Earlier Age,"
        Hamilton [Ont.] Spectator, 25 May 1946 [PU].

L46-82 "Have You Read...?" Los Altos [Calif.] News, 30 May 1946
        [PU].

L46-83 "Bound to Be Read," Corona [Calif.] Independent, 31 May 1946
        [PU].

L46-84 ANON. "Fiction: The Bulwark," Virginia Quarterly Review,
        22 (Summer 1946), lxxv. Repub. Salzman, p. 712; See
        I72-2.

L46-85 PRESCOTT, ORVILLE. "Outstanding Books: The Bulwark," Yale
        Review, 35 (Summer 1946), 767. Repub: Salzman, p. 712;
        See I72-2.

L46-86 WALCUTT, CHARLES CHILD. "Naturalism in 1946: Dreiser and
        Farrell," Accent, 6 (Summer 1946), 263-68.

L46-87 ANON. "Literature: The Bulwark," United States Quarterly
        Booklist, 2 (June 1946), 89.

L46-88 GALLOWAY, MYRON J. "Christian or Communist?" "Index" Maga-
        zine (Montreal), June 1946, pp. 18-21 [PU].

L46-89 HICKS, GRANVILLE. "The Library: Theodore Dreiser," American
        Mercury, 62 (June 1946), 751-56. Repub: Kazin and
        Shapiro, pp. 219-24 (as "Theodore Dreiser and The Bulwark");
        See I55-1. Salzman, pp. 705-09; See I72-2.

L46-90 MATCH, RICHARD. "The Bulwark by Theodore Dreiser," Tomorrow,
        5 (June 1946), 73.

L46-91 WADE, MASON. "Books of the Week: The Bulwark," Commonweal,
        44 (14 June 1946), 220. Repub: Salzman, p. 704; See
        I72-2.

L46-92 Halifax [N.S.] Chronicle, 15 June 1946 [PU].

L46-93 HALL, GERTRUDE. "Book Review," Sausalito [Calif.] News,
        20 June 1946, p. 5.

L46-94 BISSINGER, LEE. "Good Reading," New York Pic, July 1946 [PU].

Reviews: THE BEST SHORT STORIES OF THEODORE DREISER

L46-95 REED, THOMAS J. "The Bulwark," Extension, 41 (July 1946), 26.

L46-96 STEINBACH, HERBERT. "Dreiser's Last Novel," Cresset, 10 (July 1946), 51-52.

L46-97 WALLACE, MARGARET. "Books: The Legacy of Theodore Dreiser," Independent Woman, 25 (July 1946), 209-10.

L46-98 FARRELL, JAMES T. "Dreiser's Posthumous Novel: A Major American Work," Call, 13 (1 July 1946), 5. Repub: Salzman, pp. 710-12; See I72-2.

L46-99 L., B. "Great American Novelist Ends Lifelong Search," Winnipeg Tribune, 6 July 1946 [PU].

L46-100 DERLETH, AUGUST. "Three Novels," Madison [Wis.] Capital Times, 14 July 1946, p. [32].

L46-101 GALANTIÈRE, LEWIS. "Reading Matters," Town and Country, 100 (Aug. 1946), 162.

L46-102 T., R. D. "Rising Materialism of Our Days," New Leader, 10 Aug. 1946, p. 10.

L46-103 FLOYD, T. M. "The Book of the Week: The Bulwark," Alabama Baptist, 10 Oct. 1946, p. 6.

L46-104 WHITNEY, FRED C. "Books in Review," El Cajon [Calif.] Valley News, 17 Apr. 1947, Section 3, p. [6]. Repub: Salzman, pp. 691-92, under incorrect date; See I72-2.

L46-105 CAMPBELL, HARRY M. "A New Dreiser," Western Review, 11 (Winter 1947), 106-08.

L46-106 ANON. "The Last of Dreiser," Pathfinder, 54 (3 Dec. 1947), 44.

THE BEST SHORT STORIES OF THEODORE DREISER (1947)

L47-1 WAGENKNECHT. EDWARD. "Best of Dreiser Short Stories in One Volume," Chicago Sunday Tribune, 6 Apr. 1947, Part 4, p. 10.

L47-2 ANON. "Slippery, Protean Everything," Time, 49 (7 Apr. 1947), 114.

THEODORE DREISER: A BIBLIOGRAPHY

WORKS ON

L47-3   HUTCHENS, JOHN K. "Short Pause for a Return to Dreiser,"
        New York Herald Tribune Book Review, 19 Feb. 1956, p. 2.

L47-4   ANON. "The Left Bank of the Wabash," Time, 67 (27 Feb. 1956),
        108, 111.

L47-5   H., R. F. "Tales of Tragedy," Springfield Republican, 4 Mar.
        1956, Section C, p. 8.

THE STOIC (1947)

L47-6   ANON. "Last Great Novel in Dreiser Trilogy," Bridgeport
        [Conn.] Sunday Post, 2 Nov. 1947, Third Section, p. B-2.

L47-7   MacGREGOR, MARTHA. "Theodore Dreiser's Last Novel," New York
        Post, 6 Nov. 1947, p. 30.

L47-8   HANSEN, HARRY. "The First Reader: Dreiser Buries Cowper-
        wood," New York World-Telegram, 7 Nov. 1947, p. 31.
        Repub: Salzman, p. 717; See I72-2.

L47-9   B[URKE], H[ARRY] R. "Dreiser Answers His Own Question in
        Final Novel," St. Louis Globe-Democrat, 9 Nov. 1947,
        Section F, p. 5. Repub: Salzman, pp. 718-19; See I72-2.

L47-10 CAROUSSO, DOROTHEE. "Theodore Dreiser's Final Novel,"
        Brooklyn Eagle, 9 Nov. 1947, p. 12. Repub: Salzman,
        pp. 717-18; See I72-2.

L47-11 FARRELL, JAMES T. "Greatness of Dreiser is Attested in Final
        Novel," Philadelphia Sunday Bulletin, 9 Nov. 1947, Book
        Review Section, pp. 1, 7.

L47-12 STOVER, FRANCES. "The Last Days of a Titan," Milwaukee
        Journal, 9 Nov. 1947, Editorial Section, p. 4.

L47-13 SULLIVAN, JULIAN T. "Book Nook: 'The Stoic,'" Indianapolis
        Star, 9 Nov. 1947, Section 4, p. 34. Repub: Salzman,
        p. 719; See I72-2.

L47-14 ANON. "The Last of Dreiser," Time, 50 (10 Nov. 1947), 116.
        Repub: Salzman, p. 720; See I72-2.

L47-15 ANON. "Unfinished Trilogy," Newsweek, 30 (10 Nov. 1947),
        85-86. Repub: Salzman, pp. 720-21; See I72-2.

394

L47-16 L[AYCOCK], E[DWARD] A. "Unchanging Dreiser," Boston Evening
        Globe, 12 Nov. 1947, p. 19. Repub: Salzman, p. 721;
        See I72-2.

L47-17 ANON. "Briefly Noted: The Stoic," New Yorker, 23 (15 Nov.
        1947), 134-35.

L47-18 BELL, LISLE. "Books and Things," New York Herald Tribune,
        15 Nov. 1947, p. 9. Repub: Salzman, p. 721; See I72-2.

L47-19 BONNER, WILLARD HALLAM. "Dreiser, Pioneer in Naturalism,
        Appears Almost Quaint in Posthumous Work," Buffalo Evening
        News, 15 Nov. 1947, Magazine Section, p. 5.

L47-20 COLBERT, PAT. "Books in Review: The Stoic," Charleston
        [S.C.] News and Courier, 16 Nov. 1947, Section E, p. 5.
        Repub: Salzman, p. 721; See I72-2.

L47-21 J[ONES], C[ARTER] B[ROOKE]. "Last, Unfinished Novel of
        Dreiser Trilogy Reveals Anew His Power and Awkwardness,"
        Washington Sunday Star, 16 Nov. 1947, Section C, p. 3.

L47-22 P[ARSONS], M[ARGARET]. "Last Novel By Dreiser," Worcester
        [Mass.] Sunday Telegram, 16 Nov. 1947, Section C, p. 4.

L47-23 SHERMAN, JOHN K. "Dreiser Power Holds in His Final Novel,"
        Minneapolis Sunday Tribune, 16 Nov. 1947, Women's News,
        Theaters, Travel, Art, Music and Books Section, p. [20].
        Repub: Salzman, p. 722; See I72-2.

L47-24 F., S. J. [STANLEY J. FRIEDMAN?]. "The Bookshelf," Harvard
        Crimson, 19 Nov. 1947 [PU].

L47-25 ALGREN, NELSON. "Dreiser's Despair Reaffirmed in 'The
        Stoic,'" Philadelphia Inquirer Books, 23 Nov. 1947, p. 3.
        Repub: Salzman, pp. 726-27; See I72-2.

L47-26 ALLEN, STEWART. "Dreiser's Last Novel: A Selected Anderson,"
        Dallas Daily Times Herald, 23 Nov. 1947, Part 6, p. 5.
        Repub: Salzman, pp. 725-26; See I72-2.

L47-27 BRANIGAN, ALAN. "Profound Novel," Newark Sunday News,
        23 Nov. 1947, Section 4, p. 10. Repub: Salzman, pp. 724-
        25; See I72-2.

L47-28 BUTCHER, FANNY. "Dreiser True Realist in His Final Novel,"
        Chicago Sunday Tribune, 23 Nov. 1947, Part 4, p. 5.
        Repub: Salzman, pp. 727-28; See I72-2.

WORKS ON

L47-29 COWLEY, MALCOLM. "Ending Dreiser's 'Trilogy of Desire,'"
New York Times Book Review, 23 Nov. 1947, pp. 7, 57.
Repub: Salzman, pp. 722-24; See I72-2.

L47-30 "Dreiser's Trilogy Complete, but His Wife Finished It,"
Columbus [Ohio] Dispatch, 23 Nov. 1947 [PU].

L47-31 SPINKS, BRIAN. "Completing the Record of a Notable Career,"
Houston Post, 23 Nov. 1947 [PU]. Repub: Salzman, p. 728;
See I72-2.

L47-32 HICKERSON, WILLIAM H. "Dreiser's Last Novel Won't Add to
Fame, Says Reviewer," Cleveland Plain Dealer, 30 Nov.
1947, Woman's Magazine and Amusement Section, p. 21.
Repub: Salzman, pp. 728-29; See I72-2.

L47-33 S., W. T. "Dreiser's Final Novel, and 'Anderson Reader,'"
Providence Sunday Journal, 30 Nov. 1947, Section 6, p. 2.
Repub: Salzman, pp. 729-30; See I72-2.

L47-34 W., E. D. "Dreiser Completes Trilogy," New Bedford [Mass.]
Sunday Standard-Times, 30 Nov. 1947, Third Section, p. 28.
Repub: Salzman, p. 730; See I72-2.

L47-35 CONROY, JACK. "Dreiser's Final Novel of Cowperwood Series,"
Chicago Sun Book Week, 3 Dec. 1947, p. 4A. Repub:
Salzman, pp. 730-32; See I72-2.

L47-36 FARRELL, JAMES T. "Dreiser's 'The Stoic' Powerful," Chicago
Daily News, 3 Dec. 1947, p. [19]. Repub: Salzman,
p. 732; See I72-2.

L47-37 MARCUSON, DR. "Books in the News," Macon [Ga.] News, 4 Dec.
1947 [PU]. Repub: Salzman, pp. 732-33; See I72-2.

L47-38 LYDENBERG, JOHN. "The Anatomy of Exhaustion," Saturday Review of Literature, 30 (6 Dec. 1947), 36. Repub: Salzman,
pp. 733-34; See I72-2.

L47-39 MORRIS, LLOYD. "Dreiser's Last," New York Herald Tribune
Weekly Book Review, 7 Dec. 1947, p. 54. Repub: Salzman,
pp. 734-35; See I72-2.

L47-40 PAULUS, JOHN D. "Dreiser's Real Place in American Letters
Recalled by 'Stoic,'" Pittsburgh Press, 14 Dec. 1947,
p. 68. Repub: Salzman, pp. 736-37; See I72-2.

Reviews: LETTERS OF THEODORE DREISER

L47-41   STEDMAN, ALEX. "Theodore Dreiser's Last Book Ends the
         Cowperwood Saga," Fort Worth Star-Telegram, 14 Dec. 1947,
         Section 2, p. 11. Repub: Salzman, p. 736, as appearing
         in Fort Worth Press; See I72-2.

L47-42   HAY, JOHN. "Books of the Week: The Stoic," Commonweal, 47
         (19 Dec. 1947), 260-61. Repub: Salzman, p. 737; See
         I72-2.

L47-43   COMPTON, NEIL. "Napoleonic Financier," Montreal Gazette,
         20 Dec. 1947 [PU].

L47-44   FARRELLY, JOHN. "Fiction Parade: Finis," New Republic, 117
         (22 Dec. 1947), 28.

L47-45   McSTAY, ANGUS. "Dreiser's Undeviating Furrow Ends with Cow-
         perwood's Death," Toronto Globe and Mail, 27 Dec. 1947,
         p. 12.

L47-46   COURNOS, JOHN. "The Reviews: End of Dreiser's Cowperwood
         Novels; Recent Books on Men of Medicine," New York Sun,
         28 Dec. 1947 [PU].

L47-47   HABICH, WILLIAM. "Dreiser's Last--Symbol of an Age,"
         Louisville Courier-Journal, 28 Dec. 1947, Section 3, p. 7.

L47-48   HARDWICK, ELIZABETH. "Fiction Chronicle," Partisan Review,
         15 (Jan. 1948), 108-12.

L47-49   WALLACE, MARGARET. "Novels in the News," Independent Woman,
         27 (Jan. 1948), 21.

L47-50   ROLO, CHARLES J. "Dreiser's America," Tomorrow, 7 (Feb.
         1948), 55-57.

L47-51   ANON. "Final Volume," Cresset, 12 (Sept. 1948), 52.

LETTERS OF THEODORE DREISER (1959)

L59-1   HANSEN, HARRY. "Dreiser's Letters Reveal His Rugged Indi-
        vidualism," Chicago Sunday Tribune, 1 Mar. 1959, Part 4,
        p. 10.

L59-2   GEISMAR, MAXWELL. "From the Banks of the Wabash," New York
        Times Book Review, 8 Mar. 1959, pp. 1, 30.

WORKS ON

L59-3   LYNN, KENNETH S. "Dreiser: Lonely and Dedicated, Angry and Confused," New York Herald Tribune Book Review, 8 Mar. 1959, p. 1.

L59-4   ANON. "Swock! Smack! Crack!" Newsweek, 53 (9 Mar. 1959), 112.

L59-5   HUTCHENS, JOHN K. "'Letters of Theodore Dreiser,'" New York Herald Tribune, 12 Mar. 1959, p. 21.

L59-6   PEEL, ROBERT. "Dreiser's Letters," Christian Science Monitor, 12 Mar. 1959, p. 15.

L59-7   WALBRIDGE, EARLE F. "Literature: Dreiser, Theodore. Letters of Theodore Dreiser: A Selection," Library Journal, 84 (15 Mar. 1959), 852-53.

L59-8   HART, JAMES D. "Dreiser's Stubborn Search for the Meaning of Life," San Francisco Chronicle, 29 Mar. 1959, This World Section, p. 14.

L59-9   HICKS, GRANVILLE. "Dreiser the Puzzle," Saturday Review, 42 (4 Apr. 1959), 16.

L59-10 WEST, ANTHONY. "Books: Man Overboard," New Yorker, 35 (25 Apr. 1959), 169-70, 173-74.

L59-11 ALGREN, NELSON. "Dreiser Hedged Out," Nation, 188 (16 May 1959), 459-60.

L59-12 SHAPIRO, CHARLES. "Our Bitter Patriot," New Republic, 140 (8 June 1959), 18-19.

L59-13 MIZENER, ARTHUR. "The Innocence of Dreiser," New Statesman and Nation, 58 (4 July 1959), 20.

L59-14 HINDUS, MILTON. "Dreiser's Prejudices," Commentary, 29 (Jan. 1960), 80-83.

L59-15 HODGINS, FRANCIS, JR. "The Dreiser Letters," Journal of English and Germanic Philology, 59 (Oct. 1960), 714-20. Reviewed with Letters to Louise.

L59-16 ROVIT, EARL H. "Robert H. Elias, ed. Letters of Theodore Dreiser," Books Abroad, 35 (Autumn 1961), 400-01.

LETTERS TO LOUISE (1959)

L59-17   GEISMAR, MAXWELL.   "Literary Friendship," New York Times Book Review, 13 Sept. 1959, p. 49.

L59-18   YAFFE, JAMES.   "Editor's Notes," Saturday Review, 42 (3 Oct. 1959), 38.

L59-19   ELIAS, ROBERT H.   "Letters to Louise," American Literature, 33 (Mar. 1961), 90-91.

M

TAPES

Included in this section are discussions of Dreiser that have been recorded on reel-to-reel and/or cassette tapes.

1970

M70-1   GREBSTEIN, SHELDON. Sister Carrie. Twentieth Century American Novel Series. Deland, Fla.: Everett/Edwards. 35 min.

M70-2   MOERS, ELLEN. A Century of Dreiser. Sound Seminar Series. New York: McGraw-Hill. 18 min.

M70-3   SPILLER, ROBERT. The Second Renaissance. Great American Writers, No. 4. Deland, Fla.: Everett/Edwards. 35 min.

1973

M73-1   LEHAN, RICHARD. An American Tragedy. Twentieth Century American Novel Series. Deland, Fla.: Everett/Edwards. 45 min.

N

THESES AND DISSERTATIONS

Dissertations subsequently published are indicated by a cross-reference to the appropriate section.

1926

N26-1   FRANKLIN, PAULINE M. "American and English Criticism of
         Theodore Dreiser." Master's thesis, U. Iowa.

1929

N29-1   SAYRE, KATHRYN K. "The Themes of Dreiser." Master's thesis,
         Columbia U.

N29-2   SPRAGUE, DEWITT C. "Some Picaresque Elements in the Novels
         of Theodore Dreiser." Master's thesis, U. Iowa.

1931

N31-1   GIBBERD, MABEL. "A Study of Dreiser's Major Characters."
         Master's thesis, U. Chicago.

1932

N32-1   BRODMERKEL, ALEXANDER H. "A Comparison of the Novels of
         Thomas Hardy and Theodore Dreiser." Master's thesis,
         Columbia U.

1935

N35-1   MAILLARD, DENYSE. "L'Enfant Américain dans le Roman du
         Middle-West." Ph.D. dissertation, U. Paris.

WORKS ON

1936

N36-1   GREENBERG, EMIL. "A Case Study in the Technique of Realism:
        Theodore Dreiser's An American Tragedy." Master's
        thesis, New York U.

1938

N38-1   ELIAS, ROBERT H. "The Romantic Stoicism of Theodore
        Dreiser: A Study of His Attitude Toward Industrialism
        and Social Reform." Master's thesis, Columbia U.

1939

N39-1   SAALBACH, ROBERT P. "The Philosophy of Theodore Dreiser."
        Master's thesis, U. Chicago.

1940

N40-1   BOWER, MARIE HADLEY. "Theodore Dreiser: The Man and His
        Times; His Work and Its Reception." Ph.D. dissertation,
        Ohio State U.

1943

N43-1   MÜLLER, IRMTRAUD. "Amerikakritik en den Hauptwerken Theo-
        dore Dreisers bis zum New Deal." Ph.D. dissertation,
        Vienna U.

1946

N46-1   ELVEBACK, HELEN B. "The Novels of Theodore Dreiser with an
        Analysis of His Other Writings." Ph.D. dissertation,
        U. Minnesota.

1948

N48-1   BLACKSIN, IDA. "Theodore Dreiser and the Law." Master's
        thesis, New York U.

N48-2   CAMPBELL, ERNESTINE B. "Dreiser as a Critic of American Po-
        litical and Economic Life." Master's thesis, Atlanta U.

Theses and Dissertations

N48-3 ELIAS, ROBERT H. "Theodore Dreiser: Apostle of Nature."
       Ph.D. dissertation, U. Pennsylvania. See I49-1.

N48-4 GUILLON, PIERRETTE. "The Influence of Balzac on the Novels
       of Theodore Dreiser." Master's thesis, Brown U.

N48-5 LIEN, VERNON M. "An Analysis of the Reputation of Theodore
       Dreiser." Master's thesis, U. Nebraska.

                              1950

N50-1 HOWELL, EILEEN. "Theodore Dreiser's Development as a
       Naturalist." Master's thesis, New York U.

N50-2 QUINN, VINCENT G. "Religious and Ethical Attitudes in Theo-
       dore Dreiser's Fiction." Master's thesis, Columbia U.

N50-3 ROBERTS, JOHN V. "The Design of Theodore Dreiser's Sister
       Carrie." Master's thesis, Columbia U.

N50-4 STEPHANCHEV, STEPHEN. "Theodore Dreiser among the Critics:
       A Study of American Reactions to the Work of a Literary
       Naturalist, 1900-1949." Ph.D. dissertation, New York U.

                              1951

N51-1 GELFANT, BLANCHE H. "The American City Novel 1900-1940: A
       Study of the Literary Treatment of the City in Dreiser,
       Dos Passos, and Farrell." Ph.D. dissertation, U. Wiscon-
       sin. See J54-5.

N51-2 HAILEY, VIRGINIA L. "Religion in the Novels of Theodore
       Dreiser." Master's thesis, Southern Illinois U.

N51-3 HOROVITZ, SYDNEY. "Theodore Dreiser, Basic Patterns of His
       Work." Ph.D. dissertation, U. Pittsburgh.

N51-4 LEVINE, RICHARD. "Characterization in Dreiser's Fiction."
       Master's thesis, New York U.

N51-5 LEWIS, ROBERT E. "Unified Reality: A Study of the Novels
       of Theodore Dreiser." Master's thesis, U. Idaho.

N51-6 OVERHULS, BARBARA S. "Theodore Dreiser's Novels: A Stylis-
       tic Study." Master's thesis, U. Oklahoma.

WORKS ON

N51-7   RANDALL, GRAY M. "The Short Story Technique of Theodore
         Dreiser." Master's thesis, U. Washington.

N51-8   SAALBACH, ROBERT P. "Collected Poems--Theodore Dreiser,
         Edited with an Introduction and Notes." Ph.D. disserta-
         tion, U. Washington. See D69-7.

                              1952

N52-1   BLACKSTOCK, WALTER. "Theodore Dreiser--The Aspirant: A
         Study of His Early Literary Career." Ph.D. dissertation,
         Yale U.

N52-2   PALMER, ERWIN G. "Symbolistic Imagery in Theodore Dreiser's
         An American Tragedy." Ph.D. dissertation, U. Syracuse.

N52-3   TULEVECH, MICHAEL C. "Dreiser's The Bulwark." Master's
         thesis, Columbia U.

N52-4   WILKERSON, JAMES C. "The Altruistic Thought of Theodore
         Dreiser in Seven Representative Novels." Master's
         thesis, U. Florida.

                              1953

N53-1   CASTLE, JOHN F. "The Making of An American Tragedy." Ph.D.
         dissertation, U. Michigan.

N53-2   KRANIDAS, THOMAS. "The Materials of Theodore Dreiser's An
         American Tragedy." Master's thesis, Columbia U.

N53-3   SHANE, MARION L. "Spiritual Poverty in Selected Works of
         Four American Novelists: Twain, Crane, Fitzgerald, and
         Dreiser." Ph.D. dissertation, Syracuse U.

N53-4   SHAPIRO, CHARLES K. "Dreiser and the American Dream."
         Master's thesis, Indiana U.

N53-5   STEINBRECHER, GEORGE, JR. "Theodore Dreiser's Fictional
         Method in Sister Carrie and Jennie Gerhardt." Ph.D.
         dissertation, U. Chicago.

Theses and Dissertations

1954

N54-1   ROBERTS, JOSEPH B., JR. "Dreiser's Social Consciousness."
        Master's thesis, U. North Carolina.

1955

N55-1   WILLEN, GERALD. "Dreiser's Moral Seriousness: A Study of
        the Novels." Ph.D. dissertation, U. Minnesota.

1956

N56-1   BERNARD, KENNETH O. "Theodore Dreiser's Determinism: A
        Detour of Faith." Master's thesis, Columbia U.

1957

N57-1   BRITTON, JOE S. "Dreiser's Views of Women." Master's
        thesis, Southern Illinois U.

N57-2   McCALL, RAYMOND G. "Attitudes Toward Wealth in the Fiction
        of Theodore Dreiser, Edith Wharton, and F. Scott Fitz-
        gerald." Ph.D. dissertation, U. Wisconsin.

N57-3   MILLER, RAYMOND A., JR. "Representative Tragic Heroines in
        the Work of Brown, Hawthorne, Howells, James, and
        Dreiser." Ph.D. dissertation, U. Wisconsin.

1958

N58-1   QUINTAL, CLAIRE-H. "Emile Zola et Theodore Dreiser."
        Master's thesis, U. Montreal.

1959

N59-1   SHAPIRO, CHARLES K. "A Critical Study of the Novels of
        Theodore Dreiser." Ph.D. dissertation, Indiana U. See
        I62-1.

N59-2   SPRINGER, ANNE MARIE. "The American Novel in Germany: A
        Study of the Critical Reception of Eight American Novel-
        ists Between the Two Wars." Ph.D. dissertation, U. Penn-
        sylvania. See J60-6.

THEODORE DREISER: A BIBLIOGRAPHY

WORKS ON

1960

N60-1 BISHOP, BERT O. "A Study of the Correlation of Theodore
Dreiser's Journalistic Experience to His Work as a Creative Artist." Master's thesis, Southern Illinois U.

N60-2 DAVIS, JOE. "The Mind of Theodore Dreiser: A Study in
Development." Ph.D. dissertation, Emory U.

N60-3 DOWELL, RICHARD W. "Three Stages of Dreiser's Determinism."
Master's thesis, U. Colorado.

N60-4 HEUSTON, DUSTIN H. "The Theistic Quest in the Novels of
Theodore Dreiser." Master's thesis, Stanford U.

N60-5 KARNATH, DAVID L. "Motive in the Novels of Theodore
Dreiser." Master's thesis, Stanford U.

N60-6 KORES, MARYJO A. "The Search for Personal Identity and
Meaning in Sister Carrie, Winesburg, Ohio, and the Novels
of Herbert Gold." Master's thesis, Ohio State U.

N60-7 RICHMAN, SIDNEY. "The World and the Dream, an Analysis of
the Pattern of Ideas in the Novels of Theodore Dreiser."
Ph.D. dissertation, U. California, Los Angeles.

N60-8 ROTHWEILER, ROBERT LIEDEL. "Ideology and Four Radical
Novelists: The Response to Communism of Dreiser, Ander-
son, Dos Passos, and Farrell." Ph.D. dissertation,
Washington U.

1961

N61-1 SIEK, EDNA H. "Social Darwinism in Theodore Dreiser's
Novels." Master's thesis, Sacramento State C.

N61-2 STAAB, WOLFGANG. "Das Deutschlandbild Theodore Dreisers."
Ph.D. dissertation, U. Mainz. See I61-1.

1962

N62-1 WILSON, JENNIE M. "A Comparative Study of the Novels of
Frederick Philip Grove and Theodore Dreiser." Master's
thesis, U. New Brunswick.

THEODORE DREISER: A BIBLIOGRAPHY

Theses and Dissertations

1963

N63-1   MAYHALL, FAN. "Religion and Morality in the Works of Theodore Dreiser." Master's thesis, Mississippi State U.

N63-2   MILLER, JERRY L. "Journey into the Twentieth Century: A
Study of Theodore Dreiser's Development as a Poet."
Master's thesis, Indiana U.

1964

N64-1   BLAKELEY, CAROLYN F. "Naturalism in the Novels of Theodore
Dreiser." Master's thesis, Atlanta U.

N64-2   HUSSMAN, LAWRENCE E., JR. "The Spiritual Quest of Theodore
Dreiser." Ph.D. dissertation, U. Michigan.

N64-3   STOKES, PETER B. "Technique and Temperament in Dreiser's
Sister Carrie." Master's thesis, Toronto U.

1965

N65-1   BIDDLE, EDMUND R. "The Plays of Theodore Dreiser." Ph.D.
dissertation, U. Pennsylvania.

N65-2   DUSTMAN, MARJORY P. "Theodore Dreiser's An American Tragedy:
A Study." Ph.D. dissertation, U. Southern California.

N65-3   FIGG, ROBERT M., III. "The Effect of Naturalism upon Form
in the American Novel from 1893 to 1925." Ph.D. dissertation, U. North Carolina.

N65-4   HAKUTANI, YOSHINOBU. "Dreiser Before Sister Carrie: French
Realism and Early Experience." Ph.D. dissertation,
Pennsylvania State U.

N65-5   LABRIE, RODRIGUE E. "American Naturalism: A View From
Within." Ph.D. dissertation, Pennsylvania State U.

N65-6   SAWICKI, ROBERT M. "Theodore Dreiser and An American Tragedy:
From the American Dream to the American Nightmare."
Master's thesis, Columbia U.

N65-7   SCHMIDTBERGER, LOREN FRANCIS. "The Structure of the Novels
of Theodore Dreiser." Ph.D. dissertation, Fordham U.

407

WORKS ON

N65-8   STORY, SUZANNE. "Human Action and Responsibility in Theodore
         Dreiser's An American Tragedy and Richard Wright's Native
         Son." Master's thesis, U. Texas.

N65-9   WILKINSON, ROBERT E. "A Study of Theodore Dreiser's The
         Financier." Ph.D. dissertation, U. Pennsylvania.

N65-10   ZEHENTMAYR, AURELIA. "Treatment of the American Businessman
         in the Novels of Theodore Dreiser." Master's thesis,
         North Texas State U.

                                  1966

N66-1   FLIPPEN, CHARLIE C., JR. "The Influence of Journalistic Ex-
         perience on Three American Novelists: Theodore Dreiser,
         Sinclair Lewis and Ernest Hemingway." Master's thesis,
         U. North Carolina.

N66-2   FRAZIER, ALEXANDER S. "The Influence of Darwinism on Theo-
         dore Dreiser's Concept of the American Businessman."
         Master's thesis, Bowling Green State U.

N66-3   FURMANCZYK, WIESLAW. "Theodore Dreiser's Worldview in the
         Light of Unpublished Materials." Ph.D. dissertation, U.
         Warsaw.

N66-4   HARMAN, WILLIAM C. "The Women in Theodore Dreiser's Novels,
         The Financier, The Titan, and The Stoic." Master's thesis,
         Bowling Green State U.

N66-5   JOHNSON, GIVEN. "The Satirical Elements in Jennie Gerhardt."
         Master's thesis, Brigham Young U.

N66-6   SALZMAN, JACK. "Sister Carrie: A History of Dreiser's
         Novel." Ph.D. dissertation, New York U.

N66-7   STOUT, REBECCA A. "The City as Setting in Theodore Dreiser's
         Jennie Gerhardt: The Role of the City in the Naturalistic
         Tradition." Master's thesis, U. North Carolina.

N66-8   SULLIVAN, WILLIAM J. "Studies on James, Dreiser and Faulk-
         ner." Master's thesis, U. Utah.

N66-9   TORRENTS OLIVELLA, M. A. "The Theme of Success in American
         Fiction from 1900-1941, with Special Reference to Dreiser,
         Lewis, Fitzgerald, and Dos Passos." Master's thesis,
         King's College.

THEODORE DREISER: A BIBLIOGRAPHY

Theses and Dissertations

N66-10   WHITAKER, ELEANOR M.   "A Descriptive Analysis of Theodore
         Dreiser's Non-Fiction Work."   Master's thesis, U. Maryland.

                              1967

N67-1   BAIRD, JAMES LEE.   "The Movie in Our Heads: An Analysis of
         Three Film Versions of Theodore Dreiser's An American
         Tragedy."   Ph.D. dissertation, U. Washington.

N67-2   DOWELL, RICHARD W.   "Theodore Dreiser and Success: A Shift-
         ing Allegiance."   Ph.D. dissertation, Indiana U.

N67-3   KRIGER, SYBIL.   "Determinism in the Writing of Theodore
         Dreiser."   Master's thesis, Kent State U.

N67-4   MOYLES, ROBERT G.   "Theodore Dreiser: The Reluctant Natural-
         ist."   Master's thesis, Memorial U.

N67-5   ORLANSKY, CLAIRE B.   "The Impact of 19th Century Scientific
         Thought on Tennyson, Dreiser, and Faulkner."   Master's
         thesis, U. Utah.

N67-6   SCHMIDT-VON BARDELEBEN, RENATE.   "Das Bild New Yorks im
         Erzahlwerk von Dreiser und Dos Passos."   Ph.D. disserta-
         tion, U. Mainz.   See I67-1.

                              1968

N68-1   ANTUSH, JOHN V.   "Money in the Novels of James, Wharton, and
         Dreiser."   Ph.D. dissertation, Stanford U.

N68-2   HEUSTON, DUSTIN H.   "Theodore Dreiser's Search for Control:
         A Critical Study of His Novels."   Ph.D. dissertation,
         New York U.

N68-3   JONES, ALAN K.   "The Family in the Works of Theodore Dreiser."
         Ph.D. dissertation, Texas Technological C.

N68-4   LE BLEU, CYNTHIA C.   "Contrasts in American Literary Natural-
         ism: A Comparison of the Degeneration Novels of Stephen
         Crane, Frank Norris, and Theodore Dreiser."   Master's
         thesis, Southwest Texas State C.

N68-5   McTAGUE, SYLVIA H.   "Dreiser the Iconoclast: His Attack on
         Marriage."   Master's thesis, U. Mississippi.

                              409

WORKS ON

N68-6   NOSTWICH, THEODORE D. "The Structure of Theodore Dreiser's
        Novels." Ph.D. dissertation, U. Texas.

                              1969

N69-1   ARNOLD, ANN J. "Naturalism in Dreiser's Female Characters."
        Master's thesis, U. Mississippi.

N69-2   BLACKSIN, IDA. "Law and Literature: Dreiser and the Courts."
        Ph.D. dissertation, Michigan State U.

N69-3   BOLCH, DOROTHY H. "Hardy's Jude and Dreiser's Clyde: The
        Spiritual and the Materialistic Approach to Naturalism."
        Master's thesis, U. North Carolina.

N69-4   BROER, BARBARA J. "A Study of Theodore Dreiser's Technique
        in The Financier, The Titan, and The Stoic." Master's
        thesis, Sacramento State C.

N69-5   DAVIS, NANCY H. "The Women in Theodore Dreiser's Novels."
        Ph.D. dissertation, Northwestern U.

N69-6   DOYLE, SUSAN F. "Dreiser's An American Tragedy: A Struc-
        tural Analysis." Master's thesis, U. Florida.

N69-7   HOPPE, RALPH H. "The Theme of Alienation in the Novels of
        Theodore Dreiser." Ph.D. dissertation, U. Denver.

N69-8   MILLER, JUANITA M. "Honore de Balzac's Influence on Theodore
        Dreiser as Revealed in the Similarities of Le Pere Goriot
        and Sister Carrie." Master's thesis, Atlanta U.

N69-9   RANDALL, ALVIA L. W. "Dreiser's Women." Master's thesis,
        Atlanta U.

N69-10 SCHNEIDER, RALPH THOMAS. "Dreiser and the American Dream of
        Success: The Early Years." Ph.D. dissertation, Kansas
        State U.

                              1970

N70-1   BLAKE, FAY M. "The Strike in the American Novel." Ph.D.
        dissertation, U. California, Los Angeles. See J72-2.

N70-2   COULOMBE, MICHAEL JOSEPH. "The Trilogy as Form in Modern
        American Fiction." Ph.D. dissertation, Purdue U.

Theses and Dissertations

N70-3   LEAF, M. "Techniques of Naturalism in the Works of Dreiser, Crane, and Norris." Master's thesis, Nottingham U.

N70-4   LINDSAY, JULIA I. "The Indictment of America in 1925: A Comparative Study of The Great Gatsby and An American Tragedy." Master's thesis, U. North Carolina.

N70-5   ROSENMAN, MONA GAIL. "The Adamsean Prototype for the Anti-Hero in the Modern American Novel." Ph.D. dissertation, Kent State U.

N70-6   SAIDLOWER, SYLVIA. "Moral Relativism in American Fiction of the Eighteen Nineties." Ph.D. dissertation, New York U.

N70-7   WHITEHEAD, JAMES FARNUM, III. "Character and Style in Dreiser's An American Tragedy." Ph.D. dissertation, U. Virginia.

1971

N71-1   BARTELL, JAMES EDWARD. "The Ritual of Failure: Pattern and Rhythm in the Novels of Theodore Dreiser." Ph.D. dissertation, U. Washington.

N71-2   BUCHESKY, CHARLES STANLEY. "The Background of American Literary Naturalism." Ph.D. dissertation, Wayne State U.

N71-3   CARLSON, CONSTANCE HEDIN. "Heroines in Certain American Novels." Ph.D. dissertation, Brown U.

N71-4   FORREY, ROBERT JAMES. "Theodore Dreiser: The Flesh and the Spirit." Ph.D. dissertation, Yale U.

N71-5   JURNAK, SHELIA HOPE. "A Study of Dreiser's Autobiographies: Dawn and Newspaper Days." Ph.D. dissertation, Tulane U.

N71-6   KUNKEL, FRAN R. "The Critical Approaches to the Novels of Theodore Dreiser, 1900-1969." Ph.D. dissertation, U. California, Los Angeles.

N71-7   MARSHALL, DONALD RAY. "The Green Promise: Greenness as a Dominant Symbol in the Quest of Eden in American Fiction." Ph.D. dissertation, U. Connecticut.

N71-8   MONTGOMERY, JUDITH. "Pygmalion's Image: The Metamorphosis of the American Heroine." Ph.D. dissertation, Syracuse U.

WORKS ON

N71-9   MORRIS, LEWIS RANDOLPH. "Philosophical Concepts in American
         Short Stories." Ph.D. dissertation, Howard U.

N71-10 POMEROY, CHARLES WILLIAM. "Soviet Russian Criticism 1960-
         1969 of Seven Twentieth Century American Novelists."
         Ph.D. dissertation, U. Southern California.

N71-11 SHELTON, FRANK WILSEY. "The Family in the Novels of Wharton,
         Faulkner, Cather, Lewis, and Dreiser." Ph.D. dissertation,
         U. North Carolina.

N71-12 WARNER, STEPHEN DOUGLAS. "Representative Studies in the
         American Picaresque: Investigations of Modern Chivalry,
         Adventures of Huckleberry Finn, and The Adventures of
         Augie March." Ph.D. dissertation, Indiana U.

N71-13 WEBER, JUDITH DOWNS. "The Autobiography of Childhood in
         America." Ph.D. dissertation, George Washington U.

N71-14 WILDER, ALMA A. "An American Tragedy: The Transformation of
         Fact into Fiction." Master's thesis, U. North Carolina.

                              1972

N72-1   BIGELOW, BLAIR F. "The Collected Newspaper Articles, 1892-
         1894, of Theodore Dreiser." Ph.D. dissertation, Brandeis
         U.

N72-2   BUCHHOLZ, JOHN LEE. "An American Tragedy: The Iconography
         of a Myth." Ph.D. dissertation, Texas Christian U.

N72-3   BURKE, JOHN MICHAEL. "A Bibliography of Soviet Russian
         Translations of American Literature." Ph.D. dissertation,
         Brown U.

N72-4   COSGROVE, WILLIAM EMMETT. "Marriage and the Family in Some
         Nineteenth-Century American Novels." Ph.D. dissertation,
         U. Iowa.

N72-5   CURRY, MARTHA MULROY. "The 'Writer's Book' by Sherwood
         Anderson: A Critical Edition." Ph.D. dissertation,
         Loyola U. (Chicago).

N72-6   PETERSON, SANDRA MARNY. "The View from the Gallows: The
         Criminal Confession in American Literature." Ph.D. dis-
         sertation, Northwestern U.

                              412

Theodore Dreiser: A Bibliography

Theses and Dissertations

N72-7   REFFETT, SID SHANNON. "Visions and Revisions: The Nature of Dreiser's Religious Inquiry." Ph.D. dissertation, U. Notre Dame.

N72-8   RIGGIO, THOMAS PASQUALE. "The Education of Theodore Dreiser." Ph.D. dissertation, Harvard U.

N72-9   SHULMAN, IRVING. "A Study of the Juvenile Delinquent as Depicted in the Twentieth Century American Novel to 1950." Ph.D. dissertation, U. California, Los Angeles.

N72-10   SMITH, MARTHA STRIBLING. "A Study of the Realistic Treatment of Psychic Phenomena in Selected Fiction of William Dean Howells, Hamlin Garland, Henry James, Frank Norris, and Theodore Dreiser." Ph.D. dissertation, U. North Carolina.

N72-11   SZUBERLA, GUY ALAN. "Urban Vistas and the Pastoral Garden: Studies in the Literature and Architecture of Chicago (1893-1909)." Ph.D. dissertation, U. Minnesota.

N72-12   TOWNSEND, BARBARA ANN. "Superstitious Beliefs of Theodore Dreiser." Ph.D. dissertation, Ball State U.

N72-13   WEIR, SYBIL BARBARA. "The Disappearance of the Sentimental Heroine Characterization of Women in Selected Novels by Robert Herrick, Edith Wharton, and Theodore Dreiser, 1898-1925." Ph.D. dissertation, U. California, Berkeley.

1973

N73-1   DICKSTEIN, FELICE WITZTUM. "The Role of the City in the Works of Theodore Dreiser, Thomas Wolfe, James T. Farrell, and Saul Bellow." Ph.D. dissertation, City U. New York.

N73-2   EHRLICH, CAROL. "Evolutionism and the Female in Selected American Novels, 1885-1900." Ph.D. dissertation, U. Iowa.

N73-3   HEROLD, EVE GRIFFITH. "A Study of the Bildungsroman in American Literature." Ph.D. dissertation, Ohio State U.

N73-4   OLDANI, LOUIS JOSEPH. "A Study of Theodore Dreiser's The 'Genius,'" Ph.D. dissertation, U. Pennsylvania.

O

PRODUCTIONS OF PLAYS

This section cites productions of Dreiser's plays and reviews of the productions. Announcements are cited also in instances when they provided the only information we could locate on a production or when they included information about the production that did not appear in the reviews.

One production was not included because of insufficient information. Folder 371 in the clipping file in the Dreiser Collection at the University of Pennsylvania contains the following announcement, clipped from about a dozen newspapers around the country and dated from as early as 11 Dec. 1915 to as late as Mar. 1916: "Another of Theodore Dreiser's plays, 'The Rag Pickers,' which will appear in his forthcoming 'Plays of the Natural and Supernatural' has been accepted for stage production by Wallis Clark. . . ." We were unable to verify that the production was actually staged, nor could we find when or where it was to be staged.

Announcements and reviews of a production are classified under the citation of the production. Because of this arrangement, the first two digits in the entry numbers for these items signify the date of the production, not the year of publication of the item. The year of publication is given in the entry itself.

An asterisk at the end of an entry based on a clipping (see 017-25) indicates that we were unable to locate the work in the place cited. In these instances, the asterisk signifies that the item does exist, but the bibliographical information may not be accurate.

MISCELLANEA

016-1   LAUGHING GAS. Opened 7 Dec. 1916 at the Masonic Temple,
         Indianapolis, Ind. Producer: Indianapolis Little
         Theatre Society. Director: Carl Bernhardt.

         Reviews:
         016-2   ANON. "Little Theater Marks Epoch in Producing
                  'Laughing Gas,'" Indianapolis News, 8 Dec. 1916,
                  p. 27.

         016-3   SAYLER, OLIVER M. "Novel Stage Experiment,"
                  Boston Evening Transcript, 22 Dec. 1916, p. 14.

017-1   THE GIRL IN THE COFFIN. Opened 28 Jan. 1917 at the St. Louis
         Artist's Guild, Knights of Columbus Hall, St. Louis, Mo.
         Producer: St. Louis Players Club. Director: A. H.
         Brueggman.

         Reviews:
         017-2   ANON. "Works of Dreiser and Bernard Shaw Given
                  by Players," St. Louis Globe-Democrat, 30 Jan.
                  1917, p. 7.

         017-3   HURD, CARLOS F. "'Girl in the Coffin' Has Drama-
                  tic Power," St. Louis Post-Dispatch, 30 Jan. 1917,
                  p. 9.

017-4   THE GIRL IN THE COFFIN. Opened 9 Oct. 1917 at the Colony
         Ball Room, St. Francis Hotel, San Francisco, Calif.
         Producer: St. Francis Little Theatre Club. Director:
         Arthur Maitland.

         Review:
         017-5   WILDE, ANNIE. "Over the Tea Cups," San Francisco
                  Call and Post, 10 Oct. 1917, p. 8.

017-6   THE GIRL IN THE COFFIN. Opened 3 Dec. 1917 at the Comedy
         Theatre, New York, N. Y. Producer: Washington Square
         Players. Director: Edward Goodman.

         Reviews:
         017-7   ANON. "Four New Plays at the Comedy," New York
                  Times, 4 Dec. 1917, p. 11.

         017-8   ANON. "'Girl in the Coffin' Is Villagers' Offer-
                  ing," New York World, 4 Dec. 1917, p. 9.

416

Productions of Plays

017-9   ANON. "Plays and Players: All American Bill by
the Washington Square Players," New York Evening
Telegram, 4 Dec. 1917, p. 10.

017-10   ANON. "The Theatre: New Washington Square Bill,"
New York Evening Sun, 4 Dec. 1917, p. 12.

017-11   ANON. "Three New Plays Given at Comedy,"
New York Sun, 4 Dec. 1917, p. 5.

017-12   ANON. "The Washington Square Players," New York
Evening Post, 4 Dec. 1917, p. 9.

017-13   P., J. A. "Washington Square Players Present an
American Programme," New York Tribune, 4 Dec.
1917, p. 9.

017-14   SHERWIN, LOUIS. "The New Play: Theodore Dreiser
and Others at the Comedy," New York Globe and
Commercial Advertiser, 4 Dec. 1917, p. 12.

017-15   ANON. "An All-American Bill at Comedy," Brooklyn
Daily Eagle, 5 Dec. 1917, p. 7.

017-16   ANON. "New Plays in New York: Mr. Dreiser,
Playwright," Boston Evening Transcript, 5 Dec.
1917, Part Two, p. 12.

017-18   DALE, ALAN. "Washington Square Players' New Bill
Is Entertaining," New York American, 7 Dec. 1917,
p. 8.

017-19   DARNTON, CHARLES. "The New Plays," New York
Evening World, 7 Dec. 1917, p. 25.

017-20   BLOCK, RALPH. "When the Theatre Wakes Up,"
New York Tribune, 9 Dec. 1917, Section 4, p. 2.

017-21   BEACH, BURTON T. "First-Night Facts from Broadway," Chicago Evening Post, 10 Dec. 1917, p. 9.

017-22   ANON. "Washington Square Players Seen in Interesting Bill," New York Clipper, 12 Dec. 1917,
p. 10.

017-23   MANTLE, BURNS. "Washington Sq. Players Win New
Laurels in a Bill of American Plays," New York
Evening Mail, 12 Dec. 1917, p. 11.

THEODORE DREISER: A BIBLIOGRAPHY

017-24   F. "The Washington Square Players," Nation, 105 (13 Dec. 1917), 675.

017-25   MODERWELL, HIRAM K. "A Critic on Broadway," Springfield Republican, 13 Dec. 1917* [PU].

017-26   SIME. "Washington Square Players," Variety, 14 Dec. 1917, p. 20.

017-27   ANON. "Washington Square Players," New York Dramatic Mirror, 15 Dec. 1917, p. [5].

017-28   ANON. "Plays and Players," Town and Country, 73 (20 Dec. 1917), 19.

017-29   MANTLE, BURNS. "Theodore Dreiser's 'Girl in the Coffin' Done by Uplifters," Minneapolis Sunday Journal, 23 Dec. 1917, Amusement Section, p. 1.

017-30   ARMITAGE, LOUISE. "Terre Haute Gives Broadway a Thrill," Terre Haute Tribune, 22 Jan. 1918, p. 3.

017-31   "Musings About Mummers," International, Feb. 1918 [PU].

017-32   POLLOCK, CHANNING. "The Washington Square Players," Green Book Magazine, 19 (Feb. 1918), 211-13.

018-1   THE OLD RAGPICKER. Opened 30 Jan. 1918 at the Colony Ballroom, St. Francis Hotel, San Francisco, Calif. Producer: St. Francis Little Theatre Club. Director: Arthur Maitland.

Announcements:
018-2   ANON. "The Little Theater," San Francisco Bulletin, 26 Jan. 1918, p. 10.

018-3   ANON. "New Bill On at Little Theater," San Francisco Examiner, 30 Jan. 1918, p. 8.

018-4   THE GIRL IN THE COFFIN. Opened 21 Mar. 1918 at the Arts and Crafts Players Theatre, Detroit, Mich. Producer: Arts and Crafts Players. Director: Sam Hume.

Productions of Plays

Reviews:
018-5   McC., E. H. "Arts and Crafts Scores Success,"
         Detroit Free Press, 17(?) Mar. 1918* [PU].

018-6   HOLMES, RALPH F. "Dreiser Play Proves Master-
         piece and Best of Arts and Crafts Work," Detroit
         Journal, 22 Mar. 1918, p. 11.

020-1   THE GIRL IN THE COFFIN. Opened 27 Jan. 1920 at the Province-
         town Playhouse, New York, N. Y. Producer: Workers'
         Theatre Guild. Director: Wayne Arey.

         Review:
         020-2   GARDY, LOUIS. "Workers' Theater Guild Makes Its
                  Debut with Three Finely Played Sketches of Rebel
                  Tendency Before Keenest Audience," New York Call,
                  27 Jan. 1920, p. 4.

020-3   THE GIRL IN THE COFFIN. Opened 8 Feb. 1920 at the Princess
         Theatre, New York, N. Y. Producer: Workers' Theatre
         Guild. Director: Wayne Arey.

         Reviews:
         020-4   ANON. "Workers' Guild in Familiar Playlets,"
                  New York Sun and Herald, 10 Feb. 1920, p. 9.

         020-5   GARDY, LOUIS. "The Stage: Workers' Theater
                  Guild Opens at Princess Theater and Hits Broadway
                  Firstnighters Hard," New York Call, 10 Feb. 1920,
                  p. 4.

         020-6   TOWSE, J. RANKEN. "The Drama: The Theatre-
                  Workers' Guild," New York Evening Post, 10 Feb.
                  1920, p. 11.

021-1   THE HAND OF THE POTTER. Opened 5 Dec. 1921 at the Province-
         town Playhouse, New York, N. Y. Producer: Provincetown
         Players. Director: Charles O'Brien Kennedy.

         Reviews:
         021-2   ANON. "Provinceton [sic.] Players in Repulsive
                  Play," New York Herald, 6 Dec. 1921, p. 14.

         021-3   "'Hand of the Potter,' Sad," New York World,
                  6 Dec. 1921* [PU].

021-4   MacGOWAN, KENNETH. "The New Play: The Provincetown Players," New York Globe and Commercial Advertiser, 6 Dec. 1921, p. 18.

021-5   TOWSE, J. RANKEN. "The Play: 'The Hand of the
Potter,'" New York Evening Post, 6 Dec. 1921,
p. 9.

021-6   ANON. "The Stage: Theodore Dreiser's 'The Hand
of the Potter' Is Remarkably Acted by the Provincetown Players," New York Call, 8 Dec. 1921, p. 4.

021-7   ANON. "St. Louis Might Lay Claim to Some Credit
Here," St. Louis Times, 10 Dec. 1921 [PU].

021-8   RATHBUN, STEPHEN. "'The Chocolate Soldier' and
'The Mountain Man' Arrive Together Monday,"
New York Sun, 10 Dec. 1921, p. 4.

021-9   SCHAUERMANN, KARL. "The Devil's Play Ground and
Work Shop," Milwaukee Leader, 10 Dec. 1921,
Saturday Magazine Section, p. [3].

021-10 HIGHBROW, THE, pseud. "At the Play: 'The Hand
of the Potter,' at the Provincetown Playhouse,"
Town Topics, 86 (15 Dec. 1921), 13-14.

021-11 LEWIN, ALBERT P. "Play Things," Jewish Tribune,
16 Dec. 1921 [PU].

021-12 DE FOE, LOUIS V. "A Misuse of the Theatre,"
New York World, 18 Dec. 1921, Metropolitan Section, p. 2M.

021-13 S., F. F. "David Belasco Honored," Cincinnati
Enquirer, 18 Dec. 1921, Section Three, p. 4.

021-14 LEWISOHN, LUDWIG. "Drama: Year's End," Nation,
113 (28 Dec. 1921), 762-63.

021-15 NATHAN, GEORGE JEAN. "Humor Lost in New Play by
Kummer: Dreiser's Play is Poor," St. Paul
Pioneer Press, 8 Jan. 1922, Second Section, p. 6.

021-16 E., G. D. [G. D. EATON?]. "'The Hand of the
Potter'--and Criticism," Michigan Daily Magazine,
22 Jan. 1922, pp. 5, 7-8 [PU].

Productions of Plays

028-1   THE HAND OF THE POTTER. Opened in Sept. 1928 at the Renais-
        sance-Buhne Theatre, Berlin, Germany. This production
        also went on tour.

        Reviews:
        028-2   Berlin Vossiche Zeitung, 22 Sept. 1928 [PU].

        028-3   STEFAN, PAUL. "Theater, Kunst, und Wissenshaft,"
                Frankfurter Zeitung, 25 Sept. 1928 [PU].

        028-4   A., E. "Theater, Kunst, und Wissenschaft,"
                Hamburg Freidenblatt, 14 Jan. 1929 [PU].

        028-5   "Bühne und Kunst," Berlin Der Tag, 21 Feb. 1929
                [PU].

        028-6   "Dreiser auf der Bühne," Die Stunde, 21 Feb. 1929
                [PU].

        028-7   Neue Freie Presse, 22 Feb. 1929 [PU].

030-1   THE BLUE SPHERE. Broadcast 4 June 1930 over radio station
        WABC, New York, N. Y. Producer: Columbia Network.
        Director: Georgia Backus.

        Announcement and review:
        030-2   ANON. "Dreiser Writes Play for Air Being Produced
                Wednesday," Brooklyn Daily Eagle, 1 June 1930,
                Section E, p. 7.

        030-3   SKINNER, JOHN. "Riding the Waves," Brooklyn
                Daily Eagle, 8 June 1930, p. A14.

038-1   THE HAND OF THE POTTER. Opened 5 May 1938 at the Portfolio
        Playhouse, London, England. Producer: Portfolio Players.
        Director: Hector Abbas.

        Review:
        038-2   ANON. "Portfolio Playhouse," London Times, 6 May
                1938, p. 14.

P

ADAPTATIONS OF WORKS

This section presents stage and screen adaptations of Dreiser's
works plus a novelization of notes and a screenplay he wrote with
Hy Kraft.   Included also are reviews and criticism of and selected
news stories on these adaptations.   Only adaptations in the United
States are cited.   Persons interested in adaptations in other
countries should consult entries C36-1 and P35-36, Margaret Tjader's
mention of adaptations in Russia on pp. 224-25 of her Theodore
Dreiser: A New Dimension (see I65-2), and a review of an Italian
television production of An American Tragedy in Variety, 28 Nov.
1962, p. 28.   Tape and filmstrip adaptations intended for classroom
use in secondary schools are also omitted.

Citations for dramatizations give the playwright or playwrights
and the date of the first performance on stage in the United States.
Persons interested in various productions of the dramatization should
consult the reviews.

Reviews, criticism and news stories are classified under the
citation of the adaptation.   Because of this arrangement, the first
two digits in the entry numbers signify the date of the adaptation,
not the year of publication of the item.   The year of publication is
given in the entry itself.

An asterisk at the end of an entry based on a clipping (see P35-
27) indicates that we were unable to locate the work in the place
cited.   In these instances, the asterisk signifies that the item
does exist, but the bibliographical information may not be accurate.

Adaptations of Works

P26-1   AN AMERICAN TRAGEDY. Dramatization by Patrick Kearney.
        Premiere: 5 Oct. 1926 at the Shubert Theatre, New Haven,
        Conn.

        Reviews, Criticism and News Items:
        P26-2   GRABE, W. C. "An American Tragedy, at Shubert,
                Best Ever," New Haven Journal-Courier, 6 Oct.
                1926, p. 2.

        P26-3   ANON. "'An American Tragedy' Scores a Triumph,"
                New York Times, 12 Oct. 1926, p. 31.

        P26-4   D[AVIS], C. B. "'American Tragedy' Evokes Ovation
                at First Performance," New York Herald Tribune,
                12 Oct. 1926, p. 15.

        P26-5   HARKINS, JOHN. "Dreiser Novel Reaches Stage,"
                New York Morning Telegraph, 12 Oct. 1926, p. 2.

        P26-6   S[MITH], A[LISON]. "Another New Play," New York
                World, 12 Oct. 1926, p. 15.

        P26-7   LAIT, [JACK]. "American Tragedy," Variety,
                13 Oct. 1926, p. 47.

        P26-8   OSBORN, E. W. "'An American Tragedy,'" New York
                Evening World, 13 Oct. 1926, p. 26.

        P26-9   COLEMAN, ROBERT. "'An American Tragedy,'"
                New York Daily Mirror, 14 Oct. 1926, p. 26.

        P26-10 P., S. L. "'An American Tragedy' Is Poignant
                Drama, Well Done," Wall Street News, 14 Oct.
                1926 [NN].

        P26-11 SAYLER, OLIVER M. "An American Tragedy," Foot-
                light and Lamplight, 3 (14 Oct. 1926), 1 [PU].

        P26-12 VREELAND, FRANK. "Dreiser Squeezes In," New York
                Telegram, 15 Oct. 1926, p. 11.

        P26-13 U[NDERHILL], H[ARRIETTE]. "An American Tragedy
                and an All-American Comedy," New York Herald
                Tribune, 17 Oct. 1926, Section 6, p. 2.

        P26-14 BRACKETT, CHARLES. "The Theatre," New Yorker, 2
                (23 Oct. 1926), 33-34.

MISCELLANEA

P26-15   ANON. "Presenting Patrick Kearney," New York
         Times, 24 Oct. 1926, Section 8, p. 2.

P26-16   ATKINSON, J. BROOKS. "American Dramatists,"
         New York Times, 24 Oct. 1926, Section 8, p. 1.

P26-17   WOOLLCOTT, ALEXANDER. "The Stage," New York
         World, 25 Oct. 1926, p. 13. Repub: Alexander
         Woollcott, Going to Pieces. New York: Putnam's,
         1928. Pp. 130-34.

P26-18   YOUNG, STARK. "An American Tragedy," New Repub-
         lic, 48 (3 Nov. 1926), 297-98. Repub: Stark
         Young, Immortal Shadows: A Book of Dramatic
         Criticism. New York: Scribner's, 1948. Pp. 72-
         75.

P26-19   ANON. "Dramatist Borrows Film Tricks to Put
         Murder Trial on Stage," New York Herald Tribune,
         21 Nov. 1926, Section 6, p. 7.

P26-20   ANON. "Stagecraft Magic Sets 'The American
         Tragedy,'" New York Times, 5 Dec. 1926, Section 8,
         Part 2, p. 9.

P26-21   P., H. T. "Play of Kearney, Novel of Dreiser,
         Both Native-Born," Boston Evening Transcript, 13
         Dec. 1926, p. 9.

P26-22   ANON. "Douglas Scores in Capitol Play," Albany
         Evening News, 5 Nov. 1929, Second Section, p. 26.

P26-23   ANON. "'An American Tragedy' Revived at Waldorf,"
         New York Times, 21 Feb. 1931, p. 15.

P26-24   LOCKRIDGE, RICHARD. "'An American Tragedy,'"
         New York Sun, 21 Feb. 1931, p. 6.

P26-25   DUDLEY, BIDE. "'American Tragedy' Evokes New
         Reaction," New York World-Telegram, 3 Mar. 1931,
         p. 16.

P30-1   AN AMERICAN TRAGEDY. Screenplay by Sergei M. Eisenstein,
         Grigori Alexandrov and Ivor Montagu. Unproduced.

         Publication:
         Eisenstein, Sergei M. The Film Sense. New York: Har-
              court, 1942. Pp. 236-42. (Excerpts)

Adaptations of Works

Montagu, Ivor. With Eisenstein in Hollywood. New York:
International, 1969. Pp. 207-341. (Complete)

Criticism:
P30-2   WILSON, EDMUND. "Eisenstein in Hollywood," New
        Republic, 68 (4 Nov. 1931), 320-22. Repub:
        Edmund Wilson, The American Earthquake. Garden
        City, N. Y.: Doubleday, 1958. Pp. 397-413.

P30-3   EISENSTEIN, S[ERGEI] M. "An American Tragedy,"
        Close Up, 10 (June 1933), 109-24.

P30-4   DONNELLY, TOM. "A Great Film That Might Have
        Been," Washington Daily News, 2 July 1946, p. 42.

P30-5   EISENSTEIN, SERGEI. Film Form. Ed. and trans.
        Jay Leda. New York: Harcourt, 1949. Pp. 96-103.

P30-6   EISENSTEIN, SERGEI. "Un Projet: l'adaptation de
        An American Tragedy." Trans. Peter Kassovitz, La
        Revue des Lettres Modernes, 5 (Summer 1958), 216-
        24.

P30-7   EISENSTEIN, SERGEI. "'An American Tragedy,'"
        Sergei Eisenstein: Notes of a Film Director.
        Ed. R. Yurenev. Trans. X. Danko. Moscow:
        Foreign Languages Pub. Co., 1959. Pp. 98-106.

P30-8   SETON, MARIE. Sergei M. Eisenstein. New York:
        Grove Press, 1960. See Index.

P30-9   MURRAY, EDWARD. "Theodore Dreiser in 'Hooeyland,'"
        The Cinematic Imagination: Writers and the Motion
        Pictures. New York: Ungar, 1972. Pp. 116-23.

P30-10 BARNA, YON. Eisenstein. Bloomington, Ind.:
        Indiana U. Press, 1973. See Index.

P31-1   AN AMERICAN TRAGEDY. Film. Screenplay by Josef von Stern-
        berg and Samuel Hoffenstein. Directed by Josef von
        Sternberg. Produced by Paramount Publix. Released in
        Aug. 1931.

        Reviews, Criticism and News Items:
        P31-2   ANON. "Foul Tactics," New York Times, 3 July
                1931, p. 20. Editorial.

P31-3   ANON. "Dreiser Halts 'Tragedy' Film," New York
         American, 16 July 1931, p. 3.

P31-4   ANON. "Court Refuses Dreiser Writ Against Film,"
         New York Herald Tribune, 2 Aug. 1931, p. 18.

P31-5   ANON. "Dreiser Loses Suit to Bar Screen Play,"
         New York Times, 2 Aug. 1931, p. 18.

P31-6   BOEHNEL, WILLIAM. "Dreiser's Story Told on
         Screen," New York World-Telegram, 6 Aug. 1931,
         p. 14.

P31-7   CAMERON, KATE. "'American Tragedy' 4-Star Film,"
         New York Daily News, 6 Aug. 1931, p. 34.

P31-8   CREWE, REGINA. "Dreiser's 'American Tragedy'
         Ponderous as Film Attraction," New York American,
         6 Aug. 1931, p. 11.

P31-9   HALL, MORDAUNT. "The Screen: Mr. Dreiser's
         Famous Story," New York Times, 6 Aug. 1931, p. 22.

P31-10   SHAWELL, JULIA. "'American Tragedy' Unreels at
         the Criterion Theater," New York Evening Graphic,
         6 Aug. 1931, p. 21.

P31-11   WALDORF, WILELLA. "'An American Tragedy,'" New
         York Evening Post, 6 Aug. 1931, p. 12.

P31-12   CHEAVENS, DAVID. "'An American Tragedy,'"
         New York Morning Telegraph, 8 Aug. 1931, p. 2.

P31-13   SELDES, GILBERT. "True to Type: Theo. Dreiser
         Indicted in His Indictment of Society," New York
         Evening Journal, 8 Aug. 1931, p. 8.

P31-14   HALL, MORDAUNT. "'An American Tragedy' on the
         Screen," New York Times, 16 Aug. 1931, Section 8,
         p. 3.

P31-15   ANON. "The New Pictures: An American Tragedy,"
         Time, 18 (17 Aug. 1931), 17.

P31-16   JOSEPHSON, MATTHEW. "Dreiser, Reluctant, in the
         Films," New Republic, 68 (19 Aug. 1931), 21-22.

P31-17   PEET, CREIGHTON. "The New Movies: 'An American Tragedy,'" Outlook and Independent, 158 (19 Aug. 1931), 502.

P31-18   BAKSHY, ALEXANDER. "Emasculated Dreiser," Nation, 133 (2 Sept. 1931), 237.

P31-19   ANON. "The Tragicomedy of 'An American Tragedy,'" Literary Digest, 110 (5 Sept. 1931), 18-19.

P31-20   KRAFT, H[Y] S. "Dreiser's War in Hollywood," Screen Writer, 1 (Mar. 1946), 9-13.

P33-1   JENNIE GERHARDT. Film. Adapted by S. K. Lauren and Frank Partos. Screenplay by Josephine Lovett and Joseph Moncure March. Directed by Marion Gering. Produced by Paramount. Released in June 1933.

Reviews, Criticism and News Items:
P33-2   SHAFFER, GEORGE. "Dreiser's Story Will Be Filmed Without His Aid," New York Daily News, 20 Mar. 1933, p. 32.

P33-3   ANON. "'Jennie Gerhardt' Is Dramatic Treat at the Paramount," New York American, 9 June 1933, p. 9.

P33-4   BOEHNEL, WILLIAM. "'Jennie Gerhardt' at Paramount," New York World-Telegram, 9 June 1933, p. 18.

P33-5   CAMERON, KATE. "Miss Sidney Lovely as Dreiser Heroine," New York Daily News, 9 June 1933, p. 52.

P33-6   COHEN, JOHN S., JR. "The New Talkie: Mr. Dreiser's 'Jennie Gerhardt,' as Indorsed by Mr. Dreiser," New York Sun, 9 June 1933, p. 18.

P33-7   HALL, MORDAUNT. "The Screen: Sylvia Sidney and Donald Cook in a Pictorial Version of a Theodore Dreiser Novel," New York Times, 9 June 1933, p. 20.

P33-8   JOHANESON, BLAND. "'Jennie Gerhardt' Great Love Story," New York Daily Mirror, 9 June 1933, p. 23.

P33-9   PELSWICK, ROSE. "Sylvia Sidney Doomed to Play Role of Unhappy Maiden Buffeted by Fate," New York Evening Journal, 9 June 1933, p. 20.

427

MISCELLANEA

P33-10 SHERMAN, AL. "Sylvia Sidney Excels; a Talkative
        Talkie," New York Morning Telegraph, 10 June 1933,
        p. 2.

P33-11 SHAN. "Jennie Gerhardt," Variety, 13 June 1933,
        p. 15.

P33-12 ANON. "Screen: Film of Dreiser's 'Jennie Ger-
        hardt' Satisfies," News Week, 1 (17 June 1933),
        30.

P33-13 ANON. "The New Pictures: Jennie Gerhardt," Time,
        21 (19 June 1933), 32.

P33-14 PARRY, FLORENCE FISHER. "On With the Show,"
        Pittsburgh Press, 24 June 1933 [PU].

P33-15 PULLEN, GLEN C. "Dreiser Film Well Acted,"
        Cleveland Plain Dealer, 22 July 1933, p. 8.

P35-1   CASE OF CLYDE GRIFFITHS. Dramatization of An American
        Tragedy by Erwin Piscator and Lina Goldschmidt. Trans.
        by Louise Campbell. U. S. Premiere: 20 Apr. 1935 at
        the Hedgerow Theatre, Moylan-Rose Valley, Pa.

        Reviews, Criticism and News Items:
P35-2   ANON. "Dreiser Play April 20," New York Times,
        31 Mar. 1935, Part 2, p. 8.

P35-3   WALDORF, WILELLA. "'Case of Clyde Griffiths'
        Next Broadway Novelty," New York Post, 29 Feb.
        1936, p. 8.

P35-4   ANON. "Theatre: 'The Case of Clyde Griffith
        [sic.],'" Daily Worker, 7 Mar. 1936, p. 7.

P35-5   ANON. "Again the Notable Talents of the Group,"
        Brooklyn Daily Eagle, 8 Mar. 1936, Section C,
        p. 3.

P35-6   PISCATOR, ERWIN. "Piscator Describes Combination
        of Cinema and Stage Technique," Sunday Worker,
        8 Mar. 1936, p. 6.

P35-7   ATKINSON, BROOKS. "Group Theater in a Skeleton-
        ized Version of Dreiser's 'An American Tragedy,'"
        New York Times, 14 Mar. 1936, p. 10.

Adaptations of Works

P35-8   BROWN, JOHN MASON. "'Case of Clyde Griffiths'
         at the Ethel Barrymore," New York Post, 14 Mar.
         1936, p. 8.

P35-9   FIELD, ROWLAND. "The New Play: 'Case of Clyde
         Griffiths,' a New Version of Theodore Dreiser's
         'An American Tragedy' Acted at the Ethel Barrymore
         Theatre," Brooklyn Times Union, 14 Mar. 1936 [NN].

P35-10   GABRIEL, GILBERT W. "'Case of Clyde Griffiths,'"
         New York American, 14 Mar. 1936, p. 11.

P35-11   GARLAND, ROBERT. "'Case of Clyde Griffiths'
         Presented," New York World-Telegram, 14 Mar. 1936,
         Section Three, p. 6C.

P35-12   HAMMOND, PERCY. "The Theaters," New York Herald
         Tribune, 14 Mar. 1936, p. 8.

P35-13   LOCKRIDGE, RICHARD. "The Stage in Review,"
         New York Sun, 14 Mar. 1936, p. 9.

P35-14   MANTLE, BURNS. "'Clyde Griffiths' vs. Expression-
         ism," New York Daily News, 14 Mar. 1936, p. 23.

P35-15   PLAYVIEWER, THE, pseud. "New Plays: 'Case of
         Clyde Griffiths,'" Bronx Home News, 14 Mar. 1936,
         p. 6.

P35-16   POLLOCK, ARTHUR. "The Theater: 'Case of Clyde
         Griffiths,' New Version of a Famous Dreiser Novel,
         Presented Imposingly at the Ethel Barrymore
         Theater," Brooklyn Daily Eagle, 14 Mar. 1936,
         p. 16.

P35-17   PRICE, EDGAR. "The Premiere," Brooklyn Citizen,
         14 Mar. 1936 [NN].

P35-18   WHITNEY, JOHN. "Broadway Last Night: Dreiser's
         'Tragedy' Through German-English Refiltering Be-
         comes Economic Commentary," Newark Evening News,
         14 Mar. 1936, p. 22.

P35-19   ANON. "Ancient Japan Lends an Idea to Broadway,"
         New York Herald Tribune, 15 Mar. 1936, Section 5,
         p. 4.

P35-20 BOLTON, WHITNEY. "The Stage Today: Groups 'Case of Clyde Griffiths' a 'Stylized' Proletarian Triumph," New York Morning Telegraph, 15 Mar. 1936, p. 3.

P35-21 ANDERSON, JOHN. "Heckler Seated in Audience Debates Drama's Entire Action with Cast," New York Evening Journal, 16 Mar. 1936, p. 14.

P35-22 FOLDES, PEGGY. "Theatrescope: 'The Case of Clyde Griffiths,' Exciting," North Side News, 16 Mar. 1936 [NN].

P35-23 GARLAND, ROBERT. "Protest and Punch Plays," New York World-Telegram, 16 Mar. 1936, p. 14.

P35-24 L., E. "Drama--Films: 'Clyde Griffiths' Excellent in Hands of Guild Theater," New York Journal of Commerce and Commercial, 16 Mar. 1936, p. 24.

P35-25 SIMON, HERMAN. "Stage and Screen: 'The Case of Clyde Griffiths,'" North Hudson Center News, 16 Mar. 1936 [NN].

P35-26 B., J. P. "The Theatre: Creatures of Circumstances," Wall Street Journal, 17 Mar. 1936, p. 8.

P35-27 REPARD, THEODORE. "Most Significant Play in N. Y.," Daily Worker, 17 Mar. 1936* [NN].

P35-28 BROWN, JOHN MASON. "Once Again the Group's 'Case of Clyde Griffiths,'" New York Post, 18 Mar. 1936, p. 12.

P35-29 G., E. "Theatre," New York University Heights News, 18 Mar. 1936 [NN].

P35-30 KAUF. "Plays on Broadway: Case of Clyde Griffiths," Variety, 18 Mar. 1936, p. 64.

P35-31 S., E. C. "'The Case of Clyde Griffiths,'" Christian Science Monitor, 18 Mar. 1936 [NN].

P35-32 SELDES, GILBERT. "True to Type," New York Evening Journal, 18 Mar. 1936, p. 25.

P35-33 NICKELL, MARION F. G. "Drama in Manhattan," Whitestone Herald, 19 Mar. 1936 [NN].

Adaptations of Works

P35-34 ANON. "'American Tragedy': Dreiser's Novel Gets New Treatment and a Class Angle," News-Week, 7 (21 Mar. 1936), 22.

P35-35 ANON. "Group Makes Dreiser's Book Vivid Social Tragedy," New Leader, 21 Mar. 1936, p. 6.

P35-36 ANON. "Latest Version of 'Clyde Griffiths' One of Four Dreiser Dramatizations; Authors Forced into Exile by Nazies," New York World-Telegram, 21 Mar. 1936, Section Three, p. 6C.

P35-37 BENCHLEY, ROBERT. "The Theatre," New Yorker, 12 (21 Mar. 1936), 24-25.

P35-38 DRAKE, HERBERT. "Case of Clyde Griffiths," Cue, 4 (21 Mar. 1936), 6-7.

P35-39 ROMER, SAMUEL. "'Case of Clyde Griffiths,'" Socialist Call, 2 (21 Mar. 1936), 11.

P35-40 W., N. "Play Reviews: Case of Clyde Griffiths," Zit's Weekly, 21 Mar. 1936, p. 6.

P35-41 "'American Tragedy,'" Erie Dispatch-Herald, 22 Mar. 1936 [NN].

P35-42 CASSAL, GOULD. "Average Intelligence; Middle-brow Commentary on the Theatrical Scene," Brooklyn Daily Eagle, 22 Mar. 1936, Section C, p. 2.

P35-43 HAMMOND, PERCY. "The Theater: Begging to Differ with Herr Piscator," New York Herald Tribune, 22 Mar. 1936, Section 5, pp. 1, 4.

P35-44 JAGENDORF, M. "The Night in New York," New York Freedom, 22 Mar. 1936 [NN].

P35-45 KEEFE, WILLARD. "The Group Again Under Fire," Baltimore Sunday Sun, 22 Mar. 1936, Section 1, p. 2.

P35-46 LEWIS, EDWARD. "The Curtain Rises," Amityville Record, 22 Mar. 1936 [NN].

P35-47 MANTLE, BURNS. "Theater Turns to Experiments," Detroit Free Press, 22 Mar. 1936, p. 15.

P35-48   PALMER, T. "This Week on the Stage: 'Case of
         Clyde Griffiths,'" This Week in New York, 22 Mar.
         1936 [NN].

P35-49   SCHRADER, FREDERICK R. "New Version," Cincinnati
         Enquirer, 22 Mar. 1936, Section Three, p. 1.

P35-50   SEAVER, EDWIN. "The New Play," Sunday Worker,
         22 Mar. 1936, p. 6.

P35-51   ANON. "New Play in Manhattan," Time, 27 (23 Mar.
         1936), 55.

P35-52   BROWN, JOHN MASON. "Divergent Opinions on the
         'Case of Clyde Griffiths,'" New York Post, 24 Mar.
         1936, p. 8.

P35-53   ROSS, GEORGE. "'Saint Joan' Is Hailed as Artistic
         Triumph of the Theatrical Year," Independence
         [Mo.] Examiner, 24 Mar. 1936, Magazine Section,
         p. 4.

P35-54   GAVER, JACK. "Up and Down Broadway," Du Bois
         [Pa.] Express, 27 Mar. 1936 [NN].

P35-55   BLUM, DANIEL C. "Broadway by Wire," Chicago
         Journal of Commerce, 28 Mar. 1936, p. 2.

P35-56   BURR, EUGENE. "The New Plays on Broadway,"
         Billboard, 48 (28 Mar. 1936), 19.

P35-57   CAHN, IRVING W. "Theatre Review: Case of Clyde
         Griffiths," Metropolitan Host, 28 Mar. 1936 [NN].

P35-58   "This Side of the Footlights," Brooklyn Citizen,
         28 Mar. 1936 [NN].

P35-59   DASH, THOMAS R. "The Theatre in Retrospect:
         'Case of Clyde Griffiths' Accents Class Angle
         Ideology and Impressionistic Technique," Retailing
         (New York), 30 Mar. 1936 [NN].

P35-60   BURNSHAW, STANLEY. "The Theater: 'Case of Clyde
         Griffiths,'" New Masses, 19 (31 Mar. 1936), 28.

P35-61   BROUN, HEYWOOD. "Tragedy in No Man's Land,"
         Stage, 13 (Apr. 1936), 35.

THEODORE DREISER: A BIBLIOGRAPHY

Adaptations of Works

P35-62   GASSNER, JOHN W. "Drama versus Melodrama," New
         Theatre, 3 (Apr. 1936), 8-10, 43.

P35-63   LEE, EDWARD. "Case of Clyde Griffiths," Promenade,
         Apr. 1936 [NN].

P35-64   ROSS, CHARLES. "The Revolving Stage," Knott
         Knotes (New York), Apr. 1936 [NN].

P35-65   SWERDLOW, IRWIN. "Labor at the Play," Justice,
         1 Apr. 1936 [NN].

P35-66   KRUTCH, JOSEPH WOOD. "Dreiser Simplified,"
         Nation, 142 (1 Apr. 1936), 427-29.

P35-67   BROWN, JOHN MASON. "What the Group and Its Play-
         wrights Think," New York Post, 17 Apr. 1936, p. 16.

P35-68   LITTELL, ROBERT. "Ubiquitous Class Struggle,"
         Today (New York), 6A (25 Apr. 1936), 16.

P35-69   MULLEN, JOHN. "A Worker Looks at Broadway,"
         New Theatre, 3 (May 1936), 25-27.

P35-70   PEACOCK, ROSCOE. Stage, 13 (May 1936), 79.
         Letter to the Editor.

P35-71   WENTZ, JOHN C. "An American Tragedy as Epic
         Theater: The Piscator Dramatization," Modern
         Drama, 4 (Feb. 1962), 365-76.

P42-1   MY GAL SAL. Film based on "My Brother Paul." Screenplay by
         Seton I. Miller, Darrell Ware and Karl Tunberg. Directed
         by Irving Cummings. Produced by Robert Bassler for
         Twentieth Century-Fox. Released in May 1942.

         Reviews, Criticism and News Items:
P42-2   "'My Gal Sal' Musical Treat," Hollywood Reporter,
         16 Apr. 1942, p. 3 [PU].

P42-3   WALT. "My Gal Sal," Variety, 22 Apr. 1942, p. 8.

P42-4   BARNES, HOWARD. "On the Screen," New York Herald
         Tribune, 1 May 1942, p. 15.

P42-5   BOEHNEL, WILLIAM. "Movies: My Gal Sal, at Roxy,
         Lives Up to the Ads," New York World-Telegram,
         1 May 1942, p. 18.

MISCELLANEA

P42-6   CAMERON, KATE. "A Nostalgic Gaiety Infuses 'My
         Gal Sal,'" New York Daily News, 1 May 1942, p. 44.

P42-7   CROWTHER, BOSLEY. "The Screen in Review," New
         York Times, 1 May 1942, p. 23.

P42-8   McMANUS, JOHN T. "'My Gal Sal' Is a Delightful
         Gal," New York PM, 1 May 1942, p. 23.

P42-9   MORTIMER, LEE. "2 Aces: 'My Gal Sal,' 'We Were
         Dancing,'" New York Daily Mirror, 1 May 1942,
         p. 28.

P42-10   PELSWICK, ROSE. "'My Gal Sal' Opens on Screen at
         Roxy," New York Journal-American, 1 May 1942,
         p. 10.

P42-11   THIRER, IRENE. "Screen News and Views," New York
         Post, 1 May 1942, p. 46.

P42-12   ANON. "The New Pictures: My Gal Sal," Time, 39
         (4 May 1942), 86.

P51-1   THE PRINCE WHO WAS A THIEF. Film. Screenplay by Gerald
        Drayson Adams and Aenaes MacKenzie. Directed by Rudolph
        Mate. Produced by Leonard Goldstein for Universal-Inter-
        national. Released in July 1951.

        Reviews, Criticism and News Items:
P51-2   BROG. "The Prince Who Was a Thief," Variety,
        6 June 1951, p. 6.

P51-3   HALL, PRUNELLA. "Screen Reviews," Boston Post,
         4 July 1951, p. 29.

P51-4   QUINN, FRANK. "'The Prince Who Was a Thief' In-
         triguing Film," New York Daily Mirror, 4 July
         1951, p. 20.

P51-5   W[EILER], A. [H]. "Tony Curtis as a Heroic
         Prince," New York Times, 4 July 1951, p. 13.

P51-6   H., L. "Gaudy 'Prince Who Was a Thief' Pleasant
         Fare at Loew's State," Brooklyn Eagle, 5 July
         1951, p. 5.

P51-7   PELSWICK, ROSE. "An Amusing Melange," New York
Journal, 5 July 1951, p. 15.

P51-8   ANON. "New Films: The Prince Who Was a Thief,"
Newsweek, 38 (9 July 1951), 95.

P51-9   POTEET, EWING. "Theodore Dreiser's Eastern Ex-
cursion," New Orleans Item, 15 July 1951* [PU].

P51-10   TINÉE, MAE. "Dreiser Story Produces Only a Boring
Movie," Chicago Daily Tribune, 20 July 1951,
Part 2, p. 4.

P51-11   ANON. "The New Pictures: The Prince Who Was a
Thief," Time, 58 (23 July 1951), 85.

P51-12   R., H. "Dreiser Tale on Screen; Other Arrivals,"
Christian Science Monitor, 24 July 1951, p. 2.

P51-13   DeBRUIN, SUE. "Capitol Film Has Princes, Palaces,
and Pulchritude," Washington Times-Herald, 27 July
1951 [PU].

P51-14   C[OE], R[ICHARD] L. "Two Kids Disport in Cala-
rabia," Washington Post, 28 July 1951, p. 10.

P51-15   HATCH, ROBERT. "Movies," New Republic, 125
(30 July 1951), 23.

P51-16   D., W. R. "Empire Film Makes Fun of 'Arabian
Nights' Story," New Bedford [Mass.] Standard-Times,
15 Sept. 1951, p. 6.

P51-17   A PLACE IN THE SUN. Film based on An American Tragedy and
Patrick Kearney's dramatization of the novel; See P26-1.
Screenplay by Michael Wilson and Harry Brown. Directed
and produced by George Stevens for Paramount. Released
in Aug. 1951.

Screenplay Publication:
Gessner, Robert. The Moving Image. New York: Dutton,
1968. Pp. 137-50. (Excerpt)

Reviews, Criticism and News Items:
P51-18   ANON. "Movie of the Week: A Place in the Sun,"
Life, 30 (28 May 1951), 47-48, 50.

MISCELLANEA

P51-19   "'American Tragedy' Filmed as 'A Place in the
         Sun,'" Pittsburgh Post-Gazette, 19 June 1951*
         [PU].

P51-20   FREEMAN, MARILLA WAITE. "Current Feature Films:
         A Place in the Sun," Library Journal, 76 (July
         1951), 1142.

P51-21   HERB. "A Place in the Sun," Variety, 18 July
         1951, p. 6.

P51-22   ANON. "Dreiser's 'Tragedy,'" New York Times
         Magazine, 29 July 1951, p. 35.

P51-23   SCHEUER, PHILIP K. "Stevens Sees Tragedy as
         Hopeful Theme," Los Angeles Times, 29 July 1951,
         Part 4, p. 1.

P51-24   BAUER, LEDA. "The Revival of Dreiser," Theatre
         Arts, 35 (Aug. 1951), 16-17, 97.

P51-25   HINE, AL. "Movies: A Place in the Sun," Holiday,
         10 (Aug. 1951), 6, 8-9.

P51-26   LUFT, HERBERT G. "As We See It," Los Angeles
         B'nai B'rith Messenger, 10 Aug. 1951 [PU].

P51-27   CARROLL, HARRISON. "'Place in the Sun' Rates
         Place Among 'Greats,'" Los Angeles Herald Express,
         15 Aug. 1951 [PU].

P51-28   REDELINGS, LOWELL E. "Paramount Film Lauded,"
         Hollywood Citizen News, 15 Aug. 1951 [PU].

P51-29   SMITH, DARR. "Film Review," Los Angeles Daily
         News, 15 Aug. 1951 [PU].

P51-30   M., W. H. "Film Reviews," Los Angeles Tidings,
         17 Aug. 1951 [PU].

P51-31   A., G. "On the Screen," New York Herald Tribune,
         29 Aug. 1951, p. 14.

P51-32   COOK, ALTON. "Film Packs 'Tragedy's' Punch,"
         New York World-Telegram and Sun, 29 Aug. 1951,
         p. 32.

Adaptations of Works

P51-33 CORBY, JANE. "Screenings: 'A Place in the Sun' Is Story of Tragic Love, at the Capitol," Brooklyn Eagle, 29 Aug. 1951, p. 10.

P51-34 W[EILER], A. [H]. "The Screen: Dreiser Novel Makes Moving Film," New York Times, 29 Aug. 1951, p. 20.

P51-35 ALPERT, HOLLIS. "Double Bounty from Hollywood," Saturday Review of Literature, 34 (1 Sept. 1951), 28-31.

P51-36 H., W. "The Modern Filming of Dreiser's 1920 Epic, 'An American Tragedy,'" San Francisco Chronicle, 2 Sept. 1951, This World Section, pp. 10, 13.

P51-37 WEILER, A. H. "'A Place in the Sun,'" New York Times, 2 Sept. 1951, Section 2, p. 1.

P51-38 HARTUNG, PHILIP T. "The Screen: But What Place?" Commonweal, 54 (7 Sept. 1951), 524.

P51-39 McCARTEN, JOHN. "The Current Cinema," New Yorker, 27 (8 Sept. 1951), 107-08.

P51-40 HANDSAKER, GENE. "'Place in the Sun' Hailed as Superb Melodrama," Pasadena Star-News, 9 Sept. 1951, p. 23.

P51-41 ANON. "New Films: A Place in the Sun," Newsweek, 38 (10 Sept. 1951), 96, 98.

P51-42 ANON. "The New Pictures: A Place in the Sun," Time, 58 (10 Sept. 1951), 96.

P51-43 HATCH, ROBERT. "Movies," New Republic, 125 (10 Sept. 1951), 22.

P51-44 PLATT, DAVID. "Dreiser's 'Tragedy' Trimmed Down to Hollywood Slickness," Daily Worker, 11 Sept. 1951, p. 7.

P51-45 ANON. "Hollywood Again Delves Into Literature of the 20s with Dreiser's 'American Tragedy,'" Des Moines Sunday Register, 16 Sept. 1951, Picture Magazine, pp. 10-11.

P51-46   SOANES, WOOD. "Furious Fan Scorches Soanes for Cooking 'Place in the Sun,'" Oakland Tribune, 21 Sept. 1951 [PU].

P51-47   M., M. "Dreiser, Bible Stories Told in Coming Films," Phoenix Arizona Republic, 23 Sept. 1951 [PU].

P51-48   PLATT, DAVID. "What Hollywood Did to Dreiser's 'American Tragedy,'" The Worker, 23 Sept. 1951, Section 2, p. 7.

P51-49   LERNER, MAX. "In the American Sun," New York Post, 26 Sept. 1951, p. 44.

P51-50   P., B. J. "Reviewing the Screen," Milwaukee Journal, 27 Sept. 1951 [Second Section], p. 4.

P51-51   ROSENFIELD, JOHN. "Dreiser's Tragedy Now Told in Terms of Our Queer Time," Dallas Morning News, 30 Sept. 1951, Part 6, p. 1.

P51-52   KASS, ROBERT. "Film and TV," Catholic World, 174 (Oct. 1951), 62-63.

P51-53   LEWIS, STEPHEN. "A Place in the Sun," Films in Review, 2 (Oct. 1951), 38-42.

P51-54   COOK, ALTON. "Another Bow to 'Place in the Sun,'" New York World-Telegram and Sun, 6 Oct. 1951, p. 6.

P51-55   CORBY, JANE. "Screenings: 'Place in the Sun' Is Topflight Job of Transferring Book to Film," Brooklyn Eagle, 7 Oct. 1951, p. 27.

P51-56   CRISLER, B. R. "New Screen Arrivals Range from the Tragic to the Gay," Christian Science Monitor, 9 Oct. 1951, p. 11.

P51-57   COE, RICHARD L. "'Place in the Sun' Rates Exactly That," Washington Post, 10 Oct. 1951, p. 9B.

P51-58   SCHIER, ERNIE. "'A Place in the Sun' Spins Absorbing Tale," Washington Times-Herald, 10 Oct. 1951 [PU].

Adaptations of Works

P51-59   COE, RICHARD L. "All Mediums Seem to Be Borrowing from Each Other," Washington Post, 14 Oct. 1951, Section 6, p. 1L.

P51-60   D., E. J. "'A Place in the Sun' Given Superb Screen Presentation," New Bedford [Mass.] Standard-Times, 17 Oct. 1951, p. 5.

P51-61   SKOLSKY, SIDNEY. "Hollywood Is My Beat," Bronx Home News, 17 Oct. 1951 [PU].

P51-62   HUGHES, ELINOR. "The Screen: A Place in the Sun," Boston Herald, 19 Oct. 1951, p. 50.

P51-63   KOWALS, LORRAINE. "Doris Arden Says," Chicago Sun & Times, 22 Oct. 1951, Section 2, p. 13.

P51-64   TINÉE, MAE. "Dreiser Story Turned into an Excellent Film," Chicago Daily Tribune, 22 Oct. 1951, Part 4, p. 11.

P51-65   SCOFIELD, DOROTHY P. "'A Place in the Sun' at the Fox-Arlington," Santa Barbara News-Press, 28 Oct. 1951 [PU].

P51-66   ANON. "'A Place in the Sun,'" Manchester Guardian, 20 Dec. 1951, p. 3.

P51-67   ANON. "'A Place in the Sun,'" London Times, 21 Dec. 1951, p. 2.

P51-68   SHULMAN, MILTON. "Much-Praised Film Is Good But Not Great," Nottingham Guardian, 22 Dec. 1951 [PU].

P51-69   POWELL, DILYS. "Highly Polished," London Sunday Times, 23 Dec. 1951, p. 2.

P51-70   DIXON, CAMPBELL. "The Stuff of Life in Dreiser Tragedy," London Daily Telegraph and Morning Post, 24 Dec. 1951, p. 4.

P51-71   HART, HENRY. "1951's Ten Best," Films in Review, 3 (Jan. 1952), 1-10.

P51-72   LOCKHART, FREDA BRUCE. "Too Small for Tragedy," Tatler, 203 (2 Jan. 1952), 10.

MISCELLANEA

P52-21 GEIST, KENNETH. "Carrie," Film Comment, 6 (Fall 1970), 25-27.

P52-22 MORSBERGER, ROBERT E. "'In Elf Land Disporting': Sister Carrie in Hollywood," Bulletin of the Rocky Mountain Modern Language Association, 27 (Dec. 1973), 219-30.

P54-1 SANDHOG. Dramatization of "St. Columba and the River" by Earl Robinson and Waldo Salt. Premiere: 23 Nov. 1954 at the Phoenix Theatre, New York, N. Y.

Reviews, Criticism and News Items:
P54-2 ATKINSON, BROOKS. "Theatre: 'Sandhog' at the Phoenix," New York Times, 24 Nov. 1954, p. 17.

P54-3 CHAPMAN, JOHN. "'Sandhog' an Unexciting Musical about an Exciting Enterprise," New York Daily News, 24 Nov. 1954, p. 36.

P54-4 COLEMAN, ROBERT. "'Sandhog' Ballad Opens at the Phoenix Theatre," New York Daily Mirror, 24 Nov. 1954, p. 25.

P54-5 DASH, THOMAS R. "'Sandhog,'" Women's Wear Daily, 24 Nov. 1954, p. 39.

P54-6 FIELD, ROWLAND. "Phoenix Presents 'Sandhog' Musical," Newark Evening News, 24 Nov. 1954 [NN].

P54-7 HAWKINS, WILLIAM. "'Sandhog' Comes Up for Air at Phoenix," New York World-Telegram and Sun, 24 Nov. 1954, p. 14.

P54-8 KERR, WALTER F. "'Sandhog,'" New York Herald Tribune, 24 Nov. 1954, p. 13.

P54-9 McCLAIN, JOHN. "'Sandhog': New Musical in a Good Try," New York Journal-American, 24 Nov. 1954, p. 10.

P54-10 SHEAFFER, LOUIS. "'Sandhog' Warm, Appealing Musical of Old New York," Brooklyn Eagle, 24 Nov. 1954, p. 6.

P54-11 WATTS, RICHARD, JR. "Of Tunnel-Building and Music," New York Post, 24 Nov. 1954, p. 11.

Adaptations of Works

P54-12 BOLTON, WHITNEY. "There Is Much That's Worthy in 'Sandhog,'" New York Morning Telegraph, 25 Nov. 1954 [NN].

P54-13 BEAUFORT, JOHN. "Fresh Arrivals On and Off Broadway: Story by Dreiser," Christian Science Monitor, 27 Nov. 1954, p. 8.

P54-14 LARDNER, JOHN. "The Theatre: The Hard Way to Hoboken," New Yorker, 30 (4 Dec. 1954), 86, 88.

P54-15 FREEDLEY, GEORGE. "Off Stage--And On," New York Morning Telegraph, 25 Dec. 1954 [NN].

P65-1 THE TOBACCO MEN. A novel by Borden Deal based on notes and a screenplay by Theodore Dreiser and Hy Kraft. New York: Holt, 1965.

Reviews:
P65-2 ROGERS, W. G. "A Filthy Weed, and How It Grew," New York Times Book Review, 23 May 1965, p. 44.

P65-3 QUINN, JOSEPH L. "Deal, Borden: The Tobacco Men," Best Sellers, 25 (1 June 1965), 115.

P65-4 KELLEY, MARY E. "Fiction: Deal, Borden. The Tobacco Men: a novel based on notes by Theodore Dreiser and Hy Kraft," Library Journal, 90 (15 June 1965), 2869.

P65-5 KENNEDY, WILLIAM. "Trite Characters of Tobaccoland Never Come Alive," National Observer, 4 (28 June 1965), 19.

P65-6 MAURER, ROBERT. "New Fiction: Roll Your Own," Book Week, 2 (18 July 1965), 12.

P65-7 DANIEL, JOHN. "Well-Trodden Corridors," Spectator (London), 216 (13 May 1966), 604.

INDEX

THEODORE DREISER: A BIBLIOGRAPHY

Anderson, Margaret   J30-1, K18-1
Anderson, Margaret Steele   L14-47
Anderson, Sherwood   A18-1, C41-3, G-7, I26-1, J24-1, J25-1, J34-1,
   J36-6, J39-3, J42-1, J53-3, J64-2--J64-3, J69-12, J72-13, K16-6,
   K16-26, K17-14, K26-30, K29-8, K31-33, K33-4, K51-9, K56-2,
   K71-12, L25-8, L47-26, L47-33, N60-8, N72-5
Andrews, Clarence A.   A00-1, J67-1
Angell, James Burrill   L11-80
Angoff, Charles   J56-1
Anisimov, Ivan   A25-1, A31-2, J68-1, K58-6
"Annual Hailstorm, The"   CA
"Another American Tragedy"   C29-5
"Anthony Hope Tells a Secret"   C98-11
Antush, John V.   N68-1
Anzilotti, Rolando   D47-1, J68-2, J71-1, K66-1
"Appearance and Reality"   A35-1, C33-4
"Apples: An Account of the Apple Industry in America"   C00-13
"Applied Religion--Applied Art"   C23-2
"April Weather"   A26-1, A28-1, A35-1
Aragon, Louis   K46-13
"Are We in America Leading Way Toward a Golden Age in the World?"
   C27-5
Arens, Egmont   K18-5
Arey, Wayne   O20-1, O20-3
"Arizona"   A35-1
"Armed for the Battle"   C94-3
Armitage, Louise   O17-30
Armour, Philip D.   C98-44
Arnavon, Cyrille   I56-1, K45-2
Arnold, Ann J.   N69-1
"Arrested"   C92-12
"Art of MacMonnies and Morgan, The"   C98-5
"Art Work of Irving R. Wiles"   C98-17
"Article 4 Hundred 47"   C93-20
"Artist, The"   A26-1, A28-1, A35-1
"Artists' Studios"   C98-25
Arvin, Newton   K35-9, L31-33
"As a Realist Sees It"   C15-7
"As If in Old Toledo"   C94-9
"As It Is with the Living"   A26-1, A28-1
"As New as New York Itself"   C06-15
"As to the Jucklins"   C96-8
"As with a Finger in Water"   A26-1, A28-1, A35-1
"Ascent, The"   A26-1, A28-1, A35-1
"Ashtoreth"   A20-1, C19-6
"Asia"   A26-1, A28-1, A35-1
Askew, Melvin W.   K62-3
Aspirant, The   A29-2

447

INDEX

INDEX

461

INDEX

INDEX

INDEX

INDEX

INDEX

INDEX

484

Maxwell, John   L25-36
May, Armand   K31-13
May, Henry F.   J59-3
Mayberry, George   A25-1, J49-4, K46-11, L46-43
Mayfield, Sara   K66-16
Mayhall, Fan   N63-1
Maynadier, Emily W.   K07-2
"Mayor and His People, A"   A19-1, C03-3
Mazets'kii, G.   K67-3
"Mea Culpa!"   C36-5
"Meaning of the USSR in the World Today, The"   C40-10, D51-1
"Meddlesome Decade, The"   C29-10
Mellett, Sue   K45-4
"Men in the Dark, The"   A23-1, C12-1
"Men in the Snow, The"   A23-1, C13-9
"Men in the Storm, The"   A23-1, C99-46
Mencken, H. L.   A25-1, B25-2, C09-13, D62-1, G-2, G-8, I26-1, I27-1,
    J17-1, J20-1, J22-3, J25-2, J39-5, J46-1, J50-5, J51-5, J56-1,
    J61-3, J66-7, J69-3, J71-7, J71-15, K16-7--K16-9, K17-9--K17-10,
    K18-1, K21-10, K25-1, K26-18, K46-26, K48-1, K58-1, K61-5--
    K61-6, K65-10, K66-5, K66-16, K71-29, L11-7, L11-36, L11-53,
    L12-1, L12-12, L12-16, L12-53, L12-64, L12-68, L13-36, L13-53,
    L14-39, L14-66, L15-51, L16-29, L16-45, L18-23, L19-3, L19-51,
    L20-26, L22-56, L23-21, L25-54, L29-19, L31-28
Mendel, Alfred O.   B39-2
Mendel'son, Moris Osipovich   I71-2
"Merchants Win, The"   C94-5
"Mercy of God, The"   A27-2, C24-3
"'Mercy' of God, The"   A27-2, C24-3, D62-1
Merrill, Flora   F25-5
"Messenger"   A35-1
"Metropolitan Favorite, A"   C96-36
Meyer, Annie Nathan   A20-2, K20-2--K20-3
Meyer, George W.   K42-7
Mezsèts, A.   A00-1, A11-1
"Michael J. Powers Association, The"   A23-1
Michaud, Régis   J26-4, J28-9
"Midsummer Mania, A"   CA
"Midsummer's Day Dream"   CA
Miettinen, Lauri   A25-1
"Mighty Burke, The"   A19-1, C11-1
"Mighty Rourke, The"   A19-1, C11-1
Mihelič, Mira   A00-1
Miller, Henry   J52-2, K26-17
Miller, Jerry L.   N63-2
Miller, Juanita M.   N69-8
Miller, Margaret   L46-66
Miller, Perry   J62-5

INDEX

INDEX

INDEX

INDEX

INDEX

INDEX

INDEX

INDEX

INDEX

INDEX

INDEX

INDEX

Ziff, Larzer A15-1, A27-1, J66-13, J67-5--J67-6
"Zither--Spring" A26-1, A28-1, A35-1
Zola, Emile J70-2, J72-4, N58-1
"Zuckerman" C92-13
Zydlerowej, Jósefy A11-1, A25-1
Zyla, Wolodymyr T. J72-4

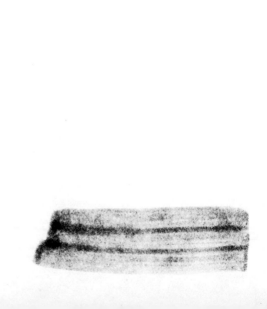